Desertification, Land Degradation and Sustainability

Desertification, Land Degradation and Sustainability

Anton Imeson

Foundation 3D Environmental Change,
Foundation For Sustainable Development (FSD), The Netherlands
University of Amsterdam, The Netherlands

WILEY-BLACKWELL

A John Wiley & Sons, Ltd., Publication

Library of Congress Cataloging-in-Publication Data

Imeson, Anton.
  Desertification, land degradation, and sustainability / Anton Imeson.
     p. cm.
  Includes bibliographical references and index.
  ISBN 978-0-470-71448-5 (cloth) – ISBN 978-0-470-71449-2 (pbk.)
  1. Desertification. 2. Desertification–Control. 3. Reclamation of land. I. Title.
  GB611.I44 2012
  333.73'6–dc23
                                                                          2011022871

A catalogue record for this book is available from the British Library.

This book is published in the following electronic formats: ePDF 978-1-119-97776-6; Wiley Online Library 978-1-119-97775-9; ePub 978-1-119-97978-4; Mobi 978-1-119-97979-1

Typeset in 9/11pt Times-Roman by Laserwords Private Limited, Chennai, India
Printed and bound in Malaysia by Vivar Printing Sdn Bhd

First Impression 2012

To my wife Jane

Contents

Preface

The land soil and water are the most precious natural resources we have. However, human actions that started 5000 years ago continue to cause an ever decreasing decline in their quality and value. More than 20 years of research has shown that desertification and land degradation can be stopped and large areas restored of their quality. Protecting and restoring the functions and services that have been lost by the land and soil is seen as the key to sustainable development and reversing climate change.

The approach of this book has been to make a synthesis of research findings and communicate the essence of these in a practical way so that the reader can have information about the causes of desertification and its nature, how it is being measured and its impact and what can and is being done about it. This book then is a study of mans impact on nature and whether limits need to be placed on the appropriation of water and land. So much work has been done that it only possible to select a few examples that scientifically underpin the conclusion.

Because processes of desertification are a consequence of culture, climate and geology, and the main drivers are land use and development, these need to be presented in a coherent framework understandable to people with different experience. This has been done in several different ways using indicators, the concepts of functions and ecosystem goods and services, systems and change, desertification response units, ecosystem health and soil quality, hierarchy theory and adaptive management. Some basic principles and key processes are explained from hydrology, erosion, soil degradation, ecology soils because these need to be appreciated by people responsible for policy and legislation. Similarly some basic principles from the economic and social sciences are applied so that the cultural drivers of land degradation give more guidance in restoration. Land use, Agriculture, and Development are important but the main thing is how people see value and treat the land unaware of the influence on processes. Desertification is a story of mans impact on earth so an effort has been made not to include too much detail regarding case studies because this can be found in the cited literature.

The book is also an introduction to and a case study of Geography, Applied Geography, Physical Geography, Natural Resource Management, Soil Conservation and Environmental Law and Environmental Politics and ethics.

The book also describes many indicators and measurements that can be made. This is particularly with respect to soil and land degradation.

Inevitably, as it is about actions and responses to desertification, the book examines and analyses the role of the UNCCD, United Nations Convention to Combat Climate Change and European Soil Conservation Policy and their influence.

However, this book is not just academic because the reader, like the author is a stakeholder. Policies that stop land degradation and reverse it could be introduced overnight but it requires seriousness, effort and organization. As the causes and processes of land degradation are similar everywhere, it is possible to treat desertification both locally and globally. At the end of the book, the Selfoss Call to Action is included so that the reader can see what is actually being thought and recommended by scientists from Environmental Law and soil conservation.

The book is organized into three main parts.

Part I, is about the Nature of Desertification.

After the scope and approach of the book are described there are three main Chapters that respectively consider respectively the causes and why it matters, Responses to Desertification and Desertification Indicators from Concept to Practice.

Chapter 1 considers the nature of desertification, its history and impact on ecosystem functions and services and the importance of life and its feedback with processes. It looks at scientific data and evidence for land degradation in research. It also discusses how and why desertification occur and the methodology.

Chapter 2 introduces the responses being made at different levels and review the causes of desertification.

Chapter 3 introduces indicator approaches, concepts and principles. It describes how selected approaches are applied in practice. It describes how indicators can be obtained from the soil and hydrological information. Resilience and stability Indicators of the different soil and land functions identified as being damaged by human actions are described. There is an introduction to water and desertification and basic principles of hydrology and soil stability.

Part 2 looks at local desertification impact and responses.

Chapter 4 describes the key processes regulating the soil and land scape functions

The hydrological and conservation functions are created and maintained and how they are related to human actions and processes in the soil and landscape. This chapter presents methods for studying change, key soil, ecological and hydrological processes. It introduces soil stability and soil response and catchment responses.

Chapter 5 is about the human impact on degradation processes. It contains an introduction to soil erosion, soil structure degradation, gully erosion, grazing impact, fire and the impacts of land use conversions. Eight short case studies from the USA, Australia, Europe and South America are used to illustrate principles. The chapter describes sediment transport data and erosion monitoring methods, impact from water resource development, Principles and Concepts of soil conservation.

Chapter 6 describes responses to land degradation from perception to action. It looks at positive experience from case studies in Europe, the United States soil conservation response of Bennett to the Dust Bowl. European soil conservation policy and responses to land degradation are described. It looks at experiences of sustainable land management obtained from the SCAPE Project into soil conservation and protection strategies for Europe. The perception is the perception that there is a problem and the action considers both the legislation and enactment of laws.

Part III is about global desertification impacts and responses.

Chapter 7 Global Desertification Today described the emergent consequence of local desertification at a global sale through land use change and the appropriation of land and water and illustrates this in Central Asia and the USA with respect to water. It describes the Millennium report and the role of the UNCCD. The impact of desertification on soil quality and functions is described. Some basic information about global fluxes is mentioned. There is a case study illustrating the impact of the financial markets and investments on land degradation. Three examples of global problems are described from Brazil deforestation, Namibia and China.

Chapter 8 looks at the impacts of desertification on ecostystem services and capital. The nature and value of natural capital is explained as are the different services provided by the land.

Finally, in Chapter 9 the way forward, the main conclusion about finding answers are elaborated in some detail, making use of the findings from international conferences and calls from action by the scientific and environmental law community.

And Part 3 is about global desertification.

Acknowledgement

Jane, Joan, Marc, David, Robert, Marlies and Manon – thank you for your feedback and encouragement when I was writing this book.

I also acknowledge the help and support of the editorial and production team of John Wiley and Sons, in particular the help from Fiona Woods. Rachael Ballard, Izzy Canning and Sarah Karim and Aishwarya are thanked for their contribution to this book and a special thanks goes to Gillian Andrews for her improvements and insights.

This book is the result of a process that began as a student and I am especially appreciative of the opportunity I had to be part of a team at Hull University with Ian Douglas, Roy Ward, Alistair Pitty, David Watts, Jay Appleton, Ian Reid, John Pitman and Les Ternan and to the NERC for supporting my PhD. Later to have an opportunity to work with Pim Jungerius and his team at the Laboratory of Physical and Geography of Soil Science of the University of Amsterdam (FGBL). Working as part of an interdisciplinary team was encouraged in the Faculty of Spatial Sciences, and I appreciate the opportunity created by others which enabled me to work in Morocco (Herman van de Wusten) in Lestoho and in Indonesia with the Free University (Theo Faber). I acknowledge the contributions made by the IGU Commissions in which I participated and who shared their research experience, particularly during field visits of the GERTEC and COMTAG Commissions (Asher Schick, Tom Dunne, Rorke Bryan, Anders Rapp, Adam Kertec, Dino Torri, Aaron Yair, Hanoch Lavee, Jean de Ploey, Anna Netto, Maria Sala, Adolfo Calvo Hans Reizebos, Theo van Asch).

I also thank the founders and members of the ESSC and the many meetings and conferences they have organised on this subject. Jose Rubio is thanked for his encouragement and many opportunities he created, most recently for example in his work with V. Andreu at the Campus de Excelencia on the human and socioeconomic consequences of desertification. I am also grateful for discussions I have had with Jeff Herrick and Luca Montanarella concerning the application of research in policy and application in the USA and Europe.

With respect to the methodology, I am grateful to Cranfield University and collaboration with Peter Allen and Janice Evans during the ERMES project in which the work of Adolfo Calvo, Pepe Rubio, Hanoch Lavee, Joachem Hill and Chico Perez Trejo is acknowledged. I am also grateful to all of those in the MEDALUS project including of course John Thornes, Jane Brandt and Nicky Geeson, Mike Kirkby. For field visits, I especially appreciate the ideas and contributions from, amongst others, Prof. Aru, Prof. Enni, Prof. Basso, Maria Roxo, Francisco Lopez Bermudez and his team as well as Costas Kosmas, Prof. Yassiglou, Prof. Puigdefabregas and Albert Sole.

I would also thank the EU DG Research for supporting desertification research for nearly 20 years. Roberto Fantechi, P. Balabanis, Denis Peter and Maria Yeroyianni are thanked for their feedback and encouragement. I would like to acknowledge the support I received in the project (EFEDA I and II, MEDALUS I, II and III), AQUDAPT, DESERTLINKS, SCAPE, LUCINDA and LEDDRA. Finally my appreciation is to the Universiteit van Amsterdam and LERG Foundation that supported the installation of the Chair in Desertification and Soil Erosion. The support of Koos Verstraten and Jan Seevink iand IBED is greatly valued for their consideration and support. Special thanks to the many research students who contributed to this work indirectly through their field research and also to the laboratory staff for the analyses.

I am very grateful for the work being done by the UNCCD and of which I have been able to make use of. I acknowledge the great efforts they are making to reduce the impacts of desertification.

Artemi Cerda offered his help on many different occasions. His investigations on sustainable and non-sustainable land use and its impact on land degradation provide real data and evidence of the nature of several processes. Also his leadership at the EGU means that land degradation has gained prominence. Michiel Curfs, Hanoch Lavee and Aaron Yair for their many contributions and insights into desertification. Dolf de Groot and the Foundation for Sustainable Development are also thanked for their support and development of the concepts of ecosystem services and capital.

With respect to soil conservation policy and land care, I am particularly grateful to the support of the Iceland Soil Conservation Service represented by Andres Arnalds and Oli Arnalds and Svein Runolfsson and for the inspiration from the Changjing River Scientific Research Institute, the soil and water conservation service and the participants of the study tours: Zhu Jiang, Xiao Xiang, Tao Xin, Yu Jicheng, Wan Caibing, Chen Wengui, He Jun, Lv Tao, Yu Jianhua, and Liu Dezhong.

I thank:

Mr. Liu Zhen, Director General of Soil Conservation Dept., Ministry of Water Resources (MWR) and Mr. Xiong Tie, Vice Commissioner of Yangtze Water Resources Commission (CWRC).

Mr. Ning Duihu, Division Chief of Soil Conservation Dept. MWR; Ms. Liao Chunyan, Director General of Soil Conservation Bureau, CWRC; and Mr. Zhou Miaojian, Director General of Auditing Bureau, CWRC.

Mr. Hu Danwen, Section Chief of Soil Conservation Bureau, CWRC in European Soil Conservation is gratefully appreciated. I am also gratefull to Hu Danwen and Piet van der Poel and Lars Anderson for their support from the EU China Europe exchange programme for their interest and support for soil conservation in Europe. Also for translating the SCAPE book into Chinese.

Thanks also to Piet van de Poel for his kindness and support in China and to Lars Anderson in Wuhan for his feedback. I thank my colleague Michiel Curfs for his support and commitment.

Finally, I would like to thank Helen Briassoulis of the Aegean University (and the other members of the LEDDRA project on Land and Ecosystem Degradation Response Assessment) for their discussions and contributions to the work Agostino Ferrara,

Koutsoukos Vassilis, Abdelkader Taleb, Ahmed El Aich, Angelo Nolè Antonella de Angelis, Artemio Cerda, Claire Kelly, Concepcion Alados, Costas Kosmas, Dan Wen Hu Geoff Wilson, Giovani Quaranta, Giuseppe Mancino HongHU LIU, Katerina Kounalaki, Luca Salvati Mina Karamesouti, Mohamed Chikahoui, Nichola Geeson, Rossanna Salvia, Ruta Landgrebe Sandra Naumann Sophia Bajocco, Zhang Pingchang Vassilis Detsis, Constantinos Liarikos Minas Metaxakis, Nichola Geeson, Panagiotis Stratakis, Thanassis Kizos and Theo Iosifides.

Denis Peter provided inspiration and motivation for writing this book. Special mention to Chico Perez Trejo and Dolf de Groot for providing the inspiration for the path which I took.

Introduction:
Scope and approach

In this book, desertification and land degradation are treated holistically from a systems perspective. By definition they are caused by human activities in the past and present, such as forest clearance, the use of fire and the use of trees for charcoal. Land degradation and desertification are therefore a consequence of man's impact on the earth's ecosystems. They are a consequence of the use of the natural resources of the land and soil by agriculture and industry and they are driven by, for example, economic activities, property development, industry and agriculture. They can in many cases be prevented or responded to by using strategies and methods to restore land and soil qualities, or by educating people regarding their relationship with and responsibility towards nature or land (Runólfsson and Andres 2004).

After reading this book the reader should have a clear understanding of how, at the local level, human actions actually affect the processes of degradation in the landscape and soil and of how process knowledge can be used to develop criteria for sustainable land use. At the global level, the links with globalization, climate change and biodiversity loss should also be clear. Throughout the book use is made of findings from field research and monitoring.

The responses being made by society to land degradation and desertification are discussed and evaluated. Part of this response is that of the United Nations Convention to Combat Desertification (UNCCD), and the way in which UNCCD addresses and defines desertification and land degradation is explained (see Chapter 3), because UNCCD has a large impact on research and it is partly responsible for governance.

The other features that distinguish this book are:

- The information about land degradation processes is based on scientifically validated peer-reviewed studies. Models are used to describe certain processes, but not to make projections.

- The impact of desertification is explained from the perspectives of functions that are occurring in a single socio-ecologic system in which both culture and landscape quality (geology and climate) constrain and limit change.

- The methodological approaches used to translate concepts of indicators and of functions, dynamic systems and adaptive management in land degradation are presented with examples.

- The book explains and adapts the basic principles of hydrology, soil degradation and soil conservation as they affect land degradation and at the same time describes key indicators and how they can be measured and used.

- The link between local and global desertification is explained.

Finally, the book discusses the strategies and methods that would enable desertification to be stopped and debates whether or not this can be done.

This book can be started in each of the three parts and most of the chapters can also be read alone.

The advantage of a process-based approach is that it allows similar problems to be treated together and it is not necessary to systematically treat desertification in each country or continent. This is because the hydrological processes and geology in combination with human actions create a limited number of field situations that repeat themselves.

Reference

Runólfsson, S. and A. Andres (2004) Soil conservation at the top of the world – conservation strategies in Iceland, pp. 1–4, *Conserving Soil and Water for Society*, International Soil Conservation Organization Conference (ISCO), Brisbane, July.

Part I
The Nature of Desertification

1
Desertification, its causes and why it matters

By definition, human induced **land degradation**, which is how **desertification** is defined, is caused by the actions of people that have a negative impact on the 'functioning' of the environment, as it is being *eco*-culturally experienced and as regards its value as a natural resource. A function is something like clean water, air and food but it can also have an aesthetic or cultural nature. Some functions can be restored and new ones created in landscapes that have become degraded with respect to their earlier state. Species and cultures differ in their capacity to survive the loss of their functions and habitat. This 'resilience' is reflected in how they are affected by land degradation and desertification. Resilience can be with respect to nature but also with respect to the economy and the social capital of people. Natural capital is provided by nature and it is the basis of all economic activity and human existence.

Sustainable land use and management are about establishing principles that can be brought into practice as a response to land degradation and desertification. In many cases land can have its quality and values restored and degradation can be put into reverse. Lost qualities or functions of the land can be restored through sustainable land management and with the help of natural processes. But in many cases changes are irreversible.

Parts II and III of this book include local and global level case studies. They describe key processes and attributes of landscapes relevant to desertification and give details of the actions that can be taken to ameliorate or adapt to it in different socio-environmental contexts. The cultural and economic pressures and drivers of land degradation are immense and much of the world is comprised of degraded landscapes. Because these are a consequence of our lifestyles, culture, attitudes and values they can be systematically changed by strategically planned human efforts. The situation is quite positive to the extent that the future does not have to be the consequence of actions that degrade the landscape; there can also be other actions that lead to restoration and the reversal of land degradation. The same socio-economic and financial forces that resulted in land degradation as a result of the critical values of natural processes being disregarded can be used to organize the responses that must be made.

> A society with cultural values that better understands how to be in harmony with nature can be attained. (*The Book of History, The Books of Zhou*, The Great Norm, p. 19 in Xiao Jietu and Li Jinquan 2008)

Desertification, Land Degradation and Sustainability, First Edition. Anton Imeson.
© 2012 John Wiley & Sons, Ltd. Published 2012 by John Wiley & Sons, Ltd.

This book introduces some of the *fundamental* principles and practices of land degradation and land and landscape management as they appear in 2011. It discusses the strategies, policies and actions that are being undertaken by different organizations responsible for land degradation and who are trying to deal with it. Successful strategies and approaches that can be used to reverse land degradation are well known and these are described.

The findings of European research on desertification were recently reviewed by an expert group for the European Community (Roxo 2009). Their intention was to raise awareness of the urgent state of land degradation in Europe and explain the current situation. It was also to show what Europe had achieved and what could still be done. As well as the severity and consequences of land degradation, the experts examined the main processes associated with it, such as soil and ecosystem degradation, erosion, salinization and wildfires; the causes such as climate change and land use practices, pollution, contamination and compaction; and the different landscapes in which land degradation is most concentrated.

More or less in parallel, an International Conference was organized by SCAPE (Imeson *et al* 2006) that brought together experts from environmental law (Hannam and de Boer 2002) and the land degradation communities. A little later, an International Forum on Soils and Society (2007) supported by the Iceland Government to celebrate 100 years' existence resulted in A Call for Action. One of the most common universal problems is that people appropriate natural resources or farm in an unsustainable way, irrespective of any law. The Brazilian Environmental Protection Agency cannot prevent the rain forest being used illegally as a source of fuel for pig iron production because it reduces the transport cost of iron ore on the way to China which generates billions of dollars each month. Or alternatively they are exempted.

The unanimous conclusion was that with the present scientific understanding, it is possible to evaluate the degree to which the actions and policies being used to address desertification are appropriate in view of scientific knowledge (Briassoulis 2010). This fortunate situation is an outcome of a large research effort in many countries and regions. There is sufficient scientific legitimacy to place land degradation at the top of the priority list of governments. This is equally true for other parts of the world, where similar knowledge and understanding has been acquired since concerns were raised at least two hundred years ago by Europeans observing the impact of land use in marginal areas in Europe but especially in South and North America.

A holistic systems based approach

When considering the nature and causes of desertification many different assumptions can be made that influence the methodology used to present what might seem to be an extremely complex environmental problem. The **traditional** approach is to evaluate the different factors ranging from matters such as geology, climate, economy and culture. It is difficult to be conclusive because it is hard to integrate and quantify factors that are always changing and uncertain.

A different way is to start **holistically** with just **one system**. Desertification can be conceptualized as if there is just one **socio-economic system** in which society finds itself with nature (for example, Huxley (1885), van der Leeuw (1998)). This way of looking at desertification was developed by several research schools in the 1990s at a time when ways of better integrating the physical and socio-economic factors affecting land degradation were being sought. In a single discipline approach it becomes clear that what is important are **people's actions** and what they do and the **relationships** between them. Addressing desertification is attainable if alternative positive cultural habits and practices are adopted since the things people do directly change the biophysical processes and alter the way in which the single system will respond.

Man and nature are in fact acting at one scale symbiotically. **Symbiosis** describes the close and often long-term interactions between different biological species. Symbiotic relationships can be necessary for the survival of at least one of the organisms involved. Relationships, therefore, matter because all life has contributed to the present state of the earth. Earthworms, trees and fungi are no less significant than humans in influencing the properties of the single socio-environmental earth system. All human actions that affect other life are important because of symbiosis and interdependence. Although symbiosis has received less attention than other interactions such as predation or competition, it is an important selective force behind evolution. Desertification then is about deserts and drylands such as the Judean desert (Figure 1.1) which may or may not be experience current degradation. It is also about the spread of desert-like conditions or features (Figure 1.1) as a result of human actions (Figure 1.2) in Valencia, Spain.

1.1 The nature of desertification

1.1.1 Concern about desertification in developed countries

Europe and America became concerned about desertification in the 1980s (Fantechi and Margaris 1986). It was postulated that desert-like conditions might spread to southern Europe from North Africa and to the south western United States from Mexico. There was similar evidence of such desertification in north east Brazil, China, Africa and India. According to Canadian meteorologist Hare (1976) who investigated this for the United Nations, it was not clear if this was the result of human causes or climate. In neither wealthy nor poor countries is there much evidence linking poverty to desertification. Poverty has very many causes and land degradation is linked to them in historical and political contexts that are about population growth, culture and exploitation of rural populations. Desertification and land degradation can be brought about by many different things such as conflict and migration, land use and farming, water use and soil contamination. It can also be brought about by the appropriation of people's natural resources and functions and these affect both developed and developing nations. Examples of strategies, policies and laws that address these are numerous (Arnalds 2005a and b).

Modern agriculture and forestry as well and the exploitation of natural resources involves using the land in ways that withholds and prevents it from doing what it once did in the way of regulating the hydrological cycle and energy balances, transformation processes and providing food chains and food webs.

It was confirmed by the EU working group on Desertification, set up by the European Soil Forum in 2005, that the higher the subsidies, the higher the land degradation because of the pressures and disruptions that these place on ecosystems. This is true everywhere because of the way subsidies affect human behaviour. The mathematics is explained in several monographs at the Santa Fe Institute, New Mexico. The main aims of forestry and agriculture are to provide resources and food and to sustain the economy and protect

Figure 1.1 The Judean Desert has a socio-ecosystem that it adapted to aridity and grazing (Credit: Anton Imeson).

(a)

Figure 1.2a The Judean Desert. Desertification is about the spread of desert-like features into humid areas as a result of vegetation clearance and agriculture and exploitation of resources (Credit: Anton Imeson).

jobs. These are the strategic goals of the U.S. Forest Service, for example, whose main mission is focused on their employees' needs and the increased production of timber. In achieving these rational goals, the natural and cultural environments are ignored and often degraded of their other functions (protection from flooding) and capital (value of this protection) is lost. Actions and practices take place that should in fact be regulated because they cause harm to the life with which we share a symbiotic dependence. For most people, the land is real estate and a provider of food and raw materials. Society has not been effective in promoting values that make us conscious of being symbiotically part

(b)

Figure 1.2b How thousands of years of social and environmental capital can be destroyed in few moments in Spain. Photograph A. Cerda 2011.

of nature. There is a limited or lack of any legal duty of care towards the environment, land and soil. There is the real possibility that the support functions of the earth are being compromised because of the disappearance of species both on land and in the sea.

1.1.2 Desertification and drylands

Today, the UN definition of desertification is that it is *'human induced land degradation in dry and sub-humid regions'* (UNCCD: United Nations Convention to Combat Desertification). Another view is that desertification occurs everywhere but that it is actually most prevalent in cold regions where the low temperatures and short growing season create fragile ecosystems that lack resilience (Arnalds 2005a and b).

A different perspective has emerged in the scientific community. The United Nations Convention to Combat Desertification (UNCCD 2011) has recently reviewed its strategy. Its main purpose is to combat poverty and increase people's standards of living in dry regions. The UNCCD has become in practice an extension of the UNDP and the FAO whose objectives of reducing poverty and giving food security reflect its new strategic goals. It has launched the next decade as the decade of desertification. It gives examples of success stories in several different countries of the world. Many of these are successful not because they reduce land degradation but because they improve the livelihoods of the people in the short term.

From the perspectives of a single system, the UNCCD is an organization that is responsible for mainly monitoring the implementing of the Convention to Combat Desertification. It is an actor in the system that we are studying and some its actions may increase, decrease or do little about the actual desertification that is happening in the world.

(a)   (b)

Figure 1.3 Desertification processes in Marocco near Beni Boufrah. (a) shows the response to land degradation in the form of terraces built by an aid organisation which failed to work and triggered badlands. (b) was taken during an extreme event and it can be seen that most runoff is from paths. The farmers own terraces were effective (Credit: Anton Imeson 2011).

1.1.3 The drivers of desertification

An obvious starting point when considering the causes of desertification is the increase in the human population from about 1 million in the Stone Age to I billion in 1850 and 6 billion in the 1990s. Technological advances have enabled man's numbers to increase and at the same time give him the tools and means with which he can cause desertification. Worst land degradation is frequently driven by top down help or investments because these ignore elementary principles regarding the nature of the processes and the aspirations of people. This is illustrated in Figure 1.3a that shows how terraces resulted in badlands when they ignored the specific properties of the soil. In Figure 1.3b, taken during a storm, that created a flash flood, that most runoff is from paths and tracks and that the terraces of the farmers were effective. In the Middle Ages in Europe monks began developing machines and tools that increased the efficiency of agriculture and this helped develop a culture that led to the agricultural revolution. It is the combined influences of technology, human numbers and culture that have made desertification and land degradation such an urgent and seemingly intractable issue. Man is one of maybe 3 million species but today consumes far more food than all of the other land animals put together. Ever since people started to use fire to improve grazing and domesticate crops and cattle, land degradation and desertification occurred and this happened everywhere. There are few areas of the world that have not been affected by the appropriation and use of water by agriculture and the altered water and salt balances that have been the result are one of the main characteristics of degraded lands. Chemicals being used in the environment are one of the most common causes of soil degradation today. The short- and long-term impact of these on people and soil organisms is well documented. When

Figure 1.4 This photograph in the area of former Atlantic rain forest in Brazil was cleared to produce coffee until there was land degradation and erosion. Now it is used for ranching and it has low productivity. In places the Atlantic rain forest is being restored but mainly the land is used for Eucalyptus in which there is no wild life and it is a kind of green desert (Credit: Anton Imeson).

the life that herbicides take out disappears, the processes in the soil that enable it to hold water and resist erosion vanish.

Most if not all of the earth's ecosystems show repeated evidence of land degradation in the past. This can easily be seen in the soil profile which provides an accurate record of past human actions, as is described in Chapters 4 and 5. This is illustrated in Figure 1.4 where mass movements of the deeply weathered soil profile have filled the valley bottom sediments. The rain forest was cleared for coffee production that resulted in land and soil degradation. Figures 1.5 and 1.6 from Bolivia are taken about 100 m apart above and below a surface into which badlands are developing and stripping the entire lacustrine deposit which is about 10 m thick. Figure 1.5 shows how sub surface flow is being triggered by the people who use the surface A2 horizon for bricks. This enables water to penetrate the erosive subsoil which disperses and is eroded creating the landscape down slope in Figure 1.6. Few soils today have escaped degradation and most have been totally changed by ploughing or grazing. That machines in the hands of man would endanger the environment was forecast by Pythagoras.

1.1.4 Restoring land and soil functions through conservation, protection and restoration

Actions by people and societies enable them to adapt to desertification and restore land. Today soil conservation and protection are important because they can be a key tool in sustainable development. Some examples of this will be illustrated in Chapters 4, 5 and 6.

It has even been possible to stop and reverse or adapt to desertification by restoring different functions and this is demonstrated in many areas such as in Murcia Province

Figure 1.5 and Figure 1.6   are taken looking east and west. This lake deposit near Tarije Bolivia has its original A2 soil horizon that is being used for bricks. Human actions trigger subsurface water movement and lead to all of the lacustrine deposit being eroded until only bedrock remains. Nothing is left of the original amazing nature and wildlife that the first settlers encountered and when everyone could live from the land. Many functions that have gone include food, water and climate regulation. Most of the vegetation is exotic (Credit: Anton Imeson).

in Spain and in the French Alps. There are many strategies and approaches to this that involve, for example, utilizing many different areas of administration and by the application of forestation, the regulation of financial markets, land tenure laws and responsibilities, and by promoting education and research. In many cases, however, if left unattended, many functions will restore themselves, as occurs on abandoned agricultural fields in different parts of the world. This is the case in Figure 1.7 taken on land that was recently used for wheat. By studying the development of the vegetation on agricultural

Figure 1.7 illustrates vegetation on abandoned agricultural fields near Mertola in Portugal. The land is colonized mainly by a species of *Cistus* and after about 12 years oak trees start to appear. The time since abandonment ranges from 2 years at the top left to 12 in the top right (Credit: Anton Imeson).

fields abandoned for different lengths of time, it is possible to compare the changes in relation to time.

More than four thousand years ago in China, ways of reclaiming desertification-affected areas and of reducing flooding were developed and recorded. In Roman times, land use policy and loans created poverty and threatened food production to the extent that laws and regulations were introduced to prevent banks charging interest, which made people poor and unable to provide the food needed in Rome. Many successful afforestation projects were carried out throughout the world with great success during the nineteenth and twentieth centuries and afforestation is seen as one of the main strategies for combating desertification.

Soil conservation and protection throughout the ages has developed principles that can be applied with and by communities to restore much of what has been degraded. It can sometimes cause harm because of the economic pressure from mechanisms such as carbon subsidies. Trees are being planted in areas that are too arid or above the tree line in the paramo of South America, for example. Proper governance and organization are needed so that activities are managed. It also requires time, which can vary from a few years to centuries. In some situations, large improvements can occur in just a few years, so that areas that are seemingly hopelessly degraded can be transformed into areas valued for other products, hunting, nature or wine production. The value of terraces is both with respect to farming and flood protection. Figure 1.8a taken along the Yangze River shows the use of terraces both for agriculture and reducing sediment supply. Knowledge about the effectiveness of different kinds of terrace construction can be validated. It is not only in China that the value of terraces is understood, it is also in Europe at Cinque Terra. Figure 1.9a, where terraces became eroded when fields were abandoned and the maintenance stopped. In Figure 1.9b terraces are being reconstructed.

(a)

(b)

Figure 1.8a and Figure 1.8b   The Chinese soil conservation service is implementing soil conservation works to prevent soil from entering the Yangtze River. The soil conservation service in China is experimenting with different techniques of terrace construction and erosion control that it applies in restoration work in much of the country (see Figure 1.8b) (Credit: Anton Imeson).

(a)

(b)

Figures 1.9a and 1.9b Restoring agricultural terraces at Cinque Terra, Italy, which has been possible because of the development of tourism and high added value products and services that exploit globalization (Credit: Anton Imeson).

1.1.5 Natural versus man-made landscapes

Actual desertification is the desertification taking place today; **historical desertification** is that which occurred in the sometimes very distant past.

Many if not most of the phenomena of degraded land observed today were caused by erosion and land degradation that occurred in the past. During the last twelve thousand years (the Holocene) man has been the main geological agent. Today, actual land degradation processes follow a) forest clearances, b) farming practices, c) the over exploitation of resources, d) grazing, e) fire and f) pollution, as they also did in the past. Today's processes might be more extreme than historic ones because of tractors, bulldozers and chemicals and the lower resilience of the soil. They degrade the soil chemically, physically and biologically, making it sensitive to erosion and runoff production. On the other hand, past erosion has made the land less sensitive to erosion because the ground surface becomes armoured by stones and only the vegetation is adapted to this human impact. As far as runoff is concerned, the soil and land are different from the past but flood runoff will be much greater today. The causes of soil degradation and the solutions are common knowledge in many societies and cultures and these are explained in Part II of the book.

Actual or present-day geomorphological processes include those of erosion (by wind and water, on slopes and in river channels) and sediment transport. These can be directly responsible for accelerated erosion and flooding, when the vegetation and the protective soil organic layers have been changed by people. Bare soil or sand is valued aesthetically in some gardens in China and Japan. Figure 1.10 was taken during a storm in Osaka Japan that created urban runoff and erosion locally.

Under relatively natural conditions, hydrological and geomorphological processes are regulated by the vegetation, ecosystem and soil, so that there is very little erosion, flooding and sediment transport. As a consequence of removing and modifying the natural system this regulation capacity can be reduced. The sensitivity of soil erosion to initial conditions means that it is hard to predict. On the other hand this is not always problem in practice because Figure 1.8 taken during rainfall along the Yangtze River shows the natural soil conservation function being performed by the forest and below it the function being provide by the farmer so that he can farm the slope. Both the trees and the farmer have the aim of using the soil as a resource and of keeping it on the slope.

Evidence of land degradation can obtained from monitoring or case studies from which changes can be quantified using key indicators of system behaviour (see Chapter 3).

Figure 1.10 Soil erosion and runoff in a street in Osaka, Japan. In this cultural setting, erosion and soil degradation may have an aesthetic value in gardens (Credit: Anton Imeson).

An indicator might be something as simple as the disappearance of rivers in Valencia, Spain or the loss of the topsoil that was once present beneath forests and which had a great capacity to retain water. This loss has occurred throughout the world with the spread of ploughing in Europe during the Middle Ages (Bork 2003).

Actual desertification can be established by recording and observing very many different desertification indicators. Desertification can be studied top down and this is the perspective of most international organizations and of remote sensing.

1.1.6 Dynamics of human–landscape interactions

Human societal groups, whether farmers or stock raisers, are dynamic agents who are continually altering the natural landscape. The consequences include the loss of the existing landscapes with semi-natural ecosystems and their soil, plant and animal life. The loss involves the protection and regulation functions and their replacement with built-up areas and urban industrial wasteland. There is functional, structural and visual degradation of the remaining open landscape and its biological impoverishment and the ecological disruption of its natural ecosystems by accelerated erosion, soil, air and water pollution and neo-technological despoliation, combined with the creation of monoculture steppes. People are actively altering the local ecology so that in this sense there is a co-evolutionary process because the relationships that underpin the dynamics of the woodlands, fields and rivers are themselves evolving dynamically. These dynamic processes depend on the **scale**. Although these changes may be incorporated into our culture in urban environments, through organic architecture and planning, very often development is informal and unregulated.

The scale of desertification in which we are interested for a specific purpose is called the **focal scale**. This could be a single point in a field, a farm or slope, or a landscape or region. **Coarse** scale processes are those that are relatively slow such as changes in property law (Goldstein 2004) or the weathering of rock which can vary from tens to thousands of years. These constrain top down the ways in which desertification can progress and express itself. For example, in the Negev Desert researchers have shown how small differences in the nature of rocks influence the surface water holding properties of the soil. This can have a stronger influence on the degree of aridity than the amount of rainfall. Aridity and drought sensitivity can depend as much on rock type and weathering as on rainfall. This is one reason why aridity indices need to consider the properties of the land as well as the rain. They are a poor indicator of desertification. Marls lose much water from evaporation or runoff.

Both the physical and social environments constrain desertification. The geology, soil and geomorphology as well as the frontiers between cultures and customs form boundaries of what are regional or landscape scale **desertification response units** (**DRUs**). The **sensitivity** of an area to land degradation and desertification can therefore be delineated according to **geology and culture**.

Culture determines how resources are perceived and valued and determines how people act and the things they do.

At any focal scale we identify as being our concern, **bottom up finer scale processes** are those that drive change. They could be for example, things such as **ploughing** the soil or the **interactions** between the vegetation and soil that influence the **infiltration**

and water holding capacity of the land. The **feedbacks and interactions** between man and **the other actors** that cause change is critical. This is beautifully illustrated in the recently published *Atlas of Soil Biodiversity* (2010) that explains the interactions between farming, soil biodiversity and desertification.

1.1.7 Land use changes

Land use changes are key to explaining desertification. This was the motivation behind the Medalus Project, supported by the European Union during which these relationships were measured and studied for more than a decade at target areas in southern Europe and elsewhere (Fantechi and Margaris 1986). It is not just the changes but rather the disregard for land capability or potential and the methods used which compact and degrade the soil structure. Figure 1.11a illustrates how badlands are being used for agriculture and Figure 1.11b illustrates how this is achieved.

In most parts of the world, there are many areas where areas that were once cleared for agriculture are now forested again (Bork 2003). This is illustrated by New York state and New England, Germany and in the Belgian Ardennes as well as in Spain, Greece and Italy. The soils and forest found today contrast greatly with those from the past. At the local scale, human actions can either bring about land degradation or they can reverse it. For example, if fine scale processes in the soil are promoted so that its **water and nutrient regulating characteristics** are improved, it can hold much more water and its temperature regime will become more moderate. **Emergent higher level benefits** will follow, such as higher crop yields, less runoff and flooding, more infiltration and groundwater for irrigation and more and clean water for urban areas. Farmers can prevent soil degradation and enhance soil functions.

The land is just like the ocean. In most seas around Europe desert-like conditions have been caused by fishing; the effects of fishing for shellfish and shrimps is particularly damaging to the biodiversity. But where the sea bottom is not dragged and disturbed for cockles, shrimps, within a few years in marine reserves there can be a remarkable recovery of the life on the sea bed. The same is true on land. When this is left alone and people stay away, after a few years there can be a dramatic improvement in life and biodiversity. **The best thing** we can do after a forest fire is usually **nothing** (Cerda 2010).

What is meant by sustainable land management is land management that produces the second situation whereby actions are taken that makes things improve. In practice this means prioritizing the **soil and water conservation** as the function rather than the crops that it can produce. It has more value. The effectiveness of traditional farming systems in combating desertification and guaranteeing food security is significant. These systems are those in which people's actions in combination with natural processes sustain the functioning of the soil and land.

The current degraded state of world is therefore an expression of man's cumulative impact during the Holocene Period. A relevant question then is can we ignore this and does it matter? The long-term carrying capacity and collapse of the earth's ecosystems might be occurring because of the depletion of life in the oceans and on land. Biologists focus on the biodiversity as an indicator of this. However, the response then is perhaps to have a policy that targets protected areas, endangered species and nature reserves rather than the entire area.

(a)

(b)

Figures 1.11a and 1.11b   are examples from Murcia, Spain, when bulldozed areas of badland soils sensitive to dispersion are cultivated. Such areas erode after the first rainfall and are not suitable as building land nor really for agriculture because of their salt and very high carbonate content (Credit: Anton Imeson).

More than half of the world's productive capacity is now being appropriated by humans for food and raw materials as well as 85 per cent of the world's water. Charles Darwin in 1834, Thomas Huxley in 1885 and Malthus in 1888 as well as Heidegger in 1935 and Leopold in 1949 were amongst the many who realized that this would inevitably result in the degradation of what they saw as the capital provided by nature for man. They thought that the growth in the human population would exceed the earth's carrying capacity (considered to have been reached in 2010). Diamond (2005) explained many examples where the collapse of civilizations were a consequence of ignoring land degradation.

1.1.8 Thresholds and different states

Desertification sometimes occurs when critical conditions are reached and the system changes into a different state. Research by systems ecologists and earth scientists have identified thresholds whereby there is a change in some condition (trigger) that leads to the system moving to a different state: in this case, from one in which there is the experience of an attractive and a not desertified existence into one that is degraded. One example is a land or soil system that suddenly loses its capacity to store water so that plants cannot live and erosion and runoff occur very frequently instead of never. Another example illustrated in Figure 1.15 is when groundwater tables are lowered and spring discharge and seepage decrease.

This idea can be easily visualized and understood by observing the soil under a plant in a garden or park and comparing what is found on bare areas and under the shrubs in the shade. Under the shrub or plant the soil is shaded and relatively cool in the summer or warm in winter but in the open it is compact because of the impact of rainfall and the lack of strength because there are no roots or substances that bind it together. In the garden it is easy to practise transforming our soil into a desert-like system or into one that is abundant with life.

A frequent consequence of the over exploitation of an area is that the landscape loses its capacity to function as a provider of clean and adequate water and protector from erosion, landslides and flooding. The system can change into another state in which processes that may be thought of as indicating the presence of natural capital, resilience, ecosystem services and complexity, are lost. The land and soil can no longer store water and retain plant nutrients. Positive feedbacks cause a progressive loss of plant cover and biodiversity and the soil becomes thinner with more frequent heat and water extremes. It can become affected by soil degradation, salinity and erosion processes. Some processes are slow, occurring across the lifetimes of several generations, and other are more or less instantaneous. They act together to trigger hazards, such as flash floods and landslides. For example, the flooding in Pakistan in August 2010 is not just the result of the Monsoon but of the land and soil degradation, causing increasingly higher amounts of runoff and at the same time reducing the capacity of the river channels with sediment eroded from the land. This process can be seen to be taking place wherever people have to cope with the floods produced by development and forest clearance, as on Caribbean islands, where rainfall is frequently highly intense. The River in Figure 1.15 suddenly lost about 80 percent of its flow because of the permits given for developers to pump water for new orange plantations. The people in the village using the water for generations had not legal protection, so what was a river fed by powerful limestone springs is transformed into an open drain.

1.1.9 Feedbacks and control

There is no effective feedback or process that links this knowledge to the actions that society and governments take at the global scale or in most countries on a national scale.

Figure 1.12, 1.13 and 1.14 show Limburg, The Netherlands, where land consolidation and farming caused many problems with erosion and flooding. The old landscape is shown in Figure 1.12 (Credit: Anton Imeson and Luuk Dorren). Research into ways of reducing erosion (Figure 1.13) resulted in regulations that have been applied and now limit erosion (Credit: Anton Imeson). Figure 1.14 shows that a large amount of loess has been lost and the underlying chalk or less fertile sediments are at or near the surface, reducing the productive function of the soil (Credit: Luuk Dorren). (Ransdalerveld, South Limburg (NL), April 2003. From Dorren.)

Figure 1.15 The Riu del Sants River in Canals which has provided the Town with water for hundreds of years and to which the town owes its existence has recently had its discharge reduced to a fraction because of the abstraction of groundwater for new orange plantations (Credit: Anton Imeson).

And even if this knowledge is present it does not stop a process in which the benefits are money and jobs. Never-the-less as the case from Dutch South Limburg illustrated in Figures 1.12 to 1.14 illustrates as a response to flooding in the villages, research was carried out to identify farming techniques that would prevent runoff and erosion. Figure 1.13 shows the experiments (set up by Frans Kwaad) during winter rainfall. This and other research were applied and further erosion and flooding largely stopped. The landscape before (Figure 1.12) and after land consolidation (Figure 1.14) is illustrated. This can be achieved by a soil conservation service that is functioning such as on the Cape Verde Islands. Figure 1.16 and Figure 1.17 illustrate the terraces in the Cape Verde Islands that enable the people to cultivate very steep slopes. Soil conservation is a response to the erosion and famines that occurred in the quite recent past. Without appropriate governance the situation will repeat itself and continue as there is no moral or cultural imperative that restrain actions.

In many developed countries, floods are responded to seriously because they directly threaten life and property. However, climate change is explained as the most common cause and the only feasible option, the improvement of the river channel capacity to convey more flood runoff. Restoring the soil and water protection of the land can be done. This would require the farmers and landowners restoring the soil structure and water capacity so that the soil could retain maybe 60 centimetres of rainfall as it once did instead of the few millimetres that is often the case today. This might cost less than the insurance paid to people on the floodplains who think that they are being flooded by **rainfall** and are not aware that it is **runoff**. In some places where rivers were on average 100 m wide, they may be now only 10 m wide because of ground water abstraction. At the same time the runoff coefficient (proportion of rainfall that reaches the river) is far higher and new sources of flood runoff have been created on agricultural and built-up lands to which rivers are not adjusted.

In most places, the causes of land degradation are a combination of present and past causes. Geological processes are cyclical. Periods of erosion are followed by periods of stability and soil formation. Accumulation of soils and sediments for perhaps hundreds of years is followed by a release that may be instant. The accumulation and release of

Figure 1.16 and Figure 1.17   Cape Verde Islands. The Cape Verde Islands has an effective soil conservation service that is helping farmers in response to and as feedback from disasters caused by soil loss and famine in the recent past (*Source:* Figure 1.17 Anton Imeson).

sediments from hillslope depressions occurs over thousands of years and the underlying causes may be the uplift of the land and down cutting of rivers. Flooding and erosion today are usually a consequence of both short-term processes and long-term adjustments in the rivers and landscapes. For the geologist, these are easy to explain but for the policy maker, they occur over time spans that are easy to ignore in the short term but which have devastating effects in the long term. Risk analysis is done mainly by hydrologists, who only look at water and inundation, not the causes of the problem from the perspectives of soil erosion, sediment balances and river channel capacity.

1.1.10 Stopping land degradation

Whatever actions people may take, the fundamental principles or laws of ecology hydrology and soil conservation influence the outcome. What is critical for human safety and well being is the ability of the land surface and soil to regulate the local hydrology and chemical balances and to protect people from floods and landslides. Population growth, development, mechanization and industrialization do not inevitably have to follow a path that damages, removes and discards ecosystem services, including the water regulation capacity of the land. Although land degradation has progressed far, the complete exhaustion of the earth's natural resources can be and is being addressed by alternative land use and management paradigms. For example, the Cover to Cover paradigm is one in which it is also mentioned that we need to find alternative ways of feeding people based on plants and animal products that are derived from temperate forest trees and plants.

Methods that have proven successful in addressing different aspects of land degradation will be discussed from bottom up and top down perspectives in Parts II and III.

1.1.11 Where is the greatest cost?

The cost of desertification and land degradation is often claimed to be greatest in drylands where there is also claimed to be most poverty. Paradoxically, some, drylands and desert margins are affected least because of the natural resilience of the vegetation. Others, however, have been shown to be very sensitive because of high rates of population growth, migration and conflicts, and taxation. Other dryland areas are rich and here degradation is high, as in parts of the south western USA, Australia and south eastern Spain, because of irrigated agricultural and water appropriation by urban areas. Amongst the most sensitive areas are cold regions, where the capacity of the land to restore its quality and functions is inherently low. Although scientists can now put a value on soil functions, at the end of the day what is lost is priceless in terms of the calamities that are occurring and the impact they have on people's lives and future security. Land degradation and desertification can actually occur anywhere, depending on the causes. Risk is not linked to a place, but to customs, cultures and actions.

1.1.12 Desertification as a loss of ecosystem functions

Land and soil degradation taking place today can be seen from the perspective of ecosystem functions. Jose Rubio and his team at the Spanish Desertification Research Institute and President of the European Soil Conservation Society have played a key role in communicating and promoting a paradigm of desertification that is based on ecosystem functions and ecosystem services. These include food, energy, clean air and water and a habitat and place where we can fulfill our lives. Biodiversity loss, climate change and flooding happen now and not in the past because of the soil and land that had capacities and properties that have been lost which enabled them to perform functions and regulate the heat and water balances. The causes of this are land and water use, land management and development. Because desertification involves almost everything, it is appropriate to consider this as one entity (McGlade 1995).

McGlade referred to land degradation and desertification as being human ecodynamics. This is the dynamics of human modified landscapes set within a long-term perspective and viewed as a nonlinear dynamic system. Desertification is therefore about the co-evolution of socio-historical and natural process and their time interaction. The idea of a function links people with the physical environment.

McGlade explains that there is no environment, there is no ecosystem, there are only socio-natural systems. What requires emphasizing is how people interact with and impact upon the dynamics of processes taking place in the soil and landscape in ways that affect how it functions and provides ecosystem services. Bottom up, the most important processes relate to land and water appropriations and change which are associated with development and the requirements of the increasing population for natural resources. Sustainable land management requires considering all of the other life on the planet (geo-ecology) in combination with our human customs and cultures as causes and explanations of land degradation and desertification.

1.1.13 Man as a geological agent

What desertification is and why it occurs can also be seen from the perspectives of geological time and process.

Geologists distinguish between the natural long-term geological rate of erosion in natural ecosystems and accelerated erosion. The valued coastal area of the Valencia Lagoon, used by tourists and for rice production was a consequence or benefit of the land degradation and forest clearance. probably during the last 5000 years.

Although man is the main geological agent today, this was not so in the past and even today other organisms can claim to be the same. Throughout geological history, periods of landscape stability have alternated with periods of instability. Figure 1.18 shows the Valencia Lagoon from the south, looking along the coastal bar that is occupied by hotels for tourists. The area shown is used for rice or fishing.

That the geological processes and causes of land degradation today are the same as hundreds or even millions of years ago is one of the basic principles of geology. Land degradation phenomena being observed may be in different stages of development and this may give the illusion of a very large spatial variability. Frequently, things that look different are just in a different phase of a cycle or in different areas of attraction. Because plants under the influence of climate adapt and change the soils in ways that reflect the fundamental properties of the rock, there is a great similarity between soils that occur on the same rock types, globally.

Soils and landscapes on granite in the USA, Australia and South Africa and France have remarkably similar minerals and soil properties that influence the way in which erosion and land degradation express themselves. This means that the geomorphology can be used as a means of stratifying the earth's surface into areas that are similar in terms of how they respond to land degradation and sustainable land management.

Land degradation and desertification processes, for example, on limestone or in pastoral communities can be understood and managed or dealt with in the same way, wherever they may be.

Figure 1.18 The Valencia Lagoon used for tourism and rice, created by erosion and land degradation in the previous centuries (Credit: Anton Imeson).

1.1.14 Desertification and vegetation

As well as being cleared by man, there are an infinite number of possible reasons why specific plants or vegetation communities might become degraded and disappear from a location. Animals and plants might not be able or willing to invest resources in maintaining their habitat so that they disappear and leave the environment that they find no longer attractive, creating bare areas.

Geomorphologists have studied the impact of humans on erosion and sediment as the human population changed during the last 8000 to 10 000 years of the Holocene Period, following the Ice Ages of the Pleicestone Period. Sediments that accumulated in lakes and floodplains provide stratigraphical evidence from which chronologies and former reconstruct land cover conditions can be constructed. The impact of land use on land degradation and erosion has been dramatic. Historical records and archaeological evidence have been linked to that from soil science and geomorphology, enabling a connection to be made between culture, land use, erosion and land degradation. The history of land degradation and desertification has been recorded in this way with great accuracy. Both seemingly insignificant interventions by people as well acts as the wholesale removal of the vegetation have an impact on land degradation depending on the constraints of higher level factors. When forests or grasslands were cleared in Europe, soil erosion increased from virtually nothing in the Neolithic period, to attain high rates when the vegetation was used for agriculture or charcoal for bronze and iron and heating so that many if not all upland areas lost their original soils, only remnants of which remain today. Many detailed reconstructions have been made by scientists throughout the Mediterranean, in Greece, Italy, and France, documenting the history of human land use impacts on desertification.

Understanding and knowing how to manage or respond to land degradation, when it occurs, is very important for land use planning and development but it essential to distinguish between past historical impacts and present ones. There are many instances of mismatches between regulations that restrict land use and the true causes of degradation or erosion which may no longer be active.

Nature with our intelligent help can cope with man's physiological needs and wastes, but she has no homeostatic mechanisms to cope with bulldozers, concrete, and the kind of agro-industrial air, water and soil pollution that will be hard to contain as long as human population is out of control (Odum 1971).

1.2 The links between global and local desertification

Figure 1.19 was developed by Cherlet at the European Joint Research Centre in 2008 as a means of illustrating the challenges in producing a new Global Atlas of Desertification. It provides a good overview of what scientists meeting at a workshop to discuss the content of a new Atlas on Desertification being produced by different international organizations wish to achieve.

In Figure 1.19a the different spatial scales are shown. One aspect of time is allowed for by having slow and fast variables. Slow variables constrain the changes that take place and fast ones drive them. For example land ownership laws that affect how people use the land and the down cutting of rivers that might trigger erosion change slowly but are important over a few hundred years.

The actions taken at the different scales link the systems at different levels. What might happen is that the levels in the middle are weakened and disappear. If all of the resources go from the local to the global system then this is what happens as an ecological footprint. If the whole world is covered with palm oil, maize or eucalyptus and incorporated into the global economic system, on the ground what happens is that the ecosystem services provided by the land such as flood protection, food and shelter are reduced. At each level there is a resilience and resistance to change that is present in the form of capital (Huxley 1885) and this is what allows the functions and ecosystem services to be provided.

1.3 Discussion: desertification as a world-wide and historical phenomenon

Desertification will be associated by many people with the Sahel region and with the droughts that occurred in the 1970s when millions of people perished. At that time climate was considered a major factor in desertification. In a report prepared for the United Nations, Hare (1976) discussed why deserts had expanded during human history and if people or the climate were the cause. There was no data available then to answer these questions but it was proposed that overgrazing caused a change of albedo, so that the surface would become cooler, there would be increased lower atmosphere stability and reduced convective activity. However, it was found it was the case in Tunisia that eroded soils were hotter and dryer so that with less evaporative cooling there is more

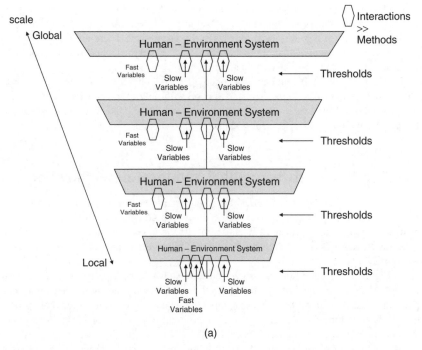

(a)

Figure 1.19a The notion of human environmental systems operating at different spatial scales. At each level different processes and indicators operate. (From Michael Cherlet 2008).

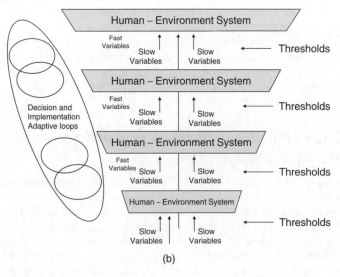

(b)

Figure 1.19b To the left, Cherlet adds Decision and Implementation Adaptive loops (Credit: Michael Cherlet).

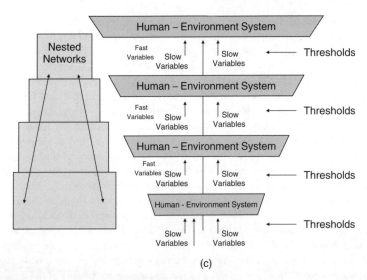

(c)

Figure 1.19c To the left, Cherlet illustrates the nested networks and the appropriation of capital as a global footprint (Credit: Michael Cherlet).

energy available to warm the soil. In either case, human induced changes in the vegetation cover have a profound impact on the climate and productivity of ecosystems and their sensitivity to desertification and grazing practices (Hanan *et al.* 1991). People's actions on the ground seemed to irreversibly affect the water and heat balances and in the short term also the climate.

It was considered possible that the changes in Africa or South America could increase the risk of desertification in Europe and North America and this was partly a motivation for European and North American research programmes that were set up to monitor the climate in Europe, Africa and the USA and Mexico. In Europe the first important workshop was held on Lesbos in 1984 (Fantechi and Margaris 1986) and this led to the implementation of large research projects such as Medalus (Mediterranean Desertification and Land Use), Efeda (European Field Experiment in a Desertification Threatened Area) and ERMES (Ecosystem Response to Land Degradation in Mediterranean Ecosystems). These had as their aims establishing the complex causes of desertification and monitoring and modeling its occurrence. It was soon established that the main drivers of desertification were land use and rural development policies, particularly those that subsidized crops. In Chapters 6 and 9, actions to combat land degradation and desertification in Europe are described in more detail.

The example of desertification on Easter Island Rapa Nui is also well known and in the research questions relatively simple. Is the cause of the complete deforestation of the palm dominated forest a climate catastrophe or was it land use? Mieth and Bork (2004) review all of the evidence in their research monograph and provide conclusive evidence from the soil that the forests were cleared by humans using slash and burn between 1250 and 1450 AD (p. 76).

Many examples of desertification are found in China, where wind and water erosion are considered to be major problems risking the harmonious development of the country. As much as 20 per cent of the affected areas are being treated in restoration projects being implemented by the Chinese Soil and Water Conservation Service, which is an important government ministry. In all regions of the world, ancient civilizations developed techniques for preventing land degradation and for restoring soil and land functions.

In the United States, desertification has recently affected many different regions, ranging from the South West, to the Great Plains, and the Eastern Seaboard from New England to Tennessee. All kinds of actions could have resulted in land degradation but the most well known examples are the impacts from the cultivation of tobacco and sugar as cash crops by colonialists. Many of the problems resulted from the mechanization of agriculture and as a consequence of the mechanization of farming. The causes of desertification were discussed and recorded at International Workshops on Desertification in Tucson in 1994. The first workshop asked the question why desertification could not be controlled. The second focused on connecting science with society. Most of the upland areas in Europe were also once forested. In the 1950s the pollen contained in ancient soil profiles found under cairns in the United Kingdom was investigated and it was concluded that these areas were at that time forested. In these areas as well, many of the thick layers of peat that held huge quantities of water have been eroded by water or wind erosion so that there has been a great loss in the water storage capacity of these landscapes. The trees were cut for fuel or to clean land, and soil erosion followed. The impact of historical land degradation can be seen almost everywhere, both by the specialist who knows what to look for and by ordinary people.

In Brazil, desertification has received much attention in many contrasted parts of the country ranging from the North East, where severe droughts were possibly caused by the reduction in precipitation as a consequence of forest clearance, in the Atlantic Rain forest along the coast, as a consequence of coffee growing, and in the areas now being developed for soya production.

Land degradation and desertification occurred in many parts of Africa for many different reasons and these include the impacts of sugar and palm oil and groundnuts in Ghana and Senegal and, of course, the impacts of wars, migration, locusts and all kinds of government policies. Many of the 175 million migrants worldwide are in fact economic migrants because of desertification and they are in effect environmental refugees. In Zimbabwe, vast areas have become degraded and desertified and the productive function of the land lost. The Rhodesian Soil Conservation that controlled and regulated farming according to the principles of soil conservation is an example of the desertification and degradation of social and institutional capital that provided feedback between farmers and their actions. Restoring the soil conservation function of the land could be the main priority of aid but in fact this link is not frequently appreciated.

From satellite observations and from the UN, the most affected areas are probably to be found in Central Asia, because of the relatively harsh climate, involving a short growing season, due to winter cold and summer droughts. These areas, as well as Alpine and cold regions in general, have fragile soils.

In general, the areas most prone to desertification today are those that have a relatively high productivity since they then have a higher human pressure. Under semi natural conditions, soil erosion is at its greatest in areas with about 400 to 500 mm of rainfall, but when the protective vegetation cover is removed it is greatest in the tropics or equatorial regions because of the high energy of the rainfall.

1.4 Discussion: life and its feedback with the environment

Viewed from space, the earth can clearly be seen to be functioning as a whole. It is characterized by global and zonal patterns in vegetation and soil. The vegetation and its ecosystems reflect the way in which plants and animals have become adapted to and were able to exploit and maintain themselves under the prevailing conditions. Deserts are found in cold or dry regions conditions where plant growth is limited by water. For much of the time, the ground surface appears or is covered with rocks. In other areas, vegetation growth is limited by lack of sunlight and energy and/or nutrients.

Deserts can occur in cold or hot dry regions. These typically occur along coastlines that have cold upwelling water along the coast and in the belts of high pressure where air that was heated along the equator descends and prevents rainfall. In desert and arid regions ecosystems have adapted to the prevailing conditions so that they are by nature resilient. Plants and ecosystems interact with the soil and rocks to create environments for themselves that help them to modify their own local climate. At the same time, they are having an impact on the regional and global climate by regulating the heat and water balances. Humans and other animals mainly require plants that can photosynthesize sunlight as a source of food or energy. In their interactions with other plants, some have gained a competitive advantage by enlisting the help of animals. These include insects, birds and man. Life has evolved, creating a habitat and environment in which to live by means of very many processes that involve the weathering and transformation of minerals by chemical processes that release nutrients and the evolution of food webs and food chains. Seen under the microscope, the interface between the atmosphere and rock, which we could refer to as topsoil, is composed out of the excrement, decomposition products and the bodies of the living organisms themselves, which may be bacteria and fungi. Larger animals, including mice, men, birds and almost all creatures, are responsible for 'bioturbation'. They mix the topsoil with deeper layers, making the area suitable as a habitat for the plants and animals that live in it.

Soil erosion under such conditions is caused by animals and plants as they go through their life cycles and seek food. Erosion and down slope creep of soil leads to the gradual accumulation of what is called slope deposit (colluvium). Organic rich layers at slope-foot positions in different ecosystems contain pollen grains that can be used to reconstruct the former vegetation cover and to identify critical moments when erosion took place. For example, in Luxemburg, investigators could identify the influence of the Romans from buck wheat pollen and land abandonment as a result of land degradation when pine pollen appeared.

An important conclusion from research is that different types of animal or plant have very large impacts on the habitat layer with which they interact and are part of. So this habitat is in fact part of their phenotype. The significance of this was established by Darwin with his research on earthworms but ecologists have long understood that any interference with the natural life in an area can have an impact on the habitat layer that has repercussions for the other life that is sharing and making use of the habitat function. In his travels in South America, Darwin describes dozens of impacts that had occurred since about 1650 as a consequence of the depletion and extinction of the incredible amount of animal life present when Europeans first arrived. He also described the loss or this organic topsoil and the massive erosion caused by cattle during the drought and speculated on the long-term consequences. Early settlers in Australia reported on the disappearance or transformation of the habitat layer when livestock from other parts of the world were introduced.

In 1834, Darwin comments on vast and ancient forest ecosystems that were still present in some islands and locations that he encountered in Chile and Argentina and compared them with what existed in Europe then, and it is easy to compare the conditions found then with those encountered today. He described how in many areas the forests had sometimes been replaced by flourishing communities producing all kinds of products, but that in others there was poverty or erosion. A frequent conclusion was the importance of culture and he analysed the reasons for failure which are still evident today.

1.5 Discussion: the adaptation of people and cultures to desertification

Most people today grow up in regions to which they naturally become attached to and which they would not describe as being degraded. The landscape and soil environment are part of our and other organisms phenotypes and we created these in the past with our actions, habits and cultures. Nevertheless, when our ancestors cut down forests in Neolithic and Bronze Ages or even in Medieval Times and today the perhaps pristine soils were lost and the landscape changed in ways that limit or benefit us today. Some of these changes we find negative because, for example fertile soils and landscapes were transformed into rocky barren areas unfit for agriculture. The soil has becomes so thin that it no longer holds enough water for crops. On the other hand at the same time fertile sediments were created in the floodplains and coastal areas providing food from land we irrigate today, hundreds or thousands of years later.

Wherever the reader may be located, he or she is quite probably living in or familiar with a region that has been severely impacted on by land degradation sometime in the past a consequence of his or somebody else's ancestors cultural customs. Land degradation and desertification do not mean that the areas have no value, but rather that they no longer provide the level of protection or the raw materials, water and oxygen that they once did. This can be dramatic as in the case of the examples from Bolivia shown in Photograph 1.6. When the first Europeans arrived in the fifteenth century this was an area of amazing biodiversity and pristine soils, more than one metre thick. Only a few remnants of these remain as a consequence of the bedrock stripping caused by land use practices, including grazing. Figure 1.20a and b illustrate the adaptive cycle idea that provides a framework for considering, scale, time and changes. In Figure 1.20b, for example this could be referring to the accumulation of organic matter in the soil, or to the soil formation, erosion.

In contrast other people live in regions where cultural practices such as that of Shintuism Japan and Feng Sui Korea and in China, or in Tuscany in Italy aim to have landscapes

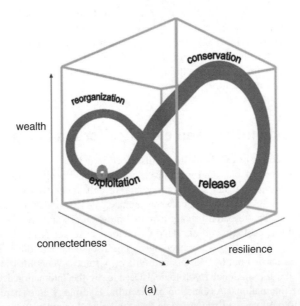

(a)

(b)

Figure 1.20(a)   The adaptive cycle and land degradation. One way of understanding change is in terms of successive stages of accumulation or conservation (for example, soil formation by weathering), release that occurs when it becomes unstable, reorganization and exploitation. This concept is applied in Gunderson and Holling (2002). The general principle is applied to land degradation in South Limburg (see Chapter 4). (Based on Gunderson and Holling 2002). (b) illustrates how different areas can be in different phases of the cycle (Credit: Anton Imeson).

that aim to be in harmony with natural processes and where there is traditionally little erosion in landscapes that retain relatively large areas of forest or natural vegetation.

Desertification is not inevitable because it invariably involves thresholds that can be predicted and dealt with when the processes and critical conditions are understood. It nevertheless requires overcoming cultural blindness as described by Huxley with respect to other people and nature.

1.6 Discussion: Data and evidence for land degradation

In subsequent sections of this book this is discussed in detail.

Primary sources of data and experience are field and monitoring experiments by people such as the author and several thousands of colleagues who set up monitoring programmes to study relationships between climate, land degradation and land use at very many places. The research usually involved programmes and projects in which the climate, hydrology, ecology, soil and land use studies were performed by geographers, landscape ecologists, geologists, archaeologists but also social and other scientists and the analysis was carried out by Masters and PhD or postdocs. Many measurements were stimulated by the International Hydrological Decade, by the International Geographical Union and the International Association of Scientific Hydrology etc. There are in some cases about 40 to 60 years of primary data that can be used to quantify land degradation and desertification. In addition to this there is some information from official government sponsored long term monitoring sites. For example, each year more than 800 scientific papers by young scientists discuss and report on research at the European Geophysical Society conferences and the abstracts and publications can be found online.

Primary measurements demonstrate that land degradation processes are extremely sensitive to initial conditions and very complex so that it is hard to model and predict, being influenced by thresholds and feedbacks. The many authors who have written many thousands of papers on land degradation research that can be found in many journals and proceedings are to some extent co-authors of this book. Very many International organizations have helped desertification and land degradation scientists organize conferences, plan meetings and visit each other's field sites.

Data collected and reported then often provides a benchmark and reference level for quantifying desertification.

Data is also provided in the form of remote sensing observations that can be used to interpret changes in surface properties as the impacts of desertification. Some countries also provide primary data and information about the climate, geomorphology, hydrology and soils.

Secondary sources of data and information are provided by Governments and International Organizations that provide data about the state of the Environment or Socio-economic conditions. Reports published by Environmental Agencies in Europe and Governments are political reflecting existing policies and add to the existing memes and social propaganda.

The Global Land Project consists of an International network of scientists investigating interactions between land use change and ecosystem goods and services. It succeeded an earlier Land Use and Climate Change Project LUCC, which is a reliable source of data and experience. There were several investigations into different aspects of desertification under the auspices of the LUCC and they provide case studies. One of its programmes is called *The consequences of land system changes* and this focuses on feedbacks between people and ecosystems, that are critical to Earth System science.

1.7 Conclusion: why land degradation and desertification occur

According to Darwin (1885), land degradation and desertification occur when the activities of people or animals are not checked and by something so that there is no limit on what they do until some threshold is reached and it is triggered. Land degradation and desertification involve three critical areas: processes, land use issues and the real causes. This has been known for a long time in Iceland where the people are very aware of the land degradation that started in about 800 AD when the settlers arrived, cut down the forests and introduced sheep. Iceland was the first country to establish a national soil conservation service in 1905 (Arnalds 2005), it has world class scientists researching restoration strategies in harsh environments and has embarked upon large restoration programmes that are restoring birch forests and recovering farmland. Today, Iceland as well is at the forefront in addressing global issues of desertification and capacity building to develop sustainable land use. Not just in Iceland but almost in every country of the world there similar experiences regarding desertification. Flooding in the UK, Madeira and the islands of the West Indies is in many ways a delayed response to the impact that land use changes have on soil functions, sometimes at the scale of centuries. In many parts of the world, for example in New Zealand, the USA, Spain and South America, it has been established that there is usually a delayed response to erosion and land sliding that can be at least one hundred years, depending on the soil and climate. In New Zealand, it was found that the intrinsic soil stability of a soil resisted erosion for 80 years. Landslides and erosion today are not always a consequent of present farming activities but of changes that took place long ago. Iceland illustrates many of the common and persistent features of land degradation and desertification. Resources are identified, targeted and exploited without concern or awareness of the future costs and with ignorance about the slow processes. Resource exploitation is market or culturally driven. Available money from financial markets may lead to people investing for example in unsuitable tractors that farmers are encouraged to buy in the 1930s (U. S. Soil Conservation 1935), or in colonial times and today to the sugar, coffee, meat and exploitation of raw materials. Treating the land as a resource and exploiting it until it is consumed is accepted in our culture, as can be observed today in Vietnam, where forests are cleared for coffee production or in Indonesia where land is cleared for palm oil and Brazil for sugar cane and soya. Dynamic models that link the economy with species and or ecosystems have been developed for fisheries and have been applied to land degradation and these demonstrate remorselessly the link between politics, the economy and land degradation. One conclusion is that when the future value of a resource is not considered it then behaves like an open resource and is just used up.

Sustainable land management to prevent land degradation could be achieved by the application of experience and process knowledge and understanding to develop strategies and methods that do not cause land degradation and which restore ecological functions so that the land and soil remain a sustainable and healthy habitat for life.

As will be discussed later, the principles of sustainable land management are well understood but they are only applied if there is a high level of political insight and resources to develop policies, laws and governance. An example of this is in China where many tens of thousands of people are providing soil conservation governance.

The soil and land and its ecosystems constitute a habitat in which humans are a species. An ecological and ecosystems paradigm of land degradation is being increasingly applied in research projects. Understanding why, how and when land degradation occurs, can be approached by using the methods that have been developed by historians and geography to be taken into account, but perhaps more than always contextual and specific but the processes themselves are invariably similar. The way round this used in landscape architecture by Lloyd Wright 1965 is to focus not on the individual effects of land degradation, because these are always different but to consider the principles in a radical way.

Because it covers a large area of science, land degradation and desertification are being investigated by people with knowledge grounded in many different disciplines and work published in contrasting types of literature with different conventions and experiences. This makes it a dynamic and continually evolving field of knowledge. The challenge is how can to develop a shared terminology with common and harmonious concepts. A common and agreed set of integrated concepts, language and terminology does not yet exist. The greatest number of people working on land degradation live in China and there is a need for joint literature and platforms for the exchange of experiences and development of common language. A particular problem is the institutional frameworks of environmental laws whereby the focus is on politics rather than science (Granger 2009).

One reason for desertification is that the different states of affairs are not given adequate attention. For example, the state of affairs of the Ministries of Agriculture or of Development decide on policy. By applying this idea of Wittgenstein, the communication challenge in land degradation could be transcended. Different states of affairs influence the validity and intentions of about what is being meant. They come from: history and archeology, the economics of rural and marginal lands, natural resource management, and geomorphology, in which man is seen as a geological agent, hydrology and water resources management, land use, including agriculture and forestry.

References and further reading

Allen, T.F.H. and T.B. Starr (1982) *Hierarchy: Perspectives for Ecological Complexity*. University of Chicago Press, Chicago, 310 pp.

Arnalds, A. (2000) Evolution of rangeland conservation strategies, in O. Arnalds and S. Archer (eds), *Rangeland Desertification*, pp. 153–163. Advances in Vegetation Sciences Series. Kluwer, Dordrecht, The Netherlands.

Arnalds, A. (2005a) *Strategies Science and Law for the Conservation of the World Soil Resources* International Workshop, Selfoss, Iceland, 14–18 September 2005. Rit LBHl nr. 4. Agricultural University of Iceland. 270 pp.

Arnalds, O. (2005b) Knowledge and policy making: premises, paradigms and a Sustainability Index Model, in *Strategies, Science and Law for the Conservation of the World Soil Resources*, Agricultural University of Iceland, Publication No. 4: 251–259.

Arnalds, O., E.F. Thorarinsdottir, S.M. Metusalemsson, A. Jonsson, E. Gretarsson and A. Arnason (2001) *Soil Erosion in Iceland*. Soil Conservation Service and Agricultural Research Institute, Reykjavik. 121 pp.

Arnalds, O. and Barkarson, B.H. (2003). Soil erosion and land use policy in Iceland in relation to sheep grazing and government subsidies. *Environmental Science and Policy*, 6: 105–113.

Aru, A. (1996) The Rio Santa Lucia Site: An integrated study of desertification, pp. 169–188, in J. Brandt and J.B. Thornes, *Mediterranean Desertification and Land Use*. John Wiley and Sons, Ltd, Chichester. 554 pp.

Bork, H.-R. (2003) State-of-the-art of erosion research – soil erosion and its consequences since 1800 AD, pp. 11–14, in *Briefing Papers of the First SCAPE Workshop*.

Brandt, J. and J.B. Thornes (2000) *Mediterranean Desertification and Land Use*. John Wiley and Sons, Ltd, Chichester. 554 pp.

Briassoulis, E. (2008) Land use policy and planning, theorizing, and modeling: Lost in translation, found in complexity? *Environment and Planning* B Vol. 35: 16–33.

Briassoulis, E. (2010) (LEDDRA Project: Land and Ecosystem Degradation and Desertification. *Assessing the Fit of Responses to Land and Ecosystem Degradation and Desertification*, EU 7th Framework Programme, http//Leddra.aegean.gr.

Burton, R.F. and G.A. Wilson (2006) Injecting social psychology theory into conceptualisations of agricultural agency: towards a post-productivist farmer self-identity? *Journal of Rural Studies* 22: 95–115.

Cerda, A. (2010) Herbicide versus tillage. *Soil and Water Losses at the El Teularet Soil Erosion Experimental Station*. Geophysical Research Abstracts (n.p.).

Cherlet, M. (2008) *Atlas Structure Overview and Needs*, *World Atlas Desertification* Discussion Expert Meeting on Defining a Roadmap of the Development of a New World Atlas on Desertification (WAD), JRC, ISPRA 3–5 December 2008.

Darwin, C. (1845) *Journal of Researches Into The Natural History and Geology of the Countries Visited During the Voyage of H.M.S.* Beagle *Round the World*. John Murray, London: 2nd edn.

Diamond, J. (2005) *How Societies Chose to Fail or Succeed*. Viking Penguin, Harmondsworth. 572 pp.

Dorren, L. K.A. and A.C. Imeson (2005) Soil erosion and the adaptive cycle metaphor. *Land Degradation and Development* 16: 509–516.

Dregne, H.E. (1983) *Desertification of Arid Lands*. Harwood Academic Publishers, London.

Falkenmark, M. and J. Lundquist (1998) Towards water security: political determination and human adaptation crucial. *Natural Resources Forum* 22: 37–51.

Fantechi, R. and Margaris N.S. (1986) *Desertification in Europe*. Proceedings of the 1984 Symposium in Mytilini, Greece. D. Reidel, Dordrecht.

Goldstein, R.J. (2004) Environmental ethics and positive law, pp. 1–37, in *Environmental Ethics and Law*. Ashgate, London.

Groot, de R.S. (1992) *Functions of Nature: Evaluation of Nature in Environmental Planning, Management and Decision Making*. Wolters-Noordhoff, Amsterdam, 315 pp.

Gunderson, L.H. and C.S. Holling (2002) *Panarchy: understanding transformations in human and natural systems*. Island Press, Washington, D.C. 507 pp.

Hanan, N.P. Prevost, Y.A. Diouf and O. Diallo (1991) Assessment of desertification around deep wells in the Sahel using satellite imagery. *Journal of Applied Ecology* 28: 173–186.

Hannam, I. (2000). Soil conservation policies in Australia: successes, failures and requirements for ecologically sustainable policy. pp. 493–514, in E.L. Napier, S.M. Napier and J. Tvrdon (eds). *Soil and Water Conservation Policies and Programs: Successes and Failures*. CRC Press, Boca Raton, Florida.

Hannam, I. and Boer, B. (2002) *Legal and Institutional Frameworks for Sustainable Soils*. A preliminary report. IUCN Environmental Policy and Law Paper No. 45.

Hare, F. (1976) *Climate and Desertification*. Report prepared for the United Nations Environment Programme. Institute of Environmental Studies, University of Toronto.

Heede, B.H. (1990) Vegetation strips control erosion in watersheds. *Research Note*. RM-499 USDA; 1., Forest Service, June.

Heidegger, M. (1954) *The Question concerning Technology and Other Essays*. Harper and Row, New York.

Helldén, U. (1991) Desertification – time for a reassessment? *Ambio* 20 (8): 372–383.

Herrick, J.E., B.T. Bestelmeyer, S. Archer, A. Tugel and J.R. Brown (2006) An integrated framework for science-based arid land management. *Journal of Arid Environments*. 65: 319–335.

Holling, C.S. (2000) Theories for sustainable futures. *Conservation Ecology* 4(2): 7 [online] URL: http://www.consecol.org/vol4/iss2/art7.

Holling, C.S. and G.K. Meffe (1996) Command and control and the pathology of natural resource management. *Conservation Biology* 10(2): 328–337.

Howard, A. (1940) *An Agricultural Testament*, Oxford University Press, Oxford.

Huxley, T.H. (1885) Selected Works of Thomas Huxley Westminster Edition containing III *Evolution and Ethics* (1893) and IV *Capital the Mother of Labour* (1890). Appeltons, 334 pp.

Imeson, A.C. (1987) Soil erosion and conservation. In *Human Activity and Environmental Processes*, ed. K.J. Gregory and D.E. Walling. John Wiley and Sons, Inc., New York.

Imeson, A.C., O. Arnalds, L. Montanarella, A. Arnouldssen, L. Dorren, M. Curf and D. de la Rosa (2006) *Soil Conservation and Protection in Europe (SCAPE): The Way Ahead*. European Soil Bureau, Ispra, Italy.

Imeson, A.C. and H. Lavee (1998) Investigating the impact of climate change on geomorphological processes: the transect approach and the influence of scale. *Geomorphology* 23: 219–227.

International Forum (2007) *Soils, Society and Global Change*. 31 August–4 September, Selfoss, Iceland.

Joyce, L.A. (1989) *An analysis of the range forest situation in the United States 1989–2040*. A technical document supporting the 1989 USDA Forest Service RPA Assessment General Technical Report RM 180 Rocky Mountains Forest and Range Experimental Station.

Kosmos, C.S., N. Moustakas, N.G. Danalatos and N. Yassoglou (1996) The Spata Field Site. The impacts of land use and management on soil properties and erosion, pp. 207–230 in J. Brandt and J.B. Thornes, *Mediterranean Desertification and Land Use*, John Wiley and Sons, Ltd, Chichester.

Lang, A. and H.R. Bork (2006) Past soil erosion in Europe, pp. 465–475, in J. Boardman and J. Poesen, eds, *Soil Erosion in Europe*, John Wiley and Sons, Ltd, Chichester, 855 pp.

van der Leeuw, S. (1998). *The Archaeomedes Project–Understanding the natural and anthropogenic causes of land degradation and desertification in the Mediterranean*. Luxemburg: Office for Official Publications of the European Union.

Leopold, A. (1949) *A Sand County Almanac and Sketches Here and Thereby*. Oxford University Press, Oxford.

Lopez Bermudez, F.A, A. Romero Diaz and J. Martinez Fernandez (1996) The El Al Field Site: Soil and vegetation cover, pp. 169–188, in J. Brandt and J.B Thornes, *Mediterranean Desertification and Land Use*, John Wiley and Sons, Ltd, Chichester.

McGlade, J. (1995) An integrative multi-scalar modeling framework for human ecodynamic research in the Vera Basin, southeast Spain, pp. 357–385, in L'Homme et la degradation de l'environnement XV Reconteres internationals de Histoire d'Antibes Editions APDCA Juan-les-Pines. 514 pp.

Malthus (1798) *An Essay on the Principle of Population as it Affects the Future Improvement of Society*. J. Johnson, London.

Mieth, A. and H.R. Bork (2004) *Ester Island/Rapa Nui Scientific Pathways to Secrets of the Past*. Man and Environment 1. Department of Ecotechnology and Ecosystem Development, Germany.

L. Montanarella, A. Cowie and U. Schneider (2007) Potential synergies between existing multilateral environmental agreements in the implementation of land use, land-use change and forestry activities. *Environmental Science and Policy* 10: 335–352.

Reining, P. (1978) *Handbook on Desertification Indicators*, AAAS Publication No. 78-7, 141 pp.

Roxo, M.J. (1994) Field site: Lower Alentejo, Portugal. In: *Medalus II, Project 1, 2nd Annual Report*, J. Brandt and N. Geeson, eds, pp. 49–57. London.

Roxo, M.J. (2009) *Lucinda Land Care in Desertification Affected Areas from Science to Application*. EU Project. See at http://geografia.fcsh.unl.pt/lucinda/

Runólfsson, S. and A. Andres (2004). Soil conservation at the top of the world- conservation strategies in Iceland, pp. 1–4 ISCO International Soil Conservation Organization Conference, Conserving Soil and Water for Society, Brisbane July 2004. Woodman *et al.*, eds, *The Breakdown and Restoration of Ecosystems*, pp. 231–240. www.tucson.ars.ag.gov/isco/isco13.

Stafford Smith, D.M and J.F. Reynolds (2002) Desertification: A new paradigm for an old problem pp 401–424 in *Global desertification do humans cause deserts*, Berlin: Dahlem. Workshop Report 88, Dahlem University Press. 437 pp.

Sutton, M.O. and E.N. Anderson (2004) *Introduction to Cultural Ecology*. Rowman and Littlefield, Lanham, MD. 384 pp.

Tongway, D. (1994) *Rangeland Assessment Manual*, Division of Wildlife and Ecology, Canberra. 69 pp.

Thornes, J.B. and Burke, S. (1996a) *Actions taken by national governmental organisations to mitigate desertification in the Mediterranean. Concerted Action on Mediterranean Desertification* (355 p) Kings College, University of London.

Thornes, J.B. (1996b) Introduction, pp. 1–11, in J. Brandt and J.B. Thornes *Mediterranean Desertification and Land Use*. John Wiley and Sons, Ltd, Chichester. 554 pp.

UNCCD (2007) *10-year Strategic Plan and Framework to Enhance the Implementation of the Convention* 2008–2009, COP 8 Madrid, 3–4 September.

UNCCD (2011) *Addressing Desertification, Land Degradation and Drought in the Context Of Sustainable Development and Poverty Eradication*, 20 September, New York.

UNEP (1991) *Status of Desertification and Implementation of the United Nations Plan of Action to Combat Desertification*. UNEP, Nairobi.

United Nations (1992) *Earth Summit Convention on Desertification*, Brazil, 3–14 June 1992. Department of Public Information, UN, New York.

USDA Forest Service (2007) *Strategic Plan* FY 2007–2012, 38 pp.

Vita-Finzi, C. (1973) *Recent Earth History*, Macmillan, London, 138 pp.

Warren, A. and L. Olsson (2003) Desertification: loss of credibility despite the evidence. *Annals of Arid Zone* 42 (3): 271–287.

Westman, W.E. (1986) Resilience Concepts and Measures in B. Dell, A. J. M. Hopkins and B.B. Lamont, eds, pp. 5–19, The *Resilience of Mediterranean Ecosystems*. Junk, The Netherlands.

Wilson, G.A. (2009) Rethinking environmental management – ten years later: A view from the author. *Environments* 36(3): 3–15.

Wilson, G.A. (2010) Multifunctional 'quality' and rural community resilience. *Transactions of the Institute of British Geographers* 35: 364–381.

Wilson, G.A. and H. Buller (2001) The use of socio-economic and environmental indicators in assessing the effectiveness of EU Agri-Environmental Policy. *European Environment* 11: 297–313.

Xiao Jietu and Li Jinquan (2008) *An Outline History of Chinese Philosophy*, (I) Foreign Language Press, Beijing, China, 434 pp.

Yair, A. and H. Lavee (1981) An Investigation of Source Area of Sediment and Sediment Transport by Overland Flow along Arid Hillslope. *IAHS Pub*. 133, pp. 433–446.

2
Responses to desertification

2.1 Finding answers

2.1.1 Ethics regarding land and all life

Many responses to desertification are planned but other things are happening unintentionally or informally as a consequence of globalization and greater access to information. It is a basic human instinct to have empathy for other people and living things and to be part of a civilization that has values and is equitable towards all. There is growing reluctance to be responsible and accountable for policies that spoil or appropriate the social, economic and environmental capital of fellow world citizens and burden them with debt for things they do not need or cannot afford. So many organizations such as the Campus of Excellence in Spain in 2008 and various NGOs are helping to adapt and change our culture by raising awareness of the true state of land degradation and the human actions causing it.

2.1.2 The United Nations Convention to Combat Desertification

The United Nations Convention to Combat Desertification (UNCCD) defines desertification in the following ways:

- '**Land degradation**' means reduction or loss of the biological or economic productivity and complexity of rainfed cropland, irrigated cropland, or range, pasture, forest and woodlands. Land degradation is often linked with food insecurity and poverty, in a cause–effect relationship.

- '**Desertification**' means *land degradation* in arid, semi-arid and dry sub-humid areas. While land degradation occurs everywhere, it is only defined as 'desertification' when it occurs in those areas. Desertification affects 70 per cent of the world's drylands, amounting to one fourth of the world's land surface.

- '**Sustainable land management**' refers to land use management practices that do not result in land degradation and which are sustainable from the perspectives of soil and land quality and biodiversity, natural capital and ecological integrity. The UNCCD emphasizes the value of traditional knowledge and practices as opposed to modern

Desertification, Land Degradation and Sustainability, First Edition. Anton Imeson.
© 2012 John Wiley & Sons, Ltd. Published 2012 by John Wiley & Sons, Ltd.

mechanical or industrial agriculture which focuses only on yields and is not integrated into the cultural systems that have evolved.

What is meant by traditional knowledge systems are systems that are sustainable because the food and crop production is integrated into the local economy and ecology. Sustainable land management therefore is in some way a strategy for protecting soil from degradation.

Kirkby (2009) has recently reviewed the changing emphasis that desertification has received since the 1950s. A complete review of the origin of the concept was given by Odingo (1990). When the UNCCD was developed it was thought that there would be many more advances in the development of the social scientists and the integration of these concerns with the physical ones and that consequently there has never been a sound scientific conceptual underpinning of what desertification actually is. This is still the case and accounts for the fact that attention being given to desertification is far less than it warrants on the basis of the impact land degradation is having on the world.

Kirkby (2009) lists the processes that cause land degradation as:

- soil erosion caused by wind and water;

- deterioration of the physical, chemical and biological properties or economic properties of the soil; and

- long-term loss of natural vegetation.

Combating desertification should occur through activities involving the integrated development of land and which are aimed to prevent or reduce land degradation, rehabilitate degraded land and reclaim desertified land.

What the UNCCD might be able to achieve is to help the governments which are responsible to tackle the cultural, ecological and ethical aspects of desertification that have been mentioned in section 2.1.1.

2.1.3 NGOs and desertification: increasing public concern and the development of a political will

That our actions are still profoundly altering the earth's water and energy budgets and the capacity of its ecosystems to support nature is obvious to anyone with internet access. Google-earth and street-view have democratized remote sensing and geographical information systems information. Some International organizations are recording and archiving information about the changes. There is a feedback to policy but this is limited because the messages are politicized and not directed back towards people or organizations with the resources and a mandate to manage responses. Land degradation and desertification are often not recognized in global programmes such as the Group on Earth Observations (GEO) and the Intergovernmental Panel on Climate Change (IPCC) assessments that consider matters in relation to systems and sectors such as forestry and agriculture. Environmental policies are mainstreamed into other policies and are not given much priority.

Table 2.1 From Desertlinks (Geeson *et al.* 2005) Concerns expressed by stakeholders in Portugal (Beja and Mertola), Italy (Agri), Spain and Greece. This table shows the problems identified in the National Action Plans for Combating Desertification.

Problems identified at the stakeholder workshops

	Beja	Mertola	Agri	Guadalentín	Lesvos
1	depopulation	depopulation	lack of water	deforestation	lack of water
2	lack of employment	advance of deserts	drought	lack of water	drought
3	drought	deforestation	deforestation	drought	increase in temperature
4	deforestation	drought	temperature increase	soil erosion	fire
5	poor infrastructure	lack of water	climate change	aridity	deforestation
6	lack of water	lack of employment	fire	desert advance	destruction of vegetation
7	desert advance	climate change	desert advance	biodiversity loss	soil and water pollution
8	soil erosion	soil erosion	ozone layer destruction	fire	depopulation

The Desertlinks Project carried out several meetings with stakeholders to identify their main concerns (see Table 2.1).

In the USA one can surf one's watershed, obtain hydrological and water quality data from catchments that have been monitored for many years and evaluate for oneself the impact of land use changes on the hydrology and erosion. It is possible to describe and estimate the water and geochemical balances of different elements and to link these to the dynamics of the processes and changes taking place in the oceans and on land and it is possible to record the disappearance of every tree. The huge demand for commodities such as beef, soya, palm oil, coffee and sugar, as well as raw materials, is having a direct impact on land use change and soils are being lost and people flooded and this can be seen more or less in real time on the internet.

Sutton and Anderson (2004), in their introduction to *Cultural Ecology*, provide a systematic account of how different human cultures are affecting the environment and of how these are explained by fundamental principles of human and group behaviour.

That the biosphere is critical for maintaining the chemical characteristics of the earth's atmosphere was described by Lovelock (1979) half a century ago. Before this, Darwin in South America had commented on the impact of the massive changes in the ecosystems that had occurred since about 1650 and 1830, when he was in Argentina and Brazil. How have and how are the degradation and disappearance of living ecosystems affected by or been responsible for the carbon dioxide in the atmosphere, which has a residence time of 200 years, and oxygen, with a residence time of about 1600 years? Animals are, of course, totally dependent on the oxygen produced by plants and how is this last affected by a decrease in the amount of photosynthesis by plants and by the additional oxygen now being consumed to weather rock exposed by land degradation and by combustion?

Today, land degradation processes are affecting almost anywhere in the world but in some cases degradation has been halted or reversed. For example, for the last 20 years the vegetation cover in the Mediterranean and parts of Africa seems to have increased.

2.1.4 Desertification and socio-economic function analysis (1992)

The socio-economic consequences of land degradation can be estimated by assessing the socio-economic functions of the environment. The chance that erosion leads to loss of the socio-economic functions of the environment can be assessed with environmental sensitivity analysis.

Socio-economic function analysis involves the evaluation of the socio-economic value of the different functions of the environment, as described by Costanza *et al.* (1997) and de Groot (1992). In order to describe and quantify the functions, the land use of the area has first to be mapped. Next, the functions of the different landscape units have to be assessed. Where possible, an economic value has to be attached to these functions. Examples of this will be given later.

Millennium ecosystem assessment

The notions of soil and ecosystem functions now have a long history in soil science and ecology. They are seen as being analogous to those of ecosystem goods and services (Costanza *et al.* 1997). The Millennium goals of the United Nations can be found on the UNDP website. These set out principles and involve intentions to address land degradation.

Millennium ecosystem assessment (MEA) authors came to the following conclusion: the capacity of ecosystems to provide goods and services is being reduced by desertification and land degradation:

> ...the changes made to ecosystems contributed to substantial net gains in human well-being and economic development. But these gains have been achieved at growing costs in the form of the degradation of many ecosystem services, increased risk of non-linear changes, and the exacerbation of poverty for some groups of people. These problems, unless addressed, will substantially diminish the benefits that future generations obtain from ecosystems.

The MEA made it clear that the degradation of ecosystem services could grow significantly worse in the next decades and is a barrier to achieving the Millennium Development Goals. They describe how the value of all of the goods and services in the world were valued. Applications of function analysis have also been developed in soil science and soil conservation. Soil quality indicators can also be used as an indicator of how desertification is affecting soil goods and services. Different soil indicators can be evaluated using a balanced score card method so that a record of the ability to provide goods and services can be kept.

2.1.5 The soil conservation and protection function of land

The functions approach was developed and applied in several different areas of science, ranging from environmental economics, nature conservation and soils. Examples of its use can be found in the European Soil Strategy. In the United States, functions are sometimes described in terms of different qualities with respect to ecosystem health. In environmental economics (de Groot 1992) and soil science, they have been helpful in developing a more harmonious and less agro-centric viewpoint regarding the value of the land. The benefits of the approach were described by Havstad (2007) and others nearly 20 years ago and these are considered further in the next chapter.

The functions provided by the land include food, natural resources, water and protection and habitat. But this has to be extended to include all life because we are part of it. The landscape in which these processes or functions exists share a common habitat of all life. The impact of desertification, for example, might be felt or experienced in terms of the impairment of so-called ecological, economic or heritage functions.

The 'function' approach has been applied in several different areas as part of the Mediterranean Desertification and Land Use project (MEDALUS). The sensitivity to desertification was approached by studying the effect of soil erosion and soil degradation on the loss of mainly production functions. In a case study, attention was given to obtaining indicators that could be used to quantify what were called *soil and water conservation* functions. This is the idea that the land is protecting people in ways that they would otherwise have to do for themselves.

Should land degradation reduce the production or ecological functions of a *land unit*, and make it unfit, for example, for cereal production or nature conservation, then the losses of these functions can be exactly quantified in terms of money or other things. The losses can also be related to the critical values of indicators, such as soil depth, that can be used to establish threshold conditions and be related to the sensitivity to desertification. However, potential benefits of new functions can be considered, such as are illustrated later in the Guadalentin catchment area in Spain (irrigation, almond cultivation and free-range pig farming).

A functional approach enables areas, which are physically or socio-economically dissimilar to be compared. This is in practice essential because in each area or country the concept of degradation is socio-economically and culturally different. Functional indicators, just like other indicators, can be defined at different scales and hierarchies, as will be explained later.

An indicator should summarize specific aspects of the effects of complex processes and also be easy to measure and relate to critical conditions. This is easily said. In practice a major problem is that simple universal indicators are impossible to find because properties of the soil and vegetation, and processes that are dependent on chemical or physical threshold conditions (for example, frost action or salt accumulation) usually limit the validity of an indicator to a specific geo-ecological domain or regions. This is exemplified by soil depth.

Consequently, because the real point of interest is not the value of an indicator such as the soil depth, but whether after erosion the soil retains after erosion its productive capacity, former soil erosion has left the soil so thin that it is now unfit for use under modern cultivation methods. To calculate and compare the sensitivity of different areas, soil depth is evaluated in its context as a function performance indicator.

The term **performance** implies that target or threshold values for an indicator can be given so that, for example, policy can be tested by the degree to which the policy is meeting its objectives. For example, when an area of land is no longer cultivated and it loses its agricultural function, desertification or some other factor that explains this has exceeded an important threshold.

Paradoxically desertification has an underlying simplicity from the perspective of the causes and processes. The solutions are also simple. Although human impact is enormous and much seems to have been irreversibly lost, there are many actions can be taken re-address the cultural causes.

2.1.6 Restoring functions, sustainable land management and land care

Although in many cases the land is in such a condition that the soil no longer protects us from flooding, scientists have found that erosion processes and land degradation are both cyclical and complex. If allowance is made for slow processes such as the weathering of rocks and the down cutting of river channels and some diffuse processes and evolution of structures and patterns to conserve water and promote biodiversity, many ecosystem functions can be restored and developed in a few years or decades.

Detailed process studies in ecosystems (Herrick *et al.* 2006) in the USA, Israel, Iceland, Spain, Australia, South America and Namibia have demonstrated concepts and techniques that can be applied in all environments. In China, there are large programmes of ecosystem restoration under way. Yair (2002) has demonstrated, in many different situations in Israel, how process knowledge can be applied to transform landscapes when the processes are understood and manipulated to kickstart ecosystems and recreate a living earth (Arnalds 2005).

Also, the ecosystem processes that can induce the restoration of landscapes and reduce or counteract desertification are conceptually much better understood so that better and more effective strategies can be employed. Lost forests ecosystems can be restored, as is happening in many places in the world, ranging from the laurel forests in Madeira to the forests above Mexico City and in many parts of China, so that people have clean water.

2.1.7 Case: Restoring the hydrological and aesthetic functions of soil and land in China and Europe

It is common knowledge that sediment yields are low from areas under natural or complete ($\geq 75\%$) vegetation cover which is in an ecologically healthy condition. Today erosion and overland runoff are increasing problems that perhaps are being enhanced by climate change, but which are definitely mainly due to agricultural practices that make soil compact, degrade soil structure and leave agricultural land without cover of crops

Figure 2.1   Soil conservation work makes it possible to cultivate these highly erodible sandy soils developed on granitic rocks in China (Credit: Anton Imeson).

during critical periods of the year. There are many examples of successful practices that manage this. In China and Europe, the benefits of extra water availability that is being provided as a benefit of soil conservation and protection can also be quantified. The benefit is also aesthetic and terraces are a form of landscape architecture that create a harmonious experience of life. The Chinese do not construct terraces like those in Figure 2.1 as cheaply as possible: instead, they try to make them beautiful, constructing the best landscape that they can.

The amount of water that can be stored in the soil and on the slopes is a key benefit. This can be measured in very many ways, ranging from remote sensing to field measurements using rainfall simulation or field experiments. Permeability, infiltration rate and soil depth are excellent indicators of how the soil water regulation function is being performed and how this relates to erosion and the soil water reservoir capacity. It was calculated by the project office team (Hu Danwen, Piet van der Poel and Lars Andersen, personal communication) that at least ten times the amount of water is stored in the soils upstream of the great Three Gorges Dam compared with the reservoir itself. Figure 2.2 shows a site where the effectiveness of a forestation project is being measured. Severe erosion occurred when the forest was cut for different reasons and the aim now is to restore a forest cover with hydrological benefits.

Land use and soil management policy should be carried out in ways that are harmonious with the maximization and optimization of the soil water regulation functions of the land. This would have the additional benefit that more water could be made available for power generation, as less would be needed for flood protection. The requirements of farmers and agriculture need to be managed by a soil conservation service which understand the processes and changes. Otherwise it is just like over-fishing and there will always be a 'tragedy of the commons'.

Conclusion

Soil and land conservation and protection are cross cutting issues that involve everyone. Our vision might include a Ministry of Soil, Water and Land Resources that makes sure that catchments regulate the provision of all kinds of services and resources in a sustainable way. Our vision could also seek inspiration from other countries such as China and New Zealand, where there are policies of integrated watershed management being developed with the aim of creating harmonious landscapes. On the other hand, we could learn from the USA, all the laws in the world won't make a difference if farmers are exempted from them.

2.1.8 Desertification and the European Community

The European Community has played an important role in promoting the International Convention to Combat Desertification. It has encouraged research and is promoting monitoring and control both in Europe and in different parts of the world. For this reason, special attention will be given to Europe in Chapters 5 and 6.

In the early 1990s the European Community became concerned that desertification might be affecting Europe. Roberto Fantechi at the Directorate General for Research who was the Head of the Environment and Climate Programme at that time decided with Professor Margaris from Greece to organize a workshop to evaluate and to respond to this at a meeting in Lesbos. This was the start of a large research effort by European scientists who launched programmes to monitor and study the complex causes of the problems. The methodologies applied ranged from remote sensing, modelling to field studies and they brought together research from the earth and social sciences. Many reports and

Figure 2.2   China, a forest restoration project in an area that was deforested for timber production. The shales weather into highly erodible material (Credit: Anton Imeson).

conclusions from this research were published in the Proceedings of an International Conference in Heraklion, Greece (Balabanis *et al* 1999).

At the Earth Summit in Rio, which established the International Conventions on Climate Change, Biodiversity and Desertification as legal frameworks for addressing desertification, the emphasis was placed on helping the affected countries in Africa and on the link with poverty and human well-being. In the United States, desertification was mainly a problem of rangelands. Several important workshops took place that stressed the challenges of connecting science with stakeholders and policy makers.

There was a paradox that whereas desertification in the USA was considered to be associated with the invasions of shrubs into areas of former desert grasslands, in Europe trees were regarded as an indication of recovery from degradation (see Chapters 4 and 6).

In Europe, the main instruments for addressing land degradation at the European scale are the UNCCD and the European Soil Strategy.

2.1.9 Responding to desertification and land degradation in Europe

European research soon showed that the main causes of land degradation were not poverty and marginalization, as in historical times, but the practices of agriculture and subsidies. The main causes of land degradation in Europe were the agricultural policy and the way in which soil was being used and managed. Responsibility for soils in Europe belongs to the Ministries of Agriculture, who are therefore responsible for the problems and threats to the soils but in reality are focusing on providing food and on helping farmers to maximize their incomes and on generating for them interventions and subsidies.

As the first stage of developing a soil protection policy, the European Commission published a soils communication in 2002 (COM 2002). The preparation of this communication was discussed with all stakeholders, including the scientific community. It highlighted and discussed the following threats: biodiversity, sealing, compaction, floods and landslides, salinization, soil erosion, contamination and organic matter. In its second phase it prioritized the development of action to specifically address these. These threats occur because of the things the farmers and others are doing so that it is these actions that require regulations.

2.1.10 Soil protection and sustainable land use in Europe

Soil protection in Europe is seen as part of the general Sustainable Development Strategy. The benefits of soil protection should be equitably made available to all. Sustainable use is defined as:

> to use the components of the environment in a way and at a rate that preserves at the long-term its multitude of functions and improve its quality including biological diversity, thereby maintaining its potential to meet the needs and aspiration of present and future generations.

It was realized that translating these into operational definitions and actions that command wide support would require much more thought, long negotiations and much vision.

Figure 2.3 and Figure 2.4 Traditional agricultural practices are being abandoned and replaced by ones that are not sustainable because of their impact on the water and soil resources. Pigs replace sheep in Murcia, Spain, and herbicides replace cover crops in Andalucia (*Source*: Figure 2.3 Imeson and Figure 2.4 A. Cerda).

This approach is important because soils are to be evaluated on the functions (goods and services) that they provide. These range from ecological and economic functions through to those that encompass amenity, recreation, heritage, psychology and well-being. Although it might not be realized, everyone is a stakeholder in this sense that we all depend on the soil for clean air, water, food and the landscape in which we exist. Although it might see like a good idea, this free range pig farming in Murcia shown in Figure 2.3 failed according to the farmer because of many problems, for example with the lack of water and contamination.

Figure 2.5 Typical impact of support measures to farmers that cause erosion because there is no guidance and control. This is why scientists think that a soil conservation service could help (Credit: Anton Imeson).

There were several important principles. The first principle is that of the 'polluter must pay'. This principle is to a large extent already applied in the United States by the U.S. Soil Conservation Service. The implications of globally accepting this principle are probably not fully appreciated by the policy community. The principle of preventative action has long been applied in soil conservation. Preventative action requires applying the principles of soil conservation and economics. Figure 2.4 shows the gully erosion that transforms the hydrology in an uneconomical and unsustainable way as a consequence of the management practice in which the farmer uses herbicides to control weeds which is in fact unnecessary. The subsidiarity principle is also appropriate to soil erosion. Soil erosion and protection problems will have local dimensions as a result of national and regional policies.

2.2 Conclusion: The causes of land degradation today

The causes of land degradation are what is happening on the ground today and in particular it is an emergent result of the common global culture in which financial investment and marketing mean that we all want the same things as cheaply as possible. The natural vegetation pattern of the earth is in fact rapidly becoming a land use map because of globalization and the dominance of a few commodities. There are a limited number of socio-environmental systems being created which are part of the ecological footprint of the areas they provide with food or raw material. As Figure 2.5 illustrates, they are not always a footprint of real food but of subsidies. This area, like many others in Europe is ploughed so that the farmer is eligible for payments, not to produce any crop, which even if it is sown is often left unharvested because the yields are very low. Subsidies, create conditions like these that are perfect for erosion and flood runoff.

Ecosystems of which the adapted vegetation was once temperate forest have been transformed into areas that are required and used to produce wheat and an artificial steppe or desert-like landscape means that much of these areas are kept free of vegetation for much of the year so that there is much erosion. As a consequence over much of America and Europe, more than a metre of topsoil and the life it once contained has vanished (Bork 2005). Elsewhere, forests have been or are being replaced to raise cattle, sugar cane or palm oil and soya but in nearly all cases there is a massive loss of soil and degradation of the land.

For tens of thousands of years man and animals have co-evolved and interacted with the soil-water-vegetation system of which they are part. The evolution of this system incorporates all of the familiar ecosystem processes and included weathering and erosion. During the Holocene Period, as the organization of man and other animals increased, huge changes in the distribution of soils and sediments took place. These were linked to domestication and grazing, fire and development of technology, etc. Many examples of how this happened in different cultures are described by Sutton and Anderson (2004).

In general soils became thinner and stonier on slopes and thicker in the valleys. How and why this happens is described in Chapter 4. In fact there was for all kinds of reasons soil resources became more and more concentrated in the valleys. At a certain moment in time, perhaps due to pressures such as drought or land use, the vegetation becomes less resilient with bare areas which then affects the microclimate and temperature.

The system could move from one state of attraction to another. The positive feedbacks that furthered these shifts were not necessarily negative as the accumulation of the soils in valleys in fact brought many benefits and rainwater harvesting and higher rates of groundwater recharge occurred on the slopes.

At the change or transition, communities and animals could exploit the same uniform resources everywhere. After the *transition* they would have to adapt by making use of the dryer or wetter sites or by adopting new strategies or ways of exploiting the natural resources.

Although it meant the loss of habitat for some, it may have been a necessary factor – necessary for the development of the ancient irrigation cultures which would benefit from the additional nutrients and water coming with the eroding soil. In the long term, erosion causes a transfer of resources which have value.

2.3 Conclusion: strategies to mitigate desertification

At a general level desertification and land degradation are a consequence of human culture, today and in the past, and of the impacts that these are having on the environment in which we live. Virtually everything we do can affect the regulating functions of the land and the ability to withstand or recover from the impacts of stresses such as drought, agriculture or wildfires. For thousands of years, strategies and techniques to prevent or mitigate the impacts of land degradation have been known.

The processes of land degradation are remarkably similar everywhere so that knowledge can be transferred and overarching principles of sustainable land use and restoration identified.

The present state of the environment itself enables us to identify areas that are sensitive to land degradation on the basis of current understanding of the cultural drivers and the ecosystem processes.

There is a big gap between the current political consensus and the nature of the problem. The way in which the UNCCD and the European Union and most developed countries regard desertification is reflected in a report on the contributions made by the EU to the Convention to Combat Desertification.

Land degradation is a social-economic problem. The underlying causes are directly related to human activities that often produce and use natural resources in unsustainable ways. Organization and practice play key roles in influencing the degree of pressure that human activities place on nature. Thus, ecological degradation and impoverishment are the products of social and economic interventions and the institutional context. They stimulate competition among diverse actors at local, national and global levels. This in turn gives rise to over exploitation of resources and exclusion from assets (productive, environmental or cultural). These social-economic interrelations, including the micro, meso- and macro-level linkages, make dealing with the agricultural economies in arid, semi-arid and dry sub-humid areas complex.

What is meant by complex, is that one avoids the ethical courage to challenge a situation in which within the cultural ecological norms of society it remains legitimate to do what one likes and to ignore the living world that is treated as an economic resource.

This approach to desertification is an example of the syndrome that desertification is a consequence of the over exploitation of natural resources because of governments, their policies and institutions.

When it is said that the problem described is a problem of sustainable development, what this means is that in fact the situation is desperate. In implementing the Convention to Combat Desertification there is the difficulty that complex environmental problems are divided into systems and sectors so that cross cutting issues such as desertification that affect everything disappear. Many different ministries are involved, including Economic Development, Environment, Agriculture and Water. In many cases, responsibility for land degradation lies with the Ministry of Agriculture, which is also responsible for agricultural policy.

In reality, however, the complex causes of land degradation are known to all and described in many studies. At a UNCCD conference in Israel and Spain, the following causes were mentioned. Money that should go to agriculture ends up in the budget of the Army or Police for security. For example, in Uganda, there had been a fourfold increase in the population in a region of Kenya because of war, food could be confiscated by armies as in Ethiopia, and there can be policies of cheap food in cities, which is also a factor of land degradation in Europe. The appropriation of land for cash crops such as sugar or palm oil and other things was recorded by Watts (1966) in Barbados but it is a common cause of land degradation in Indonesia and South America. There are many instances of land degradation and poverty occurring when farmers were required to pay tax or pay back loans, which also occurred during Roman times.

Environmental policy in Europe aims to integrate desertification and soil protection into other policy areas wheras in China these are valued at the level of a Ministry.

References and further reading

Arnalds, O. – AUI (2005) *Strategies, Science and Law for the Conservation of the World Soil Resources*, Workshop, Selfoss, Iceland, 14–18 September. Rit LBH1 Nr 4, Agricultural University of Iceland. 270 pp.

Arnalds, O. (2010) Dust sources and deposition of Aeolian materials in Iceland. *Iceland Agricultural Science* 23: 3–21.

Balabanis, P., D. Peter, A. Ghazi and M. Tsogas (1999) *Mediterranean Desertification: Research Results and Policy Implications*. EUR 19303. European Commission, DG-Research.

Bork, H.-R. (2003) State-of-the-art of erosion research – soil erosion and its consequences since 1800 AD. *Briefing Papers of the first SCAPE Workshop*, C. Boix-Fayos, L. Dorren and A.C. Imeson, 11–14.

Braat L.C., S.W.F. Van der Ploeg and F. Bouma (1979) *Functions of the natural environment: an economic-ecological research*, Institute for Environmental Studies, Free University Amsterdam, Amsterdam. 73 pp.

Costanza, R., R. d'Arge and R. de, Groot, *et al*. (1997) The value of the world's ecosystem services and natural capital. *Nature* 387: 253–260.

Darwin, C. (1845) The voyage of the Beagle (Keynes, R. D. ed. (2001). *Charles Darwin's Beagle Diary*. Cambridge: Cambridge University Press.

Dorren L. K.A. and A.C. Imeson (2005) Soil erosion and the adaptive cycle metaphor. *Land Degradation and Development* 16: 509–516.

Downing, T.E., H. Dowlatabadi and R.J. Fernandez, *et al*. (2007) Global desertification: building a science for dryland development. *Science* 316: 847–851.

Fantechi, R. and N.S. Margaris (1986) *Desertification in Europe* (Proceedings of the 1984 Symposium in Mytilini, Greece). D. Reidel, Dordrecht.

Geeson, N., G. Quaranta and R. Salvia (2005) *A participatory approach to identifying indicators to soil biodiversity: empirical evidence from the northern Mediterranean countries*, Desert links Report, Desertlinks, Kings College, London. 10 pp.

Groot, de R.S. (1992) *Functions of Nature: Evaluation of Nature in Environmental Planning, Management and Decision Making*. Wolters-Noordhoff, Amsterdam: 315 pp.

Gunderson, L.H. and C.S. Holling (2002) *Panarchy: Understanding Transformations in Human and Natural Systems*. Island Press, Washington, D.C. 507 pp.

Hannam, I. and B. Boer (2002) *Legal and Institutional Frameworks for Sustainable Soils. A preliminary report*. IUCN Environmental Policy and Law Paper No. 45.

Havstad, K.M. and J.E. Herrick (2003) Long term ecological monitoring. *Arid Land Research and Management* 17: 389–400.

Havstad, K.M., D.C. Peters and R. Skaggs, *et al*. (2007) Ecosystem services to and from rangelands of the western United States. *Ecological Economics* 64: 261–268.

Herrick, J.E., B.T. Bestelmeyer, S. Archer, A. Tugel, and J. R. Brown (2006) An integrated framework for science-based arid land management. *Journal of Arid Environments* 65: 319–335.

Holling, C. S. (2000) Theories for sustainable futures. *Conservation Ecology* 4 (2): 7. [online] URL: http://www.consecol.org/vol4/iss2/art7.

Huxley T.H. (1893) *III Evolution and Ethics* and *IV Capital the Mother of Labour* (1890). In *Selected Works of Thomas Huxley*. Westminster edn, Appeltons. 334 pp.

Imeson, A.C. (2009a) Desertification and ecosystem services, in *Human and Socio-economic Consequences of Desertification*, J.L Rubio and V Andreu, eds. Campus de Excelencia, Universidad las Palmas, 272 pp.

Imeson, A.C. (2009b) Responding to desertification in Spain from Charles Darwin to John Thornes, pp. 71–77, in *Advances in Studies on Desertification Contributions to the International Conference on Desertification in Memory of Professor John B. Thornes*, A. Romero Diaz, F. Belmonte Serrato, F. Alonso Sarria and F. Lopez Bermudez, eds. 732 pp. Universidad de Murcia.

Imeson, A.C., O. Arnalds, L. Montanarella, *et al*. (2006) *Soil Conservation and Protection in Europe (SCAPE). The Way Ahead*. European Soil Bureau, Ispra, Italy.

Lovelock, J.E. (1979) *Gaia: A New Look at Life on Earth*. Oxford University Press, Oxford.

Kirkby, M.J. (2009) Desertification: The broader context, pp. 41–50, in *Advances in Studies on Desertification Contributions to the International Conference on Desertification in Memory of*

Professor John B. Thornes. A. Romero Diaz, F. Belmonte Serrato, F. Alonso Sarria and F. Lopez Bermudez, eds. 732 pp. Servicio de Publicaciones, Universidad de Murcia.

Mieth, A. and H.R. Bork (2004) *Ester Island/Rapa Nui Scientific Pathways to Secrets of the Path. Man and Environment* 1.

Moss, T. and H. Fichter (2000) *Regional Pathways to Sustainability Experiences of Promoting Sustainable Development in Structural Funds Programmes in 12 Pilot Areas*. European Commission. EUR 19401, 174 pp.

Rubio, J.L. and E. Bochet (1998) Desertificaion indicators as diagnosis criteria for desertification risk assessment in Europe. *Journal of Arid Environments* 39 (2): 113–120.

Rubio, J. and V. Andreu (2009a) Campus of Excellence, in *Human and Socio-economic Consequences of Desertification*. J.L Rubio and V. Andreu, eds. Campus de Excelencia, Universidad las Palmas. 272 pp.

Rubio J.I. and V. Andreu (2009b) Desertification and migration, pp. 69–91, in *Human and Socio-Economic Consequences of Desertification*. J.L Rubio and V. Andreu, eds. Campus de Excelencia, Universidad las Palmas. 272 pp.

Sutton, M.O. and E.N. Anderson (2004) *Introduction to Cultural Ecology*. Rowman and Littlefield, Lanham, MD. 384 pp.

Thornes, J.B. and S. Burke (1996) *Actions taken by national governmental organisations to mitigate desertification in the Mediterranean*. Concerted Action on Mediterranean Desertification (DRAFT 355 pp). Kings College, University of London.

UNEP (1991) *Status of Desertification and Implementation of the United Nations Plan of Action to Combat Desertification*. UNEP, Nairobi.

United Nations (1992) *Earth Summit Convention on Desertification*, Brazil, 3–14 June 1992. Department of Public Information, UN, New York.

Watts, D. (1966) *Man's Influence on the Vegetation of Barbados, 1627 to 1800*. University of Hull Occasional Paper in Geography Series, Department of Geography, Hull.

Wilson, G.A. (2009) Rethinking environmental management – ten years later: a view from the author. *Environments* 36 (3): 3–15.

Wilson, G.A. and H.Buller (2001) The use of socio-economic and environmental indicators in assessing the effectiveness of EU Agri-Environmental Policy. *European Environment* 11: 297–313.

Yair, A. and A. Kossovsky (2002) Climate and surface properties: hydrological response of small arid and semi-arid watersheds. *Geomorphology* 42 (1–2): 43–57.

3
Desertification indicators: from concept to practice

3.1 Introduction

3.1.1 Why desertification indicators are needed?

Desertification has been defined by Dregne (1983) as

> the impoverishment of terrestrial ecosystems under the impact of man, it is the process of deterioration in these ecosystems that can be measured by reduced productivity of desirable plants, undesirable alterations in the biomass and the diversity of the micro and macro-fauna and flora, accelerated soil deterioration, and increased hazards of human occupancy. (Dregne, 1983)

People and organizations need information about land degradation and desertification for many reasons, the main one being that they find environmental problems much too complex to understand. The reasons for tackling desertification are apparent at the abstract level illustrated in Figure 3.1 but to connect with people more emotional approaches are effective (Figure 3.2, linking it to loss of infrastructure (a), lives flooding (b), and livelihoods (c)).

The UNCCD (United Nations Convention to Combat Desertification) established early on the requirement for information about the nature and state of desertification in different countries in the form of indicators. It lacked the resources or mandate to have its own scientific programme. It therefore depended on other organizations such as the FAO, UNDP, World Bank and UNEP, European Union, China and the USA for scientific knowledge and underpinning. It established a Committee on Science and Technology (hereafter CST) (CST 1997) of experts to advise it. Their many reports can be found on the UNCCD website. One of its first wishes was to have information on benchmarks and indicators. They wanted to be able to exchange information and compare in a non-arbitrary way how serious desertification was in different countries and also monitor the implementation of the Convention. There was a real difficulty of getting resources and media attention, like those accorded climate change and biodiversity. Climate and biodiversity seemed much easier to define, measure and demonstrate than changes in land degradation and desertification.

Desertification, Land Degradation and Sustainability, First Edition. Anton Imeson.
© 2012 John Wiley & Sons, Ltd. Published 2012 by John Wiley & Sons, Ltd.

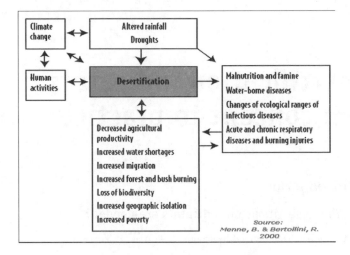

Figure 3.1 Why indicators are needed.

Figure 3.2 The reality of desertification is revealed in the field by tragic situations showing how desertification impacts on peoples farms and infrastructure (Lesotho Figure 3.2a), homes and lives (Marocco) and livelihoods (sand and shrub encroachment affecting ranchers in New Mexico) (Credit: Anton Imeson).

In reality, it is the other way round. It is possible to establish very accurately what has taken place in the world during the last hundred years in the way of land degradation. The consequences in the forms of floods, food security, warmer temperatures and the over exploitation of resources and the disappearance of natural habitats are evident.

The Convention had the opportunity to scientifically demonstrate that biodiversity loss and climate change are in fact consequences and indicators of land degradation.

The Convention hoped that indicators on desertification would be a key to gaining access to the knowledge that only rich but also organized countries could afford. Many countries have supported the Convention with research. The CST provided Guidelines for its indicator requirements. The FAO and UNDP with many other organizations set up a global programme to collect indicators for a Land Degradation Assessment (LADA).

Indicators can function as symbols and be given emotional significance such as the disappearance of the spotted owl and the migratory Atlantic salmon. The public acceptance of an indicator is critical. Through indicators, scientists help legitimize political choices. Consequently ethical considerations cannot be avoided. Indicators can be seen as a means of promoting equity but to attempt this risks the scientific legitimacy and objectivity that is critical for public support. Can desertification be what we want it to be without scientific verification? The UNCCD Guidelines for indicators is part of the broader UN strategy for sustainable development. They reflect the policy mandate for pursuing community based natural resource management as a strategy for community economic development (Gunter and Jodway 1999). Indicators can be used to demonstrate that things are getting better or worse and to show how effective action has been in achieving this. Therefore, indicators enable the scientist to communicate his knowledge of environmental risks to stakeholders who can act upon it. But, on the other hand, they can become an instrument for monitoring and control. Whereas the scientist is concerned with validity and accuracy, the policy formulator is looking for simplicity and clarity. It is soon evident that scientists often propose much more complex and difficult indicators than are usually hoped for by policy makers. Instead of just a few indicators, there are hundreds that look at all of the factors involved and which meet resistance from those who need to collect data. Indicators are in fact selected mainly because of the availability of data, even though they may be inappropriate.

From the policy perspective, indicators are particularly needed when there is danger of being overwhelmed by the sheer volume of information, which instead of helping – hinders decision making. Indicators must get information into the correct form so that decisions can be based on it. A good indicator presents information in a clear and usable form at the right time to those who need it. Just a few key headline indicators are all that is wanted. The paradox is, that these are readily available and easy to obtain if scientific definitions of desertification processes are used and all of the factors are integrated by a key value. Many hydrological parameters and measurements, for example, enable change to be monitored; changes in the water balance, river discharge, water storage and runoff connectivity, for example, are easy to measure and enable man's impact on ecosystem services to be quantified – also by remote sensing.

From the shared viewpoints of scientists and policy makers, an indicator should summarize specific aspects of the effects of complex processes and also be easy to measure and relate to the main issues. Key indicators can be effective when they really do this.

Much effort has been put into indicators, both by organizations responsible for desertification and by scientists and practitioners who are trying to support the Convention. Rubio and Bochet (1998), for example, were among the first to develop procedures for describing how indicators could be used in practice and they stressed that indicators are integrated and synthetic information that can provide data on threshold levels, status and evolution of relevant physical, chemical, biological and anthropogenic processes.

3.1.2 The land, water and nature as natural indicators of desertification

A desertification indicator should in some way summarize the dynamics of the complex processes that have led to or are leading to desertification. It should also provide a sensitive and early warning of impending desertification and be cheap and easy to measure and understand. The soilzone of the biosphere, at the interface of atmosphere and lithosphere, is in the front line with respect to the threat of desertification. It might be expected to yield useful indicators and this is in fact the case. On the other hand, the causes of desertification are all driven by land use practices and changes, so that key indicators can also be looked for as a consequence of these activities and the pressures they cause. They also impact on water and nature where very many indicators are present.

Almost a quarter of a century ago, the Nairobi Seminar on Desertification resulted in the publication of a *Handbook on Desertification Indicators* (Reining 1978). The recommended physical indicators included soil depth, organic matter, soil crusts, dust and sandstorms, salinity and alkalinity and relative reflectance (Reining 1978). Such 'indicators' are within given contexts correlated with land degradation. However, research in the intervening and earlier years suggest that there are certain limitations when deriving indicators from soil and which complicate their interpretation:

1 The soil is also a function of several other factors (notably, time, parent material and slope) that influence its properties and behaviour and it also has dynamic properties that influence its response.

2 Desertification processes need to be treated at different spatial and temporal scales. Desertification at one scale may lead to the redistribution of resources and the reversal of desertification at another. Scale concepts must be included in indicator schemes. Disturbance and degradation may be part of the natural long-term functioning of the system (see Chapter 4).

3 Land degradation is a biased concept reflecting the values of people and their socio-economic and cultural situation. In other words, it is a question of culture.

Because people and the causes are left out, the relationships of these with the causes is tacit and difficult to act upon. For example, all of the aforementioned indicators, from soil depth, to relative reflectance, could be caused by anything from over exploitation of ground water, the destruction of the vegetation cover, fire and/or overgrazing and it could be affected by locusts, war or a cheap food policy in favour of urban areas or by the appropriation of land for export crops.

How land desertification and land degradation were defined at the start of the implementation of the UNCCD convention by scientists as working definitions were in some ways an obstacle to progress, because it was not clear how to respond. The definitions were too partial to enable the real causes of desertification to be established and dealt with. For example:

- Land degradation is any process that results in loss of biological or economic productivity from the soil-vegetation-water system.

- Land degradation is the substantial decrease in either or both of an area's biological productivity or usefulness due to human interference.

- Land degradation means reduction or loss, in arid, semi-arid and dry sub-humid areas, of the biological or economic productivity and complexity of rain-fed cropland, irrigated cropland, or of processes, including processes arising from human activities and habitation range, pasture, forest and woodlands resulting from land uses or from a process or combination patterns, such as: (1) soil erosion caused by wind and/or water; (2) deterioration of the physical, chemical and biological or economic properties of soil; and (3) long-term loss of natural vegetation (UNCED 1992).

All of these definitions are valid at the general conceptual level and may be true but they are descriptive.

3.1.3 Stakeholder opinions

During the last decade in Europe especially but also as a result of the UN, there was a movement to involve stakeholders and policy needs to help define research objectives. This had a large impact on the research questions. The participatory approach can be valuable in giving ownership and finding out how people perceive desertification. The Desertlinks Project (Brandt and Geeson 2003) was one of several EU projects on desertification indicators. It exploited knowledge from Target Areas in Greece, Italy, Portugal and Spain, from which there were many years of data, and tried to make this available to the National Action Programmes of Annex 4 (Northern Mediterranean) Annex of the Convention. An example of one of these surveys is shown in Chapter 2. Amongst the outcomes of the project were reviews of indicator concepts (Imeson 2002), functional indicators (Imeson 2003) and the DIS4ME indicator system (Brand and Geeson 2003) (the latter can be consulted online as an expert system to learn about issues such as land abandonment, forest fires, water and salinization). The philosophy was that whatever type of desertification problem a person might have, the Dis4me system could help him with explanations and indicators. This approach resulted in many hundreds of indicator descriptions, some key headline indicators as well as several compound indices. The process was very bottom up and followed very closely the Guidelines of the UNCCD. The question being asked is what evidence of desertification do I have? According to the amount of evidence, an area is considered to be more or less sensitive to desertification.

The basic idea that if the stakeholder says there is a problem then this is legitimate. It means there is a high possibility that scientific understanding about processes is constrained by the frameworks and objectives of UNCCD and EU policies. The aim is the contentment of stakeholder and policy makers, leaving the problems that the scientist might have found for the future stakeholder dialogues.

Communicating and explaining indicators to stakeholders is in any case difficult because so many studies are being done in parallel and there is an overload of information that describes risks rather than actually what has happened and why. Indicators are most easy to explain when they are based on processes that can be discussed bottom up. This is the case with the field assessment methods described later.

3.2 Approaches to desertification indicators

There are very many different concepts and frameworks for people to have used for desertification indicators. Some of these are listed in Table 3.1.

3.2.1 Overview of some concepts and their application

Capital generating wealth

Over tens, hundreds or thousands of years all organisms including man built and created physical and social structures that represent different forms of capital – social, economic and physical. All that is needed is some measure of this capital and an assessment of how it is threatened. This notion was in fact developed more than 130 years ago by Huxley (1890). Putting at the centre of our consideration the 'Habitat Function' of the land or soil for micro(organisms) and the landscape as a habitat for people is a more simple and applicable scenario to thinking of the soil or land as an economic resource for people and the services it provides them.

What makes it more or less attractive? For the soil organisms whose activities creates the water and nutrient services or functions of the soil it is relatively simple to understand. For people it is more difficult and complex because they are influenced, among other things, by their psychological needs and these are influenced in turn by social control, consumerism and ideology. Very many, if not most, people chose to behave in a way that is benevolent to others, including nature, and this attitude can be learnt. Now this is exploited by charities and environmental marketing but it can also be applied to making, protecting and restoring our habitat as something more attractive (Xiao and Li 2008). Acts that benefit the restoration of capital generating nature will lead to increases in the water regulating, soil conservation function as well as creating employment. Chinese society has for thousands of years benefited from the capital of the knowledge of how to manage water and protect the soil. It has also confronted some of the drivers of land degradation, which include population growth and job creation.

Desertification occurred in the past and today (both in society at general but also in the soil) when capital was neglected because alternatives become more attractive (e.g. alternative jobs, trade), or there may be a competitor who tries to exploit your capital or to claim it by means of war. This alternative income has the same effect as subsidies and cheap energy. People are not dependent on the value of what they are producing so they can neglect it (see Huxley 1890).

Complex systems: organizations and structures in society and nature created by processes

The Theory of Complex Systems is based upon the principle that systems such as landscapes can generate their own structure, through the mutual interaction of self-reinforcing

Table 3.1 Overview of some of the indicator concepts and approaches mentioned in this chapter (Credit: Anton Imeson).

Approaches and terms	Description – Comment	Concept/indicators
DPSIR	Driver, pressure, state, impact, response (DPSIR) described extensively, for example, in the EU Soil Strategy working groups and environmental agencies	Systems idea
Rangeland health	Method for assessing health using biological and physical indicators Guidelines produced that are now operational	Uses concepts of state and transition, resilience and functions
Functions and ecosystem services	Functions and services provided by nature are damaged by desertification	Applied for the evaluation of nature
Soil conservation function	This book and increasingly being proposed for policy Illustrated by example from Portugal	Leads to identification of key indicators at different scales
Soil quality	Soil quality. Developed in the USA.	Soil functions
Soil change	Quality for agriculture mainly Working group of SSSA	Soil quality indicators. Soil stability is a key indicator. Work in progress
Land and soil habitat function	The soil as a habitat for life and man	An old concept explained by Huxley (1885)
The earth as a resource for all life	How attractive is it that we should invest in our future	Functions, natural capital Attractivity
Hydrology and water balance	**Water is a key indicator** of present desertification	Hydrological cycle
Soil moisture	Makes apparent the degraded state of the world and the causes evident.	Critical water requirement
Infiltration	The system is not providing its conservation function	Floods and droughts
Soil erosion		Indicator of soil conservation function
Sediment load		Human impact on vegetation and soil

(continued overleaf)

Table 3.1   (*continued*)

Approaches and terms	Description – Comment	Concept/indicators
Dynamic and complex systems	Applied in models. Operationalized by Desertification Response Unit method	Hierarchy theory
DRUs: Desertification Response Units	(See section 3.4.4) (See Van de Leeuw 2001)	Interactions between scales Thresholds Patterns and structure give resilience and capital Direction of change
Adaptive management and panarchy	Explains changes and incorporates many of the above ideas	Included hierarchy theory and resilience
Human use and appropriation of environment, land and water	Most of the worlds land and water is used by humans. Water is returned contaminated to rivers and oceans.	Key indicators are disappearance of rivers, spread of desertified areas Natural disasters and famines Climate change. Included biodiversity
Sustainable land use and traditional knowledge	Assessment methodologies vary but these require all functions of the land to be considered as well as change	Very many indicators that can be judged from field assessments and direction of change
Key indicators	Things that summarize complex system behavior of single system with a feedback to human actions	For example, soil stability, runoff and water balance, sediment yield' Subsidies and ignorance

processes of elements at different temporal and spatial scales. The fact that these systems appear to be at some stable equilibrium is that the components that we can currently observe are linked to other components in ways that reinforce their very existence. However, what has recently become apparent is that hidden behind this average view of the landscape system is the potential to become something else, potential landscape structures that could express themselves in very different patterns and flows. Spatial Patterns: from micro-structuring to landscape patterns (including vegetation patterns, soil water patterns, soil horizon patterns), and in the pattern of villages. This is included in the idea of the Central Place Theory and used in regional planning and logistics.

Just as a beaver evolves to build lakes, so mankind has evolved to exploit and use resources and in doing so changes the way the world is and how it functions.

Desertification and globalization involves in some ways the incorporation of the affected areas resources and capital into the economic system of the richer regions or countries who have more power. Structures and patterns that are not maintained by work, money or energy gradually decay, such as abandoned agricultural terraces and rural villages. Migrate to areas where the resources become available such as Europe and North America or poverty follow. This idea is taking place in Somalia where the appropriation of the fishing by Europe and other countries leaves the people with no livelihood in a desert country and this is sometimes said to be a motivation for piracy.

It is simple to record and monitor things to see if things are getting better or getting worse. This means that not just the rate but also the directions of a processes matter. Therefore a single value of an indicator cannot measure the direction of change and establish whether things are getting better or worse. If the process is going in the wrong direction, action might be needed, even if it seems very slow.

When trying to explain and predict behaviour in terms of the different factors that influence decisions, the results that follow are invariably weak or inconclusive. We can never know a person or landscape well enough to know how or why they do things and to be able to predict behaviour with certainty. It can be explained more convincingly that people do what they find most attractive, and formalize this mathematically using non-linear systems theory.

3.3 Global and regional indicators of land degradation and desertification

At global and continental scales, the 'geography' of desertification can be mapped using different types of indicator, usually derived from remote sensing or statistically analysed data. In most cases indicators just consider one facet of desertification (such as the evaporative efficiency of water use or the HAPP (Human Appropriated Primary Production) or do not use spatially explicit data. Many maps of desertification describe indicators and risks that are hypothetical and their values are at the general level. They are mainly cartographic products aimed at awareness-raising and lack substantive data needed to give confidence in their application to land use decision making.

Therefore the need is for the collection of data and information that enables desertification phenomenon to be geographically categorized and mapped. This involves both identifying where, at what rate and why land degradation is taking place and how it is impacting on people.

Both physical systems and human societies seem to move towards a limited number of areas of attraction. State and transition models have been applied to describe how a more productive and valued system providing many societal functions can suddenly be replaced by one that is perceived as degraded and which is of little use. Soil erosion and nutrient loss or overgrazing can trigger this. Similarly in social systems, behavioural psychologists have shown that people are motivated by wanting to do things that they find attractive and rewarding. If an urban lifestyle seems to offer more advantages rural land will be abandoned, particularly if rural areas are threatened or over taxed.

Combating desertification from this perspective involves increasing the resilience (maybe as capital) of both ecological and socio-economic systems. Restoration involves restoring lost functions and services.

Desertification indicators have also been developed to be used globally and region-ally. On the home pages of the different National Committees of the UNCCD, maps of indicators can frequently be found. They usually include indicators that were agreed on at regional UN meetings but there is a large variety.

Examples of indicators are those developed by Kirkby and associates in the *Medalus* target area studies (Kosmas 1999). These had a scale of about 1:10 000 to 20 000. At a coarser regional scale other desertification sensitivity indicators were developed and validated with a) regional precipitation and vegetation data obtained from remote sensing and existing land cover information and b) indicators from the target areas. In principle, differences occurring within target areas inferred by regional scale indicators enable differences in sensitivity resulting from underlying factors of geology, geomorphology and climate to be used as a basis for stratifying the selection of field sites where studies are being made to validate the use of indicators.

Information on coarse scale indicators is provided by Sommer *et al.* (2011). In addition up to date information can be found at DeSurvey (2010), which is developing remotely sensed tools for monitoring desertification. This makes extensive use of the regional scale erosion model.

A difficulty in explaining and communicating regional scale indicators is that they refer to abstracted conditions existing in hypothetical $4\,km^2$ or $100\,km^2$ or larger pixels. Although they can be verified in terms of the field experience and expert judgement, a strict validation is seldom possible and the uncertainty cannot be statistically analysed. Nevertheless these indicators express the generalized effects of the underlying factors that influence, for example, erosion and they enable potential desertification sensitive hotspots to be identified. They are relevant for coarse scale issues.

3.3.1 Discussion: old versus innovative approaches to indicators

A challenge with desertification indicators is that the scientific innovations that were made in the 1990s until about 2005, when new paradigms were developed and tested, was not followed up and today there is a reluctance for people to move away from a land evaluation approach in which different factors are assessed and then recombined as different qualities. Applications of more efficient methodologies that seemed to have transcended many problems are very few.

Many soil erosion and conservation scientists still use methodologies that employ models to predict or combat erosion that are basically a development of the Universal Soil Loss Equation (USLE) (Wishmeier and Smith 1978). The paradigms are statistical and based on analysing different factors in ways that the developers of the model would consider misuse and abuse (Wishmeier 1976).

There are three practical challenges that indicators must meet. The first is to protect and conserve the soil before erosion has damaged or removed it. This requires early warning. Are existing soil monitoring systems up to this task? Do new developments in global monitoring systems (GMS) enable emerging problem areas to be identified in time and dealt with? Google-earth and street-view as well as Ladar enable high resolution changes in the vegetation and ground elevation to be applied in land degradation processes.

The second challenge is to promote sustainable land use practices that make erosion unlikely or virtually impossible. Much effort was put into this area and processes are well understood. However, there is perhaps an overemphasis being placed on biodiversity as a general indicator of sustainability, and too often soil loss, erosion and runoff are politically linked to arguments that promote the needs of combating global climate change rather than being simply associated with poor (non-sustainable) land use management and planning.

The challenge faced by indicators is in the area of evaluation. It will be necessary to monitor the efficiency and effectiveness of soil conservation and protection actions that aim at reversing desertification by restoring functions. Here indicators that enable reference or base level conditions to be documented are useful, as will be described later (Pellent *et al.* 2005).

Actions to prevent and control soil erosion are only needed on a small percentage of the total area and even then for only a limited number of years. This might be because the causes disappear, the system recovers or there is no land or soil left or people adapt. It is evident from the adaptive cycle and its four phases (page 33). Today soil conservation is concentrated in areas where erosion has just occurred and changed the system.

Land degradation resulting from some kind of human action continues until it is regulated by some feedback that leads to it being stopped. For example, a traditional feedback would be that because erosion reduces the soil productivity, the activity would be abandoned as the land lost value as capital. The soil might either recover or be degraded. However, in practice feedbacks are influenced by perceptions choices and values. They are also influenced by subsidies, interventions and markets.

In facing the challenges mentioned earlier, the starting point should be that it is human actions and customs making it possible at a specific location for a limited period of time. Whether or not erosion and desertification will occur depends on the chance that critical conditions will be met. This is about what people do and how the land is used and managed. Even in areas undergoing severe erosion, 95 per cent of the soil being lost is from only a few per cent of the total area. That is except in areas where there is a heavy use of herbicides, the soil is poisoned, when everywhere can be affected. Indicators should enable the affected areas to be identified not simply to be detected but also for managing desertification reversal. In such cases herbicide use is a reliable indicator of land degradation worldwide.

The requirements of indicators can be examined from the perspectives of concerns expressed by different actors. Three types of concern are formulated: according to whether they are scientific or technical, policy driven or (affected person) victim related.

Scientific concerns relate to the legitimacy of indicators. A simple indicator of land degradation requires a simple and accurate definition of the thing in itself. This requires defining both the temporal and special scales and exactly what is meant by something subjective and culturally anchored. If we start by disaggregating an erosion problem into DPSIR this takes us away from the holistic framework that is needed to make the choice of indicators self-evident but which just need to be put into action.

Rather than predict what will happen in the future, the approach should be to devise indicators that explain where we are now and what is happening. What will happen in the future will depend on what actions are taken.

3.4 Applying selected concepts in practice

Some of the concepts and frameworks listed in Table 3.2 can be used to obtain indicators in ways that are illustrated here.

3.4.1 DPSIR

The DPSIR (driver, pressure, state, impact, response) approach has been used by the European Environment Agency for its Soil Strategy and is used in many other organizations. Its potential as an instrument for soil conservation has often been analysed. Many environmental issues can be explained from a kind of systems perspective that is in some ways very useful because it links the effects (impacts) to the causes (pressures and drivers) as well as the solutions (responses). This is very convenient for agencies or organizations such as the OESO and the European Environmental Agency which want to demonstrate and communicate progress being made in identifying and dealing with the problems that are within their mandates.

It is described by Wilson and Buller (2001) as a typological indicator hierarchy developed by the OECD from about 1993 onwards and described and developed in various OECD publications, for example see OECD (2001). This approach has been favoured by statistical services such as Eurostat and by the European and National Environment Agencies. It is currently being applied to the European Soil Strategy. Its application to erosion

Table 3.2 Examples of questions being asked when selecting an indicator methodology (Credit: Anton Imeson).

What is observed	Typical questions	Indicator approaches
Evidence of changes in state and condition	Is there a soil erosion problem today or one that is imminent?	Indicators of rangeland health (see Pellent *et al.* 2000)
Evidence from critical factors affecting erosion and soil degradation	Are critical threshold values of factors known to influence erosion being reached?	Erosivity, erodibility, cover, slope, carrying capacity, etc.
Loss of functions and quality	Are the critical functions of the soil being lost thus threatening sustainability?	Soil water regulating and production functions
Loss of viability	Is the present exploitation of the soil sustainable? Is the natural economic and ecological capital being maintained?	Loss of soil, organic matter and biodiversity and habitat function
Loss of resilience	Can the soil remain within its current state of attraction?	State and transition thresholds schemes
		Adaptive management
		Panarchy

by the European Environmental Agency (EEA) is described in detail in EEA (Gentile 2003) and it is being used also for its proposals for a monitoring framework for Europe (Soilnet). This is quite different from the framework described by DG-Agriculture (2001).

It is a problem that although a specific case of an issue (e.g. soil erosion in Italy) could be analysed in terms of DPSIR, the most appropriate indicators would depend completely on the scale and context of the specific case. Moreover, these indicators are unlikely to have a similar meaning or value outside of the specific case being considered. In other words, DPSIR indicators are obtained by abstraction for the case in hand. These have to be considered at the appropriate level of the generalization. They cannot be validated or used at the detailed scale from which they were abstracted because there is as yet no way of doing this.

The UN Sustainable Development programme found that it was much more effective to focus more on the issues. The first cut should be in relation to the concerns of people in the light of the issues such as, for example, 'soil loss' and 'forest fires'. In the real situations when the causes of erosion are obvious, the DPSIR checklist may be extremely useful and valuable for describing problems. This does not mean, however, that it is a good source of practical indicators. An excellent overall headline indicator could stand alone without being buried in noise produced by other indicators that are decided on in committee and have influenced the outcomes.

A basic issue concerns the political legitimacy of soil erosion and conservation indicators that policy makers must take into account.

The Working Group on Desertification (Costello *et al.* 2004) analysed desertification according to the DPSIR for Europe and this provides a useful example of the strengths and weaknesses of the approach.

3.4.2 The soil itself an indicator of land degradation and desertification

The world's climate and vegetation can be classified as belonging to specific categories or types. Differences in climate that influence the vegetation type relate to the fact radiation, nutrients or moisture work as limiting factors. As a consequence soils occur in a zonal sequence as one moves from the tundra and temperate and tropical regions to the equator.

A strange fact is that there are so few soil types and that soils look remarkably similar. Nearly all soils reach a limited depth because of feedbacks affecting water and nutrients. There a limited number of states of attraction that are expressed in how soils look and behave. One reason also is that they have become similar because of the practices of agriculture by humans but also because of the role of the vegetation and organisms in the soil responsible for its development.

Whether or not one state or another exists depends on some critical condition being reached. For example, there is the classic threshold related to whether all of the calcium is leached by rain from the soil or not. On the dry side, there are **pedocals** on the wet, **pedalfers**. On one side, calcium will always accumulate and on the wet side the soils will become acid. This zone of attraction can be observed at a continental scale but it can also be seen on a single slope or even in a field or can be seen to be varying from day to day when the dynamics of water soluble salts in the landscape are followed. Another process of attraction is in relation to how organic matter and the humus form profile. This can lead to a situation in which organic matter accumulates on top of the soil or in the other state it is mixed by animals through the soil profile. Soil either has organic matter accumulating on the surface or it is mixed through the profile by organisms, and in each of these different states (known as humus forms) indicators have different meanings.

A transect that cuts across different zones enables areas that are similar with respect to specific conditions to be compared. They offer conditions for controlled experiments. This is important with respect to best practices and restoration. A comparison of cold mountainous areas with short growing seasons in Central Asia, South America and North America on similar soils enables the impacts of different management practices to be seen. Also they enable conditions that are more extreme to be compared. They enable a warning to be given about the negative impacts of specific activities. If something inadvertent happens on soils in North America, lessons can be transferred elsewhere.

There have been many studies of desertification along transects and these look at the combined influence of climate and land management.

At different scales and levels and in many ways, the land and soil can be used as a source of easy to measure and effective land degradation and desertification indicators. The land and soils are the habitat of all organisms and are part of its genetic phenotype. We can measure the current value of the soil in terms of **soil health or soil quality indicators** and also see how past human activity affected soil processes causing degradation. The word health refers to the soil habitat and how it functions. Humans are not usually included as an indicator but at the landscape level they are part of this system so that human health is also an indicator. Comparisons can be made between the health of human populations and the health of the soil as influenced by food nutritional quality and toxicity.

The transect approach in which the soil is evaluated in terms of specific indicators will enable trends in the impact of desertification to be reported.

A transect cuts across different soils and enables us to observe them as functioning systems.

3.4.3 The value of the universal soil loss equation (USLE)

Although the USLE was described earlier to be a very poor instrument for predicting erosion, it is also a really rich and important source of knowledge and experience. Many of the things it contains can be used to derive indicators that have great value in themselves independent of the equation. It also provides a general and easily understood and explained framework for understanding and integrating soil erosion and conservation issues as part of the overall framework for finding solutions to the challenge of sustainable land use.

Much of people's understanding of erosion processes went into the development of the equation, which therefore incorporated the paradigms of the time from soil conservation. This knowledge was critical in helping the USLE become widely applied. It correctly identifies the vegetation cover as being the most important factor, and concepts such as **'erosivity'** and **'erodibility'** and of **'protective vegetative cover'** from this framework have been used to define very successful erosion indicators. These can be evaluated by indicators such as the Fournier erosivity index, the IE30 index and the 'C' Factor from the Wischmeier (1976) equation. In the case of erodibility, this can be done using the 'k' factor or soil aggregation indices.

Although, it is true that indicators such as these may be useful for identifying and analysing potential problems or hot spots, and for comparing the effectiveness of different soil protection strategies, they are only relevant for a very limited range of processes and issues unless they are supported by field measurements and analysis. They can be incorporated into other concepts.

Deterministic modelling frameworks that integrate the effects of different erosion processes have been developed by Medrush, Pasera and other projects (but they have not usually been very successful in predicting actual erosion rates that can be validated). One difficulty is that in most cases models try to model the erosion caused by individual rainfall events. Field measurements of erosion have shown that actual soil loss is extremely sensitive to the initial conditions of soil moisture as well as to all kinds of biological processes and the interactions between organisms and the soil and that it is these influences that need to be taken into account. Each time it rains, the system changes, plants grow and the hydrology and processes are affected (Ludwig *et al.* 2005).

3.4.4 Land degradation: the desertification response unit principle

The principle is explained here because it underpins the choices of indicators discussed later.

The basic research requirement is to be able to assess how a particular area will be affected by the processes of desertification. A frequently suggested approach is to collect basic information about existing conditions from monitoring and field experiments. This data can then be used for the parameterisation of mathematical simulation models that can be used to extend the results beyond the site of measurement and evaluate different scenarios of desertification.

Processes and hierarchy

Traditionally, the difficulty in capturing the dynamics of arid and other ecosystems has always been the seemingly overwhelming spatial variability in biotic-abiotic interactions which tends to reduce the applicability of any model derived from local experimentation. Rainfall simulators enable processes to be observed at different scales and these can be performed on experimental plots to test different treatments (such as in Figure 3.3 examing the relationship between management treatments and soil loss) or in Figure 3.4 in Crete, where measurements are being made in siitu. Variability has tended to be viewed as a statistical problem, to be solved by means of appropriate sampling methods where the spatial variability can be assumed to be random and the underlying mechanism can be found if enough samples are taken. However, some time ago, research on the processes which generate spatial patterns (Imeson *et al.* 1996) indicates that these are usually hierarchically organized structures that have evolved from biotic-abiotic interactions. They, therefore, can actually serve to gain an understanding of the processes which generate the patterns observed at different spatial and temporal scales, generating the structures and patterns which we perceive as the landscape. Figure 3.5 illustrates the hierarchical sequence of interlinked structures that can be found in semi-arid regions beginning from those found microscopically in the soil and extending at the highest hierarchical level to the general landscape. Desertification research has concentrated on these processes and their hierarchical interlinkages at each of the indicated scales.

The results of dynamic systems modelling tend to support the above. Model runs show that the spatial patterns in water movement on slopes (Imeson *et al.* 1996), when used as input into simple spatial dynamic systems models of plant-soil interactions, results in the emergence of a structured vegetation pattern comparable to that found on the slope.

Desertification Response Units (DRUs)

DRUs may be thought of as clearly definable land units that have, by virtue of their process-response structures, a characteristic response to desertification processes. The

Figure 3.3 above and Figure 3.4 below. Fieldwork in Spain above studying runoff on experimental plots (Credit A. Cerda 2011) and at Crete (Omalus) below, applying the Desertification Response Unit concept to obtain indicators (Credit: Anton Imeson).

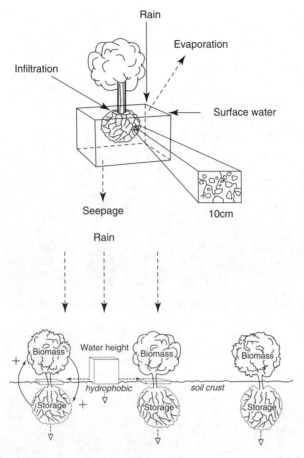

Figure 3.5 Interactions or processes at different scales result in patterns and structures in the landscape that provide a source of indicators that can be monitored. This is the basis of the DRU concept (Credit: Anton Imeson).

process-based approach used for defining DRUs allows us to evaluate, at larger spatial scales, the possible changes in their collective response regimes to impacts such as changes in land-use practices, fire, grazing, extreme climatic events. The assessment of the evolutionary changes in the DRUs is characterized in terms of the dynamic properties of soils as they interact with the changes in plant communities, and their effect on the more slowly-changing properties of soils. Figure 3.5 is a very specific case of a more general situation in which two different subsystems evolve with high or low infiltration rates. This can change from season to season, the hydrophobic conditions may be under the plants and the low infiltration rates could be caused by biological or other types of crust and compaction from trampling.

To put the DRU concept into practice, practical methods for characterizing DRUs are required. At the DRU scale, of geographically identifiable land units in the landscape

Figure 3.6 and Figure 3.7   The response unit approach can be applied in many situations. In Figure 3.6 The landscape in N. E. Brazil (Roxo 2006 Lucinda) and in Figure 3.7 to the postfire recovery of vegetation (Credit A. Cerda).

Figure 3.8 Desertification response units under Arctic conditions (Credit: Anton Imeson).

that have specific soil and vegetation patterns, the initial characterization focuses on identifying the desertification-sensitive processes. These DRUs are generally larger in size than experimental plots from which research data is obtained, so that the research at the experimental plot scale can be used to characterize the units in terms of their soil properties, vegetation cover, and other attributes that are useful in identifying these units in remotely sensed images.

At each spatial scale the identified processes operate at distinct temporal scales as a *nested hierarchy of processes*. These include the structuring mechanism of soil aggregation at the patch level, the spatial structuring mechanisms at the plot-slope level, the water redistribution and movement patterns, and the spatial interactions among DRUs at the landscape level. Each of these levels of the hierarchy can be characterised in terms of patterns of flows which define their degree of coherence and resilience. In the next section we explain what we mean by resilience and how it can be used in understanding the process of desertification. The response unit approach can be applied in many situations that range from North East Brazil (Figure 3.6), post fire recovery of vegetation in Spain (Figure 3.7) and the Arctic (Figure 3.8). In all three figures, patterns can be observed at the three scales of the soil aggregation, the vegetation patch and the response unit. It is much more practical to approach spatial variability in this way because average conditions occur nowhere.

3.5 Desertification, resilience and stability

The concept of resilience in the context of non-equilibrium systems has been defined as the degree to which a system can be changed or disturbed and still recover (O'Neill *el al*. 1986). What this means in less theoretical terms is that systems tend to react and re-structure in response to disturbances; and instead of degrading, these ecosystems seem to absorb and thrive on what could be considered an impact. For example, the research undertaken by Pradas (1994) on the effects of fire on Mediterranean ecosystems illustrated how these systems can recover from fire in four to five years, even though there might be significant changes in the vegetation communities. Figure 3.9 shows one of the areas studied four years after a fire and here the bare areas because of their hydrophobic behavior provided rainwater harvesting from the larger trees and vegetation bands that developed.

Resilience is an evolved emergent property of an ecosystem, and it can be affected by the way in which human activity changes its structural properties.

There are three aspects of landscapes that need to be considered before relationships between human impact and desertification can be understood. These are 1) the stability or inertia of soil-plant systems with respect to external change; 2) the existence of threshold conditions related to internal system behaviour; and 3) the resilience of soil-vegetation systems.

It is well known that erosion systems are characterized by threshold conditions that usually have to be transgressed before erosional processes are initiated or accelerated. For example, the energy and volume of water delivered by an extreme rainfall event would generate lower infiltration rates and high volumes of runoff that would exceed critical sediment entrainment thresholds. It might at first be thought that it would be a simple matter to seek out critical erosivity thresholds that could be related to erosion and to see how these would be affected by human activity and possible climate change.

However, threshold conditions are not associated in a simple way with processes external to the soil-plant system subject to erosion. For example, Schumm (1977) points out that they are also related to thresholds *intrinsic to the system*, which means that the stability of the erosional system is continually evolving. The thresholds of erosion may be very different in adjacent drainage basins because the erosion-deposition environment is at a different stage in its evolution. This is why morphologically similar terraces along adjacent rivers may have different ages.

The possible effects of human-induced impacts observed in one location are difficult to translate to another unless they are placed in an evolutionary context. A clear example on Mediterranean hillslopes concerns the difficulties that arise in trying to compare rates of erosion and desertification in areas of matorral and forest. It is impossible to understand differences in degradation rates and processes unless these are related to fire effects, taking into account the post-fire evolution of the matorral and forest. For example, a comparison of erosion processes on north and south facing slopes 12 years after a fire in Valencia (Cerda *et al.* 1995) revealed the persistent effect on desertification of the slower post-fire recovery of vegetation on the south-facing slopes. Whereas on north-facing slopes, the vegetation cover had recovered and degradation was no longer occurring, on the south-facing slope large bare areas with a high erodibility were still degrading.

Sometimes neither external nor intrinsic changes result in instability and desertification because negative feedback processes bring back the ecosystem to its original state. Relationships between parameters, such as rainfall intensity and soil loss, tend to occupy specific domains to which they are, as it were, attracted. On occasions, relationships may shift to another domain characterized by different relationships and sometimes by different processes. Continuing with an example taken from a study on forest fires (Imeson *et al.* 1992), it appeared that provided a burnt forest soil in Catalonia is shaded by regenerating vegetation within about five years, the soil will retain a non-degraded structure

Figure 3.9 This photograph, taken two years after a forest fire in Catalonia, illustrates how the vegetation was able to respond quickly to recover after the fire, provided that the ground surface was not trampled. Indicators need to consider the responses of the vegetation to fire but also to identify critical conditions such as a vulnerable soil structure (Credit: Anton Imeson).

with a high water retention and aggregate stability (Ubeda *et al.* 1990) so that the forest will recover to its stable domain. If regeneration is slow because of drought, fire or grazing, a loss of structure occurs in the upper five centimetres of the soil, suddenly altering water pathways and soil moisture storage characteristics (Figure 3.9). Processes of soil structure regeneration become rather suddenly spatially structured, being high under plants and low on un-vegetated patches, so that a persistent patchy vegetation pattern develops in what might be called a desertified domain.

Emergent properties of landscape systems tend to generate many possible trajectories which the landscape could evolve to, each with different properties. And associated with each one of these is a likelihood of degradation and loss of biological potential. In this context it becomes clear that understanding resilience as a dynamic force in landscape evolution is fundamental, not only to understanding the processes threatening landscapes into regimes which a landscape can irreversibly degrade to, but also as a key to successful land-use management strategies for preventing or reversing the process of desertification. These are discussed in Chapters 5 and 6.

In conclusion, if we examine the implications of the above arguments, in terms of landscapes that have evolved under a high degree of stress from grazing, fire and extreme climatic events, we should expect to find a high degree of resilience and stability in terms of their response to continued disturbance. However, many landscapes have in fact lost the structures that impart stability due to processes of land degradation, terracing and cultivation and these landscapes are likely to be affected considerably by the kinds of impacts which are associated with modern land-use systems, added to the effects of possible climate change which might occur.

3.5.1 Key processes at different scales

At the **patch scale**, changes in the ability of a soil to absorb, store and conduct water can result from the changes that occur in the surface and subsurface structure of the soil. On the surface, for example, there are changes in the air–soil interface produced by the emergence of plants, formation of biogenic and structural crusts. Beneath the surface, soil microbiological activity leads to the growth, evolution and decay in the surface area number and/or size of aggregated soil particles. The term 'aggregation' is used in a general way to collectively describe all of these effects that enhance the water and nutrient retention properties of the soil. The balance between processes that either enhance or reduce actual or potential aggregation is therefore critical. The chemical, microbiological and other processes responsible for the state and condition of soil aggregation at different scales has been studied. For the purpose of this chapter, it may be assumed that firstly, the rate of stabilization and growth are related to the level of microbiological activity, and the degree of entanglement of smaller particles is dependent on fine roots and fungal hyphae; and secondly, that the rate of decay reflects the supply and rate of mineralization of organic matter. At the patch scale, both aggregation and decay are dependent on temperature and rainfall, and in particular vary with the degree of shading, soil organic horizon development, stoniness and soil moisture availability. Figure 3.10 illustrates the very strong influence of the vegetation and the sometimes very strong soil aggregation observed after a very intense tropical storm near Cairns, Australia. The storm produced much runoff but the roots of the trees (Figure 3.10a) and grass (Figure 3.10 c and d) enable both types of vegetation to protect themselves and survive hurricanes.

Parameters that can be used to study the structures produced by aggregation processes include those that can be obtained directly from measurements of aggregate size distributions: measurements of the water stability and dispersive characteristics of soil particles and parameters that can be derived from studies of thin-sections. Soil moisture retention characteristics of differently structured and aggregated materials can be obtained from in-situ experiments and soil moisture and temperature data used to estimate the potential for aggregate enhancement by (micro)biological activity.

At the **response unit** scale, the key processes related to water availability are a) those that redistribute the precipitation to cause relatively wet and dry subsystems and b) those related to the position of the plot that influence the radiation receipt, evapotranspiration and precipitation (aspect, altitude and topographic position). The key process here is the redistribution generated within the plot because it reflects differences in the hydraulic and surface properties (crust development, stones, water repellent behaviour). Some of the processes are emergent properties produced by the dynamics of aggregation processes at the patch scale; others may be the result of relatively constant site characteristics, for example rock jointing, soil depth and slope angle, or of completely different processes produced by grazing, trampling and fire. In many cases, however, differences between the patches from which the response unit is composed reflect the aggregation dynamics at the plot scale as well as responses of plants and animals to the moisture or dry microenvironments that either reinforce or reduce the differences under the impact of fire and grazing. These responses lead to the emergence of the structures in the soil at this scale.

Parameters for describing processes at this scale can be obtained from process studies of vegetation-soil-runoff generation that make use of natural or simulated rainfall. Air

(a)

(b)

(c)

(d)

Figure 3.10a, b, c and d These photographs, taken after heavy rain in North Queenland, Australia, illustrate how tropical plants and grasses withstand rainfall intensities of hurricanes (e.g. 16–20 cm/hour) – much better than the sugar cane fields do. With sugar cane, the plants are removed and there is flooding (Credit: Anton Imeson).

photographs are useful for establishing trends in vegetation patterns over longer periods of time.

At the next higher scale of the **landscape response unit and slope** the reallocation of water between different response units is important. As at the response unit scale, some of the structures observed could be emergent properties but others are not. Very much depends on the nature of the lithology, and geological structure and geomorphology, all of which, determine the potential for change. The impact of water reallocation at the drainage basin scale involves water movement over long distances by pathways not considered at the patch or response unit scale.

The reallocated water transports both nutrients and sediments and is reflected in the short term by the distribution of truncated and colluvial soil profiles and in the vegetation patterns present at this scale. However, at this scale, processes occurring over longer time spans (hundreds to thousands of years) also need to be considered. The greatest changes occur during extreme periods of degradation when erosion can lead to the loss of the soil (water and nutrient retaining medium) producing an irreversible desertification, for example on hard limestone where the rate of soil regeneration requires tens of thousands of years. Repeated fires on hard limestone have lead to the irreversible degradation of the former forested slopes in Valencia that can now only support a matorral cover.

At the slope and catchment scales, different runoff and erosion processes than are important at the patch and response unit scale can be important. Preferential subsurface water movement (percoalation and throughflow) in relation to the local soil and lithological conditions often explains the patterns of response units that are found on a slope. Also important is the process of subsurface saturation overland flow and the generation of runoff by this process on partial or variable source areas. Rill and gully erosion are often the result of hydrological processes that occur at this scale.

Parameterizing processes at this scale can be done from estimations of water storage potential changes obtained from field measurements, estimations of the potential for percolation and subsurface saturated overland flows. It is useful to develop an historical framework for future change that can be based on a reconstruction of the former erosion history that can be derived from studies of sediments and colluvium. Hydro-geological and pedological field studies can also be used to establish linkages between different parts of drainage basins. The potential for rill and gully development can be evaluated from diagnostic slope and soil characteristics.

3.5.2 Interactions at different scales and desertification states

To illustrate how the processes just described interact, a simple model of desertification can be envisaged in which we consider the impact of progressive degradation beginning at the patch scale and proceeding upwards to the scale of the landscape response unit. Three stages of desertification are recognized during which water transfers take place at increasingly larger scales. As we go from stage 1 to stage 3 there is a stepwise loss of structure at the lower scale. Erosion can make shifts from state 1 to state 2 or 3 irreversible.

State 1: Complete vegetation cover returns because of large structural resilience, short period of degraded vegetation cover; no important loss of soil structure.

State 2: Patchy vegetation develops because rainwater and nutrient harvesting are reinforced at the patch scale.

State 3: Hillslope vegetation reflects major transfers of water and sediments from desertified areas of slope with no patchy vegetation to areas with patchy vegetation.

This sequence of vegetation patterns is frequently observed in arid areas.

State 1

Beginning at a randomly located patch, shaded by vegetation, the rate of soil stabilisation R^s and aggregation processes is greater than the rate of destabilization R_d so that the water and nutrient retention capacity of the soil are optimal. If disturbance (fire, grazing, trampling) occur there will be a period during which R_d will exceed R_s. If this situation persists because of drought, repeated fire or continued grazing, eventually within a period of months or years depending on the resilience of the soil, the soil surface will experience a change in structure, becoming more erodible and less well structured, having a higher bulk density and lower water retention capacity. Alternatively it could develop local biogenic crusts or water repellent behaviour. Any change in this direction will mean that small amounts of rainfall will infiltrate preferentially where structure is less degraded or altered, usually adjacent to plants. In other words, rainwater reallocation takes place at a micro-scale. The degree of resilience of the soil structure in combination with the chance pattern of rainfall and the landuse incidents (grazing, fire, etc.) will determine whether the vegetation will return to its original state or whether a bifurcation point will be passed and the soil-vegetation will pass into the second domain of patchy vegetation.

State 2

When water reallocation at the patch scale becomes important, this is reinforced by many plants that have developed all kind of mechanisms for harvesting rainwater. By effectively concentrating the rainfall that runs off from bare patches, interception and by altering the patterns of infiltration and water storage a heterogeneous pattern of soil hydrological characteristics develops that is rather resilient with respect to change. Any disturbance such as fire or grazing reinforces the rainwater harvesting mechanism facilitating the regrowth of the inpatch plants. The intrapatch plants, should they recover, during wet years or seasons provide a means for initiating a return to state1, provided that soil degradation has not lead to a loss in soil volume. This is less likely to happen on stony soils where the surface is armoured by residually accumulating stones.

State 3

In very dry and degraded areas the vegetation patches may be degraded so far and for so long that even the infiltration rates close to the vegetation patches or clumps become low. Rainfall may be lost as runoff from a large section of a slope and may infiltrate at some more favourable location down slope, or in the river channel. Loss of infiltrating water accompanied by erosion means that the recovery of vegetation on the upper desertified slopes becomes less but that there is an improvement in conditions elsewhere. This condition is less easily reached on stony soils than on sandy or silty ones.

The patterns of vegetation at different scales provide information about both the resilience of the location and the importance of water reallocation at different scales.

3.5.3 Landscape functions, ecosystem health, and soil quality

As already described earlier in this book, the soil may be thought of as performing environmental functions or services to people or society. Soil quality indicators enable soils to be evaluated in terms of the provision of these functions. The notion of health is applied by comparing the differences between soils that have had their functions degraded and those that are from healthy reference areas. This approach has recently been adopted and applied to all of the rangelands throughout the United States (Pellent *et al.* 2005). In Table 3.3 below an overview is given of the different types of function and the impact that desertification has on them.

An essential aspect of the soil quality and ecosystem health approach towards indicators is that they are both subjective, reflecting the values and culture of the user. Because the indicator is intimately linked to the user, and because all situations are complex but unique, it is not possible to compare areas by means of the actual values of what is measured but instead in terms of the way in which functions are being performed.

The adoption of the rangeland health indicator programme in the USA is a major advance. This scheme could be used for rangelands throughout the world and its value has been demonstrated outside of the USA in Mongolia, Europe and South America. It can be used on cropland.

The concept of soil functions is increasingly being advocated for sustainable resource management for more than 20 years (see, for example, Kimpe and Warkenten 1998 and Shaxson 1998) and this is now an integral part of the EU Soil Strategy and in the USA National Soil Resource Inventories.

Desertification can be defined as it is experienced, namely in terms of the irreversible loss of the currently valued 'production' and 'ecological' functions. From the perspective of functions, there is a strong resemblance between concepts and indicators of desertification and concepts of soil health or quality (Doran and Jones 1996; Doran and Parkin 1996; Harris *et al.* 1996; and Karlen *et al.* 1997). The indicators of soil quality summarized by Karlen *et al.* (1997) and the concepts they propose are all appropriate to desertification. Desertification indicators, like indicators of soil health and soil quality, reflect a deterioration in the performance of the soil with respect to its ability to deliver its expected services. Ideally, the degree of desertification can be quantified by comparing the desertified soil with one at a healthy reference location, if it is available.

In the example from Portugal given here, the soil and water conservation function, in which the soil also protects people from offsite flooding and erosion, is developed.

A function or service of the environmental system can be defined as:

- Properties of the environmental system which are maintained by components, interactions and processes of the system. The function can be seen as a potential or actual supply of the environmental system.

- The set of processes that result from interactions among the biotic and abiotic components of the ecosystem (Landres 1992).

Functions are initially defined for a systematic assessment and evaluation of natural and semi-natural ecosystems, in order to achieve the conservation and sustainable utilization of nature and natural resources (Braat *et al.* 1979; De Groot 1992). They are also useful for identifying, defining and comparing degraded environmental systems.

Table 3.3 Functions provided by land and soil and the impacts of land use and appropriation of water (Credit: Anton Imeson).

Function	Description	Potential impacts
Regulation functions		
1. Water supply	Better groundwater availability and moisture retention, through good infiltration of rainfall	Loss of ground water resources
2. Water regulation	Lower runoff and flood risks, due to good infiltration of rainfall, or to retention of water in ecosystems.	Loss of surface water resources, and/or increased flood risks
3. Soil retention	Vegetation cover important against erosion	Increased erosion leading to loss of productive capacities of the soil and/or to sedimentation
4. Soil formation and maintenance of fertility	By litter formation and organic matter addition, or by accumulation of sediments.	Loss of resilience of ecosystems because of negative impacts on the soil formation processes
5. Carbon sequestration	Sequestration of carbon in biomass	Loss of the amount of carbon sequestered
Production functions		
6. Food supply	Production of dryland crops	Loss of productive capacity of the land
7. Grazing	Sheep and goat grazing.	Loss of pasture quality
8. Raw material	Fibre for fabrics	Loss of possibilities to extract raw materials
9. Genetic resources	Old cultivated varieties, or wild plant species diversity	Loss of genetic diversity
Habitat functions		
10. Refugium	As habitat for natural species	Loss of biodiversity and nature
Information functions		
11. Recreation	Drylands may provide opportunity for tourism and recreation, including outdoor activities.	Loss of opportunities for recreation
12. Historic information	Heritage value of traditional agricultural practices	Loss of historic information
13. Aesthetics	Valuable scenery	Loss of scenery
14. Existence/bequest value	Desert landscapes or water resources may have special value in regions of water scarcity	Impacts on landscapes

3.5.4 Natural or vital capital provided by nature

This extract from Huxley (1890) expresses the essence of the concept:

> Now, herbaceous and all other green plants stand alone among terrestrial natural bodies, in so far as, under the influence of light, they possess the power to build up, out of the carbonic acid gas in the atmosphere, water and certain nitrogenous and mineral salts, those substances which in the animal organism are utilised as work-stuff. They are the chief and, for practical purposes, the sole producers of that vital capital which we have seen to be the necessary antecedent of every act of labour. Every green plant is a laboratory in which, so long as the sun shines upon it, materials furnished by the mineral world, gases, water, saline compounds, are worked up into those foodstuffs without which animal life cannot be carried on. And since, up to the present time, synthetic chemistry has not advanced so far as to achieve this feat, the green plant may be said to be the only living worker whose labour directly results in the production of that vital capital which is the necessary antecedent of human labour. (Huxley, T.S., *Capital – The Mother of Labour*. Collected Essays IX)

3.6 The soil and water conservation and protection functions

Desertification was explained as occurring when valued ecological and economic functions are lost. One of these functions is the soil and water conservation function. This supports all of the other functions because without this the soil will disappear and there will be no food production or water. This function therefore protects all of the vital capital of Huxley (1890). The vital capital lost is the capacity of the fertile top soil to produce valued crops which cannot be done so easily on the soils that remain and land is often abandoned. The vital capital of the people near Schruns in Austria is being protected by these forests (Figure 3.11) from rockfall, avalanches and landslides. Without this it would not be safe to live in the valley. The soil protects people in the same way but this service is mainly disregarded.

Function performance indicators can be used to study this. This can be done at different scales to characterize how well a soil is performing its soil and water conservation functions. Key indicators are to be found in the soil aggregation behaviour, infiltration characteristics and in the response of the soils, slopes and catchments to extreme rainfall. Responses at coarser scales can be explained by indicators at finer scales. Examples of developing and applying such indicators are described for two areas near Mertola, Portugal, in the Alentejo. Some difficulties associated with applying indicators to desertification are discussed, in particular the question of long-term changes and resilience. How this works is explained in Chapters 4, 5 and 6.

With respect to desertification, the most basic function of the ecosystem is **the soil and water conservation function**. Consequently, the task of obtaining desertification indicators involves identifying and underpinning parameters that can be used to evaluate the performance of this function.

Figure 3.11 In Austria, people deliberately plant protection forests to prevent damage from falling rocks and avalanches and in this way make use of the soil conservation and protection function; they manage trees for this purpose (Credit: Anton Imeson).

Very many soils in areas experiencing desertification in southern Europe have been studied in areas that are considered to be affected by desertification. Many indicators have been proposed and tested. This was done to see how they performed in monitoring change and also to identify critical threshold values that enable degraded soils to be distinguished from those not at risk.

3.6.1 The water and nutrient regulation functions of the soil

The loss of water and nutrient regulating functions can be caused by the deregulation of several processes. Water regulation functions require a soil medium which is able to store and retain water, which is closely related to the maintenance of soil porosity and permeability. This is in turn, is favoured by the aggregation of primary particle in larger water-stable aggregates. The aggregation processes are a consequence of biological activity of the soil and reflect the dynamics associated with it.

Water-stable soil aggregation can be considered as an indicative of the success and failure of biological activity in creating and maintaining the water and nutrient regulation function which, in turn, favours retention of available soil moisture and water and nutrient transport. This biological activity depends on there being both a sufficient input of suitable organic matter and periods of time during which soil moisture and temperature do not limit the activity.

In a large extent of desertified areas, the loss of vegetal cover brings about a diminution of soil organic matter. This reduction has a direct effect on soil structure by the weakening of the soil aggregates. The weakened soil aggregates break into smaller ones upon the impact of the raindrops, the slacking caused by wetting and the cultivation. Small aggregates and primary particles fill the soil pores on its surface and lead to the formation of crust, reducing infiltration. The degradation of the structure on the surface has a negative effect on the biomass productivity of the soil by reducing water availability for plants and hampering the re-vegetation. Thus, the loss of water and nutrient regulation function bring about a feedback self-accelerated mechanism that, if not arrested, accelerates land degradation.

In more arid soils, the water regulating function is often regulated by dispersion of clay minerals. Dispersion conditions are frequently found in soils that contain low amounts of salt but where a large proportion of this consists of sodium. The clay dispersion is a climate-sensitive process. A climatological threshold above or below which the soil is being either flocculated or dispersed has been proposed for southern Europe (Lavee *et al.* 1996 and 1997). Where the annual precipitation is below about 400 mm yr^{-1} dispersion is a key process that regulates infiltration. The areas of soil affected by dispersion vary both temporally according to the amount of rainfall, and spatially, anywhere salt accumulates in soil.

3.6.2 Soil and water conservation function at the slope and landscape level

The landscape can be seen as a mosaic of hydrological or ecological response units whose spatial arrangement is the result of the processes of water, nutrients and sediment transport at hillslope and catchment scales. These processes are regulated by positive feedbacks between the vegetation, soil and water that reinforces the redistribution of rainfall and runoff within each unit.

The degradation of water and nutrient regulation functions of soil caused by land degradation and desertification can result in an increase of runoff and erosion at coarser scales (hillslope and catchment scales) and the reduction of landscape performance for soil and water conservation. This is reflected in three responses emergent at hillslope scale:

1 Changes in the distribution of sediment and runoff source and sink areas. There are changes in the size, behaviour and location of sink and sources of water and sediments on slopes.

2 A general loss of soil depth at sources sites and a potential increase at accumulation sites.

3 An increase of hydraulic connectivity between bare patches, increasing runoff volumes during extreme rainfall events.

At catchment scale, the impact of desertification because of the loss of soil and water regulation function is a change of hydrological and erosive response, which manifest itself as:

1 Higher discharge peaks and sediment loads after extreme events.

2 Increasing fluvial erosion on river banks.

3 Channel incisions and ephemeral gullies development resulting from heavy winter rainfalls.

4 Silting up of reservoirs and other water storage structures.

5 Spreading pollutants on valleys and down slope areas. However, at the catchment scale in Arizona shown in Figures 3.12 and 3.13, desertification is indicated by the loss of the native grassland and its replacement by Mesquite and other shrubs, and wind erosion and dust deposition are important.

3.6.3 The value of in-situ field measurements of indicators

People's actions may bring about changes in soil properties that can be measured in time and these are often correlated with things such as the organic matter content, soil bulk

Figure 3.12 and Figure 3.13   show views of the Jornada long term study site in New Mexico (Credit: Anton Imeson).

density, the albedo and the electrical conductivity. When changes in such properties are monitored or mapped (Kosmos 1999), it becomes apparent that soils are very different in terms of their sensitivity to the causes of desertification. Critical threshold values of indicator may be deduced from the damage to or disappearance of the functions that they are being used to monitor. When properties such as the above are used as indicators it takes a great amount of work to measure them, there is a high degree of spatial variability, and a great number of sampling issues, such as mixing and changes that occur in transit and with storage. In fact, the seemingly high resolution of laboratory data is misleading. It is much more accurate to record properties of the soil that are dynamic directly in the field using methods and techniques that have been developed for this. This was the motivation behind the soil test kit that was developed in the USA for use with stakeholders.

There are a number of methods and indicators available that capture the complex behaviour of the soil that are influenced by human activity. Examples include the dispersion test (Emerson 1967 and Loveday and Pyle 1973), slaking tests and indices (how soil responds to wetting, the Jornada soil stability kit test (Herrick *et al.* 2001), soil crusting indices or roughness indices, etc. The hydrological function can be measured in the field using the inversed auger hole method, the crust permeability test and by using rainfall simulators to record things such as the time from rainfall to ponding or runoff. Many such measurements were made in this area of calcareous marls and limestones near Lorca, Spain. Most of the highly variable annual rainfall is trapped by the vegetation or other sinks. The appearance of the land varies greatly from season to season and year to year.

At a coarser scale, patterns in the vegetation cover and the relationship with the soil properties is usually evident. What are important also are the source areas of runoff. When it rains, where does the water come from? And what are the mechanisms that are involved whereby it can reach the river?

Indicators such as the above enable key functions of the land to be quantified and then for the effects of management and human actions to be observed. Why things happen at a particular place and not another depends on things such as the way in which animal life in the soil is increasing the permeability in the top 20 cm of the soil and the way in which people are decreasing it. Figure 3.14 from Antrim in Northern Ireland shows a very common situation in when specific types of sediments occur along lake, river or coast shores. Erosion is greatly influenced by groundwater and positive pore pressure and by the properties of clay that affect water movement and stability. Slope instability and mass movements are often human induced because of the impact of people on subsurface seepage and drainage. This is very common in the Great Lakes region of Canada and the USA.

3.6.4 Water stable soil aggregation as an indicator

The loss of water and nutrient regulating functions can be caused by the deregulation of several processes. Water regulation functions require a soil medium that is able to store and retain water. This depends on the soil porosity and permeability being maintained. This is in turn favoured by a soil in which the primary particles are aggregated into larger water-stable agglomerations. The processes of agglomeration is often dependent on biological activity and the inputs of organic matter. Since biological activity depends on favourable temperature and moisture conditions; it is easy to see how more

Figure 3.14 Land degradation processes near Antrim, Northern Ireland. In contrast to Australia, rainfall intensities are low and there is little surface erosion. On the other hand, erosion is caused by the influence of land use on subsurface water movement and drainage (Credit: Anton Imeson).

unfavourable climatological circumstances affect soil properties. However, other ecological and pedological processes also come into play so that relationships and causes are often complex.

Nevertheless, the *water stable soil aggregation* of a soil can be indicative of the successor failure of biological activity in creating and maintaining the water and nutrient regulation function which in turn favours retention of available soil moisture and good transmission characteristics. This depends in turn on there being both a sufficient amount of food (suitable organic matter) and periods of time during which soil moisture and temperature do not critically limit biological activity. A reduction or diminution in soil stabilization will only lead to a loss of function in soils where this process is important. When this is the case, soil aggregation indices can provide good indicators of desertification. When this is not so, for example, in clay soils, alternative indicators are appropriate. Figure 3.15 illustrates an application in The Netherlands. The simple test requires counting the number of standard water drops required to break down a standard aggregate sufficiently to pass through a standard sieve. The relative strength of aggregates and there changes in time can be compared. In Figure 3.16 what is important here is the differences in soil properties between the sandy top soil and the clayey sub soil. This is an example of a texture contrast soil and of the risk that they present when ploughed and left exposed to a heavy autumn rainfall event.

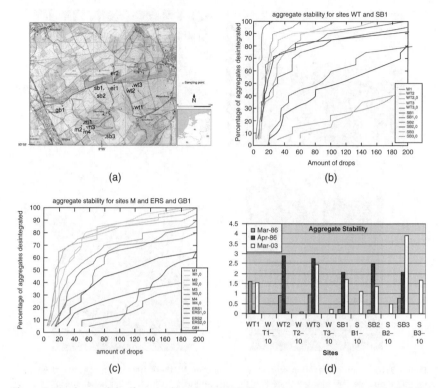

Figure 3.15a, b, c and d   (from A v/d Lockant 2006) The number of water drop impacts that the soil can withstand without breaking has proved to be a simple and useful indicator of water stability. There was an excellent correlation with the Jornada test. It can be used to compare different sites and seasonal trends. (m = maize, sb = sugarbeet, w = wheat and g = grass).

3.6.5 Clay dispersion as an indicator

In soils that are more arid, frequently where there is a tendency for clay minerals to disperse, there are important physico-chemical processes that affect the water regulation functions. Such conditions are frequently found in soils that contain low amounts of salt but where a large proportion of these consist of sodium. There is a threshold described by the Sodium Adsorption Ratio (SAR Value) and electrolyte concentration, above or below which conditions lead to the soil being either flocculated or dispersed. With dispersion, soils become more compact, fine pores become blocked and infiltration rates are lowered by an order of magnitude. For this reason, simple dispersion and infiltration tests provide good indicators of the risk of dispersion. Figure 3.17, illustrates this threshold. What it means is that during the first minutes of rainfall, because of the extreme low salt content, dispersive conditions occur but a few minutes later the salt content could be high enough to flocculate the clay. It is important therefore to use distilled water for rainfall simulation and other experiments. Infiltration rates can be an order of magnitude higher if tap water is used instead of dioinised water.

Figure 3.16 Runoff and erosion during an autumn storm in Catalonia in a hazelnut plantation where there has been dispersive soil (Credit: Anton Imeson).

3.6.6 Herbicides or other chemicals

The water regulating function is also influenced by at least two other activities. Chemicals can poison the soil biota, for example dissolve organic compounds from eucalyptus, heavy metals from mines, and agro-chemicals can, either through the effects they have on clay dispersion, or on the soil biota, be responsible for the decline of the soil aggregation. Runoff and erosion processes can concentrate chemicals in the soil creating toxic sinks and sources because of the way in which clays and organic matter are concentrated by runoff and sedimentation processes. How the desertification response unit method can be applied to identify risks from chemical time bombs was illustrated in the Guadalentin catchment in Spain (Imeson *et al.* 1998a).

Soil crusting, sealing and slaking

The degree and rate at which the soil surface becomes smoother under the influence of rainfall has been quantified into indicators by authors such as Boiffoin and

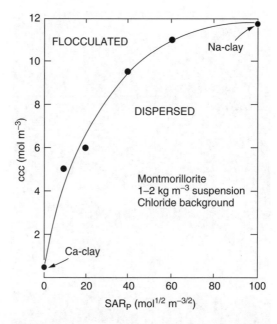

Figure 3.17 This illustration shows the nature of the dispersion threshold that depends on the proportion of sodium in the soil and dilution by rainfall. SAR, the sodium adsorption ratio, is used as an indicator of soil stability (Credit: Anton Imeson).

Monnier (1986). These are sometimes referred to as slaking or crusting indices. When an unstable soil is gradually or suddenly wetted it breaks down into micro aggregates that blend or fuse together to form a compact surface crust. This crust may be hard when dry but it reduces the rate of infiltration and frequently becomes soft when moist. There are several crust classification schemes that can be used as indicators of the processes that have resulted in the crust formation. Crusts may lead to the development of sink and source areas of runoff and infiltration. Soil stability is highly irregular in most places. Under plants it is high, due to the effects or roots and infiltrating moisture and the positive influence of shade. In the open, the surface soil is usually unstable because of the lack of organic matter and the inhospitable micro-environment for organisms.

Soil stability is influenced by the proportion of binding to non-binding substances. Consequently, soils become more stable as the clay and organic matter contents increase. Material that consists of the weathering products of highly calcareous marls is often highly unstable. Sodium clays can be very hard and dry but when moistened, clays may readily disperse or swell and this can be a factor in rill and gully erosion.

3.6.7 Slope and catchment level indicators

The soil on a slope is a store of minerals, water and nutrients. Together with the vegetation it prevents erosion from occurring. If the fine scale processes (described as first-order processes) regulating the fine scale functions are diminished, erosion and runoff at the slope scale are affected. Three indicators of this are:

1 Changes in the distribution of sediment and runoff *source and sink* areas on the slope.

2 A general loss of *soil depth* at source sites and an increase at accumulation as well as changes in the runoff mechanisms and amounts, and the amount of sediment reaching the river.

3 An increase in the *connectivity* of slope runoff processes. There is a gradual change in the pattern of vegetation (sink areas for runoff) and areas of runoff production. Changes in the vegetation patterns can provide early warnings of soil degradation issues.

Changes in soil depth on impermeable rocks sometimes result in a positive feedback, where by the more shallow it becomes the more likely erosion is to occur.

The soil and water conservation function can also increase so that things get better. This can be through the natural regeneration of the vegetation as on abandoned land. For example, this can occur on abandoned land or during a succession of wet years, if there is an increase in the water storage capacity of the soil-vegetation system. However, the function can also be decreased by overgrazing and fire. Under semi-natural vegetation the soil and water conservation function is provided by the development of the storage opportunities by weathering and interactions between organisms and mineral material. This is why the parent material is so important. On farmland it can be increased by ploughing. In other words, in time the soil can often become thicker and deeper and store more resources and possess more capital.

Some examples of the use of infiltration and vegetation patterns as indicators are demonstrated by the patterns of infiltration that occur on land abandoned for different periods of time, as described by Calvo-Cases (2003). The importance of connectivity of the hydrological system is has been well demonstrated by Tongway (1994) in Australia, who showed how this is indicative of the degree of grazing and degradation.

On cultivated land, a soil and water conservation function is affected and to some extent performed by tillage and by the construction of terraces. Additions of manure or chemical fertilizers can have a positive effect, promoting higher storage and stability. However, the effects can also be negative. The long-term effect of terracing is to accumulate soil and to create a potential time bomb should abandonment occur and maintenance no longer be forthcoming. Also on cultivated land, ploughing and tillage erosion affect the long-term degradation of the soil by means of gravitational effects. Increasing stoniness can also indicate the loss of fine soil particles that are harvested with root crops. As an example above in Table 3.4 some results are shown when the soil and water conservation function was assessed with simple indicators in Portugal. Part of the research aimed to identify the characteristics of the areas that were runoff sources. These were identified in the field after heavy rainfall. These were classified into the categories shown under the heading source areas. (P is for path). It was then observed which of these produced eroded sediment and details of the crust were recorded. Then a series of experiments were performed. The trickle irrigation test measures the permeability of the crust, the torvane gives a measure of the shear strength.

Table 3.4 Assessment of Soil and water conservation Function Performance at a fine scale near Mertola, Portugal (Credit: Anton Imeson).

Source Area	Crust Type	Sediment Production yes/no	Final Infiltration rate		Soil Stability		Function Performance score
		Occasional Observations	*Trickle Irrigation Experiment*	*Rainfall Simulations*	*Torvane*	*Dispersion test*	
Rd	compaction	+	1	4	2	2	- - -
Ab 0–5 Ru	structural/ erosional	+	1	n.a.	2	1	- - - -
Ab 0–5	erosional	-	1	1	3	3	+
Ab 0–5$_{ns}$	erosional	-	2	n.a.	3	2	+/-
Ab 5–10	erosional	-	4	2	3	3	+ + +
Ab 10–15	erosional	-	1	4	3	4	+ + +
Ab 15–20	erosional	-	1	1	3	4	+
Wheat	structural/ erosional	+ +	2	3	3	1	- -
PDep.	depositional	+ + +	3	n.a.	1	1	- - - -
PStr.	structural	+ + + +	2	1	1	1	- - - - - - - -
Btree	erosional	-	1	n.a.	4	4	+ +
BTree$_{ns}$	slightly erosional	-	5	n.a.	3	4	+ + + +
Tramp	trampling	-	4	n.a.	n.a.	3	+ + +
Tramp$_{ns}$	no distinct crust formation	-	5	n.a.	n.a.	4	+ + +

n.a.: not available

3.6.8 Regional and high order catchment level indicators

At the catchment scale the river channels and slopes may also store colluvium, alluvium and water. The performance of this function can be assessed by catchment scale assessments of erosion that describe sinks and sources and the amount of erosion that is produced by extreme events. For example, near Mertola, the channel incisions and ephemeral gullies resulting from heavy winter rainfall were used as an indicator of this catchment scale sensitivity. The ephemeral gully incision summarized the failure of the catchment to perform its soil and water conservation function at this scale. Important thresholds can also be obtained from analysis of the hillslope topography, with field measurements, air photographs or digital elevation data.

3.6.9 Desertification sensitive areas

This method has proved popular with many countries following its adoption with several of the National Action Programs. Its benefits are that in a short time with available data it is possible to make a map that can be combined with erosion prediction maps (Kosmos 1999).

The method was developed in Target Areas that were known to be sensitive to desertification and for which there was a high degree of data availability. This methodology was developed under the leadership of Kosmos (1999) and co-workers who applied it in different countries. It later became developed as a component of the Desertlinks Project on indicators. The Indicator system developed was also adapted by the FAO and it contributed to the LADA indicator methodology mentioned earlier.

This led to the development of the Environmentally Sensitive Area methodology. The overall objectives of that research were a) to develop the conceptual and practical tools for identifying critical areas for desertification; b) to establish threshold conditions for desertification; and c) to enable the different Target Areas to be compared. The ESA method requires establishing the spatial patterns of both the existing land degradation and of the factors that influenced it. These patterns were identified by means of 'key indicators of soil, climate and management qualities' to which critical values could be given. The approach had to be both simple and flexible in order to cope with different physical and socio-economic conditions, and different levels of data availability and knowledge of the underlying causes of desertification. The great contrasts between the target areas in Spain, Italy, Portugal and Greece, as well as the complexity of the desertification problem, prevented the simple transfer of indicators between target areas. Nevertheless, the indicators could be used and combined by weightings to classify areas as being either critical, potential, or at no-risk of desertification (Kosmos 1999). The data that was collected and used for validating the ESA methodology was later used with additional data and information for Desertlinks Indicator System (DIS). It is the intention that the DIS should be a tool that the National and Regional Action Programmes of the UNCCD find useful.

3.7 Spatial variability and discontinuity

Many studies of hillslope hydrology have demonstrated that under (semi) natural conditions there may be a pronounced spatial variability in infiltration and runoff. Yair and co-workers at Sde Boker described such discontinuities on rocky desert slopes and showed how these discontinuities were exploited by plants. They found that the concentration of infiltrating water by rocks and stones resulted in stony deserts receiving about 60 mm of rainfall being ecologically less arid than silty or sandy deserts receiving twice as much rainfall. Yair and co-workers (Kuhn 2004) emphasized the importance of soil surface properties in determining the aridity of dry areas. Later work has shown that infiltration is spatially structured in many environments and that this spatial structuring is usually related to plant distribution. Yair later showed that even in desert dune areas at Nizzana, surface runoff was generated by crusts on undisturbed dune surfaces and where the water eventually accumulated, shrubs would grow. The surface properties that create discontinuity in runoff and structure the infiltration on a slope may be quite different. Under Mediterranean forest (Imeson 1991) and on coastal dunes it is a hydrophobic effect produced in the first case by plant exhudates and in the other by algae. In other cases, it could be the result of macropore flow produced by shrinking and swelling and by the soil fauna.

In an arid region, a spatially discontinuous infiltration creates opportunities for vegetation that would not exist if infiltration were the same everywhere. Water does not have to wet all of the soil and it reaches deeper layers from which it is not lost so rapidly by evaporation. In some cases, spatially discontinuous infiltration patterns are static, being determined by the jointing of rock outcrops and the position of large stones. In others, they may vary through seasonal changes in crust properties or from a dependency on soil moisture, as in the case of water-repellency.

Tillage

Tillage is one of the main processes of land degradation and soil erosion and examples of it are shown in the case studies. There are many indicators and models that are able to make accurate models to explain current soil conditions.

Grazing

Grazing and its management is a major source of heterogeneity and discontinuity as is illustrated in the Northern Mediterranean. Here, as in many regions, areas that once were covered by forests have degraded into shrublands. The overall productivity of these lands is very low and many lands have been abandoned. The livestock farmers that still use the land for grazing receive subsidies from the government according to the numbers they possess. Although low intensity grazing is advised, the carrying capacity is usually exceeded and land overstocked because the animals receive supplementary feed. Without subsidies the grazing would probably end but the persistence of unsustainable practices leads to further deterioration of the land. The main impacts are:

- The reduction in the amount and diversity of natural vegetation by exploitation and clear-cutting of forest lands, overgrazing the pastures, burning forest and shrublands.

- The overexploitation of the water resources and especially the groundwater, of which the levels usually drop and springs disappear.

- The soil sealing by livestock expansion leading to a loss in the water conservation by the soil and pollution and accelerated soil erosion.

- The expansion of irrigated agriculture for livestock.

This can be observed by active rills and gullies that damage tracks and cause poor accessibility; a drop in the elevation of the water table and the presence of xlerophyl species and saline soils; less cover so that the shallow soils hold less water have more extreme temperatures and higher erodibility. This all leads to increase of overland flow and erosion.

For example, indicators for land degradation pressure may be: slope-steepness, soil-depth, exposition, vegetation cover, etc. Triggers may be grazing or fire, and may be indicated by trampling paths, stocking rates, burnt area, etc. Impact may be a loss of the soil and water conservation function, being indicated by reduced infiltration capacity. Figure 3.8 was taken from an intensively grazed area in Lesbos and many indicators can be observed. As the non palatable often thorny vegetation increases following the fires that are periodically used to remove it, so animals are forced to walk on an increasingly smaller surface of paths. The shrubs themseleves maybe hundreds of years old and have roots that extend many meters into the weathered rock.

In reality, grazing is very complex and indicators depend on whether the state of affairs are those of animal husbandry, ecologists or soil conservation. Very much depends on the context in which grazing is being considered.

Today, at the coarsest scales the largest impacts are on the water and water quality which affects flood plains. This can be monitored quite simply as can the impacts of grazing. Gathering points, wells and fences have proved to be good indicators.

3.7.1 Self assessment by stakeholders

One of the critical requirements of the UNCCD was that people in the affected areas should be able to measure their own indicators and apply these to their own situation. This was to be done both to identify the threats but also to see if the actions being taken were effective in combating desertification. In practice, in areas experiencing land degradation, people are intuitively aware of the degradation and erosion and are often collecting data and information that can be extremely effectively used as indicators to mobilize political commitment to soil conservation and protection. When people have a strong relationship with the land and have a sense of place and history, this brings with it an understanding of the changes that are taking place and a discussion of indicators is largely academic. However, when this link is absent, indicators may raise awareness of changes and the responses that can be taken.

The indicator field assessment method

This method enables the user to identify the measurements that he wants to make according to his needs. They are linked to the concept of soil quality which are described in detail on the soil quality website. What does the soil do for you? What functions does it perform? One of these is a soil conservation function. As described earlier, the soil conservation functions can be provided by people (e.g. soil conservation works) or by animals and plants (stable soil structure). The use of soil functions is explained as a separate soil conservation approach later. The methods were developed by amongst others Herrick and co-workers in the USA in 2008.

When soil loss occurs it is usually as a consequence of land degradation processes, which can include the effects of erosion processes themselves. These include wind and water erosion processes, soil contamination, decline in organic matter, acidification, sealing, and compaction. They all influence the quality of land to provide habitat or a place

Figure 3.18 Heavily grazed area in Lesbos illustrating many impacts of grazing (Credit: Medalus and Anton Imeson).

to live, not only for humans, but also for a wide variety of other living forms and natural processes that influence and are influenced by climate change as well as people. Land quality criteria such as, for example, landscape or biodiversity are under direct influence by the aforementioned degradation processes and therefore cannot be easily separated from them as changes in one causes changes in the other. Knowledge on the status of the land is essential not only for corrective but also for preventive actions in order to avoid changes that are irreversible or difficult to manage. In this way, importance of assessment and monitoring degradation processes can easily be seen as crucial prereq- uisite of actions. The current legal network set by the European Union encourages each country to establish acceptable risk levels based on the common criteria. In this way each country is encouraged to set its own priorities to address in respect to land resource (soil) conservation.

A state and transition framework means that in this case some kind of pressure pushes the system from an existing stable reference state to one that is degraded.

The stakeholder is provided with a tool kit of methods that they use to measure and assess land degradation. The tool kit approach demonstrates the opportunity for low cost on site monitoring of crucial parameters to help the management of land. Field measurements provide more relevant and accurate information than laboratory ones. How was this method tested in Latvia? The conclusions of a UNDP-Latvia workshop were that:

• An appropriate soil kit will enable the user to understand and monitor the changing soil conditions in the fields around him which are a consequence of his own management and natural processes.

• It has the potential to provide up-to-date relevant information to the farmer so that he can make decisions that save him money from unnecessary activities and which make him money because his soil becomes more productive.

At the same time, the data collected from soil kits can be developed into a monitoring system that enable the authorities to have critical necessary information about their soils. If similar data is used elsewhere this will enable the exchange of information. It is particularly important that the user has a clear vision of why he needs the measurements, what he is doing and how it can help him with his data needs.

Soil testing kits have a very long history in soil science, particularly with respect to soil fertility assessments. Although professional tool kits are being marketed and available, it is much better to design soil kits that are specific to the region.

As well as being relevant for soil erosion and land degradation, the measurements in a kit should be of indicators that reflect the different goods and services that the land and soil are providing. These can relate, for example, to the productive function of the soil (including moisture and temperature), to the ability to regulate water and nutrients. It is helpful to have the tool kit include measurements that are specific to soils that have special characteristics and problems: for example, peat soils, soils on flat areas that have poor drainage (polders), highly clayey soils and soils that contain high concentrations of soluble salts and carbonates, or rocks and stones. The way in which the tests are used and the way in which the results are interpreted will depend on things such as this. This why it is useful to stratify an area according to topography and soil sediment type. Figure 3.19 adapted from Herrick and others summarizes the phases of the different activities or components of the approach described above. This scheme is refined with the stakeholders who will actually be responsible for the work. Instead of productive potential it could be any other function that was to be improved. The feedback in the figure between what is done and the response is a very important management and learning device.

It is always the case that field data are more reliable than laboratory data. The advantages of many field measurements are that they are in fact much more useful and accurate than laboratory measurements. They can also be done by the farmer who learns from doing them. This is particularly the case for dynamic soil properties (permeability, structure, compaction, thermal properties, soil moisture, pF and pH, etc.). Furthermore, the user is able to investigate differences in the field and quantify the impact that his management is having. Management costs are much less if they are targeted at specific locations where field measurements identify requirements or approaching problems. It is not so much what you measure but that you understand the relationship to the changes you are trying to detect. There are many guidelines for interpreting the stability of the soil from repeated

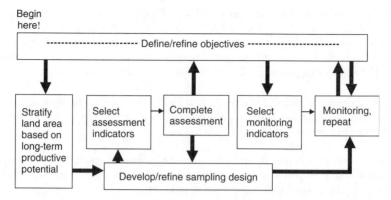

Figure 3.19   How the tool kit is applied in land degradation assessment (After Herrick *et al.* 2008) (Credit: Jeff Herrick).

measurements of either the soil surface or the soil aggregate size distribution. Farmers can make their own photographic guides so that they can identify areas of unstable soil.

3.8 Hydrological indicators of desertification

There are very good reasons for considering the world water problem an issue of desertification. For this reason, some concepts and principles from hydrology are introduced in this and the following chapters. Water-soil-vegetation form one system and this has responded and adapted to the actions of people. Figure 3.19 and 3.20 show salt accumulation in the soil at the mouth of a river . This is the iconic process that destroyed Civilizations until people learnt to manage soil salinity and sodicity. Salt accumulation is an excellent indicator of the salt and water balance in a soil and landscape. In Figure 3.19, the shrinking and swelling of the soil indicates its low permeability. In Figure 3.20, the salt is accumulating as a result of evaporation and capillary rise. This is in this case a natural process taking place in an estuary as well as a being a consequence of the dam.

Global indicators

At the coarsest scale, the hydrological records present in most countries provide a rich and excellent source of desertification indicators. People have changed ecosystems more rapidly and extensively in the last 50 years than in any other period to meet rapidly growing demands for food, fresh water, timber, fibre and fuel. The policy of many organisation today is to attempt to meet the water requirements of 12 billion people in 2030 by smarter or intelligent management of soil and water so that food and water security can be achieved. This is not actually a realistic policy. It might be accomplished but it would have a deadly impact on life and ecosystem processes. There are correlations between population density, forest area and human well being so that a smarter solution would be to intelligently manage demand. The USGS had been scientifically monitoring and keeping track of these changes at a very high level of resolution at thousands of locations. Data and information on the world's rivers are available on request.

Figure 3.20 The lower Guadiana River, Spain, showing the tidal contact zone where interactions take place that have been greatly impacted upon by dam building, contamination mining (Credit: Anton Imeson).

Falkenmark calculated that during the last 300 years the proportion of human appropri-ated water has increased from virtually nothing to 70 per cent (Falkenmark and Lundquist 1998). The impact of this on the ecosystems and inhabitants is immense. In the United States, the average width of rivers in many regions today is only about 10 per cent of what is was 100 years ago. The loss of economic and cultural functions that have accompanied the disappearance, diminution or contamination of rivers as a consequence of land degradation is in the order of trillions of dollars, that is an added cost of the agricultural, industrial practices and other things that people are doing. By changing the water and energy balances, this is also driving climate change.

Local and regional scale

The importance and value of water means that it is intensively monitored and hydrology is a rich source of knowledge. Relationships between land use change and the func-tioning of the hydrological system are very hard to pin down because so many other things are involved. Urbanization and waste disposal and contamination are degrading the hydrological services provided to people but these are also producing features that are expressions of land degradation.

Some frequently used hydrological concepts and terms are explained here, together with their relationship to land degradation.

Local scale indicators of desertification are described and some methods of measuring them are illustrated.

3.8.1 The water cycle

The water cycle is a biogeochemical cycle and it plays a key part in the cycling of other biogeochemicals. Nearly all the phosphorus that is transported is carried absorbed to the sediment that is eroded from the land. The eutrophication of lakes is primarily due to phosphorus, applied in excess to agricultural fields as fertilizers, and then transported by runoff. Both runoff and groundwater flow play significant roles in transporting nitrogen from the land to lakes and sea. Runoff also plays a part in the carbon cycle, again through the transport of eroded rock and soil. The water cycle is powered from solar energy. Eighty-six per cent of the global evaporation occurs from the oceans, reducing their temperature by evaporative cooling.

Human activities that alter the water cycle include: agriculture alteration of the chem-ical composition of the atmosphere, the building of dams, deforestation and afforestation, groundwater use, water abstraction from rivers and urbanization.

3.8.2 Human impact on water and desertification

Irrigation, drainage, and impoundment have has a major impact on the land and water discharge for more than 5000 years. Controlling water to grow crops has been the primary motivation for human alteration of freshwater resources. Today, of course, demands for fresh water are for irrigation, household and municipal water use, and industrial uses. There has been a dramatic increase in water appropriation during the last century as well as during the past 300 years. A timeline of human water use was provided by Allegra (2008).

12 000 yrs ago: hunter-gatherers continually return to fertile river valleys

7000 yrs. ago: water shortages spur humans to invent irrigation

1100 yrs ago: collapse of Mayan civilization due to drought

mid 1800s: faecal contamination of surface water causes severe health problems (typhoid, cholera) in some major North American cities, notably Chicago

1858: 'Year of the Great Stink' in London, due to sewage and wastes in Thames

late 1800s–early 1900: Dams became popular as a water management tool

1900s: The green revolution strengthens human dependency on irrigation for agriculture.

World War II: water quality impacted by industrial and agricultural chemicals.

1972: Clean Water Act passed; humans recognize need to protect water (Allan 2006).

The Global Water Crisis: The world population and demand for fresh water are increasing. The land is considered to be able to support the growing population with water and food, for the next 50 years on aggregate but there are many areas of water scarcity where demand exceeds supply. There is, however, a pending crisis of water mismanagement and mismanagement of water resources. Desertification and land degradation might be part of the tradeoff with the environment.

Is one tradeoff desertification?

According to Allegra (2008), symptoms of physical water scarcity include severe environmental degradation, such as river desiccation and pollution; declining groundwater tables; water allocation disputes; and failure to meet the needs of some groups. Some 1.2 billion people live in river basins where the physical scarcity of water is absolute (human water use has surpassed sustainable limits). Another 500 million people live in river basins that are fast approaching this situation.

Water scarcity as an indicator of desertification

Water scarcity is defined from the perspectives of individual water users, not according to the water available on the basis of the hydrology of an area and the available water. Water insecurity is when people lack secure access to safe and affordable water to consistently satisfy their needs for drinking, washing, food production, and livelihoods. An area is water scarce when a large number of people are water insecure. About three billion people live in areas facing water scarcity, and more than 1.2 billion of them – one fifth of the world's population – live in areas of physical water scarcity. Another 1.6 billion people live in basins that face economic water scarcity, where human capacity or financial resources are likely to be insufficient to develop adequate water resources even though adequate water in nature is claimed to be available.

Physical water scarcity occurs when available water resources are insufficient to meet all demands, including minimum environmental flow requirements. Arid regions are most often associated with physical water scarcity, but an alarming new trend is an artificially created physical water scarcity, even where water is apparently abundant. This is due to the over allocation and overdevelopment of water resources, leaving no scope for making water available to meet new demands, except through interbasin transfers. There is not enough water to meet both human demands and environmental flow needs.

3.8.3 Consumptive water use

This is water used by agriculture and not returned to streams after use (evaporation from reservoirs and lakes and transpiration from irrigated crops that consume much water, such as cotton and alfalfa). Irrigated agriculture is responsible for most consumptive water use and the decline in surface runoff and groundwater levels. An extreme example is the Colorado River, which has most of its water diverted to irrigated agriculture, so that in a normal year no water at all reaches the river's mouth. The same has happened in very many parts of the world.

Agriculture is responsible for 87 per cent of the total water used globally. In Asia it accounts for 86 per cent of total annual water withdrawal, compared with 49 per cent in North and Central America and 38 per cent in Europe. Rice growing, in particular, is a heavy consumer of water: it takes some 5000 litres of water to produce 1 kg of rice. Compared with other crops, rice production is less efficient in the way it uses water. Wheat, for example, consumes $4000\,\mathrm{m^3/ha}$, while rice consumes $7650\,\mathrm{m^3/ha}$.

Much water use is non-consumptive, which means that the water is returned to surface runoff. But it is usually contaminated. The WHO estimates that more than 5 million people die each year from diseases caused by unsafe drinking water, and lack of sanitation and water hygiene. The figures in the provided in the next sections 3.8 were taken from Allegra (2008) who reviewed estimates in the cited sources and they should be thought of as indicative.

3.8.4 Human appropriation of runoff

Asia has 69 per cent of world population but 36 per cent of global runoff. South America has 5 per cent of world population, and 25 per cent of runoff. The Amazon River accounts for 15 per cent of runoff and this is accessible to 25 million people (0.4 per cent of world's population): estimate poses the Amazon River to be 95 per cent inaccessible. Runoff in Zaire may be 50 per cent inaccessible. The mainly unused northern rivers flowing to the Arctic have an average annual flow of $1815\,\mathrm{km^3/yr}$, 95 per cent considered to be inaccessible. Together, this amounts to $7774\,\mathrm{km^3}$ or 19 per cent of total annual runoff, leaving $32\,900\,\mathrm{km^3}$ geographically accessible (but does not correct for many northern rivers with large flows relative to their population sizes) (Allegra 2008). Temporally availability: about 27 per cent of global runoff ($11\,100\,\mathrm{km^3}$) is renewable ground water and base river flow. The rest is flood water and harder to capture. The present storage capacity of large dams totals $5500\,\mathrm{km^3}$, of which $3500\,\mathrm{km^3}$

is used to regulate river runoff. Adding together base flow and surface runoff controlled by dams gives total stable flow. Correct for spatially inaccessible flows yields and estimate of available runoff (AR) as 12 500 km^3/yr (Allan 2006)).

What is the fraction of Available Runoff (AR) now used by humans? Withdrawals: agricultural withdrawals = average water application rate (12,000 m^3/ha) × world irrigated area (240 × 10^6 ha in 1990) = 2880 km^3. Assuming 65 per cent is consumed, 1870 km^3. Industrial water use is estimated at 975 km^3 and roughly 9 per cent (90 km^3) is consumed. The remainder is discharged back into the environment, often polluted.

Municipal use is estimated at 300 km^3 per year, of which 50 km^3 (17 per cent) is consumed.

Evaporation from reservoirs is estimated to average 5 per cent of gross storage capacity of reservoirs (5500 km^3) or 275 km^3/yr. In-stream flow needs are estimated from pollution dilution, assuming that this suffices to meet in-stream needs. A common dilution term is 28.3 litres per second per 1000 population. Using the 1990 population yields a dilution requirement of 4700 km^3. If half of water received adequate treatment, the dilution requirement is reduced to 2350 km^3 /hr.

Combining these estimates indicates that humans appropriate 54 per cent of AR. Human use of ET (18,200 km^3) plus runoff (6780 km^3) constitutes 30 per cent of total accessible renewable fresh water and 23 per cent of unadjusted value.

3.9 Water in the soil and landscape

3.9.1 The soil moisture storage capacity

The water storage capacity of the soil is the water that is available in the soil for use by plants, excluding obviously water that moves quickly though the soil under the influence of gravity as well as the water bound by strong forces to mineral surfaces. The storage capacity therefore depends on both the volume of soil and the volume of available pore space that can retain water against gravitational forces. In the context of desertification, this indicator is related to the production and regulation functions of soil quality. Changes in water storage capacity can be used as an early warning of desertification.

Water storage capacity is an excellent and appropriate desertification indicator with a long history of use in the context of water and soil management. It has been extensively used by hydrologists in the calculation of the soil–water balance and it is used in scheduling irrigation amounts. It is a valuable indicator because it directly describes how the soil is functioning.

Changes in water storage capacity can be attributed to soil degradation processes and soil biological activity. The water storage capacity is influenced by the depth to which rainfall penetrates the soil. The vertical differences in storage capacity in the soil affect both the subsequent evaporation of water and crop productivity. The erosion of the soil results in a loss of storage capacity.

Soil organisms produce many of the pores in a soil that enable a soil to store water. Organisms also produce substances that make pores able to retain their coherence when the soil is wet. A decrease in water storage capacity may be giving an early warning that the resilience or regenerative capacity of a soil is being affected by desertification.

If a soil cannot store as much water and nutrients as before, it will produce less biomass and there will be a positive feedback in which the storage capacity decreases.

Soil texture and rocks weather into regolith and soils that have characteristic pore-size distributions.

How it can be measured

Storage capacity can be measured experimentally in situ. A soil is saturated and covered by plastic to prevent evaporation and allowed to drain against gravity so that the *field capacity* is known. There are many procedures for measuring the energy with which water is held in the soil. Soil moisture suction can be converted to a measure of soil pore size distributions. Values can also be calculated by keeping a soil water balance account. This requires measuring or calculating the difference between evaporation and precipitation. Extensive and very useful guidelines are available from the FAO. Soil thin sections can be used and pore size distributions measured automatically under the microscope.

3.9.2 Plant water availability and critical water requirements

Water availability is dependent not just on the amount of rainfall but rather on the amount of water that can be stored. If rain falls on concrete or coarse sand and gravel it will quickly drain away and is not available for plants.

The water storage capacity can be related to the critical water requirements of plants and vegetation and in this way provide an indication of the suitability of the soil for a specific use. There is a huge database kept by the FAO describing plant water requirements and how these are related to soil water storage capacity. Typically a 10 cm layer of soil might have a storage capacity that ranges from 2 to 6 cm. This can be also measured with respect to the energy holding water in the soil and in this case the soil suction (pF) is a good measure of availability. Available water is that occurring in the range of suctions occurring between field capacity and the wilting point.

Key questions then are why and how do land degradation and desertification influence this property?

3.9.3 Runoff processes and mechanisms

When rain falls there are many different mechanisms and these are influenced greatly by desertification in different ways. More information can be found in Chapter 4.7 on Water.

For simplicity it is possible to think of four different mechanisms of runoff and these are very briefly:

- Horton Overland Flow. If the rainfall intensity exceeds the infiltration rate, once the surface storage is full overland flow can occur on a slope and when this reaches a river this can be thought of as surface runoff.

- Throughflow or interflow. Water that enters the soil moves down slope through the soil until it reaches the river channel. It may be either rapid or slow, delayed through flow.

- Flow through pipes, tunnel or macro pores.

- As unsaturated flow through fine pores.

There are several different processes that occur and explain the pattern of runoff producing areas in drainage basins and these are explained next.

Hydrologists often focus on more on modelling the amounts of runoff without necessarily verifying what is happening in the field. Consequently, the models that model water flow are calibrated to give accurate results but they do not always describe the processes of runoff generation that are actually happening. There are frequently differences that result from the assumptions made in the models that are very great. There are also problems because key processes that can have a huge impact on runoff and erosion are often impossible to include, for example, the development of soil surface crusts and entrapment of air in the soil, the soil water chemistry and water repellent behaviour. These will be illustrated later.

This is important for land degradation because it is important to know exactly where sediment and runoff comes from in order to propose and locate soil conservation or other measures. The nature of the runoff producing mechanisms are changed completely as a consequence of land use changes and practices. With soil management it is possible to change the processes to either increase or decrease runoff.

In conclusion it is useful to look at the feedbacks with the soil and management systems that occur and change over time as trees grow and the soil evolution takes place.

The question posed here is: How are the regulating functions (e.g. buffering and soil moisture storage) that control water amount and quality affected by environmental change? Which changes are critical for soil and groundwater contamination and which changes critical for specific types of plant or community? What are the drivers of these changes, how do the functions respond and how can they be measured?

The impact of these changes or impaired functions can be observed in the rivers and groundwater.

3.9.4 Sources of runoff and sediment

Hydrologists have long known that certain small areas in a drainage basin provide most of the runoff reaching a river. Such areas have been described as 'partial' or 'contributing' areas by some and as 'variables source areas' by others. Kirkby and Chorley (1969) were some of the first to present an overview and a theory of this topic. The work of Hewlett and Hibbert (1967) on variable source areas in the USA and by Dunne and Black (1970) in New England had a large impact on hydrological modeling because they provided theories that enabled runoff production zones to be identified. It was also shown by Sklash and Farvolden (1979) that runoff could be generated at locations where the soil water has a capillary fringe at or close to the surface.

In many areas it was found that the infiltration capacity of the soil is very variable. There are source and sink areas of water on hillslopes. Water from a runoff producing zone travels downslope to a sink which might be a short distance. In desert and semi arid areas, the vegetation patches are very often sinks where water enters the soil. Runoff production from a source area can be important for vegetation as it enables a reallocation of the water and nutrients on a slope, making it possible for plants to practise rainwater harvesting.

One of the ways that plants increase their ability to hold water is by making the soil hydrophobic or water repellent when it is dry. This enables small amounts of rainfall, say, just a few mm, to bypass the upper soil layer and provide water to roots that might be beneath it at, say, 10 to 30 cm. This layer also reduces evaporation.

What are the relationships between soil runoff producing mechanisms and soil properties and soil behaviour? The different hydrological processes and mechanisms mentioned earlier have feedbacks with the physical, chemical and biological properties of soils. These are sensitive to changes in climate, land use or other perturbations and they impact on water and water quality.

3.9.5 Soil behaviour and soil responses to rainfall

These are two notions being used by many to investigate the interactions between soil degradation, hydrological processes and human activity.

When soil material is subject to the impacts from rainfall or to contact with flowing water, it can respond in different ways, which will be described in more detail later in Chapter 3. These include, dispersion, swelling, slaking and flocculation and include the effects of water repellency and consistency. These can be studied by laboratory and field experiments. Indicators and useful indicators have been found to be the consistency index of de Ploey, and soil stability indices and aggregate stability.

The response of the soil can also be studied by rainfall simulation experiments and in this case, things measured include, the soil moisture and how water moves into the soil (wetting front behavior), the time it takes water to pond on the surface and the time to produce runoff and the amount and nature of the sediment and chemicals in the runoff.

Feedbacks between vegetation and runoff

The spatial pattern of runoff and sediment source and sink areas of course reflects feedbacks between water, plant growth and bare patch development (Tongway and Ludwig 1994; Ludwig and Tongway 1995). Soil water dynamics and vegetation dynamics are thus functionally related and vegetated and bare-ground patches may form interconnected units within the larger mosaic. The spatial pattern of vegetated and bare patches within such a mosaic determines if and how patches interact and strongly affects the downslope routing of water, sediments, nutrients, seeds, etc. Therefore, patterns in vegetation and soil are indicators for ecosystem functioning and hillslope hydrology.

The usefulness of pattern as an indicator in land degradation studies comes, on the one hand, from its building blocks, i.e. vegetated and bare patches, which govern the location and pattern of source and sink areas. For example, a measure of the extent and distribution of the bare patches within the mosaic can be an important index to characterize the erosion vulnerability of a certain area. On the other hand, the pattern can also be used at a broader scale to study the length or continuity and the intensity of downslope routing of water and soil material.

A number of ways exist to describe and characterize spatial patterns. Five pattern indices that can be used to describe and quantify are:

- the extent and distribution of vegetation patches (perceived as runoff and sediment sink areas);

- the extent and distribution of bare areas within the vegetation-bare soil mosaics (perceived as runoff and sediment source areas);

- the capacity of vegetated patches (sinks) to catch runoff and sediment;

- the connectivity between different source areas.

Three concepts from landscape ecology (lacunarity, contagion and fragmentation) can be used to identify the degree of contagion and gap distribution within the vegetation mosaic.

References and further reading

Adeel, Z., and U. Safriel (lead authors) (2005) Dryland systems, in R. Hassan, R. Scholes, and N. Ash, eds, *Millennium Assessment, Ecosystems and Human Well-being. Volume 1: Ecosystems and Human Well-being: Current State and Trends*. Island Press, Washington, pp. 623–664.

Allan, D. (2006) *Human Appropriation of the World's Fresh Water Supply*. University of Michigan. Available online from http://www.globalchange.umich.edu/globalchange2/current/lectures/freshwater_supply/freshwater.html (Accessed 03/06/2008).

Allegra, C. (2008) *Final Report Water Cycle* IUCN. Gland, Switzerland. August. 38 pp.

Aradottir, A. L. and Arnalds, O. (2001). Ecosystem degradation and restoration of birch woodlands in Iceland. In: F. E. Wielgolaski (ed.), *Nordic Mountain Birch Ecosystems*, pp. 293–308. Man and the Biosphere Series, Vol. 27. UNESCO, Paris, and Parthenon Publishing, Carnforth.

Arnalds, A. (2000). Evolution of rangeland conservation strategies, in O. Arnalds and S. Archer (eds), *Rangeland Desertification*, pp. 153–163. Advances in Vegetation Sciences Series. Kluwer, Dordrecht, The Netherlands.

Arnalds, O., E. F., Thorarinsdottir, S. M. Metusalemsson, A. Jonsson, E. Gretarsson, and A. Arnason (2001) *Soil Erosion in Iceland*. Soil Conservation Service and Agricultural Research Institute, Reykjavik. 121 pp.

Arnalds, O. and Barkarson, B. H. (2003) Soil erosion and land use policy in Iceland in relation to sheep grazing and government subsidies. *Environmental Science and Policy*, 6: 105–113.

Bird, S. B., J. E. Herrick, M. M. Wander, and L. Murray (2007) Multi-scale variability in soil aggregate stability: implications for understanding semi-arid grassland degradation. *Geoderma* 140: 106–118.

Boatman N, C., R. Stoate, C. R. Gooch, *et al.* (1999) *The Environmental Impact of Arable Crop Production in the European Union, Practical Options for Improvement*.

Bergkamp, G., M. M. Bakker, L. K. A. Dorren, H. Looijen and J. De Vente (1997) *Soil and water conservation in the Alentejo region (Portugal)*. Medalus working paper 73, 69 pp.

Boiffoin, J. and G. Monnier (1986) Infiltration rate as affected by soil surface crusting caused by rainfall, pp. 210–217, in F. Callebaut, D. Gabriels and M. De Boodt, eds, *Assessment of Soil Surface Sealing and Crusting* ISSS Flanders Research Centre For Soil Erosion and Soil Conservation. Ghent.

Boix-Fayos, C., A. Calvo-Cases, A. C. Imeson, M. D. Soriano Soto and I. R. Tiemessen (2001) Spatial and short-term temporal variations in runoff, soil aggregation and other soil properties along a Mediterranean climatological gradient. *Catena* 33: 123–138.

Bolwidt, L. J. and P. C. van Leuzen (1997) *Indicators of land degradation. Soil erosion research to determine the health of land units in the Baixo-Aleentejo, Portugal*. Report, University of Amsterdam.

Braat, L. C., S. W. F. van der Ploeg and F. Bouma (1979) *Functions of the Natural Environment: An Economic-ecological Research*, Institute for Environmental Studies, Free University Amsterdam, Amsterdam: 73 pp.

Brandt, J. and N. Geeson (2003) DIS4ME: *Desertification Indicators System for Mediterranean Europe*, Desertlinks Project, Department of Geography. Kings College, London.

Burton, R. F. and G. A. Wilson (2006) Injecting social psychology theory into conceptualisations of agricultural agency: towards a post-productivist farmer self-identity? *Journal of Rural Studies* 22: 95–115.

Calvo-Cases, A., C. A. Boix-Fayos and A. C. Imeson (2003) Runoff generation, sediment movement and soil water behaviour on calcareous (limestone) slopes of some mediterranean environments in southeast Spain. *Geomorphology* 50:. 269–291.

Cerdà, A., A. C. Imeson and A. Calvo (1998) Fire and aspect induced differences on the erodibility and hydrology of soils at La Costera, Valencia, south-east Spain. *Catena* 24, 289–304.

Costello, V. and A. Arnoldussen, S. Bautista, *et al.* (2004) *European Soils Strategy*. Working Group on Erosion Task Group 6 on Desertification Final Report DG, 33 pp.

CST (1997) *Supplementary report on work on benchmark and indicators*, note by the Secretariat, Rome29 September–10 October. CST Agenda Item 6 UNCCD/COP(1) 3? Add.1, 5 pp.

DeSurvey (2010) *A surveillance system for assessing and monitoring desertification*. Project Co-ordinator: Prof. Juan Puigdefabregas. Estacion Experimental de Zonas Aridas (EEZA-CSIC), Spain.

DG-Agriculture (2001) *A Framework for Indicators for the Economic and Social Dimensions of Sustainable Agriculture and Rural Development* (39 pp).

Doran, J. W. and T. B. Parkin (1996) Quantitative indicators of soil quality: a minimum data set, in J. W. Doran and A. J. Jones, eds, *Methods for Assessing Soil Quality*. SSSA Special Publication 49, Madison, pp. 25–38.

Doran, J. W. and A. J. Jones (1996) Preface in *Methods for Assessing Soil Quality*. Soil Science Society of America Special Publication. Madison, Wisconsin, USA, pp. xi–xiii.

Dorren, L., F. Berger, A. C. Imeson, B. Maierand F. Rey (2004) Integrity, stability and management of protection forests in the European Alps. *Forest Ecology and Management* 195(1–2): 165–176.

Dregne, H. E. (1983) *Desertification of Arid Lands*. Harwood Academic Publishers, London.

Duniway, M. C., Snyder, K. A. and J. E. Herrick (2010) J.E. Spatial and temporal patterns of water availability in a grass-shrub ecotone and implications for grassland recovery inarid environments. *Ecohydrology* 3: 55–67.

Dunne, Y. and R. D. Black (1970) Partial area contributions to storm runoff in a small New England watershed. *Water Resources Research* 6: 1296–1311.

EEA *Assessment and Reporting on Soil Erosion* (2003) Technical Report 94 (edited by A.R. Gentile).

Emerson, W. W. (1967) A classification of soil aggregates based on their coherence in water. *Australian Journal of Soil Research*, 5: 47–57.

Falkenmark, M. and J. Lundquist (1998) Towards water security: political determination and human adaptation crucial. *Natural Resources Forum* 22: 37–51.

Falkenmark, M. and J. Rockström (2004). *Balancing Water for Humans and Nature: The New Approach in Ecohydrology*. London: Earthscan.

Fantechi, R. and N. S. Margaris (eds) (1986) *Desertification in Europe*. D. Reidel, Dordrecht.

Groot, de R. S. (1992) *Functions of Nature: Evaluation of Nature in Environmental Planning, Management and Decision Making*. Wolters-Noordhoff, Amsterdam, 315 pp.

Gunter, J. and S. Jodway (1999) *Community-based Natural Resources Management: A Strategy for Community Economic Development, draft CED for Forest Based Communities Project*. Simon Fraser University, Burnaby, British Colombia, Canada. 32 pp.

Gustafson, E. J. (1998) Quantifying landscape spatial pattern: what is the state of the art ? *Ecosystems* 1: 143–156.

Hannam, I. D. 2000. Soil conservation policies in Australia: successes, failures and requirements for ecologically sustainable policy. pp. 493–514, *in:* E. L. Napier, S. M. Napier and J. Tvrdon, eds, *Soil and Water Conservation Policies and Programs: Successes and Failures*. Boca Raton, Florida: CRC Press.

Haring, R. (1996) *Areas sensitive to erosion identified by means of air photo interpretation in the Medalus Target Area*. Manuscript. Dissertation University of Amsterdam, available author.

Harris, R. F, D. L Karlen and D. J. Mulla (1996) A conceptual framework for assessment and management of soil quality and health. In: J. W. Doran and A. J. Jones, eds, *Methods for Assessing Soil Quality*. SSSA Special Publication, pp. 61–82.

Helldén, U. (1991) Desertification – time for a reassessment? *Ambio* 20 (8): 372–383.

Herrick, J. E., W. G. Whitford, A. G. de Soyza, *et al*. (2001) A field soil aggregate stability kit for soil quality and rangeland health evaluations, *Catena* 44: 1, 27–35.

Herrick, J. E., B. T. Bestelmeyer, S. Archer, A. Tugel, and J. R. Brown (2006) An integrated framework for science-based arid land management. *Journal of Arid Environments*. 65: 319–335.

Herrick, J. E. and J. Wright (2007) Ecological services to and from rangelands of the western United States. *Ecological Economics*. 64: 261–268.

Herrick, J. E., B. T. Bestelmeyer and K. Crossland (2008) Simplifying ecological site verification, rangeland health assessments, and monitoring. *Rangelands*. 30: 24–26.

Hewlett, D. and A. R. Hibbert (1967) Factors affecting the response of small watersheds to precipitation in humid areas, in W. E. Sopper and H. W. Lull, eds, *Forest Hydrology*. Pergamon Press, New York. Republished in *Progress in Physical Geography* 32 (20): 288–293.

Holling, C. S. and Meffe, G. K. (1996) Command and control and the pathology of natural resource management. *Conservation Biology* 10: 328–337.

Huxley, T. H. Selected Works of Thomas Huxley Westminster Edition containing III *Evolution and Ethics* (1893) and IV *Capital the Mother of Labour* (1890). Appeltons, 334 pp.

Imeson, A. C. (1987). Soil erosion and conservation, in *Human Activity and Environmental Processes*, ed. K. J. Gregory and D. E. Walling. John Wiley and Sons, Inc., New York.

Imeson, A. C. (1999). Soil degradation: the data problem and its solution, pp. 25–30, in *Desertification Convention Data and Information Requirements*. Edited by S. Enne, D. Peter and D. Pottier.

Imeson, A. C. (2002). Indicators for land degradation in the Mediterranean basin, pp. 47–55, in G. Enne, Ch. Zanolla and D. Peter, *Desertification in Europe. Mitigation Strategies and Land Use Planning*. EUR 19390, 509 pp.

Imeson, A.C., O. Arnalds, L. Montanarella, *et al*. (2006) *Soil Conservation and Protection in Europe (SCAPE). The Way Ahead*. European Soil Bureau, Ispra, Italy.

Imeson, A. C., L. H. Cammeraat and H. Prinsen (1998a) A conceptual approach for evaluating the storage and release of contaminants derived from process based land degradation studies: an example from the Guadalentín basin, Southeast Spain. *Agriculture, Ecosystems & Environment* 67(2–3): 223–237.

Imeson, A C., H. Lavee, A. Calvo and A. Cerda (1998b) The erosional response of calcareous soils along a climatological gradient in Southeast Spain. *Geomorphology*, 24: 1: 3–16.

Imeson, A. C. and H. Lavee (1998) Investigating the impact of climate change on geomorphological processes: the transect approach and the influence of scale. *Geomorphology* 23: 219–227.

Imeson, A. C., F. Perez-Trejo and L. H. Cammeraat (1996). The response of landscape units to desertification. In *Mediterranean Desertification and Land Use* (ed. J. Thornes and J. Brandt), pp. 447–468. John Wiley and Sons, Ltd, Chichester.

Jolley, L. and J. J. Goebel (2010) National ecosystem assessments supported by scientific and local knowledge. *Frontiers in Ecology and the Environment*.

Karlen, D. L, M. J. Mausbach, J. W. Doran, *et al*. (1997) Soil Quality: A concept, definition and framework for analysis. *Soil Sci. Soc. Am. J.* 61: 4–10.

Kimpe, C. R. de and B. P Warkentin (1998) Soil functions and the future of natural resources. *Advances In GeoEcology* 31: 3–10.

Kirkby, M. J. and R. J. Chorley (1969) Erosion by water on hillslopes, in *Water, Earth and Man*, ed. R. J. Chorley. Methuen, London.

Kirkby, M. J., A. C. Imeson, G. Bergkamp, and L. H. Cammeraat (1996). Scaling up processes and models from the field plot to the watershed and regional areas. *Journal of Soil and Water Conservation* 51(5): 391–396.

Kosmos, C. (1999) *Manual on Key indicators of Desertification and Mapping Environmentally Sensitive Areas to Desertification.* Medalus European Union 18882.

Kuhn, N., A. Yair and M. K. Grubin (2004) Spatial distribution of surface properties, runoff generation and landscape development in the Zin Valley Badlands, northern Negev. *Israel Earth Surface Processes and Landforms* 29: 1417–1430.

Landres, P. B. (1992). Ecological indicators: Panacea or liability. In: D. H. McKenzie, D. H. Hyatt and V. J. McDonald, eds, *Ecological Indicators*, pp. 1295–1318. Elsevier Applied Science, New York.

Lavee, H., S. Pariente and A. C. Imeson (1996) Aggregate stability dynamics as affected by soil temperature and moisture regimes. *Geografiske Annaler* 78 A: 73–82.

Lavee, H., A. C. Imeson and S. Parientes (1997) The impact of climate change on geomorphological processes and desertification along a Mediterranean-Arid climatological gradient. *Land Degradation and Rehabilitation.*

van der Leeuw, S. and S. C. Leygonie (2000) *A long term perspective on resilience in socio-natural systems.* Paper presented at the workshop on system shocks and system resilience held in Abisko, Sweden, May 22–26.

Loveday, J. and J. Pyle (1973) The Emerson dispersion test and its relationship to hydraulic conductivity, CSIRO Australian Divisions of Soils Technical Paper, 15: 1–7.

Ludwig, J. A., B. P. Wilcox, D. D. Breshears, D. J. Tongway and A. C. Imeson (2005) Interactions between vegetation and runoff in semiarid landscape: an ecohydrological framework. *Ecology* 288–297

Middleton, N. and D. Thomas (1997) *World Atlas of Desertification.* Arnold, London.

Millennium Ecosystem Assessment (2005) *Ecosystems and Human Well-being: Desertification Synthesis.* World Resources Institute, Washington, D.C.

OECD (2001) Organization for Economic Cooperation and Development (OECD) *Environmental indicators for Agriculture*, Methods and Results, Vol. 3, 416 pp.

O'Neill, R. V., D. L. de Angelis, J. B. Waide, and T. F. H. Allen (1986) *A Hierarchical Concept of Ecosystems.* Princeton University Press. Princeton N.J. 253 p

Pellent, M., P. Shaver, D. A. Pyke and J. E. Herrick (2005) *Interpreting indicators of Rangeland Health* (Technical Reference 1734-6) United States Department of the Interior, 45 pp.

Pradas, M., A.-C. Imeson and E. van Mulligen (1994) The infiltration and runoff characteristics of burnt soils in NE Catalonia, pp. 229–240, in M. Sala and J. L. Rubio, eds, *Soil Erosion as a Consequence of Forest Fires.* Georforma Ediciones, Zaragoza, Spain. 275 pp.

Reining, P. (1978) *Handbook on Desertification Indicators*, AAAS Publication No. 78-7, 141 pp.

Reynolds, J. F., D. M. Stafford Smith, E. F. Lambin, *et al.* (2007) Global desertification: building a science for dryland development. *Science.* 316: 847–851.

Roxo, M. J. (1993) Field site Investigations, Lower Alentejo, Beja and Mertola, Portugal. In: *Medalus I; Final Report*, J. B. Thornes and J. Brandt, eds, University of Bristol, UK: 406–432.

Roxo, M. J. (1994a). *A acção antrópica no processo de degradação de solos a Serra de Serpa e Mértola.* Thesis, Universidade Nova de Lisboa, 387 pp. (In Portuguese).

Roxo, M. J. (1994b) *Field site: Lower Alentejo, Portugal.* In: Medalus II, project 1, 2nd annual report, J. Brandt and N. Geeson, eds., London, pp. 49–57.

Roxo, M. J. (2009) *Lucinda Land Care in Desertification Affected Areas from Science to Application.* EU Project (http://geografia.fcsh.unl.pt/lucinda/).

Rubio, J. L. and E. Bochet (1998) Desertification indicators as diagnosis criteria for desertification risk assessment in Europe. *Journal of Arid Environments* 39 (2): 113–120.

Schumm, S. (1977) *The Fluvial System.* John Wiley and Sons, Ltd, Chichester.

Shaxson, T. F. (1998) Concepts and indicators for assessment of sustainable land use advances. *Geo-Ecology* 31: 11–19.

Sklash, M. G. and R. N. Farvolden (1979) The role of groundwater in storm runoff. *Journal of Hydrology* 43: 45–65.

Sommer, S., C. Zucca, A. Grainger, M. Cherlet, R. Zougmore Y. Sokona, J. Hill, R. Della Peruta, J. Roehrig, and G. Wang (2011) Application of indicator systems for monitoring and assessment of desertification from national to global scales. *Land Degradation and Development* 22: 184–197.

Tongway, D. (1994) *Rangeland Assessment Manual*, Division of Wildlife and Ecology, Canberra (69 pp), *Breakdown and Restoration of Ecosystems*, pp. 231–240. Plenum Press, New York.

Turner, R.M., L.H. Applegate, P.M. Berghold, S. Gallizioli and S.G. Martin (1980) *Arizona Range Reference Areas*, USDA, Forest Service, General Technical Report RM-79 34p Fort Collins, Colo.

Ubeda, X., M. Sala and A. C. Imeson (1990) Variociones en la establilidad y consistencia de un suelo forestal antes y despues de ser sometido a un incendio. 1 Reunion Nacional de *Geomorfologia*, Turuel 1990. 677–685.

UNCED (1992) Conference, *United Nations Conference on Environment and Development*. Rio de Janeiro, 3–14 June. (Informal name, The Earth Summit).

UNEP (1991) *Status of Desertification and Implementation of the United Nations Plan of Action to Combat Desertification*. UNEP, Nairobi.

Warren, A. and L. Olsson (2003) Desertification: loss of credibility despite the evidence, in *Annals of Arid Zone* 42(3–4): 271–287.

Westman, W. E. (1986) Resilience concepts and measures, in B. Dell, A. J. M. Hopkins and B. B. Lamont, eds, pp. 5–19, *The Resilience of Mediterranean Ecosystems*. Junk, The Netherlands.

Wilson, G. A. (2009) Rethinking environmental management – ten years later: a view from the author. *Environments* 36 (3): 3–15.

Wilson, G. A. (2010) Multifunctional 'quality' and rural community resilience. *Transactions of the Institute of British Geographers* 35: 364–381.

Wilson, G. A. and H. Buller (2001) The use of socio-economic and environmental indicators in assessing the effectiveness of EU Agri-Environmental Policy. *European Environment* 11: 297–313.

Wishmeier, W. H. (1976) Use and misuse of the universal soil loss equation. *Journal of Soil and Water Conservation* 31, 1, 5–9.

Wischmeier, W. H. and D. D. Smith (1978) *Predicting Rainfall Erosion Losses*: A Guide to Conservation Planning. *Agriculture Handbook* No. 537.

Xiao Jietu and Li Jinquan (2008) *An Outline History of Chinese Philosophy* (I). Foreign Language Press, Beijing. 434 pp.

Yair, A. and H. Lavee (1981) An investigation of source area of sediment and sediment transport by overland flow along arid hillslope. *IAHS* Pub 133, 433–446.

Part II

Local Desertification Impact and Response

4
Key processes regulating soil and landscape functions

4.1 Introduction

4.1.1 Land use change and functions affected

When forests are converted into agricultural land and/or when land use practices are changed, the impact on the ecosystem is considerable, as is similarly the case when the changes are from agricultural land to forest. How do human activities that alter processes affect the provision of the functions provided by the land and ecosystems? Desertification occurs when these changes lead to the loss in the capacity of the landscape to sustain itself or to recover from disturbance (Briassouli 2011).

When an area or region or loses the capacity to provide clean water, or protection from natural hazards, or from climate change, what actually takes place in the soil and landscape that causes this to happen? What are the processes involved and what has been the best practice experience in counteracting them?

Figure 4.1 illustrates the enormous magnitude in the differences of the water-holding capacity and soil erodibility of different types of land use in Europe.

4.1.2 Scientific consensus about the key processes

There is a wealth of information that is available from the many conferences and workshops that have been organized to study the impact of land use change. These conferences have been supported by several international research organizations, such as the International Geographical Union (IGU), the European Society of Soil Conservation (ESSC) and the International Society for Scientific Hydrology (IASH). There has been support for international commissions working on desertification (LANDCON) and the impacts of land use on environmental change (GERTEC). The World Association of Soil and Water Conservation (WASWC) organizes annual conferences and meetings and the International Soil Conservation Organization (ISCO) provides further information. Researchers have been able to compare processes from different parts of the world and a consensus has been able to be developed regarding the nature of key processes in different environments.

Desertification, Land Degradation and Sustainability, First Edition. Anton Imeson.
© 2012 John Wiley & Sons, Ltd. Published 2012 by John Wiley & Sons, Ltd.

| Grassland | Wheat | Maize | Production forest | Natural forest |

	Grassland	Wheat	Maize	Production forest	Natural forest
1	0.2	4.0	8.0	2.5	0.5
2	20	5	2	8	80
3	0.6–1.1	0.8–1.3	0.9–1.5	0.8–1.8	0.7–1.0
4	0.15–0.8	0.12–0.4	0.2–0.5	1.0–0.2	1.5–0.4
5	30	0.9	0.8	5	10

Key

1 = Erosion rates [t/ha]
2 = Time to ponding [minutes] (rainfall intensity cm/hr)
3 = Bulk density [g/cm^3]
4 = Storage capacity range [cm/m^2]
5 = Final infiltration capacity [mm/hr]

Figure 4.1 Landuse in relation with runoff, erosion and water storage (Credit: SCAPE and Luuk Dorren).

4.1.3 Key processes and functions

The following processes and functions are involved:

1 The processes that regulate how water is held in the soil and on slopes (water provision function).

2 The interacting physical, chemical and biological processes that regulate the stability and behaviour of the soil, in terms of its capacity to resist erosion and movement (soil protection function).

3 The processes that regulate the heat and water dynamics in the soil (habitat function).

4 Hydrological and sediment transfer processes.

5 The productive function of the soil which is influenced by the above.

Actions that drive change are a result of the weather and weathering (wind, rain, hail and flowing water), gravity, and the actions of different life forms (ranging from bacteria to ants, termites and worms, through to higher animals like plants and man). The latter includes the actions taken by species to exploit, manipulate and transform nature as a resource and habitat.

For simplification, it is helpful to focus on a few key processes and their measurement. These are:

1 The storage and movement of water at different scales.

2 The behaviour and response of the soil with respect to its erodibility (intrinsic sensitivity of soil to erosion) and water storage capacity.

3 The effects of different species on their habits and natural resources.

4 Interactions between vegetation, water amount and the energy and heat.

5 Runoff and erosion.

Processes and patterns as indicators of hydrological performance and soil conservation
One key idea introduced in Chapters 1, 2 and 3 is that the processes move water, sediment and nutrients and transport material in ways that lead to the emergence of both two-dimensional patterns on the surface and three-dimensional structures in the soil. These are then emergent features of processes. Both the movement (e.g. flow of water with sediment and chemicals) as well the patterns or structures can be monitored. The elements of the patterns can be described at different scales and in terms of fractal and network characteristics.

In time and with energy, systems develop increasing complexity and a greater fractal dimension so that the surface to area or volume of things increases. For example, in the soil that develops on abandoned land, the complexity and surface area of the soil particles increases as organisms create habitats for themselves and develop an ecosystem that increases in complexity and function in time.

When a soil is water-stable, it can retain its water-holding capacity easily during rainfall and breaks down into larger fragments. This stability is a reflection therefore of the hydrological, capital and presence of soil regulation and protection functions.

Both the impact of raindrops and flowing water, both on and in the soil, transports fine particles further than the coarser ones by a process of sorting whereby light particles are carried further than heavier ones. Another case is when as in Figure 4.2 in Iceland the surface is locally affected by the growth of ice needles and frost heaving. In channels formed by flowing water, deep and shallow sections are formed, known as pools and riffles. Eroding rills and river channels develop alternating wet and dry or deep and shallow reaches because of the complex mechanics and interactions that affect the entrainment and deposition of sediment. These can be clearly seen in the river in Portugal shown in Figure 4.3, where there are also river bars. Erosion on a slope leads to the accumulation of areas that are rich or poor in organic matter, clay and nutrients. Stones on a path kicked by walkers can create polygons. Another example is the way in which land use around a village becomes zoned in relation to the distance of travel or the way in which there is a pattern of villages according to central place theory. Patterns and structures may sometimes be a way in which resilience is expressed and if these generate value they are also an expression of human, economic and natural capital. When it rains, therefore, the rain does not fall on a field that is uniform but on one in which there are structures and patterns, some caused by previous rainfall but some caused by people. Patterns of land use and wealth reflect flows of capital, knowledge and power. With land degradation, patterns and structures are threatened.

Patterns when the actions that caused them have ceased

Not all patterns are actively being created, and they are, in a sense, fossil. They were created by the activities of life that is no longer present. They are significant because the resources are trapped in structures from which they are released and they also form a natural resource. Some structures persist for a long time and have a large impact on land

Figure 4.2   Patterns are very significant in cold areas such as in this photograph in Iceland. Bare areas are subject to needle ice growth and frost and the material is transported by wind. Plants trap sand and create differences in microclimate (Credit: Anton Imeson).

degradation processes. The agriculturally abandoned area in Figure 4.3 contains many elements that are fossil in terms of their cause but which have a very persistent impact on processes.

It may be that either a) there is little change and the pattern constrains the process and things are static or b) the patterns are being actively changed by a key process.

It is observed that when so much water is being extracted from the natural systems by people or that it is contaminated by pollution, the processes of change that would normally take place and lead to growth and progression will no longer occur.

In very many cases the life that was responsible for creating something in the soil or land has become extinct. In this case the resources that were used are released and become available to be re-incorporated into the phenotype of other animals or plants. Worms or ants may disappear so that they no longer transform the soil, a river may be dammed so there are no high flows to maintain pools and riffles, or people may abandon an area because it is economically marginal so that the terraces collapse and are no longer maintained. Figure 4.4 from Spain illustrates a common fate of many agricultural terraces when they are no longer maintained.

This is why the extinction of a species or its loss is significant. At a larger scale, land abandonment means that the people who, for example, created the Dahessa landscapes in Spain and the similar Montado landscapes in Portugal, or who built the terraces in Cinque Terre, are no longer able to maintain them and these resources can be exploited for something else or return back to a natural system that on a world scale at least contributes to the health of planetary-level ecosystem functioning.

Landslides occurring in Mediterranean areas, often linked with degradation of the vegetation cover and poor maintenance of cultural landscapes due to land abandonment, have raised the attention of decision makers in many countries.

Figure 4.3 Note the patterns and structures in the river and on the slopes that form as has been described. Pools and riffles can be seen in the channel. Location: Portugal, The Alentejo (Credit: Anton Imeson).

Figure 4.4 Terraces enable farmers to cultivate steep slopes and control erosion. They mimic banded vegetation patterns. Credit A. Cerda 2011.

Terraces provide a structure that mimics that provided by banded vegetation in semi-arid areas. Banded vegetation patterns enable resources to be concentrated and enable plants to grow where there is limited water or land.

When groundwater is abstracted from rivers and pumped from aquifers, the impacts on the environment at a large scale are immense because the patterns in human activity and the natural vegetation that were dependent on this no longer receive the resources required to sustain them or locally may have too much water at an inconvenient time. A good example is the village of Canales in Valencia. The village is located at large limestone springs that have been the source of energy and water for the municipality and irrigation of the flood plain for many centuries. But in 2010 the discharge of the springs declined by about 80 per cent. Licences given to people to use groundwater by people in the headwater areas will not be revoked by the Valencia Provincial Government who see it as an issue of Water Rights, and not of hydrology and desertification. However, the

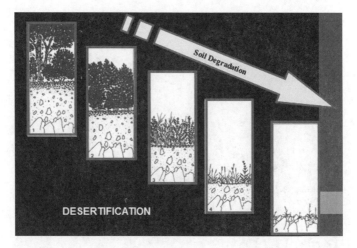

Figure 4.5 This diagram sketches the profiles found as sites become more degraded and the biodiversity and water holding capacity of the soil less. Credit A Cerda 2011.

main point is that it is not just Canales that has lost its water, it is the life of all the other thousands of springs and seepage points across the region, with critical habitat functions, that are affected, so that the resources that they created degrade and are lost. In the same area of Valencia, Figure 4.5 summarizes the relationship between the vegetation and soil on the one hand and the degree of degradation on the other. What this figure therefore demonstrates is the impact of forest clearance, grazing and fire on the soil profile. The relationship between the degree of degradation and the water balance is dramatic.

The observer and multi-level phenomenon

The role of the observer in relation to the scale of a pattern is relevant (Allen *et al*. 1984) because observations and relationships are observed at the level of readily perceived objects (say, organisms) and at other levels, such as ecosystems. How are they to be recognized at lower levels? For example, how is complexity observed under the microscope? The authors point out that there is a distinction between structural entities such as trees and people and successive levels such as a tree and a forest. On the level at which trees are recognized, the interesting behaviour involves how different trees interact with each other.

Vegetation patches exist as entities at a certain level and the question is then how do these interact? At the forest level the distinction between trees is lost, so that boundaries are important. It is explained that levels can be linked if phenomena such as primary production are common to both levels. This applies also to water availability, as well as many hydrological parameters which also correlated with primary production and can also be measured at multiple levels.

Because water and erosion can be observed at different levels, they are discussed in some detail in this and the next chapter.

In Table 4.1, the types of measurement that are frequently used to study processes according to land use and scale and different levels of land cover type are shown.

Table 4.1 Types of measurements used to study processes according to scale and land cover type.

State/condition	Scale	Indicator of process
Cultivated	Fine	porosity, organic matter, depth, bulk density
	Medium	terraces, contour ploughing, roughness
	Coarse	terraces, linear erosion, runoff
Transitional	Fine	crust, soil aggregation pattern, depth, bulk density, roots, soil fauna
	Medium	vegetation, soil and infiltration patterns, local erosion and runoff soil fauna
	Coarse	slope scale erosion and runoff features
Semi-natural	Fine	Soil aggregation, soil fauna, bulk density, porosity
	Medium	patterns in soil and vegetation
	Coarse	runoff at slope scale.

4.2 Fine scale processes

Fine scale processes always play an important role in land degradation because they can explain many things that **emerge** at higher scales and which change how the three services are provided. This knowledge helps threshold conditions to be explained and predicted. Some examples will be given as illustrations.

Soil compaction

For example, very many soils in Europe suffer from sub-soil compaction through the use of heavy machinery. This means that when it rains, a saturated layer of moving water can develop at a depth of about 30 to 40 cm. Under such conditions **discontinuous rills** can form when the soil becomes saturated and the whole layer of the top soil can be washed away and lost. This is the case when the top soil has a very low coherence or stability when wet.

Compaction can in this way be one of the **critical conditions** required for **gullies** to form. It also leads to the development of subsurface flow paths (**pipes and tunnels**) that can transport chemicals and pollutants to the river system, as in the Brie Plateau of France where millions of euros are spent purifying water for Paris.

Whether or not rills (small channels) and gullies (large incised channels) form depends on critical conditions. These may involve the dynamics of the aggregation processes in the soil, the response and stability of material when subject to rapid or slow wetting. In other words, the way in which the soil regulates and provides **soil protection to the people by providing a service at the slope and catchment level** depends on how the soil aggregation processes are managed at the fine scale. It has been possible to successfully prevent erosion from occurring today in, for example, Limburg in The Netherlands, by managing the soil structure so that the water regulation and soil protection functions are restored. This involves using cover crops and grass strips. Management involves improving the quality of the soil for life so that these increase soil water-holding capacity by creating a greater porosity and fractal area. Basically, it is the organisms in the soil as well as plant roots that create pores and spaces that enable the hydrological service to be restored and this usually occurs naturally at no cost.

4.2.1 Processes involved

Many processes are involved but include the following:

1 The activities of the **meso-fauna** in the soil, for example earthworms and ants.

2 **Soil aggregation** processes that are affected by soil organisms and physio-chemical behaviour. There can be sudden losses or gains in of the stability and strength of the soil as a result of **swelling, dispersion, flocculation** and **slaking**.

3 Transport and **weathering** processes in the soil that lead to emergent and slow changes in density and **water-holding capacity** and the accumulation of hard compact layers.

4 Movement and accumulation of **(water-soluble) salts** in the landscape.

5 Displacement and loss of soil as a consequence of **ploughing** and other farming activities.

6 Displacement of soil and stones on slopes by people and animal (**creep**).

7 Interfering with the population dynamics and the food chain (top predator effect).

8 The keeping and herding of livestock.

9 Cutting and clearing trees.

10 The use of fire.

11 Infiltration and runoff processes.

Some of the processes may be very slow but they can have a sudden emergent impact at a coarser scale. They are all processes in which the accumulation and release of material, patterns and structures occurs in different ways and can be linked in the adaptive cycle metaphor (Chapter 3). The importance of the management by the farmer is great. Figure 4.6, shows a delicate soil that is sensitive to surface sealing and erosion. The farmer uses this to his advantage to skillfully monitor and manage his crop, often creating microterraces to trap eroding soil and water and to make use of this as his resource. Figure 4.7 from Valencia, illustrates the skillful creation of a terracced landscape so that the production function can be maintained. Terraces were a major innovation many thousands of years ago because they enabled agriculture to be carried out on steep slopes. When terraces are build by bulldozer and not by hand they often lead to erosion because the soil functions are impaired.

Figure 4.6 Fine scale processes in action in a field in China. The farmer manages the structure so that it enhances plant growth and reduces runoff and erosion. The stability of the soil is a key indicator but its value depends on the context. This soil has a high silt and clay content. The soil at the back has a surface crust produced by the impact of raindrops (Credit: Anton Imeson).

Figure 4.7 Provision of soil and water conservation function by trees and terraces in Valencia Spain. Courtesy of A. Cerda 2011.

Figure 4.8 Illustrating the impact of terraces on reducing erosion and creating areas of high infiltration that form sinks for infiltrating water that comes from the sources upslope (Credit: Anton Imeson).

Figure 4.8 illustrates different methods of controlling erosion being tested on experimental slopes. Experiments such as this are valuable for translating concepts into practical actions and for dissemination to farmers.

4.2.2 Soil structure and stability as a key components

Research has shown that one of the most important indicators of the sensitivity to land degradation and soil quality is the stability of the soil structure. This is influenced by the mineral composition of the soil. Put simply, the very fine colloidal material in the soil which is smaller than about 2 to 4 microns, and which is composed of clay and organic matter, may be thought of as something that acts to bind and hold the coarser silt and sand grains together. The way in which the soil and clay behaves in water when it is wetter is important. If the soil easily breaks up into colloidal particles then it has a low stability. Also important but in different ways are the influences of the soil biota on the soil and the way it influences the hydrology and erosion. More details will be given later but the aim here is to show how these fine scale processes have an impact that acts at very coarse scales.

Earthworms

The importance of earthworms for soil formation was described by Darwin (1884). He also measured how earthworms bury artifacts and stones and influence soil fertility. Creating soil conditions in which earthworms cannot function is easy because they have specific soil requirements. The long-term importance of worm activity is illustrated by a case from Luxembourg. A fine scale process may be very important also at coarser scales. Jungerius and van Zon in 1982 realized that the activity of worms today in forests could explain the different rates of erosion on the Luxembourg Sandstone and Keuper Clay. Jungerius and van Zon (1982) were able to compare the different rates of land degradation on the different geological formations in Luxembourg. They did this by analysing the volcanic ash in the soil that came from the Eifel Mountains which can be used like cesium −134 to date soil erosion. They found that what influenced erosion most was the mixing of the soil by worms and other fauna.

Rocks that were sometimes weak could, through soil formation, develop hard pans or crusts that enabled the formation to resist erosion and develop cuestas or escarpments. They found that on the Lias Clay, earthworms were eating and removing all of the litter produced by oaks, hornbeams and hawthorn before April. As a consequence, the clay soil was exposed to rain splash erosion and runoff developed and drained from the cracks that were formed. The large number of earthworms was due to the fertility of the soil which was not always used for agriculture because of its physical properties (too high clay content). The sandstone areas, in contrast, produced podzols and acid conditions that resulted in lower amounts of soil loss as the soil was too coarse or acid for worms to thrive. The relative attractiveness of the different lithologies to animals is a major factor affecting erosion rates. This applied in the past to agriculture when there were no hidden subsidies.

In addition to this, worms can totally transform the hydrology of catchments and influence land degradation in very many ways. The activities of worms are responsible for creating the structures, in this case worm tunnels, shrinkage cracks and areas of bare soil, that enable water to drain the soil and move either on the surface as overland flow or as throughflow. They create wet and dry areas that improve the conditions for the hawthorn and hornbeam trees that provide the litter they eat.

4.2.3 Clay behaviour and land degradation processes

Between about 2 and 30 per cent of most soils are made up of very fine particles finer than 2 microns in size. This material mainly comes from the weathering of rocks or from dust and it is important because it has a very large surface area and it can influence soil behaviour and soil degradation responses. Clay has a negatively charged surface that can attract positively charged particles. Another source of fine material is fine organic matter which interacts with the clay and contributes to its function as a storage site for nutrients and water. Some clays shrink and swell and they have a high adsorption capacity. How clays behave is affected by fertilizers, farming and pollution.

In books about soils and mineralogy, clays are explained from the points of view of physics and chemistry. For the present purpose, these processes operate at a scale that is far finer than we need to consider, so this can be left to geochemistry. What is relevant is how specific types of clay property constrain processes that affect how soils provide the functions of soil protection (how soil protects people, not how we protect the soil), habitat, and water regulation.

How, and if, a clay **swells** is relevant because when this happens there is a natural swelling limit and a shrinkage limit. Swelling and drying create pores that influence how at three levels of the soil itself, the slopes and the drainage basin regulate water movement.

Clay behaviour can sometimes explain many different land degradation phenomena, ranging from flash floods in deserts; hyper-concentrations of sediment in rivers; mudflow and landslides; and the reduction of the infiltration rate of a soil to virtually zero.

On the other hand, clay minerals can act as a binding material in the soil, giving it coherence and strength, and they provide a storage place for plant nutrients and other things.

Clay and fine organic matter are critical then mainly because they explain certain things about many different processes that influence the functions being described.

The key processes considered here are physio-chemical processes that take place at a very fine microscopic scale. They determine how clay particles behave when they are in suspension or in the soil. Clay can stick together to form **flocculated plates** that settle quickly to the bottom in a suspension. Clay particles can repel one another and stay in suspension and be **dispersed**. Thus, clay particles which are smaller than 2 microns will either flocculate to form plates that attract one another or they will swell or disperse. If flocculation tales place, the particles which are formed are what are called **micro aggregates** and they are 2 to 50 microns in size. The way clay behaves is very critical because it has a very large impact on many emergent hydrological and land degradation processes. There are **chemical thresholds** whereby a system can switch from a dispersed into a flocculated state and these have a great influence on the mechanical thresholds of erosion processes.

When clay is dispersed in rivers it can lead to **hyper-sediment concentrations** occurring. In the soil it can reduce infiltration rates to almost nothing and in the deserts this often happens and causes flash floods. Investigating clay minerals and establishing their chemistry and mineralogy requires a specialized laboratory but the behaviour of clay can be observed and studied using simple **dispersion and flocculation tests**.

Evidence for it can be seen when water becomes cloudy or milky. It can occur under a few different sets of conditions. One of the experts on soil dispersion is Emerson (1967) who developed a simple dispersion test for characterizing the response of different soils to irrigation water or erosion. This test is very easy to do and the reader should try it with the soil which he/she has available. The gully shown in Figure 4.9 was photographed in an area of pipe and tunnel erosion that indirectly is a response of dispersive soil to farming. The rate of erosion is extreme and several centimeters of soil can be lost in a year.

4.2.4 Clay dispersion and runoff in a hyper-arid desert

The dust carried by the wind in deserts can contain clay particles that are sometimes dispersive when it rains. When it rains these swell and seal the soil in a few minutes, thus creating favourable conditions for flash floods. The Nahel Yahel watershed was established by Asher Schick (1978) to investigate the hydrology and erosion processes in hyper-arid areas.

The Nahel Yahel experimental watershed was established in the hyper-arid region of Israel as a site for long-term measurements of processes. This research station is the only one existing in any hyper-arid area with long-term measurements.

Yair and Klein (1973) decided to investigate the paradox that the rocky scree slopes in arid areas produced very high amounts of runoff during small amounts of rainfall. Normally, gravels and boulders can absorb bucket loads of water tipped on them. This is the case on scree slopes in cold and more humid regions. In these regions, clay dispersion is less common. They set up field plots to measure runoff and under rainfall simulation experiments to observe how runoff was produced. When they examined the ground surface, they found that below the upper gravel layers on the surface, there was a layer of fine

Figure 4.9 and Figure 4.10 Examples of the impact of clay dispersion on soil erosion and land degradation processes in Bolivia. Figure 4.9 shows a gully in an agricultural field near Tarije. Figure 4.10 from A. Cerda shows similar processes today in Valencia (Credit: Anton Imeson).

material. As much as 17 per cent of this was clay. What they found was that the threshold rainfall amount needed to produce runoff on a wet slope was 3 mm and on a dry one 2 mm. Their conclusion was that surface properties are extremely important in generating runoff and that paradoxically the steeper slopes produced less runoff than the more gentle ones.

The sediment concentrations in runoff were relatively high, being 15 700 p.p.m on one plot.

The explanation for why there is so much runoff is the influence of the clay and silt which is windblown dust that is supplied from far away. It contains clay that was formed in soils long ago in Africa or Asia. In a number of later experiments in different regions of Israel, Yair and co-workers demonstrate the importance of surface properties in influencing how they respond to rainfall and desertification. They found that it was in wetter periods, when there was more input of dust and loess in the rainfall, that there was paradoxically more ecological aridity and less water for people because more of it was lost to evaporation.

The two processes illustrated in this section (clay dispersion and worm activity) are very sensitive to human actions and they are critical in understanding the causes and finding solutions. In addition there are many other processes contributing to soil stability through the activity of life in the soil, in particular bacteria and fungi, and termites and ants, and some of these will be described later. If no allowance is made, then the consequence is the erosion problem illustrated in Valencia in Figure 4.10 and from Bolivia.

Conclusions

Many problems of land degradation and desertification occur because these and a few other natural processes are not taken into account. For example, microrhyzoa influence these processes of soil aggregation and provide a means whereby plants can access and store nutrients. In industrialized agriculture, this ecosystem service is deliberately ignored or else illuminated and replaced by applying a huge amount of fertilizer. Paradoxically such processes provide a tool for sustainable land management.

Another critical phenomenon is the water repellent behaviour of the soil and the way this regulates water availability and movement. This is the process whereby the soil is made hydrophobic by the plants in places so that water is concentrated at specific locations in the soil to the advantage of plant and seed germination.

These key fine scale processes illustrated operate at very fine scales, at microns or centimeters, but they affect and bring about differences at the level of the field and landscapes. They are processes that enable the soil to protects us from flooding and erosion and provide us with an environment that also is productive.

Fine scale processes such as these are present everywhere but how they act depends on the time and place. Fine scale processes are greatly influenced by land use and agriculture which can create soils that are dispersive and have a weak structure. Both the worms and the farmer can reduce the sensitivity of the land to erosion. Human activities can support functions that these processes provide.

4.3 The provision of the hydrological function, runoff and sediment transport

In Chapter 3, the hydrology and the water balance were described as indicators. The discharge of rivers reflects the storage of water and the different types of runoff process.

In addition, the fine scale processes in the soil, such as worm activity and clay dispersion that take place in the soil, regulate and influence water storage. Any changes in these or comparable processes are directly observed in runoff processes.

Some of the most practical resources available are in the climatological and hydrological records that are kept by most countries and which enable the effects of land use and management changes or of development to be quantified. For example, in the United States around most cities there are catchments or watersheds with more than a hundred years of river flow and sediment load measurements. The impact that the growth of cities and agricultural abstractions had on rivers can be seen. They document the abstraction of the water by cities, for industry and agriculture and at the same time enable the impact on water quality to be seen. Hydrological data enable us to directly observe and study how the different geological formations and drainage basins are regulating and responding to human impacts, including land use changes.

Change in the runoff from a small drainage basin is a sensitive indicator of the land use and land use changes that are taking place. The basic principles and terms of hydrology are explained on educational sites in different countries, as, for example, by the US Geological Service Water Resources educational and training resource.

In many other countries there have been long-term studies of key processes that look at the interactions between people, water, vegetation, soil and land degradation. Hydrologists tend to focus on present day conditions and relationships between rainfall and runoff, groundwater or water availability. Geomorphologists and geologists by contrast study changes in the landforms over longer periods of time and the processes that are responsible. They introduce longer timescales, feedbacks and a systems approach that enables them to understand and explain, for example, the impact of Europeans on land degradation in south western USA, the Atlantic rainforests of Brazil, and the impact of land use changes in the Ebro Valley on the sedimentation in the valleys. Drainage basins in which key processes have been studied can be thought of as open systems in and through which water moves and transports sediment. The weathering of rock and the input of dust and sand are sources of material. Sediment and dissolved substances are transported from the slopes to the valley bottoms by the processes of rainwash, splash erosion and surface flow (subsurface flow through channels and pipes and by mass movements). These are natural processes of erosion and a normal part of how natural systems function.

Under semi-natural conditions these processes are usually extremely slow and it can take hundreds or thousands of years for a few centimetres of sediment to accumulate in the valley bottoms. The deposit that accumulates is known as colluvium and it is very important as a source of pollen or other evidence that enables it to be dated.

Most sediment is transported by different types of biological process and splash erosion and not by overland flow, which is described later, which occurs during accelerated erosion, or unless the soil is water repellent. Unless there is some very extreme event, there is very little flood runoff or erosion. In time under natural conditions the soils and vegetation increase in depth and water-holding capacity so that most rainfall passes through the soil in which old growth vegetation is present. Such studies are relatively few because they are expensive to develop, manage and maintain. They may be thought of as reference locations where knowledge about key processes was obtained.

An important experimental location in Murcia Spain is shown in Figure 4.11 being visited by a fact finding mission from China hosted by Professor Asuncion Romero Diaz at the research centre in the Department of Geography. Another scientist,

Professor Lopez Bermudez, has been monitoring desertification and land degradation for more than 30 years and his region is a Spanish and European Target Area for the Spanish National Action Plan to combat desertification. Research is being done concerning the dispersion and piping which are key processes in explaining the badland landscape.

The Walnut Gulch Experimental Station is operated by the USDA to evaluate the effect of land use and conservation on water and sediment yield of arid and semi-arid rangelands. The data and research findings provide much information about the nature of the processes in arid and semi-arid areas and about how they are affected by human activity.

The precipitation is about 288 mm per year and dominated by a summer rainfall, most of which falls in small storms of limited extent. Winter storms are of greater extent but lower intensity. Many small dams were set up to measure erosion rates and these were described by Renard in 1984 (See Renard *et al* 2008).

In many cases, processes have been compared in paired drainage basins in which all conditions excepting land use are the same. This is illustrated later.

Discussion: land use impacts on processes in catchments

Experimental drainage basins such as those mentioned earlier have often been treated as a dynamic system in which there is a kind of quasi-stable equilibrium between the hydrology, vegetation and the soil. It will be able to accommodate variations in the climate and extreme weather conditions. It was explained in Chapter 1 that land use, climate change and interference with the life present will bring about adjustments in the functioning of the system that could be experienced as land degradation and desertification. It has also been shown that most drainage basins become periodically unstable because of slow processes that change the hydrology gradually over hundreds of years. When some rocks weather, they produce clays which gradually change their properties in time as they age. The changes can make soils that were permeable become impermeable.

The impacts of land use change are relatively simple to identify and quantify and they can be directly observed:

For example:

1 The effective precipitation (the amount of rain that actually enters the soil).

2 The amount and distribution of water in the soil.

3 The amount and location of water and sediment being displaced on the slope and arriving in the river channel and the sea.

4.4 The protection function of the land and erosion

One of the biggest impacts of people's activities is to impair the protection function of the vegetation and soil. Removing the vegetation has the added effects of decreasing evapotranspiration and interception losses so that rainfall events can produce much more runoff. These changes mean that the soil becomes much hotter or colder depending on the season.

In the natural environment, the vegetation and its ecosystem are protecting people from erosion.

In the Alps, forests are grown to protect people from rock fall. Forest restoration projects have always been a strategy for combating land degradation in Spain and France.

Erosion under natural conditions

This is affected by many things which include the climate, the slope of the land and topography and the vegetation cover, as well as the nature of the rocks and soils. A distinction is sometimes made between erosion which is natural or geological and accelerated erosion which describes the effects of man. Erosion processes move sediment from the upper part of the slope and deposit some of it at the slope foot or in a flood plain or river. The top layer of the soil is in fact gradually being moved downslope by biological processes such as those resulting from the activity of earthworms, moles and wild pigs and any other kind of animal including elephants, porcupines, termites and lyre birds. Soil exposed on the ground surface can be transported by rainsplash action and is sometimes attached to leaves that are transported by the wind. Depending on the amount of biological activity, the rate of erosion and deposition can be very high. Counter-intuitively, the erosion rate by such processes in areas of very high biological activity in forests can sometimes be greater than that outside of the forest. The transport distances are usually short. The sediment moved has a high stability and it is a normal process that leads to the creation of different soil conditions along slopes that lead to differences in soil depth and soil particle size, and fertility.

In most cases of erosion, the transport distance of most sediment is very small, and this is also the case in agricultural fields. Only a very small part of sediment displaced actually leaves a field. Erosion processes have an important effect, however, because when transport and deposition take place, material is deposited in separate size categories. This leads to the separation of clay, silt and sand or gravel and the development of crusts. These have a great influence on water storage and movement and on evaporation and the concentration of organic matter and toxic substances.

When the vegetation is removed

When there is a disturbance of the vegetation cover, as is described, for example, later in the case studies and experiments that form part of this book, runoff and erosion rates can increase dramatically several orders of magnitude. The reasons for this are that the soil can become compacted because of trampling or from the impact of raindrops or hail, and subsurface soil horizons are exposed on the surface and these may have a high clay content, and be sensitive to slaking or dispersion. What happens exactly depends on how the existing ecosystem is affected and examples of different responses are shown in the examples and photographs given later.

Some of the eroded sediment at such times is deposited as a colluvial layer at the slope foot where it remains as a thin layer that records evidence of the erosion processes that were responsible for it. It is possible to interpret the recent erosion history of slope using the evidence it contains and these might be particles of charcoal, clay coatings that indicate that the soil fragment came from upslope and was formed during different climate conditions, as well as fragments of pottery.

4.5 The long-term impact: the vigil network sites in the USA

In the 1960s a fluvial geologist (Leopold 1962) realized that there were no records being kept of the changes taking place in the alluvial rivers so he promoted the establishment of a network of small drainage basins and other selected sites where simple measurements could be made to record changes over long periods of time. At that time the interest was in the aggregation or filling up of the river channels with sediments that were being supplied from land eroded at some point in the past. The idea was to do things that would in the long term demonstrate relationships between land use change and the processes that were going on in the river channels.

In 1974 Emmett, who had participated in the project, pointed out that one of the main findings of the first analysis near Santa Fe was that by far the greatest source of sediment aggrading in the river channel was coming from the hillsides where it was being eroded by sheet erosion. In 1880 the river channels in this part of the USA had started to erode into their channels but it seemed that this process of down cutting had ended. At the time of writing (Emmett's work), there were more than 100 Vigil Network sites in the USA and worldwide the American geologists were promoting the installation of similar networks so that a global database could be obtained in different environments. The Vigil Network was started in 1962 and it was coincidental with the International Hydrological Decade (IHD) in which experimental catchments were set up throughout the world.

Emmet analyses as an example the changes recorded at Last Day Gulley, which is a small ephemeral stream channel that has in the past gone through different phases of degradation and aggradation. It is located in the valley of the Popo Agie River, 1.5 km northeast of Hudson Wyoming. The main vegetation was composed of sagebrush (*Artemesia tridentate*) and Cactus (*Opuntia* sp.) and grasses of the grama species (*Bouteloua*) and the vegetation cover varied from 30 to 35 percent. The measurements were used to calculate the erosion rates and sediment budgets during the ten-year survey period. Amongst the many things described, Emmett found that average rate of aggregation was about 0.76 cm per year so that the channel would be filled in 200 years. It was found that about one third of the sediment eroded as sheet erosion on the slopes was accumulating in the channel.

The data were also analysed in relation to climate change. When Emmett was writing there was a debate still going on regarding the relative importance of climate change and land use as an explanation for the epicycles of valley trenching and alluviation in the arroyos, not just in the south western USA but in many other regions.

Leopold in 1950 had concluded that the cutting had begun in 1880 because of the high amount of precipitation then, but that it had been aggravated by degradation caused by overgrazing. However, an analysis of the precipitation record for Santa Fe, which goes back to 1849, revealed no trend in the mean annual precipitation and overgrazing had only affected a small part of the area in which the down cutting was taking place. Further analysis of the precipitation had suggested that the period 1880 to 1940 was characterized by a decrease in amount but that there were more rainy days per year.

The Vigil Network data illustrated the value of measurements in being able to record the changes that were taking place and to understand quantitatively today what the consequences are of past human actions.

Schumm (1977), also in the same general region, found that there was a relationship between the incision of gullies and the slope of channels in the river and he said that whether or not there was incision reflected a threshold that reflected the energy of the runoff and its ability to erode the channel bed. There was no simple relationship with the climate or land use and he developed a theory of complex response. The concepts of complex response and geomorphological thresholds are important for interpreting relationships between measured human impact and erosion.

They mean that there is no simple relationship between precipitation and climate, on the one hand, and the amount of sediment coming out from the other end.

4.6 Hydrological response: what happens to the land when it rains

Studying how the land, slope or soil responds to rainfall has proved an excellent means of gaining insight into how both the processes already mentioned operate. Relationships with land management on these can also be quantified this way.

The hydrological and erosional responses can be studied during natural rainstorms but it can also be studied using rainfall simulators.

Difference response systems or states of attraction can occur so that according to which prevails, different response systems may occur at different times of the year, and during periods of extreme weather conditions.

Processes affecting the response

All of the processes that have been mentioned influence how land reacts to rainfall. This reaction is both dynamic and also influenced by things that people, animals and plants do. For example, if the soil is made water repellent by chemicals released by plants, water will avoid certain areas and move along preferential pathways to deeper layers of the soil.

It may even cause runoff downslope and reduce evaporation. If there is a change in the nature and intensity of biological activity this will affect the infiltration rate and the amount of runoff.

In many situations the characteristics of the soil that influence how it responds to rainfall are a reflection of the microbiological processes that regulate the growth or disappearance of water-stable aggregates and dispersed soil.

Pores and agglomerations in the soil

Different processes in the soil result in the evolution and destruction of the porosity. There are micropores, mesopores and macropores which hold either air or moisture. Pores are continually being formed and destroyed at the same time that they are being mixed by bioturbation and ploughing. As well as the micro fauna, the meso-fauna, such as worms and ants, as well as all ground living animals are critical in maintaining and regulating the water holding capacity of the soil in this way.

In time, the surface to volume ratio of the soil increases, the bulk density becomes low and the material may be quite loose. In agricultural soils the main source of pores is often that provided by harrowing or ploughing. In forest soils disturbances are caused by tree fall as well as by animals. A very common process today is the disturbances produced by wild pigs or boars. At the other extreme pores are caused by ice, shrinking and swelling, root and plant growth and by bacteria as they mineralize the soil. The bulk density is often good indicator of the degree to which the life in the soil has resisted processes of degradation.

Tisdale and Oades (1982) developed the concept of hierarchy in soil aggregation which explains how the forces binding particles of different sizes together lead to the creation of very fine clay domains a few microns in size, micro aggregates and meso-aggregates. Micro aggregates are bound by polysaccharides that are secreted into the soil and they are very dynamic. Coarser aggregates are bound by fungi and fine roots and these can form in a few years to transform a soil positively.

There are many chemical and physical processes that affect land degradation processes and just one of these will be described, as it greatly influences land degradation. This is the process of dispersion and flocculation that is caused by sometimes only a small amount of salt in the soil. It is important, for example, when rocks contain a lot of clay that shrinks or swells, or where the soil is saline or sodic. Under such conditions clay minerals can spontaneously disperse to produce a milk-like suspension containing gells that blocks pores and prevents water from entering the soil. This is the process of clay dispersion that has already been mentioned.

Another extreme case is the swelling of clays that contain bentonite clay such as those in Canada and the USA. This is the case in many of the badland areas of Alberta Canada and many parts of the USA such as Dakota. Sometimes the clays present will swell when they are wet so that the rock is transformed into a porridge-like substance that slides into the river channels.

Badlands

Badlands are areas in which there is a very rapid response to runoff, where infiltration rates are low and where there is a characteristic topography (see Figures 4.11 and 4.12). Badlands occur in very many parts of the world but particularly in specific types of material that develop characteristic surface features. The material is often very strong when dry but becomes weak and highly erodible when wet. Often there is an extremely high salt content.

4.7 Water

Introduction

Water is a major factor in land degradation and desertification in many different ways. Knowing how rocks, landscapes, the soil and vegetation regulate the provision of hydro-logical and climate services under different climates is important because these functions can be easily lost or damaged and in some cases easily restored.

Water requirements and water availability as a driver of desertification

Water availability is a critical issue because it underlies many of the desertification problems experienced in all regions. In most countries there is an orographic effect whereby the rain increases with altitude and people in the valleys depend on the water resources in the mountains. The inhabitants of most dry regions are aware of existing water resources and these have already been fully exploited and in many cases already been subject to degradation so that soils tend to be saline and waterlogged. When water resources are developed, this has a great impact on other functions, particularly when groundwater is over exploited and stream flow impaired or polluted by return flow from agricultural land. This is the case in most of the world.

In more humid regions, above about 350 mm of rainfall, the semi-natural vegetation or pasture protects the soil from soil erosion and soil sodicity. The higher the amount and intensity of rainfall, the greater is the capacity of the soil to erode and transport soil and this is what happens in humid areas when soil is left unprotected, particularly where the energy of the rainfall is high.

There is critical amount of water required by the existing vegetation and land users and when this is not met, for example during droughts or because of groundwater level decline, trees valued by the community can die and disappear. In such cases people talk of water scarcity. Examples of this can be found in Portugal and Spain with the increased mortality of certain oak trees and in the USA where the Pondrosa pine is retreating.

Water resources become an issue when it is perceived as an issue of desertification when people experience that less water is available for their use at a time when it is needed. Very frequently the water balance can be used to obtain a rough assessment of water issues.

The water balance and hydrological cycle

Many measurements have been proposed for expressing water availability and how this is linked to desertification. This is possible because all of the components of the hydrological cycle are connected in the cycle which can be described by the so-called water balance equation:

$$P = Q + ET +/- (S$$

where P = precipitation, Q = runoff, ET is the evapotranspiration and (S is the change of water in storage in the soil and rocks which can be solved for any area and for any period of time, such as a week, a month or a year. It can also be solved for a compartment for any specified area such as the soil, a lake, a forest or a field. Thus if there is less water available in river, soil or lake it can be because there has been either more ET and Q or less P. Thus if we want an indicator for how much water is available in the soil, as groundwater or as runoff in the river, it is possible to measure these directly (as a change in soil moisture content, change in groundwater level or change in river water amount) or to use a known relationship that these may have with another more easily measured component of the hydrological cycle or system component.

Soil water availability

How much water is available in the soil and how is it affected by land use?

The water storage capacity of the soil is the water that is available in the soil for use by plants, excluding therefore water that moves quickly though the soil under the influence of gravity as well as the water bound by strong forces to mineral surfaces. The storage capacity depends on both the volume of soil and the volume of available pore space that can retain water against gravitational forces. It was explained earlier that this volume depends mainly on life in the soil since pores are continually being degraded and need to be replaced as they are in the top soil.

Soil and rocks weather into regolith and soils that have characteristic and different soil pore-size distributions. Changes in water storage capacity can be used as an early warning of desertification.

Soil loss and erosion can be important because when soil that could once store water has gone it may be impossible for plants to survive dry periods where previously there was no problem.

Water availability is an excellent and appropriate desertification indicator with a long history of use in the context of water and soil management. It has been extensively used by hydrologists in the calculation of the soil–water balance and it is used in scheduling irrigation amounts. It is a valuable concept because it directly describes how the soil is functioning.

As will be seen, changes in water availabilty can be attributed to soil degradation processes and soil biological activity.

The depth of wetting and water penetration

The water availability is influenced by the depth to which rainfall penetrates the soil. When it rains and water enters the soil, there is a wetting front that moves into the soil. This wetting front may be smooth. Cerdà (2005) and Calvo the inventor of the Calvo rainfall simulator have performed several thousands of rainfall simulation experiments in Spain and they have studied the way in which the depth of water penetration is influenced to rock type, vegetation, stones and water repellent behaviour. Yair *et al* 1980 have shown that in the arid and semi-arid areas of Israel, the depth of wetting is critical in determining how much water is available for the ecosystem. Marls that contain clay are arid because water is easily and quickly evaporated from marls and loess, in comparison with rocky limestone.

The vertical differences in storage capacity in the soil affect both the subsequent evaporation of water and crop productivity. The erosion of the soil results in a loss of storage capacity and this has always been considered as a major factor of desertification.

Life in the soil is responsible for the pores in a soil that enable a soil to store water. Organisms also produce substances that make the aggregates and pores between them stable and able to retain their coherence when wet. A decrease in water storage capacity may provide an early warning that the resilience or regenerative capacity of a soil is being affected by desertification.

If a soil cannot store as much water and nutrients as before, it will produce less biomass and there will be a positive feedback in which the storage capacity decreases.

Storage capacity can be measured experimentally in situ. A soil is saturated and covered by plastic to prevent evaporation and allowed to drain against gravity so that the field capacity is discovered. Field capacity is the amount of water a soil can retain after drainage. There are many procedures for measuring the energy with which water is held in the soil, using, for example, tensiometers and porous blocks. Soil moisture suction can be converted to a measure of soil pore size distributions. Lysemeters can also be used. Values can also be calculated by keeping a soil–water balance account. This requires measuring or calculating the difference between evaporation and precipitation. Extensive and useful guidelines are available from the FAO. Soil thin sections can be used and pore size distributions measured automatically under the microscope. There is no need to study the entire range of soil suction values. It is possible to measure the high energy suction as a good and sensitive indicator of soil structure stability.

Water availability and limitations

Water availability depends not just on the amount of rainfall but also on the amount of water that can be retained and stored in the soil. If rain falls on concrete or coarse sand and gravel, it will quickly drain away and will not be available for plants. Plants modify and adapt their environments so that they can store more water. This is reflected in the vegetation and soil patterns and structures mentioned earlier (Ludwig *et al.* 2005).

On agricultural land, land management is used to manage the soil structure so that evaporative losses are minimized. The water storage capacity can be related to the critical water requirements of plants and vegetation and in this way provide an indication of the suitability of the soil for a specific use. A large database is kept by the FAO describing plant water requirements and how these are related to soil water storage capacity. Typically a ten-cm layer of soil might have a storage capacity that ranges from 2 to 6 cm. This can be also measured with respect to the energy holding water in the soil and in this case the soil suction (pF) is a good measure of availability. Available water is that occurring in the range of suctions occurring between field capacity and the wilting point.

Runoff and infiltration processes

If the main interest is in understanding how land use changes affect the provision of hydrological services that protect us from flooding and sedimentation, then this is the focal scale.

Changes in runoff pathways and connectivity can be seen as an emergent effect of the processes just described in the soil. Land degradation and agriculture mean that hydrology changes from one in which transfers were taking place over short distances with a very dense pattern of sink and source areas, to one in which most of the runoff moves from the slope to the valley bottom.

The process whereby water can enter the soil when it rains is known as infiltration. It is a dynamic property which is at first relatively high, say 5 or 6 cm/hour, and then either quickly drops to about nothing on soils that disperse or otherwise remains at about 4 cm/hour on forest soils that have the benefits of a high amount of capital in the form of a good soil structure.

Infiltration is a key process in desertification because it is a key mechanism with respect to soil moisture availability, natural and induced rainwater harvesting, evaporation and runoff on slopes to rivers. Most hydrological literature on infiltration is about modelling the process so that runoff from slopes can be estimated.

If water can infiltrate into the soil, it will provide water and transport nutrients that encourage plant growth and development. This has at least three positive effects. The soil is physically protected by leaves from raindrop impact, the roots and organic matter in the soil encourage the development of a soil ecosystem, which in turn makes the soil able to withstand the impact of raindrops and increases the infiltration rate so that there is a positive feedback loop in which things can improve.

Runoff is significant because it erodes, transports and deposits sediment. In many different parts of the world, land degradation scientists have established experimental catchments to study the mechanisms of runoff generation in relation to land use and climate. Runoff generation processes are very sensitive both to initial conditions in the soil and to human interventions.

During the last decades, earth scientists in particular have been studying how land use change and climate change are affecting the functioning of the hydrological system. They have realized that man is the main geological agent. Land use changes, urbanization and waste disposal and contamination are causing changes that affect runoff at all scales. The amount of runoff flow is measured or calculated as a discharge. What is relevant in this section are the processes by which runoff is generated at these different scales. Two contrasting things are happening that are affecting runoff and the next scale up, which is the catchment scale.

In the river channels the following is happening:

1 There is a dramatic decrease in river flows due to the appropriation of water by people. This is accompanied by a decrease in peak river discharges.

2 On the other hand, there is huge loss of water storage on the slopes, so that there is much more surface runoff. This is the effect of land degradation.

3 These two effects and the models that hydrologists use mean that floods are underestimated. Whereas when there were lots of sinks and sources on the slope and the models were calibrated, only a 2–10 per cent of discharge would come from the slope, under the current situation perhaps 40–60 per cent of rainfall runs off.

Rainfall acceptance

A few key properties of the ground surface influence what is called the rainfall acceptance characteristics. This is an indicator of how much water the soil can accept and it enables the effect of soil degradation to be translated into an indicator that is functional.

Things affecting this include the presence of a surface seal or crust, and the large pores beneath this that contain air, the water repellence characteristics, the amount of water already in the soil that reduces storage and the suction of water into the ground, the roughness of the surface which prevents air from being entrapped and reducing water entry and the chemistry and viscosity of the rain or runoff. Also important is the chemistry of the soil, particularly the presence of small amounts of sodium that can promote swelling, dispersion and crust formation. The texture and mechanical composition also play a role. Rainfall acceptance rates are usually always very high in soils that have a very stable structure for various reasons and at the start of rainfall in the absences of hydrophobic behaviour. Rainfall acceptance rates, just like infiltration, are either very low or very high but they are remarkably uniform for patches or surface conditions that appear similar.

An assessment of the rainfall acceptance rate is very simple and it can be done using a self-constructed rainfall simulator (see later Chapter 6).

The time to ponding, sorptivity and the infiltration envelope

The relationship between the rainfall intensity or amount and the amount of rain that will enter the soil (infiltration rate) is called by hydrologists the infiltration envelope. The critical measurements are the time to ponding or the time to runoff at a given rainfall intensity. Ponding occurs when a water film appears on the surface and this could be a few or a large percentage, depending on the time or context.

During experiments to measure ponding times it was found that a parameter known as the sorptivity is a good indicator for this. The sorptivity describes the maximum amount of water that the soil can accept and it is calculated from measurements that determine how much water can enter the soil and how this decreases in time. It can be estimated from the graph showing the relationship between the square root of the time and amount of infiltrated water.

Parlange and Smith (1978) developed the equation below that can be used to calculate time to ponding from sorptivity and saturated hydraulic conductivity measurements made with a rainfall simulator.

$$Tp = S2 \ln[r/r - ksat)]/2 \ ksat$$

where tp = time to ponding, S = sorptivity, R = rainfall intensity and Ksat = saturated hydaulic conductivity (use 1/3 of the final infiltration rate). This relationship has been used in many studies to establish spatial variations in runoff in relation to land use and other matters.

The effect of crust on infiltration, erosion and air entrapment

The crusts and seals have other effects on processes not mentioned yet. Firstly, they often prevent water passing through them because water cannot move so well from fine pores to coarse ones as there is a negative pressure. This means that pores beneath a crust stop water from both infiltrating and evaporation. The reduction in evaporation from a crusted surface and the extra strength it has sometimes also make it resistant to water and wind erosion. When it rains very heavily water cannot infiltrate unless the air that is in the soil escapes. This is why infiltration is higher on rough soils than on smooth ones. Introducing straws and holes into a soil so that entrapped air can escape can dramatically increase infiltration rates.

Runoff generation processes on slopes

When runoff occurs on a slope it has been found to be the result of several different mechanisms.

One of the most influential studies was that carried out by Horton (1945). Horton developed a theory of catchment runoff. This was important because of his infiltration theory of surface runoff, and explanations for sheet and rill erosion. Basically he considered the peak flow in rivers to be caused by overland flow. Overland flow was the runoff that occurred on slopes when the infiltration capacity of the soil was less than the intensity of the rainfall. When there was sufficient overland flow to exceed the critical energy required for flow to entrain sediment, channels would be incised and these would migrate upslope by headward recession.

An excellent overview of runoff processes can be found in Ward and Robinson (*Principles of Hydrology*). This is from the perspectives of the hydrological system and the water balance. They draw attention to and describe the different mechanisms of runoff production and describe the different pathways water follows from when it falls as rain to the moment it reaches the river channel and ocean. There are several different mechanisms of runoff mechanisms and these are very briefly:

1 Horton Overland Flow. If the rainfall intensity exceeds the infiltration rate, once the surface storage is full overland flow can occur on a slope and when this reaches a river this can be thought of as surface runoff.

2 Saturated overland flow and return flow where flow develops above a saturated soil or imperable area.

3 Throughflow or interflow. Water that enters the soil moves downslope through the soil until it reaches the river channel. It may be either rapid or slow, delayed through flow.

4 Flow through pipes, tunnel or macro pores in the soil.

5 As unsaturated flow through fine pores.

6 As groundwater flow including flow through cracks and fissures in the rock.

Today field hydrologists often focus on more on modelling the amounts of runoff. However, the models that model water flow are calibrated to give accurate results but they have no information at all about what is really happening in the field and if the organisms that transform the properties of the soil and are left out or approached probabilistically.

This is important for land degradation because it is important to know exactly where sediment and runoff comes from in order to propose and locate soil conservation measures. The nature of the runoff producing mechanisms are changed completely as a consequence of land use changes and practices. With soil management it is possible to change the processes to either increase or decrease runoff.

In conclusion, it is important to consider the feedbacks with the soil and management systems that occur and change over time as trees grow and the soil evolution takes place.

4.8 Nature, natural capital and land degradation

Discussion

Huxley (1893) pointed out the services that different organisms have provided for themselves can be thought of as the investment in a kind of capital they require in order to be able to have an environment that they find attractive to reproduce and invest in. Part of this work includes all of the cycles and transformations in the soil that mean that humans have access to the energy of the sun. The global significance of the feedback of life with the environment has been discussed in Chapter 1.4 (page 30).

Everywhere nature has adapted and modified the environment. There has been a co-evolution in the landscape of the organisms that are present and the environment and in a sense they should have a kind of copyright that we reward. Plants that are adapted to arid conditions have evolved many ways of overcoming scarce or seasonal availability in water and in creating locally relatively moderate conditions. In rocky deserts and where there is grazing or fire pressure, plants invest capital in their root systems, so that there can be high amounts of organic matter in the cracks between rocks. Annual grasses (e.g. wheat) and weeds invest in seeds and not in the soil capital that they therefore can deplete. Plants and ecosystems interact with the soil and rocks to create environments for themselves that help them to modify their own local climate. In rocky deserts and where there is grazing or fire pressure, plants invest capital in their root systems, so that there can be high amounts of organic matter in the cracks between rocks. Annual grasses (e.g. wheat) and weeds invest in seeds and not in the soil capital that they therefore can deplete. At the same time, this has an impact on both the local climate and culture of the pastoralist or framer who access the capital generated by plants directly or through animals. Animals mainly require plants that can photosynthesize sunlight as a source of food or energy. In their interactions with other plants, some have gained a competitive advantage by enlisting the help of animals. These include annual grasses like wheat that have evolved an alliance with man.

Life has evolved and created a habitat and environment in which to live from minerals by means of very many processes that involve the weathering and transformation of minerals by chemical processes that release nutrients and the evolution of food webs and food chains(see Odum 1971). Seen under the microscope, the interface between the atmosphere and the rock, something which we could refer to as top soil, is composed of the excrements and decomposition products and the bodies of the living organisms themselves which may be bacteria and fungi. Larger animals, including mice, men, birds and almost all creatures, are responsible for something called bioturbation. They mix the top soil with deeper layers, making the area suitable as a habitat for the plants and animals that live in it and thicker and thicker. And now today bioturbation is mainly caused by the tractor and the bulldozer. Ecosystems were adapted to the kind of bioturbation produced by mammals but perhaps in the past other animals now extinct were able to do the same. The huge number of animals that were in South America 500 years could also be destructive. The difference with us today is that this is made possible only with huge subsidies of energy (Odum (1971)) so that we can do things at several orders of magnitudes higher than nature has adapted to. The future will inevitably require geo-engineering aimed at replacing the capital services provided by nature artificially, or by restoring them.

Soil erosion under natural conditions is caused by animals and plants as they go through their life cycles and seek food. Harmful erosion is not caused so much by man seeking food, it is caused by using the soil and land as an expendable resource and allowing land degradation to occur. Land is perceived just as an area not as a three dimensional living entity upon which we depend.

An important conclusion from research is that in a sense, promoting life in the soil to restore hydrological functions and natural capital is also the strategy of restoring biodiversity. The significance of life as a requirement of a soil is obvious to ecologists have long understood that any interference with the natural life in an area can have an impact on the habitat layer that has repercussions for the other life that is sharing. Because the amount of carbon in the soil has become important for the climate change convention, degraded soil can especially provide such a service. Many forest restoration projects supported in this way may increase the natural capital economically but not necessarily ecologically because they have the single goal of carbon sequestration. During the last 300 years there has been a massive loss or the organic top soil and the massive erosion afterwards created large areas of shallow soils with bedrock and weathered material at the surface.

Early settlers in Australia reported on the disappearance or transformation of the thick organic rich layer of top soil when livestock and feral animals from other parts of the world arrived. This also transferred carbon to the atmosphere.

In 1834, Darwin comments on the for him vast and ancient forest ecosystems that were still present in some islands and locations that he encountered in Chile and Argentina and compared them with what existed in Europe then and it is easy to compare the conditions found them with those encountered today. He described how in many areas the forests had sometimes been replaced by flourishing communities producing all kinds of products, but that in others there was poverty or erosion. A frequent conclusion was the importance of the culture and lifestyle. He analysed the reasons for failure which are still evident today.

It is important to note that very few of these benefits provided by nature come from the direct labour of man (Huxley 1890) and the ones most at risk from desertification are the indirect consequence of other forms of life creating its own habitat and environment which benefits humans as well.

4.9 Soil stability

The strength of soil material and its behaviour under pressure is something that can be measured and assessed in many ways. One approach is by measuring the stability of aggregates by, for example, a water drop impact test and another is by shaking a sample of soil in water and comparing the degree of breakdown in various ways. Measurements and changes in soil stability have been found to be a good indicator of land degradation processes. It can be used to deduce how well several soil functions are performing.

It is the case that a stable soil surface are either a) able to accept precipitation as infiltration and/or b) resist processes of slaking and dispersion that lead to the formation of crusts. A stable soil surface favours the penetration and storage of moisture. In addition it indicates if there is resilience in the system. Stable soils also resist wind erosion (except for peat) and breakdown under raindrop impact. It is relatively easy to measure and can be estimated in many different ways.

Soil surface stability indices are relatively sensitive to change and they may provide early warning of soil and land degradation. Changes are often correlated with changes in organic matter, soil organisms and water soluble salts because these are related to dispersion and slaking.

The degree and rate at which the soil surface becomes smoother under the influence of rainfall has been quantified into indicators by means of photographs and classification schemes. These are sometimes referred to as slaking or crusting indices. When an unstable soil is gradually or suddenly wetted it breaks down into micro aggregates that blend or fuse together to form a compact surface crust. This crust may be hard when dry but it reduces the rate of infiltration and frequently becomes soft when moist. Crusts contribute to the heterogeneity in the infiltration of water, so that there are sinks and sources of runoff and infiltration and as a consequence a mix of humid and arid micro sites.

Soil stability is highly irregular in most situations because of the processes already mentioned. Under plants it is high due to the effects or roots and infiltrating moisture and the positive influence of shade. In the open, the surface soil is usually unstable because of the lack of organic matter and the inhospitable micro environment for organisms. Soil stability is influenced by the proportion of binding to non-binding substances. Consequently soils become more stable as the clay and organic matter contents increase. Material that consists of the weathering products of highly calcareous marls is often highly unstable. Sodium clays can be very hard and dry but when moistened, clays may readily disperse or swell and this can be a factor in rill and gully erosion.

Permeability measurements also provide good indicators of stability if made specifically for this purpose.

4.10 Soil response and soil behaviour

Many soil erosion process researchers have investigated what they call responses.

They underpin their work with concepts from both soil behaviour and hydrology to investigate the interactions between soil degradation and hydrological processes. When soil material is subject to the impacts from rainfall or to contact with flowing water, it can respond in different ways. These include dispersion, swelling, slaking and flocculation and include the effects of water repellency and consistency. These can be studied by laboratory and field experiments. Indicators and useful indicators have been found to be the consistency index of de Ploey and soil stability indices and aggregate stability.

The response of the soil can also be studied by rainfall simulation experiments and in this case, what is measured includes the soil moisture and the wetting front behaviour, the time it takes water to pond on the surface and the time to produce runoff, and the amount and nature of the sediment and chemicals in the runoff, as was described earlier.

Soil structure and its evolution

The soil structure is a term used in soil to describe the way in which the soil material is organized and affected by different processes. Different types of structure are shown in the table in the Appendix. The soil can have no structure in which case it is described as either massive or single grain. Structure can be weak, medium or strong according to how well it is developed.

When we examine the soil it is frequently composed of material that is aggregated and these aggregated pieces of ground have characteristics that reflect the type of structure.

A natural development or evolution of the soil structure occurs over time. In the top soil, biological and climatologic processes result in the transformation of homogenous material with a high bulk density into a material that is composed of agglomerated particles separated by voids. In such cases structure becomes finer in time and there is an increase in the fractal dimension.

Granular and Crumb structure usually results in favourable conditions for water retention and this is what is found usually where there are many roots, such as under grass and in some forests.

Slaking is the spontaneous breakdown of soil material in water. This can lead to the loss of structure and the formation of a surface crust that inhibits infiltration. Soil structure is strongly influenced by small amounts of water soluble salts that promote shrinking, swelling and dispersion. This results in soils that are very hard when dry but soft and weak when wet. They have a high bulk density, and a prismatic or columnar structure. Such soils are prone to piping, rill and gully erosion. Soil structure is strongly related to soil age as it is affected by mineral transformation and weathering. It is also affected by climate. In relation to desertification, the impact of organic matter and salt are important. The development of soil structure is seen as positive when it increases the capacity of the soil to retain water. High temperatures, trampling and tillage will lead to a decline in structure. On the other hand, shade, moisture and nutrients promoting plant growth will lead to its development. For the expert, soil structure is a sensitive indicator of soil health and of how the soil is being affected by desertification. In areas with a patchy vegetation, there is a great heterogeneity in the structure of the surface soil with a good structure being found where the soil is shaded. Stones promote good structure because the fine soil between stones is usually relatively moist.

Soil structure a consequence of several processes. Plant growth, soil erosion and ecosystem resilience are all related to it. When the soil is exposed on or near the soil surface, its structure rapidly responds to environmental factors such as climate (including water and temperature effects), and macro and micro organisms. Different types of structure have specific physical, chemical, and morphological properties closely related to the climate and parent material.

Soil structure and water availability

There is no simple relationship between the amount of rainfall and water availability because it depends also on the properties of the rock and the way these influence the infiltration and evaporation processes. Soil arrangement, structure and behaviour play a part in this.

Water availability in natural and managed systems is affected by the physical size, arrangement and composition of particles in the soil as well as by how these react (swelling, dispersion, flocculation, slaking and consistency, mentioned earlier) and upon being exposed to water.

In dry regions, there is an ecological aridity is related more to the depth of water penetration in the soil or rocks and this depends on the type of rock or sediment and the way it weathers into what is called a regolith. Badlands such as those shown in Figure 4.11 and Figure 4.12 occur. In Figure 4.12, nothing remains of the original soil before Europeans settled the region, except for a few places where there seems to be a preserved on isolated pedestals.

In different parts of the world or at different times of the year, biological activity is limited by temperature, moisture and sunlight and these limitations provide the context in which desertification is taking place in different countries. Figure 4.11 shows a badland area near Murcia being visited by Chinese soil conservation experts. Water availability is very low in this marl landscape in which badlands have formed near Murcia. This is because of the very high silt and clay content and carbonate contents.

4.11 Catchment response, hydrology and the soil

For many years hydrology was dominated by the conceptual runoff model of Horton, in which he developed an infiltration equation and model of surface runoff. In this model,

Figure 4.11 Badlands developed in saline marls that are prone to tunnel erosion. This shows a Chinese soil conservation study tour at one of the research sites of the University of Murcia's Department of Geography (Credit: Anton Imeson).

Figure 4.12 Examples of badlands from Bolivia. This area has had its water regulation function impaired by farming. Only a few remnants of the former top soils are found in the region following a process of bedrock stripping (Credit: Anton Imeson).

runoff by infiltration excess overland flow on slopes was assumed to be the source of the peak discharges in rivers. He assumed that river discharges at other times were a result of the saturated and unsaturated movement of water through the soil to the river, which he called interflow. Researchers found that runoff peaks occurred in forested drainage basins without any overland flow being needed. As a consequence, many hydrologists recognized that certain small areas in a drainage basin provide most of the runoff that reaches rivers. Such areas have been described as partial contributing areas or as variable source areas. In practice, as can be seen in several illustrations, runoff producing source areas occur along tracks and at places where the soil has been trampled. This can occur at camp sites. Where tractors turn in fields, the soil is compacted twice so that these places are also partial areas. Most partial areas are close to the rivers because the soil is moist and the capillary fringe is close to the surface.

When it rains the water that is in the river can have a complex origin and be a mixture of groundwater, channel precipitation and flow from partial or variable source areas. This means that there are runoff source and sink areas that mean that water from a runoff producing zone travels downslope to a sink. In desert and semi-arid areas, the vegetation patches are very often sinks where water enters the soil. Runoff production from a source area can be important for vegetation. The continuity of flow paths is something that land use practices influence greatly. Soil conservation measures can reduce the continuity of flow and prevent water from leaving slopes.

An overview of different frameworks used to explain runoff production in semi-arid areas is given by hydrologists in Australia, for example, Ludwig (2005). The process-based framework developed by Australian landscape ecologists is an excellent basis for sustainable management of water resources. Key elements of this are described elsewhere.

4.12 Discussion: vegetation patterns as responses to land degradation processes

Many of the world's semi-arid landscapes are characterized by a spatially discontinuous vegetation-cover, reflecting the limited availability of water and nutrients. It has been found that such vegetation patterns importantly govern the location of runoff and sediment source and sink areas. Directly upslope of vegetation clusters, such as large tussocks and vegetation bands, sediment and organic matter are trapped. Generally, this leads to higher infiltration rate upslope compared to downslope of the vegetation patch. Furthermore, bare soil patches act as sources of overland flow and vegetated patches as sinks. This spatial differentiation of sources and sinks is a dynamic property of many semi-arid and arid ecosystems and feeds back to plant growth as well as bare patch development. Soil water dynamics and vegetation dynamics are thus functionally related and vegetated and bare-ground patches form interconnected units within the larger patch mosaic. The spatial pattern of vegetated and bare patches within such a mosaic determines if and how patches interact and strongly affects the downslope routing of water, sediments, nutrients, seeds, etc. Therefore, patterns in vegetation and soil may be used as indicator for predicting response. For example, a measure of the extent and distribution of the bare patches within the mosaic can be an important index to characterize the erosion vulnerability of a certain area. Several hydrologists have illustrated with model simulations of semi-arid landscape systems, that a banded pattern could be about 10 per cent more efficient at capturing runoff than a stippled pattern.

The different hydrological processes and mechanisms mentioned earlier are connected and are often associated with and have feedbacks with the physical, chemical and biological properties of soils. These are sensitive to changes in climate, land use or other perturbations and their impact on water quality.

The significance of ice and frost

However, Figure 4.2 shows that similar patches occur under the prevailing conditions. What is important is that the vegetation creates more temperate and less extreme conditions. In Iceland the role of the vegetation is to also protect against the formation of needle ice which occurs outside the shrubs and is responsible for the area remaining uncovered and exposed to wind erosion as well as rain.

4.13 Controlled desertification experiments

There are many examples where people have undertaken controlled experiments to induce desertification and study the response. A number of experiments were done to increase infiltration and runoff by suppressing natural vegetation. Chemicals were and are frequently used to bring about changes in the hydrology. The ecological and environmental damage and costs were often not considered as significant in relation to the benefits that more water would bring.

Suppression of channel side vegetation to increase streamflow

As an example of this methodology, the research reported by Ingebo (1971) is of value. He reports the success of an experiment in 1968 and 1969 in a 246-acre drainage basin with a vegetation of chaparral. It is located in the Whitespar catchment, 6 miles southwest of Prescott Arizona. If there could be an increase in the duration of streamflow this would be of great benefit. He used a paired watershed approach in which one catchment was treated. The most abundant shrubs were *Quercus turbinella* and true mountain mahogany (*Cerocarpus montanus*). In the first experiment the chapparal vegetation in a zone along the river channel and colluvial footslope was replaced by grass; in the other it was manipulated. It was about 75 feet wide. The aim was to remove deep-rooted plants and these were treated with chemicals (fenuron).

The second treatment resulted in an 85 per cent increase in runoff and was in this sense successful because flow continued much longer than in the untreated catchments. The vegetation suppression rates were 32 to 54 per cent with the second treatment.

References and further reading

Agassi, M., I. Shainberg and J. Morin (1981) Effect of electrolyte concentration and soil sodicity on infiltration rate and crust formation. *Soil Science Society of America* 45: 848–851.

Allen, T. F. H., R. V. O'Neill and T. W. Hoekstra (1984) Interlevel relations on ecological research and management: Some working principles from Hierarchy Theory. General Tech Report RM 110. Rocky Mountain Forest and Range Experimental Station, 11 pp.

Ambers, R. K. R., D. L. Druckenbrod and C. P. Ambers (2006) Geomorphic response to historical agriculture at Monument Hill in the Blue Ridge foothills of Central Virginia. *Catena* 65: 49–60.

Anderson, P. W. and S. D. Faust (1963) *Changes in quality of water in the Passaic River at Little Falls, New Jersey as shown by long term data*. U.S. Geological Survey Professional Paper 525. D p D214–D218.

Arden, E. F. and G. Garcia (1973) *Seventeen year sediment production from a semi arid watershed in the southwest*. USDA Forest Service Research Note RM 248.

Ben-Hur, I. Shainberg, D. Bakker and R. Keren (1985) Effect of soil texture and $CaCO_3$ content on water infiltration in crusted soils related to water salinity. *Irrigation Science* 6: 281–294.

Bradford, J. M., P. A. Remley, J. E. Ferris and B. Santini (1986) Effect of soil surface sealing on splash from a single water drop. *Soil Science Soc America* 50: 1547–1552.

Bolt, G. H. and F. F. R. Koenigs (1972) Physical and chemical aspects of the stability of soil aggregates. *Mededling Fakulteit Landbouwwetenschappen State University of Ghent Belgium* 37: 955–973.

Briassouli (2011) (LEDDRA Project: Land and Ecosystem Degradation and Desertification. *Assessing the fit of responses to land and ecosystem degradation and desertification*, EU 7th Framework Programme, http//Leddra.aegean.gr.

Breshears, D. D., O. B. Myers, C. W. Meyers, *et al*. (2009) Tree die-off in response to global change-type drought: mortality insights from a decade of plant water potential measurements. *Frontiers in Ecology and Environment* 7(4): 185–189.

Cerdà, A. (1996) Seasonal variability of infiltration rates under contrasting slope conditions in Southeast Spain. *Geoderma* 69: 217–232.

Cerdà, A. and S. H. Doerr (2007) Soil wettability, runoff and erodibility of major dry-Mediterranean land use types on calcareous soils. *Hydrological Processes* 21: 2325–2336. (doi: 10.1016/j.catena.2008.03.010).

Chinen, T. (1987) Hillslope erosion after a forest fire in Etajima Island, Southwest Japan. *Processus et mesure de lérosion*. Ed du CNRS 1990210.

Chirono, E., A. Bonet, J. Bellot and J. R. Sanchez (2006) The effects of a 30-year old Aleppo pine plantation on runoff, soil erosion and plant diversity in a semi-arid landscape in south eastern Spain. *Catena* 65 (1): 19–25.

Churchwood, H. M. and R. H. Gumm (1983) Stripping of deep weathered mantles and its significance to soil patterns, pp. 73–81, in Thompson, Moore and Northcote, *Soils and Land Use in Soils: An Australian Viewpoint*. Division of Soils, CSIRO, Melbourne.

Clarke, M. A. and R. P. D. Walsh (2006) Long-term erosion and surface roughness change of rain-forest terrain following selective logging, Danum Valley, Sabah Malaysia. *Catena* 109–123.

Cook, G. D. and R. C. Dalal (1992) Structural degradation of vertisols under continuous cultivation. *Soil and Tillage Research* 24, 47–64.

Corbane, C., P. M. Andrieux, Voltz, *et al*. (2008) Assessing the variability of soil surface characteristics in row cropped fields: The case of Mediterranean vineyards in Southern France. *Catena* 72: 79–90.

Crouch, R. J. (1976) Field tunnel erosion: A review. *Soil Conservation Journal of New South Wales* 98: 111.

Dalal, R. C. and Mayer, R. J. (1987) Long-term trends in fertility of soils under continuous cultivation and cereal cropping in Southern Queensland. 1. Overall changes and trends in winter cereal yields. *Au Au Journal of Soil Research* 24: 265–279.

Daniels, L. G. (1989) Degradation and restoration of soil structure in a cracking grey clay used for cotton production. *Australian Journal of Soil Research* 27: 455–469.

Dawin Charles (1845) The Voyage of the Beagle (Keynes, R. D. ed. (2001). *Charles Darwin's Beagle diary*. Cambridge: Cambridge University Press.

Darwin, C. (1882). *The formation of vegetable mould, through the action of worms, with observations on their habits*. London: John Murray. 7th thousand. Corrected by Francis Darwin. F1364

Diaz Hernandez, J., L. J. Yepes amd A Romero Diaz (2009) Minor forms in a badlands landscape framework, pp. 231–233, in *Advances in studies on Desertification Contributions to the International Conference on Desertification in Memory of Professor John B. Thornes* (ed. A. Romero Diaz, F. Belmonte Serrato, F. Alonso Sarria and F. Lopez Bermudez, 732 pp, Universidad de Murcia Editum.

Emerson W.W. (1967) A classification of soil aggregates based on their coherence in water. *Australian Journal of Soil Research,* 5: 47–57.

Emerson, W. W. (1983) Inter particle bonding, pp. 477–498, in Thompson, Moore and Northcote, *Soils and Land Use in Soils: An Australian Viewpoint*. Division of Soils, CSIRO, Melbourne.

Emerson, W. W. (1991) Structural decline of soils, assessment and prevention. *Australian Journal of Soil Research* 29: 905–921.

Emmett, W. W. (1974) Channel aggredation in the Western United States indicated by observations at Vigil Network sites. *Zeizschrift fur Geomorfologie* 21: 52–62.

Epstein, E. and W. J. Grant (1967) Soil losses and crust formation as related to some soil physical properties. *Soil Science Soc Amer Proc* 31: 547–550.

Fryirs, K. A., G. J. Brierley, N. J. Preston and M. Kasai (2007) Buffers, barriers and blankets. The (dis)continuity of catchment scale sediment cascades. *Catena* 70: 49–67.

Finlaysion, B. L. and N. R. Wong (1982) Storm runoff and water quality in an undisturbed forested catchment in Victoria. *Australian Journal of Forest Research* 12: 303–315.

Fischer, W. C. (1984) Wilderness Fire Management Planning Guide. General Tech Report INT 171, Ogden UT US Department of Agriculture, Forest Service, Intermountain Research Station. 56 pp.

Fournier, F. and S. Henin (1962) Etude de la forme de la relation existant entre lecoulement mensuel et le debit solide mensuel. *Int As Sc Hydology* 59: 353–358.

Garcia Alvarez, A. and J. J. Ibanez (1994) Seasonal fluctuations and crop influence on microflora and enzyme activity in fully developed soils of Central Spain. *Arid Soil Research and Rehabilitation* 8: 161–178.

Gillman, G. P. and D. F. Sinclair (1987) The grouping of soils with similar charge properties as a basis for agrotechnology. *Transfer Aust J Soil Res* 25: 275–285.

Golodets, C. and N. Boeken (2006) Moderate sheep grazing in semiarid shrubland alters small-scale soil surface structure and patch properties. *Catena* 65: 285–291.

Goreham, E. (1961) Factors influencing supply of major ions into inland waters, with special reference to the atmosphere. *Geological Society of America Bulletin* 72: 795–840.

Greacen, E. L. and R. Sands (1980) The compaction of forest soils. *Australian Journal of Soil Research* 18 (2): 163–189.

Greacen, E. L. and J. Williams (1983) Physical properties and water relations, pp. 499–530, in Thompson, Moore and Northcote, *Soils and Land Use in Soils: An Australian Viewpoint*. Division of Soils, CSIRO, Melbourne.

Gregorich, E. G., R. G. Kachanoski and R. P. Veroney (1988) Ultrasonic dispersion of aggregates distribution of organic matter in size fractions. *Can Journal of Soil Sci* 68: 395–403.

Harvey, A., E. M. J. Larsen and M. F. Jurgensen (1981) Rate of Residue Incorporation into Northern Rocky Mountain Forest Soils. Research Paper INT 282. Intermountain Forest and Range Experimental Station.

Hallsworh, E. G., A. B. Costin and F. R. Gibbons (1953) Studies in pedogenesis in New South Wales. *Journal of Soil Science* 4 (2): 242–255.

Hargett, O. L., J. A. Phillips and H. J. Kleiss (1982) Soil variability and fertility considerations affecting the establishment of erosion control vegetation on Piedmont roadcuts. *Journal of Soil and Water Conservation* 228.

Haycock, N. E. and T. P. Burt (1993) Role of flood plain sediments in reducing the nitrate concentrations of subsurface runoff. A case study in the Cotswolds. *UK Hydrological Processes* 7: 287–295.

Herrick, J. E., W. G. Whitford, A. G. de Soyza, *et al*. (2001) Field soil aggregate stability kit for soil quality and rangeland health evaluations. *Catena* 44: 27–35.

Hibbert, A. R. (1979) *Managing Vegetation to Increase Flow in the Colorado River Basin*. General Technical Report RM 60. 27 pp.

Horton, R. E. (1945) Erosional development of streams and their drainage basins; hydrophysical approach to quantitative morphology. *GSA Bulletin* 56 (3): 275–370.

Huxley, T. H. (1893) III *Evolution and Ethics* and IV *Capital the Mother of Labour* (1890) *Selected Works of Thomas Huxley*, Westminster Edition, Appeltons, 334 pp.

Ibanez, J. J., R. Jimenez Ballesta (1990) Sistemos y termodinámica en edafogenesis 1. Los suelos y el estado de equilibro termodinámico, *Rev Ecol Biol Soc* 27 (4): 371–382.

Ibanez, J. J., M. C. Lobo, G. Almendros and A. Polo (1983) Impacto del Fuego sobre algunos ecossistemas edaficos de clima mediterraneao contienental en la zonz centro de Espana. *Boletin de la estacion Central de Ecolgiia* 12 (24): 27–42.

Ibanez, J. J., Jimenez Ballesta R. and Garcia Alvarez A. (1990) Sistemos y termodinámica en edafogenesis 1. Los suelos y el estado de equilibro termodinámico, *Rev Ecol Biol Soc* 27 (4): 371–382.

Ibanez, J. J., M. C. J. C. Simon sw Benito and R. Jimenez Ballesta (1987) Consideraciones ecológicas acerca de la microfauna en los pastizales y suelos turbososde la alta montana en el sistema Central Espana. *Boletin de la estacion Central de Ecolgiia* 16 (31): 63–70.

Imeson, A.C., O. Arnalds, L. Montanarella, A. Arnouldssen, L. Dorren, M. Curf and D. de la Rosa, *et al*. (2006). Scape. The Way Ahead Printed by Drukkerij Uitkijkpost Heiloo, The Netherlands EUR 22187 EN available in Chinese 139 p.

Ingebo, P. A. (1971) Suppression of Channel side chaparral cover increases streamflow. *Journal of Soil and Water Conservation* 26 (2): 79–81.

Ireland, H. A., C. F. S. Sharpe and D.H. Eargle (1939). Principles of gulley erosion in the Piedmont of South Carolina. *USDA Technical Bullentin* 633p.

Isbell, R. J., R. Reeve and J. T. Hutton (1983) Salt and sodicity, pp. 107–117, in Thompson, Moore and Northcote, *Soils and Land Use in Soils: An Australian Viewpoint*. Division of Soils, CSIRO, Melbourne.

Jansson, M. B. (1988) *G. Annaler*. A global survey of sediment yield. 70 Series A. 81–98.

Jungerius, P. D. and H. van Zon (1982) The formation of the Lias Cuesta (Luxembourg) in the light of present day processes on forest soils. *G. Annaler* 64 A 3–4: 127–140.

Kadomura, H., T. Imagawa and H. Yamamoto (1983) Eruption induced rapid erosion and mass movements on Usu Volcano Hokkaido. *Zeitschrift fur Geomorfologie* N.F. Supp Bd 46: 123–142.

Kasnin Grubin, M. and R. Bryan (2007) Lithological properties and weathering response on badland hillslopes. *Catena*: 68–78.

Katra, I., H. Lavee and P. Sarah (2008) The effect of rock fragment size and position on top soil moisture on arid and semi-arid hillslopes. *Catena* 72: 49–55.

Kilgore, M. and G. A. Curtis (1987) *Guide to Understorey Burning in a Ponderosa Pine Larch Fir Forests in the Intermountain West*. US Dept of Agriculture, General Tech Report INT 233, Ogden UT US Department of Agriculture, Forest Service, Intermountain Research Station. 39 pp.

Koenigs, F. F. R. (1961) *The mechanical stability of clay soils as influenced by the moisture conditions and some other factors* PUDOC Wageningen. *V.L.O.* 67: 7.

Kvaaerno, H. S. and L. LiOlygarden (2001) (eds) Excursion Guide International Symposium on Snowmelt Erosion and Related Problems. 59 pp.

Leaf, C. F. (1974) *A model for predicting erosion and sediment yield from secondary forest road construction*. USDA Forest Service Research. Note RM 274.

Leopold, L. B. (1962) TheVigil Network. Bull. *IASH* 7(2), 5–9.

Loveday, J. and B.J. Bridge (1983) The Management of salt affected soils, pp. 843–855 in Thompson, Moore and Northcote, *Soils and Land Use in Soils: An Australian Viewpoint*. Division of Soils CSIRO Melbourne

Ludwig, J. A., D. J. Tongway, D. Freudenberger, *et al.* (1977) *Landscape Ecology: Function and Management*. CSIRO, Melbourne, Australia.

Martinez, J. A. (1976) The evaluation of soil properties as it relates to the genesis of volcanic ash soils in Costa Rica. *Soil Sci Soc AmJ* 40: 895–900.

Meade, R. M. (1969) Errors in using modern stream load data to estimate natural rates of denudation *Geol Soc Americ Bull* 80: 1265–1274.

McHenry, J. R. and J. C. Ritchie (1977) Estimating field erosion losses from fallout cesium 137 measurements, pp. 26–33, in Errosion and Solid Matter Transport Sympossium Paris, July 1977 *ERDA E* 49–7–3029.

Moore, I. D. and G. J. Burch (1986) Physical basis of the length slope factor in the Universal Soil Loss Equation. *Soil Science Soc Am Journal* 50: 1294–1298.

Naveh, Z. (1992) A landscape ecological approach to urban systems as part of the total human ecosystem. *J. Nat Hist Mus Inst Chiba* 2: 47–52.

Norton, L., D. Schroeder and W. C. Moldenhaeuer (1988) Differences in surface crusting and soil loss as affected by tillage methods, pp. 64–71, *International Symposium on the Assessment of Soil Surface Sealing and Assessment.*

Odum, E.P (1971) *Principles of Ecology*, Saunders College Publishing, Philadelphia, 574 p

Onda, Y., W. E. Dietrich and F. Booker (2008) Evolution of overland flow after a severe forest fire, Point Reyes, California. *Catena* 72: 1.

Olive, L. J. and W. A. Rieger (1988) Problems of assessing the impact of different forestry practices on coastal catchment in New South Wales, Chapter 14, in *Fluvial Geomorphology of Australia*, pp. 283–302, Academic Press of Australia.

Papy, F. and J. Boiffin (1988) Influence des systems de culture sur les risqué derosion par ruissellement. II: Evauation des possibilities de maitrise du phenomenon dans les exploitations agrocols. *Agronomie* 8: 745–756.

Ploey, J. de and D. Gabriels (1980) Measuring soil loss and experimental studies, pp. 63–108, in M. J. Kirkby and R. P. C. Morgam, *Soil Erosion*, John Wiley and Sons, Ltd, Chichester.

Ploey, J. de and H. J. Mucher (1981) A consistency index and rainwash mechanisms on Belgian loamy soils. *Earth Surface Processes and Landforms* 6: 319–330.

Ploey, D. and A. Yair (1985) Promoted erosion and colluviation. A proposal concerning land management and landscape evolution. *Catena* 12: 105–110.

Poesen, J. W. A. and H. Lavee (1991) Effects of size and incorporation of synthetic mulch on runoff and sediment yield from interills in a laboratory study with simulated rainfall. *Soil and Tillage Research* 21: 209–223.

Puigdefabregas, J. and G. Sanchez (1996) Geomorphological implications of vegetation patchiness on semi arid slopes, Chapter 47, pp. 1027–1060, in *Advances in Hillslope Processes*, John Wiley and Sons, Ltd, Chichester.

Renard, K.G., Nichols, M.H., Woolhiser, D.A., Osborn, H.B. (2008). HYPERLINK "http://www.tucson.ars.ag.gov/unit/Publications/PDFfiles/1857.pdf" A brief background on the U.S. Department of Agriculture Agricultural Research Service Walnut Gulch Experimental Watershed. *Water Resources Research*. Vol. 44, W05S02, doi:10.1029/2006WR005691.

Rice, R. M., F. B. Tilley and P. A. Datzman (1979) A watershed's response to logging and roads: South Fork of Casper Creek, California 1967–1976. Res Paper PSW-146. 12 pp. U.S. Forest Service Department of Agriculture, Berkeley, California.

Riezebos P. A. and R. T. Slotboom (1974) Palynology in the study of present day hillslope development. *Geologie en Mijnbouw* 53: 436–448.

Riley, S. J. (1984) Effect of clearing and roading operations on the permeability of forest soils, Karuah catchment, New South Wales. *Forest Ecology and Management* 9: 283–293.

Riley, S. J. (1980) Implications of current models of runoff production to soil conservation practice. *Geographical Survey* 9: 1.

Sang-Arun, J., M. Mihara, M. Y. Horaguchi and E. Yamaji (2006) Soil erosion and participatory remediation strategy for bench terraces in northern Thailand. *Catena* 65: 258–264.

Schouten, C. J. (1983) Budget if water and its constituents for Lake Taupo New Zealand Dissolved loads of rivers and surface water quantity quality relationships. *I.A.S.H. Pub.* 141: 277–297.

Schumm, S. (1977) *The Fluvial System.* John Wiley and Sons, Ltd, Chichester.

Swanson, N. P., A. R. Dedrick and H. E. Weakly (1965) Soil particles and aggregates transported in runoff from simulated rainfall. *Trans ASEA* 437–440.

Targulian, V. O. and P. V. Krasilinikov (2007) Soil system and pedogenic processes: self-organisation, time scales and environmental significance. *Catena*, 71: 373–381.

Ternan J. L, A. G. Williams, A. Elmes and R. Hartley (1996) Aggregate stability of soils in Central Spin and the role of land management. *Earth Surface Processes and Landforms* 21: 181–193.

Ternan J., L. A. G. Williams, A. Elmes and C. Fitzjohn (1996) The effectiveness of terracing and afforestation for erosion control on Rana Sediments in Central Spain. *Land Degradation and Development* 7: 337–351.

Ternan J. L., A. G. Williams, A. Elmes and C. Hartley (1996) Aggregate stability of soils in Central Spain and the role of land management. *Earth Surface Processes and Landforms*: 181–193.

Thompson, C. H., A. W. Moore and K. H. Northcote (1983) *Soils and Land Use in Soils: An Australian Viewpoint.* Division of Soils, CSIRO, Melbourne.

Tisdall, J.M. and Oades, J.M., 1982: Organic matter and water-stable aggregates in soils. *Journal of Soil Science* 33, 141–163

Tisdal, J. M. (1978) Ecology of earthworms in irrigated orchards, Chapter 39 in Modifications of soil structure (eds w.w. Emerson, R.D. Bond and A. Dexter) Wiley, New York.

Trimble, S. W. (1974) *Man Induced Soil Erosion on the Southern Piedmont. 1700–1970.* Soil Conservation Society of America, Ankeny, Iowa.

Wallis, F. P. and I. L. James (1972) Introduced animal effects and erosion phemomena in the Northern Urewera Forests, *New Zealand Journal of Forestry* 17, 21–36

Yair, A. and M. Klein (1973) The influence of surface properties on flow and erosion processes on debris covered slopes in an arid area. *Catena* 1: 1–18.

Yair, A. and H. Lavee (1985) An investigation of source areas of sediment and sediment transport by overland flow along arid hillslopes. Erosion and Sediment Transport Measurements proceedings of the Florence Symposium IAHS 133, pp. 433–446.

Yair, A. and H. Lavee (1985) Runoff generation in arid and semi arid zones to 320. 183-22- in *Hydrological Forecasting*, John Wiley, New York.

Yair, A., D. Sharon and H. Lavee (1980) Trends in runoff and erosion processes over an arid limestone hillside, Northern Negev, Israel. *Hydrological Sciences Bulletin* 25 (3): 243–255.

Zehetner, F. and W. P. Miller (2006) Erodibility and runoff-infiltration characteristics of volcanic ash soils along an altitudinal climosequence in the Ecudorian Andes. *Catena* 65: 201–213.

5
Human impact on degradation processes

5.1 Introduction

In Chapter 4, runoff and erosion were described as sometimes being emergent processes that occurred when the soil structure degraded and critical conditions were met. In this chapter the focus is on human impact and erosion and what to do about it. Positive feedbacks and scale mean that all life has the capacity to change things at different levels of scale. For example, coral produces reefs that transform the coastal marine systems, beavers by constructing dams transform river channel dynamics and termites, and the deposition of eroded soil as dust is a source of nutrients elsewhere. It is the agents of wind and water and the processes of erosion and sediment transport that propagate these effects.

There are two extremes. In degraded areas, the landscape is adapted to human actions and there is little sensitivity; this might also be the case in natural landscapes. Although human actions might change conditions and processes very easily, it depends very much on what is being done and the context. Just the simple presence of people or hunting can trigger changes that lead to erosion by processes such as splash erosion and litter transport. Responses of the ecosystem can be very rapid and critical soil properties can change from day to day or week to week. It was found by Lopez Bermudez (1995), in Medalus field experiments, that annual plants, as well as shrubs, could produce coarse water stable aggregates around themselves that increased the infiltration rate within a few years by an order of magnitude. Although it could take hundreds of years for the soil to resemble its original state, nevertheless soils formed around annual plants transformed the soil structure with fine roots, during their annual cycle, well enough to prevent erosion. The approach of this chapter is to use local field study results to illustrate specific impacts.

Some useful conclusions about soil erosion are that over a period of several hundred or a thousand years most erosion takes place during a relatively short period during a few extreme almost catastrophic events when particular combinations of circumstances existed.

The dryer and more arid the climate, the longer the period between major erosion events. In the Atlantic rain forest of Brazil, virtually no erosion occurred between a catastrophic time about 8000–9000 years ago and the 1800s when coffee was introduced as a crop. In Europe, studies often show that erosion occurred when something happened and that this was usually in the form of some technical innovation in farming, such as the

Desertification, Land Degradation and Sustainability, First Edition. Anton Imeson.
© 2012 John Wiley & Sons, Ltd. Published 2012 by John Wiley & Sons, Ltd.

introduction of a new crop or an agricultural implement, and extreme rainfall associated with periods of volcanic activity.

Much of land degradation in the past and today began with the development of the iron manufacture in China in about 500 BC. Trees were required for charcoal to manufacture the iron tools and implements for farmers and armies. Today this continues where the remaining large forest areas are being cleared for charcoal and farmland in Brazil to make pig iron for export to China. A major factor for the past prosperity of China was the scientific and organisational capacity of its civil service with respect to agriculture and land and water management.

When erosion occurs, it usually only affects a relatively small area. Ninety per cent of erosion occurs on 5 per cent of the area during a small percentage of the time. Over thousands of years, the actual 5 per cent of the area being affected will change. It is characterized by a cycle in which weathering or deposition leads to the increase thickness of soil until a critical point is reached when conditions change and promote mass movements or erosion. The fact that periods of erosion and instability follow periods of weathering and soil formation can therefore be a consequence of both extrinsic and intrinsic causes.

The organic soil that accumulates on the surface under vegetation has important characteristics that affect both the micro climate and hydrology. It was found in infiltration experiments all over the world that the forest litter or duff can retain sometimes as much as 3 or 4 cm of water, which is used by the vegetation and soil fauna. As a consequence, hydrological processes and temperature are regulated by this layer and there will be more runoff and much less evaporation if it is lost. At the patch scale, the soil surface is exposed to higher temperatures and often there is too much radiation for plant roots to be attracted to the surface. There is less biological activity in the top soil which is hotter and dryer so that negative soil degradation pathways occur and surface seals develop. Surface seals can also be favoured by the accumulation of dust that contains swelling clays or by sodium. As water is the medium in which nutrients are transported, this also has a large impact on plant growth.

5.2 Soil erosion processes

Soil particles are moved and transported by rainfall and flowing water but even more so by ants, worms, termites and by cultivation, trampling and land levelling. All of these have been extensively measured and studied.

A characteristic feature of soil erosion processes are thresholds: if conditions stay within a certain range, a critical soil erosion process might not occur and there will be no immediate occurrence. Nevertheless if erosion occurs today, it may be the delayed response of changes that took place tens or even many hundreds of years ago.

Erosion occurs mainly as a result of the following agents and processes:

1 By wind erosion: the wind exerts a force on the soil that affects particles of a specific size (coarse silt and sand) when these are not bound together by organic matter, roots or clay.

2 By rain splash erosion. Rain and hail transport soil particles by splash action. Soil particles are eroded by overland flow if more water falls as rain than can enter the soil.

3 By rill, pipe, tunnel and gully erosion. These are formed by or carry flow that becomes channeled. Shrinking and swelling and tillage can lead to subsurface compaction and above this rills and pipes can form in the soil through subsurface erosion. This kind of erosion can also occur wherever flow from roads, paths or fields is concentrated but it requires suitable sediment. The formation of some gullies and pipes occurs in rocks and soils that are erodible and unstable when wet but hard when dry.

4 By tillage erosion whereby the soil is moved downslope by ploughing.

5 By various farming operations: for example, soil is removed in root crops.

6 By trampling by animals and humans.

Figure 5.1, shows the impact of acid sulphate mine waste and mine drainage water. The extensive area affected near Santo Domingo can be seen on Google Earth.

5.2.1 Erodibility

Erodibility is a useful term used to describe the intrinsic sensitivity of the soil to erosional forces that are described as having erosivity. The erosivity of the rain is related to its intensity, drop-size, chemical content and energy and momentum of falling water drops.

The pattern of erosion on agricultural land is frequently explained in terms of the factors that influence it. These are the energy of the rainfall and runoff (erosivity), the erodibility or sensitivity of the soil to erosion, slope conditions, and the vegetation cover and protection provided by crops and also by soil management. Figure 5.2 was taken about one hour after the start of rainfall and about 20 minutes after the start of overland

Figure 5.1 This slide from the Alentejo (Portugal) shows the impact of acid mine water leaking from a drainage pipe that makes the land toxic so that plants can not grow (Credit: Anton Imeson).

Figure 5.2 Taken at the start of runoff during a rainstorm in Habin Province, China. Note the dispersion. Shallow proto rills are starting to form and they act as drains (Credit: Anton Imeson).

flow, at the top of the slope and field. The runoff is just starting to develop shallow rills. The clay rich soil is relatively strongly aggregated when dry but clay dispersion is taking place where there are large rain drop impacts.

The term erodibility describes the intrinsic ability of a soil to resist erosion. If all of the water can infiltrate into the soil (on sand), if the land is flat, the soil has very stable aggregates resulting from specific types of clay or organic matter, and if it has many stones, accelerated erosion by water is usually limited. A stable and porous soil structure often develops under growing plants and this can make erosion very unlikely during most years. Soil organisms, in creating a habitat for themselves, bind the soil with polysaccharides and roots and increase the resilience. In silty soils, animals are very important in creating pore spaces. High rates of erosion are often correlated with low levels of organic matter but the real problem is the destruction and poisoning of the soil ecosystem and the effects of compaction. In this sense, when erosion does occur, it is a reflection of the degradation of the soil structure and an indicator of desertification.

5.3 Response of soil structure to cultivation and farming

When land is converted from forest, strong water retaining surface soil may persist for many years. Soil degradation can be consequence of many different processes and it depends very much on management. In Figure 5.3, it is possible to see the more or less derelict land left as a consequence of exposing the erodible subsoil in which pipes and tunnels could develop. The land and soil surface when the soil was farmed is present at a few places elsewhere. The extent of degraded areas such as in Figure 5.4 are very

Figure 5.3 and Figure 5.4 Areas with highly erodible soils near Tarije in Bolivia that became degraded and abandoned. These surfaces are the former sub soil horizons after perhaps one or two metres of soil has been eroded since European settlement (Credit: Anton Imeson).

great as are the consequences for the hydrological processes and functions. Figure 5.5 shows similar erosion processes at a construction site, which was not completed because the properties could not be sold.

That soil degradation can occur on different soils as a result of cultivation is a subject that has received much attention in soil physics and agriculture. In many parts of the world, experiments have highlighted a number of key processes and impacts. The organic matter content decreases as well as the characteristics of the soil structure that create problems. In a keynote paper, Dalal and Mayer (1987) described and postulated an exponential decrease in time to a steady state in the organic matter content of soil used for farming after forest removal.

Figure 5.5 Soil erosion on highly erodible marls used as a construction site in on an area of badlands, Murcia Spain (Credit: Anton Imeson).

The scientists at the Queensland Wheat Research Institute in Australia have undertaken many studies that help them understand better the structural degradation that is occurring on their highly clayey soils known as **vertisols**. Similar or somewhat problems on clay soils have been investigated in many other areas under comparable conditions, for example in North Israel and the USA, but they also occur on reclaimed soils in the Ijsellmer in Holland.

One of the findings of Cook *et al.* (1992) at Toowoomba was that they could predict the saturated hydraulic conductivity (permeability) of the soil from the dispersed silt + clay contents, which are easy to measure. The hydraulic conductivity and dispersion are both affected by how clay behaves and this is influenced by the percentage of exchangeable sodium in the soil (ESP). Stones or rock fragments (Figure 5.6) tend to be removed from the soil by farmers because they are thought to reduce the volume of soil for plants and make cultivation difficult. On the other hand they have been shown to have very many positive effects, especially in arid areas. They accumulate because of many processes ranging from frost action, to kicking by animals. Under rocks there is often a higher permeability and organic matter content because it is a preferred habitat for soil animals.

The ESP was highest at the soil surface because of evaporation and it increased steadily with the length from 0 to 64 years. Nevertheless, these were initially also quite high at between about two and four years. This accumulation is a relatively slow process that at some time will trigger a change of state in terms of soil behaviour.

Soil erodibility and its seasonality in Spain

An important conclusion from section 5.3 is that times of biological activity in the soil are favourable for the formation and stabilization of soil aggregates. Seasonal contrasts in Continental areas can produce periods that are alternatively favourable and unfavourable

Figure 5.6 Stones can be very favourable because they can armour the surface, protect the fine particles from erosion and encourage infiltration (Credit: Anton Imeson).

to biological activity and soil stability. Garcia Alvarez and Ibanez (1994) have looked at the influence of crops and climate on the processes occurring at times that are favourable, that is, Spring, and Autumn, when it is difficult for biological activity to take place. What is unfavourable is the rapid alteration of hot and cold or wet and dry conditions that occur because of irregular rainfall or alternations of hot and cold conditions.

At Gualdalajara in Central Spain, Garcia Alvarez and Ibanez measured the enzyme activity in different soils to establish different impacts. An evergreen oak stand was used as a reference for the natural vegetation. In this they found a clear stratification with more intensity near the surface. In the shrub vegetation and cereal crops, the stratification disappears. In cereals areas, there are fewer microorganisms, particularly actinomycites and fungi. Farming reduces the density of microorganisms. Their results suggested that farming reduces the catalytic capacity of the soil. What they concluded is that there is a loss in the capacity for the soil to self organize and that this increases with the degree of human impact.

They explain that unfavourable conditions in the soil in the Autumn produce conditions in which there is a release of nutrients and an opportunity to exploit these resources. The release of nutrients is more beneficial in the Spring when there is a greater enzymic activity. In Figure 5.7 a field site is shown where continuous measurements were made of soil moisture and temperature, and the evolution of the soil structure for about 6 years . The results were published in many papers by Calvo and colleagues at the Department of Geography in Valencia. In this area of about 300 mm of annual rainfall there are many worms and snails under the Stipa plants that can be seen. Figure 5.8a shows a Gerlach runoff collection device. Figure 5.8b, a worm that consumes the *Stipa* roots which extend several meters into cracks in the limestone rocks.

Figure 5.9 gives information about the erosion rates in Spain as measured at different scales. In areas such as Figure 5.7, they are currently very low because of the limited human activities.

(a)   (b)

Figure 5.7 and 5.8 (a and b)   Part of the ERMES target area in the near Benidorm being investigated by Calvo and associates as a study of processes along a climatological gradient in Alicante.

5.4 Gully erosion

The term gully is used to describe several different forms of linear erosion. They may be V or U shaped and may be formed as a consequence of many different circumstances.

For many reasons gullies are not located randomly throughout the world but instead are concentrated in certain regions. Some areas may be predisposed to gully erosion for geomorphologic reasons related to base level changes such as recent faulting or mass

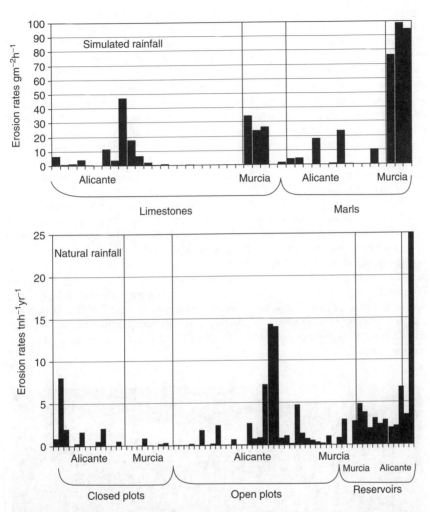

Figure 5.9 Erosion rates from studies done in the areas of Alicante and Murcia since the late 1980s by different research groups. Different methodologies are used, classified as rainfall simulation experiments (above) and data collected at different scales under natural rain (bottom graph). (The data presented are derived from Bautista *et al.*, 1996, 1999; Boix *et al.*, 1994, 1998; Bouma and Imeson, 2000; Calvo-Cases *et al.*, 1991, 2003; Castillo *et al.*, 1997; Cerdà *et al.*, 1995, Cerdà and Navarro, 1997; Cerdà, 1993, 2001; Imeson *et al.*, 1998; Martínez-Mena *et al.*, 2001, 2002; Llovet *et al.*, 1994; López-Bermúdez *et al.*, 1998; Verstraeten *et al.*, 2003; Sánchez *et al.*, 1994). Erosion rates in Alicante and Murcia (Spain). An overview of results, methods and scales of study of the last two decades.

(Authors: Carolina Boix-Fayos1, Martínez-Mena, M.1, Calvo-Cases, A.2, Castillo, V.1 From Scape).

movements. Other areas of gully erosion are confined to sediments having particular material characteristics. A specific concentration of gullies is also present in sub-humid semi-arid or even desert areas where they are associated with dispersive sediments and regoliths. This category of gully is highly sensitive to environmental change. Although gully erosion is often associated with various human impacts or interventions, gully erosion has a very long history. For example, in Natal, paleo-gullies contain datable materials that suggest ages that go back to at least 200 000 BP. There are several feature of gullies formed in dispersive materials that make them particularly sensitive to climate change. One reason is that because the erodibility of the weathered deposits is high, the mechanical energy required to evacuate sediment from gully channels is minimal. Gully erosion is nevertheless sensitive to the way precipitation influences the processes of gully side wall erosion and piping. Most gullies are enlarged by a process of headcut retreat that occurs during periods of growth.

Gullies found in dispersive materials have a number of common features with respect to where they occur, the erosion processes, how they respond to human activity, and relations with hydrology. Gully erosion is particularly severe following the clear cutting of pristine forest and its use for cash crops in areas where there are thick sensitive layers of regolith (weathered rock). Darwin in his diaries described many such areas in South America but they are very common throughout the tropics. What gully initiation requires is suitable erodible sediments. When these are exposed on the surface as in Figure 5.10 this type of process can be observed. The material being eroded in Figure 5.10 is not in situ. It is likely to be a colluvial deposited as a consequence of the first forest cleatances and land use practices that resulted in the erosion of the red Mediterranean soils that were then present and which no longer exist.

Figure 5.10 Erosion processes in Valencian orange fields as a consequence of the managment practices. Photo Cerda 2011.

5.5 Grazing and erosion

The domestication of livestock and herding of animals is an ancient activity that has a number of influences on land degradation and erosion. Animals can make the soil compact and encourage concentrated runoff. Saturated or Horton (1945) overland flow and erosion take place (explained in more detail later in this chapter) and at the same time that animals trample and displace rocks and stones downslope and they consume or destroy vegetation that is protecting the soil. But animals can also have positive impacts that reduce runoff, for example by adding nutrients that promote plant growth and which reduce runoff. Research is very difficult because the interactions and feedbacks between plants–animals–erosion occur over tens or even hundreds of years, and they involve the use of fire as a means of improving plant palatability and also changes in management practice. In some cases, erosion features in areas of present day high grazing intensity are the result of erosion perhaps many tens or hundreds of years ago and cannot be attributed to today's flocks.

The concept of overgrazing means that farmers realize that they will damage the land if they keep more livestock than the carrying capacity of the land warrants. Traditionally, the livestock numbers kept by pastoralists would be related in very complex ways to the availability of pasture and grazing opportunities. However, similarly to today, there would always be social or land use policy pressures on pastoralists to manage their livestock in a way that at times risked erosion.

In Europe livestock was traditionally a symbol of wealth for the old Germanic and Celtic tribes so they would probably maintain stocking rates at the maximum.

Research by Trimble and Mendel (1995) has shown that, where cattle range freely, the cow is perhaps the most important agent of erosion in the world today. Using areas for cattle that were traditionally used for raising sheep or pigs is a major reason for much soil erosion in parts of the Alentejo (Roxo 2009). In many tropical areas, such as those in Bolivia, cows graze very steep slopes and destroy the vegetation and displace large volumes of earth downslope in their search for food. Figure 5.11 show the landscape near Omalus in Crete, that was a research area of an ecosystem degradation study carried out along a climatological gradient from Omalus to the coast. Figure 5.11a, is an overview of the Omalus depression which is circular so that it is possible to look at the relationship between grazing and aspect. Most grazing pressure then seemed to be the west facing slopes, that were preferred. Figure 5.11b shows the animals kicking stones downslope, and this is an extremely important impact. The vegetation in the area provides too little feed for the number of animals, so there is relatively much trampling along pathways. Goats and sheep play an important role in traditional farming but there is great pressure on common and public land.

This is partly because of the heavy weight of the cow and the impact of trampling and displacing soil downslope. The occurrence of soil erosion processes induced by most grazing animals is related to the intensity of the trampling and this is connected to the location of so-called watering and gathering points where animals congregate as well as the location of fences.

The huge increase in livestock (particularly pigs) but also sheep and beef has its impact in the areas where the feed is produced. The production of irrigated livestock feeds in the dry Mediterranean regions is a major factor in the decline of the local groundwater. The overstocking and soil degradation is only possible because of the importing of feed from

(a)   (b)

(c)   (d)

Figure 5.11a, b, c and d These show the ERMES field site at Omalus, Crete at the time of the research. This area was formerly forested. Photo b shows the impact of fire and grazing on the vegetation. As the vegetation recovers after a fire, the area on which the goats can walk becomes smaller (Credit: ERMES and Anton Imeson).

other European countries. There is no relationship between the number of livestock and the carrying capacity. This is happening all over Europe, not just in the Mediterranean.

The effluents produced by animals leak into rivers, making the summer low flow discharges of many Mediterranean rivers toxic. The over application of manure has resulted in the degradation of soil structure so that many soils have become much more sensitive to erosion.

In Lesbos in Turkey Govers and Poesen (1998) measured the effect of sheep walking across a hillside on downslope movement of rocks. In Israel Yair (1995 personal communication) showed that grazing animals were responsible for most sediment found at slope foot positions. The erosion in Israel had a beneficial effect because it concentrated sediment at the slope foot where it could be farmed and it reduced the depth of soil on slopes so that there was more rainwater harvesting and infiltration for use downslope.

Xu (2006) reports on the dust sand storms in and around the Ordos Plateau in China and how they are influenced by land use change and desertification. He relates the frequency of dust storms to the area of desertified land at the level of counties. The precipitation in his study area increased from the northwest to the southeast from 150 mm to 400 mm. Most dust comes from fluvio lacustrine deposits and it occurs when the fragile steppe vegetation is damaged by grazing and cultivation. Xu says that when these stop, the quality of the land improves and erosion also stops.

Grazing and small scale soil surface structure was investigated by Golodets and Boeken (2006) in Israel. They found, in the northern Negev, that moderate grazing had a significant effect on soil structure and vegetation patterns. Grazing increased bare soil and halved the size of vegetation patches on mounds. Even low grazing intensity had significant effects on the spatial heterogeneity of semi arid shrub land. It is known that heavy grazing (Ludwig *et al*. 1977). reduces the size and abundance of shrub patches in the landscape, but the results here show that low grazing also has an impact.

On range lands it was noted by that the authors that where at some locations in Saudi Arabia these had been managed sustainably, these were dominated by highly productive grasses. In most areas, however, livestock was at a level far beyond the carrying capacity. What happens in the Middle East is that camels and goats which are not selective remove many more species than sheep or cattle did, when these can no longer survive. Rangelands also provide fuel for cooking, which is also removed. Nomadic and transhumance grazing systems have benefits.

5.6 The impact of fire on land degradation processes

The relationships between erosion, fire and desertification are paradoxical in the Mediterranean. In 1991 Rubio and Sala (see Rubio *et al*. 1991) organized a workshop that reviewed all of the then current research findings. The surprise conclusion, which still holds today, is that except under special circumstances fire mostly positively improves the ability of a soil to retain water and increases its fertility. Only where soil temperatures exceeded a critical value of about 400–600 degrees did soil erosion increase. Mediterranean forest trees and shrubs have adapted or altered soil properties so that water is usually trapped. These properties (high porosity, water repellent induced rainwater harvesting structures) mean that water remains on the slopes and will not cause erosion, unless the soil is very thin or has had these positive properties damaged by trampling. Where very high rainfall amounts can sometimes occasionally occur, as along the Mediterranean coast in Valencia, then there is a risk of erosion, perhaps once every ten years (Rubio *et al*. 1991). However, normally, the vegetation resprouts and soil properties improve so that three or four years after a fire there is no risk of erosion. But, even when erosion does occur, soil particles are trapped by resprouting vegetation and there is a positive effect. It is the case that following a fire there is less evaporation and organic matter, so there is more water available for resprouting trees.

If fires themselves do not result in erosion, why then does erosion recently often follow a fire? Research has indicated two main reasons. Firstly, there is the professed fear of postfire erosion and the question of the availability of money to protect people from the risk. Instead of fencing off the forest and keeping people out so that the vegetation can recover, soil conservation protection measures are constructed, burnt trees are taken out of the forest and often seedlings are planted. Trampling and soil profile compaction and inversion occur. All of these actions destroy the capacity of the soil to retain water and prevent erosion. Highly erodible B and C horizon material is often exposed on the surface. At the same time, the soil is made bare, runoff is concentrated and very often rill and gully erosion are caused.

The second reason why erosion occurs is that the trees grown in plantations are exotic and have not developed soil properties or a fire hydrology that is adapted to the local conditions.

Another (third) reason is because of grazing. The first plants that grow after the fire are generally rich in nutrients and favoured by sheep and goats. Although there are often regulations that should protect the plants from grazing, in practice they often still get eaten and in the process, the weak soil, which has a fragile week house-of-cards structure, gets trampled.

In conclusion, forests fires and wildfires generally do not usually cause erosion in themselves, so there is no need to panic. What mostly causes erosion are the postfire activities of the community, who are extracting a living and exploiting the situation. Preventing erosion could also be achieved by keeping people off the land and allowing nature to recover.

5.7 Case 1: Blue Ridge Foothills

Ambers *et al.* (2006) present an interesting case study that provides an example of the long-term changes caused by human impact. The region of the Blue Ridge Foothills, central Virginia, suffered severe amounts of gully erosion in the past and the methods that were developed to control gulley erosion are described in the classic paper by Ireland *et al.* (1939) in which they describe and recommend principles for controlling gully erosion that are still being used today. Trimble in 1974 had pointed out the influence that soil conservation had on the sediment dynamics of rivers and he later drew attention to the way in which the magnitude of erosion rates is greatly overestimated in models that lack feedbacks with land use and geomorphological thresholds.

Ambers *et al.* (2006) look at the detailed field evidence at Monument Hill (2006) and concluded that the following happened:

- 1760: Deforestation and agriculture were introduced: the impact was sheet erosion and the aggradation of the river channel. This continued until 1830

- 1830: Gully erosion started and the land was abandoned with perhaps the channelization of the river beds. This continued to about 1865

- 1865: Forest regrowth and soil stabilization. There was a rapid incision of the rivers until about 1900 and the continued growth of the forest until today, when there is some forest thinning.

Ambers *et al.* conclude that this response is typical of the region. They say that sediment production rates averaged 130 tons per hectare per year from 1776 to 1888. The peaks in erosion rates reported by Trimble occurred in 1920 which they say happened because his study area was settled later. The legacy of past agriculture has a really long-term impact on rivers.

What this means at a different scale is illustrated by the next case.

5.8 Case 2: Human impact in the Atlantic States

This area in the USA has been studied by many people. In 1969, Meade (1969) summarized what was known at that time. He writes that human activity had increased the sediment loads in streams draining the Atlantic States since the first European settlers landed. In the Chesapeake Bay region there are records describing the forest clearance and cultivation methods of tobacco which resulted in clear streams becoming muddy and formerly deep harbours filling with sediment washed from upstream farms. According to Meade, in 1950, 2 million tons of sediment was still being deposited each year. Soil conservation measures on land that was formerly eroded have meant that there have been some reductions in sediment loads between 1934 and 1953, but nevertheless vast amounts of sediment were still being delivered to the rivers. But it was not just agriculture but also coal mining in Pennsylvanian rivers that was a cause and at certain locations 10 per cent of the sediment was found to be coal.

Meade also analyses the impact of man on the dissolved material carried by streams and he reports on the measurements of Anderson and Faust (1963). In the Passaic River of New Jersey, in 1963, half of the flow was used for domestic and industrial supplies. Coal mines and agriculture add fertilizers and pesticides so that the situation was chronic. Meade estimates that as a consequence, sediment and dissolved loads are at least four times what they were before European settlers arrived.

Almost twenty years later in 1988 Margareta Jansson (1988) from the University of Uppsala published a global survey of sediment yield. This was one of a series of papers on sediment yields and global variations in erosion rates. The question being asked was how the global variations in sediment yield were being affected under current human influences.

It was found that, as is well known, the size of the drainage basin has a critical role to play and that the amount of sediment output per unit area decreases with size and that the greatest variability within a region is in the output from small catchments. Factors other than climate play a dominant role. Nevertheless, rainfall amount, intensity, snow and temperature and evaporation all play a role. If the river gradients are low, negative outputs can occur, for example in the Yangtze River. Jansson analyses relationships between runoff and sediment discharge and finds that these in fact do not exist, except locally.

5.9 Case 3: Impact of forest logging in California Casper Creek

The importance of roads as sources of sediment

When roads are constructed on sloping land, they profoundly change the hydrology. The nature of these impacts and changes has been given much attention because road building and construction is also a major source of runoff. This has been demonstrated all over the world.

When scientists began to compare the first quantitative measurements on sediment yields and budgets from measurements that were started in about 1970 onwards, it soon became clear that in many cases most of the sediments were being supplied from roads and tracks and not from the forested slopes.

Examples of this finding came, for example, from studies made by Froehlich and Slupik (1991) in forested catchments in the Carpathians. In the United States, studies in the Pacific North West, by Reid (1981) illustrated this. In virtually all forested catchments, the main sources of flood runoff and sediments were unsurfaced roads and tracks.

Logging in California Casper Creek

A valuable example of the impacts of forests and roads on processes is reported by Rice *et al.* (1979). They studied the response to logging and roads in the South Fork of Casper Creek, in the Jackson State Forest near Fort Bragin California, between 1967 and 1976. It is a classic paired water shed experiment in which two similar drainage basins are compared before during and after treatments. In 1962 the authors say that the age of the forest that was logged was 85 years. During the experiment logging seemed also to trigger a landslide and dam break. The experiment was designed to measure the impact on stream flow peaks and sediment loads. It was expected that the increase in water yield would be small. Like most rivers in the region, most sediment is carried during peak flows.

Between 1963 and 1967, for four years, there was a period of calibration, then between 1968 and 1971, roads were constructed and in 1972 logging began. The experiment therefore first measured the impact of road construction and in the second phase, logging and roads together. Soil erosion rates were measured in large rectangular plots of about 201 metres wide and 322 metres long. Rice *et al.* describe the response to logging as dramatic. Deviations of sediment yield in the South Fork of Casper Creek from the amount predicted from observations in North Fork, 1963 to 1976, were studied. The main changes were that the nature of the sediment supply to the river changes. Before, treatment sediment was described as being supply limited. After treatment, it was dependent on the amount of flow and discharge controlled.

In the discussion, concern about the soil loss is played down. During road construction and logging, little consideration was given to erosion control or control of water. Work was inexpertly done and ephemeral channels used as skidways; furthermore, no regard was had to hydrology or slope stability. The work was considered to have permanently damaged forest productivity for at least 10 to 15 per cent of the area. In evaluating the impact of erosion, Rice *et al.* say this is minimal in relation to the total amount of soil left, but the other functions of the soil that are being lost are not considered.

The impact on water quality was concluded to be a major concern and the existing aquatic systems were unable to maintain themselves with the new runoff regimes and sediment loads.

5.10 Case 4: Karuah Forest, New South Wales, Australia

The effect of clear cutting and road operations is also illustrated by the research of Riley (1984) in New South Wales, but he looked at the impact on the soil permeability and infiltration. He worked in the Karuah Forestry Commission where the relief was 500 metres and the rainfall above 1500 millimetres per year. He investigated the effects of different types of disturbance of the soil which had a 10-centimetre-thick ecto organic A horizon. He compared uncleared and cleared forest and sites along a road. The road sites were used for the transport of heavy machinery. The soils were the brown and yellow podzollic soils which have a texture contrast (they have been mentioned earlier elsewhere (see Hallsworth *et al.* 1953). The properties, or responses, he measured included the sorptivity (infiltration measurement, also explained elsewhere). This describes the maximum rate at which water can enter the soil and it can be used to calculate ponding times to predict runoff responses.

Riley found that the logging operations reduced the ability of the forest ground surface soil to transmit water and that the greatest reduction was for the roads. His mean values of sorptivity decreased from a range of 275 to 89 to 7.5 mm. On roads, it decreased 100 fold and on the forest soil, three- to five-fold. The saturated hydraulic conductivity decreased eight-fold. His conclusion is that this will and does lead to a large amount of runoff production on roads and the reduction in throughflow to the river.

5.11 Case 5: Afforestation in Spain

This case is different because it is about change to forest, not from forest. The Aleppo Pine (*Pinus halepensis*) afforestation has always been considered as one of the principal strategies for addressing land degradation and it is promoted everywhere, in addition because of the perceived benefits of reducing sediment yields to rivers. The government planted 2.5 million hectares in Spain with this tree and it is said to have increased the tree cover of Spain by 75 per cent. It has colonized extensive areas of abandoned land, and in Alicante, for example, accounts for 90 per cent of the tree cover (Chirono *et al.* 2006). Its distribution is encouraged by fire and is has been planted in both semi-arid areas that had a steppe of shrubland vegetation cover or in the more humid regions of oak forest. In a number of cases, there have been problems because of the impact of the techniques used for preparing the site with bulldozers, and for other reasons, so that the success rates are not always high and the trees have a bonsai appearance. In other cases, where the trees do grow, there are frequent fires and hydrology is disrupted.

An important analysis was reported by Chirono *et al.* (2006) who established plot experiments on trees that had been planted 30 years previously. Their findings were analysed statistically rather than according to processes and they focus on the relationships between forest cover and runoff percentages. Statistically, there is a threshold at about 30 per cent vegetation cover at which a tree cover in general prevents erosion.

The conclusions, for the semi-arid areas near Alicante that they studied, were that the grassland and shrub communities were equally good in reducing runoff and at the same time retaining richness and diversity of species.

5.12 Case 6: Soil erosion impacts in Europe

An overview of historical soil erosion and conservation in Europe is given by Lang and Bork (2006). The consensus is that the areas most affected by erosion are in the Northern Loess Belt and in the Mediterranean region. Mountain and northern regions, with short growing seasons and frost, are also affected by erosion.

In western Europe (e.g. England and western France), most water erosion occurs during the Winter months when soil profiles are saturated and this may be caused by low intensity storms. Going eastwards, high intensity summer rainfall storms become more important in causing erosion, so that in Central Europe erosion occurs mainly during the Summer (as is also the case in China, much of the USA, in Brazil and Australia). However, rainfall increases with altitude, and the central European, Italian and French mountain areas have frequent erosive summer thunderstorms, that occasionally produce comparable Summer rainfall. The annual variability, however, is high. Land use and management practices in central Europe have had to adapt to high rates of erosion risk.

In northern Europe, most erosion occurs during the Spring period of snowmelt. In areas where the soil freezes in the Winter before it is covered with snow, there tend to be erosion problems in the Spring. In south-eastern Europe, the Carpathian Mountains and the Danube basin have more continental climate conditions, but there is much erosion in the mountains of Romania as a result of forest clearance. However, towards the south-east in the agricultural areas, Summer droughts become more of a problem and steppe-like areas are found.

Limestone and karst areas are very common in the northern Mediterranean region and on the large Mediterranean Islands. Particularly in the mountains of Crete, and in areas of Slovenia, Dalmatia, Greece and Italy, as a result of intensive grazing, there may be rocky desert-like areas that resemble those in China. In Crete, most rainfall occurs in Winter but in some specific areas of the northern Mediterranean it is more evenly distributed throughout the year, or it has a maximum in the Summer. In Spain, there are extensive areas of limestone in south-east and central Spain which are quite humid and which are in many ways comparable with China.

Historical erosion in economically marginal areas

At the end of the last century, many areas of Europe that were agriculturally marginal suffered from land degradation and erosion and there was a subsistence economy and much poverty on occasion. In the Mediterranean area, the population in the rural areas was usually very high. Land use practices and conditions resembled those found in parts of Morocco today. Erosion was often caused by policies put in place by the then governments to achieve national self-sufficiency in wheat or rice production. On the other hand, there were a number of afforestation projects in degraded mountain areas that transformed landscapes. A major feature of the Mediterranean region is the litoralization of the population when people moved to the major cities and the coast. People moved to the coast and cities for social reasons, not just because land degradation had made agriculture unproductive. Figure 5.12 and 5.13, illustrate several paradoxes. This area is in the boreal forest zone where and by normal standards very marginal for most arable crops, especially wheat. After the war the traditional mixed farming in the region was changed and all of the animals were moved away from relatively flat areas that could be converted into large fields. This desire to have agricultural land in Norway is political and cultural. Figure 5.12 illustrates the arable landscape that was created by land levelling and which breaks up the monotony of the endless forest. The perception is that there is too little flat land and that it is worthwhile to increase the cultivable area, for aesthetics and national food security. It is made possible by subsidies but in order for the farmers to receive enough money they are allowed to cultivate slopes that are too steep because there is a shortage of flat land. Figure 5.13 shows the soil erosion plots in Norway being used to quantify erosion models such as the USLE.

Figure 5.12 and Figure 5.13 Erosion from wheat fields in Norway (Credit: SCAPE and Anton Imeson).

It is of special interest that in some areas of Europe (notably France, Spain, Portugal, Belgium, the Netherlands, Germany and Italy) there are records showing the long-term positive impact of afforestation and other soil conservation on the sediment load and erosion of rivers (Ternan *et al* 1996). There are several studies of sediment budgets in catchments of different sizes.

Limestone areas with rocky desertification are very extensive, particularly in Spain, Greece, France and Slovenia. Many limestone areas that were formerly barren and occupied by a large number of farmers are now forested. These provide an example of how voluntary depopulation can lead to the recovery of ecosystems. In the case of the Mediterranean region, forest fires increase, stimulated by subsidies that provide income.

Provided that human influence is small, erosion is everywhere limited, with the exception of areas that are geomorphologically unstable and affected by tectonic processes and uplift. Similar types of rock weather into similar types of regolith and soil so that the geology and soils can be used as a basis for transferring information between regions. Areas that are similar geomorphologically and hydrogeologically have many processes and conditions that are similar so that soil conservation strategies and approaches in these areas are comparable.

Conclusion

The main drivers of soil degradation and erosion in Europe today are cultural, ethical and financial that result in society accepting practices and habitual behavior that results in actions that deregulate, destroy and ignore the critical processes in the soil and landscape described. Elsewhere, the illegal or legal use of natural vegetation for wood and charcoal and its conversion into land used for palm oil, coffee, sugar and soy, and so on, are carried out in an unsupervised and unmanaged way. People deprived of their natural and economic capital cause land degradation elsewhere and put pressure on resources. Soil erosion and land degradation are affecting many areas in Europe and occur in association with unsustainable agricultural practices, irrigation, fire, salinization, sodicity and overstocking. On site erosion is particularly prevalent in areas with fragile and sensitive soil conditions, such as those that occur in mountains, in areas affected by sodicity and salinity, and in areas where there are repeated forest fires or overgrazing. Areas affected by uplift caused by isostatic uplift and neo-tectonics are sensitive.

However, in virtually all European countries, soil and land degradation have similar causes. The worst examples of erosion problems are usually associated with land levelling and the construction of terraces. Afforestation programmes whereby trees are planted in areas that are too dry or cold are common and these also cause erosion. Most erosion and land degradation is the result, therefore, of government or EU policies that promote land use change or which tolerate land use practices that degrade the soil structure and its capacity to regulate the hydrological processes. Both Norway and Portugal, four thousand kilometres apart, have policies that support and subsidize wheat production in areas that are unsuitable.

5.13 Case 7: Human impact in the Central Cordillera of Columbia

Twenty years ago a project was set up by Van der Hammen and others to describe and record the characteristics of the ecosystems present along a transect in Columbia running from the Ria Magdalena in the east to the River Cauca in the west. This was one of a number of studies in Columbia that were made to establish and describe conditions in areas that were then largely forested but the forest areas were being lost at a very rapid rate. Detailed information about this specific case study can be found in the Imeson and

Vis (1982). The data are interesting because they illustrate and synthesize very clearly many of the relationships described earlier in the present book.

Along the transect, the following altitudinal zones were described by Imeson and Vis at p. 42. The transect crosses:

- The paramo at 3800 to 4700 m.

- The Andean Forest, 2400 to 3800 m.

- The Sub Andean Forest, 1500–2400 m.

- The warm tropical lowland below 1150 m.

Imeson and Vis examine the effects of forest clearance on soil erodibility and soil erosion rates. They state that most of the changes in soil characteristics that affect soil erodibility are related to changes in the soil micro climate. This is exactly the same as in Mediterranean case studies. The insulating effect of the vegetation and litter is eliminated so that the amount of incoming radiation reaching the ground surface increases. The rate of decay of soil organic matter increases considerably. The decreasing loss of organic matter is also caused by the lower rate of net primary production.

5.14 Case 8: Bolivia Tarije

Present-day environmental change and environmental degradation in the Central Andes have been attributed mainly to post-colonial intensification of land use and subsequent population increase (Libermann Cruz and Qayum, 1994). However, the influence of pre-Colombian civilizations cannot be excluded and several authors report overgrazing and erosion processes during Inca times (Baied and Wheeler, and Messerli *et al.*, 2000). Moreover, the Central Andes is a tectonically active region which has also been affected by climate change. The Central Andes is, therefore, a relatively dynamic and complex region where the causes of environmental change are difficult to analyse and unravel. The research data were collected in carefully selected target or case study areas in the region around the Central Valley of Tarija, South-Bolivia. This was an ideal location containing the three main types of Central Andes ecosystems within in a relative small area (i.e. sub Andean valley, high Andean plateau (Altiplano) and inter Andean valley). Incorporated into the project objectives was the additional goal of identifying both the degree and causes of land degradation. As long-term monitoring was not feasible and long-term data sets were not available, direct and indirect indicators were used to assess environmental change.

For more detailed investigations, small catchments were selected to study erosion processes at the patch and hill slope scales. Another objective was to relate soil and water quality and vegetation cover with present land uses. By studying the impact of grazing on soil and vegetation properties, the effects of present land use could be evaluated. The main research area in Bolivia is located near the city of Tarija in the south of Bolivia and consists of three distinct ecosystems representative the Central Andes. This includes the sub Andean valleys that lie at the fringe of the eastern ranges where the Andes are bounded by the Amazon or Chaco basin; the extensive highland Andean plateaux (Altiplano); and the inter Andean valleys that cut through the Altiplano. The climate in the sub Andean valleys ranges from semi-arid (679 mm yr^{-1}) in the centre to semi-humid (1000 mm yr^{-1}) near the mountain front. Winters are characterized by a long dry period of eight months and most precipitation falls in high intensity summer storms. Maximum daily precipitation in summer time in the semi-arid area ranges from 20 to 60 mm. In general, the semi-arid zones are situated at lower altitudes between 1800 and 2000 masl and humidity increases with altitude. Climatic conditions on the highland plateau are semi arid and the yearly average is 298 mm. Precipitation falls in the four summer months with daily maxima ranging from 8 mm to 25 mm. The largest area is situated mostly between 3600 and 3900 masl, except for the mountain peaks that reach altitudes of 4700 masl. In the bottom of the inter Andean valley, the climate is semi-arid and the average annual precipitation is about 320 mm. Maximum daily precipitation amounts range from 5 mm to 45 mm and these occur during intense summer thunderstorms. The inter Andean valleys follow an altitudinal gradient that falls from 3600 masl near the Altiplano to 2600 masl in the valley bottom.

5.15 The sediment load and soil erosion

The sediment load of rivers can provide information about on-site soil erosion. It enables the nature and the sources of sediment to be to some extent identified. Any increase in sediment load can be used to identify the occurrence of erosion caused by polluters. Problems can be identified by the soil conservation service and dealt with. Sediment is a major carrier of phosphates and other chemicals that cause eutrophication. In the long term, the positive impacts of land management may be demonstrated. The slope of the sediment discharge–water discharge rating curve will become less steep and this will be an indication that conditions in the entire catchment are better. The reasons why the sediment load is not ideal are several. Relationships between sediment concentrations and hydrological parameters (precipitation, discharge or peak discharge) are highly variable because of the different processes that influence the supply of sediment to the river, the composition and nature of the sediment (organic matter, size distribution, mineralogy, etc.) and the erosivity and erodibility of the soil). An unknown percentage of the eroded soil will be deposited on the slopes and remain as colluvium. Channel erosion will also contribute much sediment to the river. Paddy fields also retain a large amount of sediment but this is not the case for upland rice. This means that the statistical strength of the relationships will be weak. The accuracy of both discharge and sediment yield measurements is low. This is because much sediment is transported at high flows. The accuracy of runoff measurements is probably no more than 90 per cent and the sediment yield calculations could be easily a factor of 2 to 5 in error.

The USLE, erosion models and sediment yields

As long ago as 1951, Anderson *et al.* established that there were good statistical relationships between erosion as calculated by the USLE and the long-term accumulation of sediment in reservoirs. Anderson (1962) and many others have established very strong statistical relationships between catchment characteristics, including geology and land use, etc.., so that they could predict erosion. The problem is that relationships change in time as conditions in drainage basins alter. There have been many recent studies in which erosion models, based on the USLE or other models, have been used to predict erosion. Recently an intermodal comparison of erosion models used data supplied by, amongst others, the author, and concluded that the models only worked when utilized by the people who developed them for their own area. There is not enough data on real erosion rates to calibrate most models and they usually exclude important processes. Under ideal conditions (detailed images, trained staff, sufficient budget including for field verification, and calibration), it is possible to use GIS and to estimate erosion and the changes that will occur as a result of management including soil conservation. The question is then which parameters can be entered into the model and how are the processes parametized? It or any model could be used to calculate what the effect of the changes on erosion might be. However, a DTM can be used to model the impact of slope on runoff generation and this is used to obtain a spatial representation of erosion. The advantages of the approach are more in the ability to apply GIS and model scenarios, rather than in any additional accuracy that would be hard to demonstrate as there is no data.

5.16 Monitoring methods to verify impact and management on erosion

There are many alternative approaches to monitoring the reduction in soil erosion that make use of on-site measurements. In considering these, consideration is given to the spatial and temporal scales being considered and also to the different types of processes involved. Sometimes indicators or indexes can be used that have been demonstrated to have value. In Table 5.1, there is an overview of the different erosion processes and of the techniques and methods that are often used to investigate them.

Rainfall simulation experiments are a valuable tool in directly estimating the amount of erosion caused by different rainfall amounts and intensities. Many countries such as Israel, Spain and the USA have made intensive surveys of infiltration and erosion indicators using simulators. These measurements can be used to validate indicators. Another use is to measure and compare soils according to the amount of rainfall needed to cause water to pond on the soil and produce overland flow. They can be used to measure differences in erodibility and to estimate the erodibility (k factor). The USLE ignores many of the processes that result in the delivery of sediment to the river. When monitoring erosion, it is advisable to be able to have methods that also quantify the rates of processes shown in the table (see Table 5.1).

Other concepts are now being used that have many advantages. These include the notion of land quality and health. In addition it is useful to have some measurements that give an overall index of the state or health of the monitoring site. It is also useful to perform the FAO soil profile descriptions. As explained in the Rangeland Health methodology (see Chapter 4).

Table 5.1   Methods of measuring the different processes or erosion (Credit: Anton Imeson).

Erosion process or factor	Simple monitoring approach method
Splash erosion and creep	Splash cups
	Splash boards
Rainwash by overland flow	A. Rainfall simulator (distilled water or rainfall) Amount of sediment, sediment concentration time to ponding, time to runoff, surface roughness, air entrapment plot characteristics stones vegetation cover, EC and ph
	B. Open plots and gutters, tracers, plot
	C. Closed plots
Surface crusting and slaking	Crust description
	Slaking index
	Dispersion test
	Aggregate stability
	Aggregate size and shape
Erodibility	Soil stability
	Liquid and Plastic limits
	Swelling (Swelling limit, Shrinkage limit)
	Swelling test
Cover	Stones and vegetation
	Protection from shading
Rill erosion	Rill description and measurement
	Mechanical strength and soil moisture
	Air photos
	Continuity of runoff and sinks and sources
Gully erosion	Gully erosion
	Type of gully
Tunnel erosion.	Soil profile characteristics, sodium
	Dispersion and swelling
Soil water retention and storage capacity	Water capacity of the soil
	Soil depth and
	Soil Compaction
	Soil rock fragment and root content

Table 5.1 (*continued*)

Erosion process or factor	Simple monitoring approach method
Soil stability	Pores (stable and unstable)
	Permeability
Runoff and sediment source areas	Rainfall Acceptance:
	Infiltration rate
	Permeability
	Sorptivity
	Patterns in the above in relation to vegetation
Human actions	For example, tillage erosion

5.17 Water resource development irrigation as responses

One of the main strategies for developing dry regions is water development. A major difficulty is that this brings with it great cost and economic sacrifice because the existing water resources are well known and have been use for generations. Economic feasibility is always a consideration, particularly when public money is used and projects tend to be greater than would be the case if local people alone were involved. The evaluation by farmers is crucial because the farmers must also invest money and time and there is always uncertainty about the market conditions. For a government, the impact of irrigated agriculture on the general level of economic activity is a main benefit. The main costs are the development of groundwater resources and irrigation system but there will be other impacts on things such as hydro electric power generation, the navigability of the river, and so on. The main negative impact however, will be in the diminished river flow and the poor quality of the irrigation water return flow. Commercial and sport fishing, as well as recreational activities such as rafting, will also be affected. Such impacts are very common everywhere and many rivers are in a degraded and desertified condition. Fluvial geomorphologists who record the hydrologic geometry of rivers have observed that the average river channel in the United States since the advent of irrigated agriculture has been reduced from about 100 metres to 10 metres during the last century. Water prices do not reflect in any way the real cost of irrigation or water abstraction for cities in dry regions. Often only the private benefits are considered.

Management of aquifers

One of the biggest drivers of desertification is the over exploitation of groundwater so that water levels decline, springs dry up and river channels disappear, carrying water that is 90 per cent effluent. The decision to exploit aquifers is a management problem. One universally agreed approach is that of the safe yield concept. This involves only pumping the same amount of water that will be replaced by recharge during the next water year. To exploit a greater amount of water is to be participating in mining. However, this is justified because heavy precipitation that occurs once every one or two decades should recharge the aquifer. This ignores the negative impact on the river ecosystem and the other functions. It is also risky because the high rainfall might not occur. There is a great contrast in the risks and management according to whether or not there are laws enacted and regulations that guard against over exploitation.

The key to desertification control and rehabilitation and increased productivity in the Near and Middle East lies in the management of the hydrological cycle (see Arar and Huss 2000).

According to some observations between 1954 and 1975, the desert southern boundary had shifted in the Sudan southwards by 90 to 100 km. Desertification manifests itself in the water logging and salinization of irrigated land, declining water tables and increased groundwater salinity. The main causes of this are poor land and water management at the field level. This has been a recurring problem since ancient times. In many parts of the Near and Middle East, irrigation has provided an initial benefit which was soon lost and farmers' incomes and living standards have dropped as farmers have had to abandon land as it becomes infertile. Any expansion of irrigation faces severe problems of natural salinity in the soils and water. It was estimated that Pakistan is losing 20 000 ha per year as a result of salinity.

Many areas have been recovered by the well-known method of constructing tube wells and draining the soil and leaching the salts and adding gypsum.

In simple hydrogeological situations, changes in the depth of groundwater depth cause an increased head of pressure in an aquifer which causes an increase in discharge at a spring. Groundwater recharge occurs when the amount of rainfall is such that it is enough to infiltrate through the soil and percolate to the groundwater. Percolation may occur very slowly though pores or rapidly along preferential joints or cracks in the rock. When percolating water reaches the groundwater, the water table rises so that there is a change in groundwater depth. This rise also leads to a rise in the groundwater level in valley bottoms or depressions where springs might reappear and rivers might flow again.

Springs can occur where the groundwater table intersects the surface. The disappearance of springs means that there has been less groundwater recharge or increased groundwater withdrawal.

The duration of zero flow in rivers has been used as an indicator of water resource availability in northern China.

5.18 Soil conservation principles and erosion

When planning soil conservation, principles used should be in relation to processes and make use of the adaptive management approach framework. This is probably the best practice for achieving integration of soil conservation measures across scales in space and time. There are several fundamental principles of soil conservation that apply universally. For water erosion by rainwash:

1 Principle: Protecting the soil from the impact force of rain and from the erosive force of wind, for example by using vegetation, plant remains, stones, or mulch. This prevents

crusting, promotes infiltration and fertility as well as the stability and resilience of the soil. *Best practice is to keep vegetation and rock fragment cover above 70 per cent.*

2 Principle: Keep rainfall on the slope, ensure that the soil is managed so that it can retain all water and that there is a high rainfall acceptance rate. Differentiate between different types of runoff generation process. *Best practice is to promote soil structure, soil health, organic matter, shading and manipulate stone and pore size distribution.*

3 Principle: Promote soil resilience. *Best practices avoid herbicides that promote erodibility, promote organic farming, promote heterogeneity (sinks and sources of runoff), reduce evaporation by manipulating soil and using hydrophobicity, stones, etc.*

4 Principle: Promote the depth of rain infiltration and reduce evaporation. *Best practice promotes soil stability, use stones and terra cotta, worms, avoid compaction. Keep in mind that under certain conditions, such as land slide prone slopes, increasing infiltration should be avoided.*

5 Principle: Avoid dispersion of clay which can dramatically lower infiltration rates. *Best practice, manage soil chemistry so that clays are flocculated, monitor soil structure and stability. Make allowance for seasonal differences in soil – water properties and interactions.*

6 Principle: Disturb the soil as little as possible and avoid compaction: *Best practice involves minimum or reduced tillage, avoiding compaction and use of heavy machinery, promoting soil life, not inverting soil profile (allow B or C horizon material on the surface).*

7 Principle: Avoid concentration of runoff water, if there is no erosion-protected (e.g. grassed) water way.

For water erosion by rill, channel and gully erosion:

1 Principle: Rills can form above a compacted subsoil. *Best practice: avoid compaction and don't create macro pores in soil that has a low stability.*

2 Principle: Gullies and rills form by the advance of headcuts. *Best practice: avoid critical conditions of flow with a Froude number above 1; avoid soil crusting and clay dispersion.*

3 Principle: Slopes: The Horton runoff model is only sometimes valid. The USLE says that erosion increases with slope steepness and length. In practice this is only on gently sloping farmland. There is no relationship between slope angle and erosion for slopes steeper than those for which the USLE was developed. *Look at the processes and sinks and sources of runoff and sediment, look for runoff caused by piping, subsurface saturation overland flow and overland flow caused by rapid groundwater rise.*

4 Principle: Manage the sediment balance of the whole catchment and understand the interactions between slopes and river channels. *Dangerous practice: Do not just reduce the amount of sediment entering a channel without evaluating the impact of this on channel erosion or the river might erode its channel and undermine bridges.*

5 Principle: Erosion at seepage points often causes gullies and landslides to occur. *Best practice: Avoid steep long slopes where unsaturated flow-lines converge and saturated areas develop (as on road cuttings). Be aware of the subsoil hydrology.*

5.19 Conceptual approaches to soil conservation

Some of the concepts that are currently being used for soil conservation applications are described here. Concepts are helpful for engaging with stake holders and for motivating and discussing soil conservation actions being taken.

Many conservation scientists have been trained to explain erosion in terms of the different factors responsible. This was the approach of the approach of the US Soil Conservation Service and it is operationalized by means of the Universal Soil Loss Equation (USLE) which considers the factors of rainfall and runoff erosivity, soil erodibility, slope, cover and management.

USLE (Universal Soil Loss Equation)

The USLE approach (also of the Revised USLE) was developed in the 1930s to evaluate and use soil erosion plot data statistically. The equation estimates a theoretical long-term rate of erosion – not the actual amount of erosion caused by an individual storm. It is a management tool. Wischmeier (1976) who developed the approach and was so worried about how it was being applied that he wrote an article entitled the 'Use and misuse of the Universal Soil Loss Equation'. It can be used for soil loss on slopes to demonstrate the possible benefit of conservation farming but the approach is not developed for monitoring nor for use in GIS. The USLE is not suitable for sediment balance or sediment delivery if the aim is management. Within specific contexts it could be helpful as a way of analysing the impact of changes in vegetation cover and rainfall in catchments. In the equation, the vegetation cover (C factor) is by far the most quantitatively important term, and this is why it is often a very practical tool while at the same time the C factor is critical but quite easy to estimate.

There was conceptually a great leap forward when systems paradigms were applied to explain erosion. Dynamic systems models could be developed linking hydrology, vegetation, erosion and land use. These models were developed at first for individual plants and in two dimensions. Gradually, they were used in dynamic GIS, as decision support tools. They could have outputs at different hierarchical levels.

Human impact on key processes

The paradox is that most many of the actions being taken to protect the soil and save biodiversity, although motivated by good intentions, have inadvertent consequences and cause damage to soil functions.

Figure 5.14   Soil erosion is important because it carries phosphates. Buffer strips protect the water because they trap eroded sediment (Credit: SCAPE excursion, Norway and Anton Imeson).

Successful approaches to managing land degradation and erosion at the catchment and river basin scale have taken consideration of the links that exist between problems of erosion and sedimentation on the one hand and the slow changes that are taking place as a result of tectonic movements, on the other. Figure 5.14 shows a soil conservation scientist demonstrating how the successful buffer strip concept is being applied in Norway. They trap sediment and the phosphate adsorbed to it, successfully improving the quality of river and lake water. What is important is the connectivity that exists between the slope and river channel and how this is influenced by people. For a theoretical consideration of this, the conceptual paper by Fryirs *et al.* (2007) is useful as a means of illustrating how the long-term interrelationships between land use change that causes erosion and the long-term movement of sediment through river channels works.

When we consider a river system, then the first approach is to identify the connectivity that exists between the erosion processes on the slope and the river channel. They describe how what are called **buffers, barriers** and **blankets** disrupt the continuity of processes along the river and on the slope, creating systems that have their linkages disrupted. Buffers, barriers and blankets decouple the erosion on the slope from the primary sediment conveyor belt. The authors use this model as a means of interpreting the different responses to rivers that are observed in the field.

What these authors do is to give a **functional** description. This feature maybe thought of as an example of patterns and structures that occur in river channels. Processes that influence the creation of such buffers include mass movements, floods, earthquakes and human activities in the river channels.

When a river is examined, it is evident that the sediment in the flood plain and river channel may have been there for very long indeed. The residence time varies from a few years to millions of years, according to the context. Buffer strips along rivers Figure 5.13

are extremely effective in filtering sediment and phosphates from slope runoff. They have had a very big positive impact in Norway in reducing river contamination. This photograph was taken during an excursion looking at the best practices being used.

Systems approaches and dynamic GIS

Examples of systems based approaches are the many dynamic systems and chaos theory models that show that erosion is sensitive to the initial soil moisture conditions. You can never know the initial soil moisture conditions well enough to know what will happen and be able to predict erosion. In dynamic GIS, models developed by the modellers, erosion and vegetation growth patterns are linked at different scales to economic models and agent based approaches. The problem is that stakeholders are not really able to take advantage of them because the organizations for whom they are developed do not have people who are really able to use them. Institutional frameworks and management are needed to be able to take advantage of them in practice. They enable the effects of land use change to be seen. They might be a good approach to looking at the impact of different soil conservation scenarios on the sediment supply or sediment budgets of large watersheds.

Models such as those mentioned require information about real world hydrological and erosion processes so that these can be parameterized. At the detailed scale, studying the infiltration process using rainfall simulators, open run-off plots, tracers or pattern analysis can be valuable.

Infiltration envelope

The infiltration (envelope) approach pioneered in Israel and America is in many ways very practical and efficient because it enables areas of runoff production to be linked to the intensity-depth-area precipitation data. Different soils respond to erosion and runoff in different ways and this varies seasonally. 'The response of soils to rainfall' approach involves estimating or measuring parameters such as sorptivity, 'time to runoff' and time to 'ponding'. These can be linked to changes in soil structure and to soil chemistry. These approaches have been developed by several research groups in Spain and The Netherlands and elsewhere (see Chapter 3 and Chapter 4).

In this approach, the fundamental concept is that of the 'hydrological or erosion response unit'. It has been found that when erosion occurs in areas that were once sinks (infiltration, accumulation of sediment) are transformed into sources. Sinks and sources occur at different scales. How do soil conservation works affect sediment sinks and sources? This is easy to evaluate with photographs, rainfall simulation and pattern analysis using simple indicators.

Desertification response units and sinks and sources

The sink and source area concept looks at patterns of runoff and sediment production and deposition on slopes and it was described in Chapter 3 and Chapter 4.

Patterns are indicators of processes. If this is known, there is no need to measure discharges; it is enough to monitor patterns. This is a great advantage because fluxes are in any case sensitive to initial conditions. Potential impacts and risk can be evaluated more accurately and effectively from patterns and structures.

The adaptive management approach places soil conservation within the framework of interacting socio-economic, cultural and bio-physical systems (Chapter 1). There is a state in which no erosion occurs and one in which erosion happens. This involves the interaction between people and their environment. There are state-and-transition-models developed in the USA. It can be shown to the farmer, for example, how his actions affect the processes in ways that result in the system remaining in a healthy state. The adaptive cycle explains the phenomenon of the accumulation release of resources in four distinct stages. Management should be appropriate to the existing stage of the cycle.

Adaptive management response

The adaptive management framework is implicitly being applied to integrate policy, processes in interacting human terms and physical systems.

France is, without specifically using the term, applying the adaptive management approach. French engineers manage the flows of sediment in rivers in a way that takes account of the interactions between hill slope and river channel dynamics over periods of at least 150 years. In Spain, the government and regions have many institutions in place that are responsible for managing sediment and erosion. These include the Government research council organizations and the hydrological services.

Applying an adaptive management framework to soil conservation could save billions of dollars because conservation measures can be tailor-made and geographically explicit. Adaptive management includes treating watersheds as systems in which there are feedbacks between land use, hydrology and sediment transport.

There are many actions that can be taken that improve the resilience of the system and reduce the chance that an area will change from one that is in a non-eroding state to one with a risk of erosion. Mulching with stones and vegetation and improving the soil as a habitat for soil fauna are effective actions that could be taken. Creating shade and heterogeneity are important, as are avoiding compaction and putting subsoil on the surface. Most Europeans have learned to value the cultural and other benefits of non farmed land around cities or elsewhere and the managers have adapted to the requirements of urban people for recreation and experiences in nature. The general response has been to manage forests and natural areas in ways that promote and diversify the functions they provide. With respect to farming there has been a response favoring either organic farming, or more intensive agriculture. The first is often part of a bottom up local economy but associated with high value products, the second to external investments and low value products for supermarkets.

References and further reading

Agassi, M., I. Shainberg and J. Morin (1981) Effect of electrolyte concentration and soil sodicity on infiltration rate and crust formation. *Soil Science Society of America* 45: 848–851.

Allen, T.F.H., R.V. O'Neill and T. W. Hoekstra (1984) *Interlevel relations on ecological research and management: Some working principles from Hierarchy Theory*. General Tech Report RM 110. Rocky Mountain Forest and Range Experimental Station, 11 pp.

Ambers, R.K.R., D.L. Druckenbrod and C.P. Ambers (2006) Geomorphic response to historical agriculture at Monument Hill in the Blue Ridge foothills of Central Virginia. *Catena* 65: 49–60.

Anderson, H.W. (1951) Physical characteristics of soils related to erosion. *Journal of Soil and Water Conservation*: 129–133.

Anderson H. W and Faust S.D. (1963) *Changes in quality of water in the Passaic River at Little Falls, New Jersey as shown by long term data:* U.S. Geological Survey Professional Paper 525 D p D214–D218

Baied, C. A. and J. C. Wheeler (1993) Evolution of High Andean Puna Ecosystems: Environment, climate, and culture change over the last 12,000 ears in the Central Andes. *Mountain Research and Development*, 13(2): 145–156.

Ben-Hur, M., I. Shainberg, D. Bakker and R. Keren (1985) Effect of soil texture and CaCO3 content on water infiltration in crusted soils related to water salinity. *Irrigation Science* 6: 281–294.

Bradford, J.M., P.A. Remley, J.E. Ferris and B. Santini (1986) Effect of soil surface sealing on splash from a single water drop. *Soil Science Soc America* 50: 1547–1552.

Bolt, G.H. and F.F.R. Koenigs (1972) Physical and chemical aspects of the stability of soil aggregates. *Mededling Fakulteit Landbouwwetenschappen State University of Ghent Belgium* 37: 955–973.

Chinen, T. (1987) Hillslope erosion after a forest fire in Etajima Island Southwest Japan. *Processus et mesure de l'érosion. Ed du CNRS* 1990210.

Chirono, E., A. Bonet, J. Bellot and J.R. Sanchez (2006) The effects of a 30-year old Aleppo pine plantation on runoff, soil erosion and plant diversity in a semi-arid landscape in south eastern Spain. *Catena* 65 (1): 19–25.

Churchwood, H.M. and R.H. Gumm (1983) Stripping of deep weathered mantles and its significance to soil patterns, pp. 73–81, in Thompson, Moore and Northcote, *Soils and Land Use in Soils: An Australian Viewpoint*. Division of Soils, CSIRO, Melbourne.

Clarke M.A. and R.P.D. Walsh (2006) Long-term erosion and surface roughness change of rain-forest terrain following selective logging, Danum Valley, Sabah Malaysia *Catena* 109–123.

Cook G.D and R.C. (1992) Structural degradation of vertisols under continuous cultivation. *Soil and Tillage Research* 24, 47–64.

Corbane, C., P.M. Andrieux, J. Voltz, *et al.* (2008) Assessing the variability of soil surface characteristics in row cropped fields: the case of Mediterranean vineyards in Southern France. *Catena* 72: 79–90.

Crouch, R.J. (1976) Field tunnel erosion: A review. *Soil Conservation Journal of New South Wales* 98: 111.

Dalal, R.C. and Mayer, R.J. (1987) Long-term trends in fertility of soils under continuous cultivation and cereal cropping in Southern Queensland. 1. Overall changes and trends in winter cereal yields. *Au Journal of Soil Research* 24: 265–279.

Daniels, L.G. (1989) Degradation and restoration of soil structure in a cracking grey clay used for cotton production. *Australian Journal of Soil Research* 27: 455–469.

Descroix, L. and E. Gautier. (2002) Water erosion in the southern French Alps: climatic and human mechanisms. *Catena* 50(1): 53–85.

Dorren, L., F. Berger, A.C. Imeson, *et al.* (2004) Integrity, stability and management of protection forests in the European Alps. *Forest Ecology and Management* 195(1–2): 165–176.

Emerson, W.W. (1967) Inter particle bonding, pp. 477–498, in Thompson, Moore and Northcote, *Soils and Land Use in Soils: An Australian Viewpoint*. Division of Soils, CSIRO, Melbourne.

Epstein, E. and W.J. Grant (1967) Soil losses and crust formation as related to some soil physical properties. *Soil Science Soc Amer Proc* 31: 547–550.

Froehlich, W (1991) Sediment production from unmetalled road surfaces Sediment and Stream Water Quality in a Changing Environment: Trends and Explanation Proceedings of the Vienna Symposium, August 1991) *IAHS Publ*. no. 203, 1991.

Fryirs, KA., G.J. Brierley, N.J. Preston and M. Kasai (2007). Buffers, barriers and blankets. The (dis)continuity of catchment scale sediment cascades. *Catena* 70, 49–67.

Garcia Alvarez, A. and J.J. Ibanez (1994) Seasonal fluctuations and crop influence on microflora and enzyme activity in fully developed soils of Central Spain. *Arid Soil Research and Rehabilitation*, 8: 161–178.

Golodets, C. and N. Boeken (2006) Moderate sheep grazing in semiarid shrubland alters small-scale soil surface structure and patch properties. *Catena* 65: 285–291.

Goreham, E. (1961) Factors influencing supply of major ions into inland waters, with special reference to the atmosphere. *Geological Society of America Bulletin* 72: 795–840.

Govers, G. and J. Poesen (1998) Field experiments on the transport of rock fragments by animal trampling on scree slopes, *Geomorphology* 23: 193–203.

Greacen, E. L. and R. Sands (1980) The compaction of forest soils. *Australian Journal of Soil Research* 18 (2): 163–189.

Greacen, E.L. and J. Williams (1983) Physical properties and water relations, pp. 499–530, in Thompson, Moore and Northcote, *Soils and Land Use in Soils: An Australian Viewpoint*. Division of Soils, CSIRO, Melbourne.

Gregorich, E.G., R.G. Kachanoski and R.P. Veroney (1988) Ultrasonic dispersion of aggregates< distribution of organic mattering size fractions. *Can Journal of Soil Sci* 68: 395–403.

Hallsworth, E.G., A.B. Costin and F.R. Gibbons (1953) Studies in pedogenesis in New South Wales. *Journal of Soil Science* 4 (2): 242–255.

Harvey, A., E. M.J. Larsen and M.F. Jurgensen (1981) *Rate of Residue Incorporation into Northern Rocky Mountain Forest Soils*. Research Paper INT 282. Intermountain Forest and Range Experimental Station.

Hargett, O.L. J.A. Phillips and H.J. Kleiss (1982) Soil variability and fertility considerations affecting the establishment of erosion control vegetatopn on Piedmont roadcuts. *Journal of Soil and Water Conservation* 228.

Haycock, N.E. and T.P. Burt (1993) Role of floodplain sediments in reducing the nitrate concentrations of subsurface runoff. A case study in the Cotswolds, UK. *Hydrological Processes* 7 287–295

Herrick, J.E., W.G. Whitford, A.G. de Soyza, *et al.* (2001) Field soil aggregate stability kit for soil quality and rangeland health evaluations, *Catena* 44 27–35.

Hibbert, A.R. (1979) *Managing Vegetation to Increase Flow in the Colorado River Basin*. General Technical Report RM 60. 27 pp.

Ibanez, J.J. and R. Jimenez Ballesta (1990) Sistemos y termodinámica en edafogenesis 1. Los suelos y el estado de equilibro termodinámico. *Rev Ecol Biol Soc* 27 (4): 371–382.

Ibanez, J.J., M.C. Lobo, G. Almendros and A. Polo (1983) Impacto del Fuego sobre algunos ecossistemas edaficos de clima mediterraneao contienental en la zonz centro de Espana. *Boletin de la estacion Central de Ecolgiia* 12 (24): 27–42.

Ibanez J.J., M.C. J.C. Simon sw Benito and R. Jimenez Ballesta (1987) Consideraciones ecológicas acerca de la micro fauna en los pastizales y suelos turbososde la alta montana en el sistema Central Espana. *Boletin de la estacion Central de Ecolgiia* 16 (31): 63–70.

Imeson, A. C. and M. Vis (1982) A Survey of soil erosion processes in tropical forest ecosystems on volcanic soils in the Central Andean Cordil *Geografiska Annaler. Series A, Physical* 64 (3/4).

Ingebo, P.A. (1971) Suppression of Channel side chaparral cover increases streamflow. *Journal of Soil and Water Conservation* 26 (2): 79–81.

Ireland, H.A., C.F.S. Sharpe and D.H. Eargle (1939). Principles of gulley erosion in the Piedmont of South Carolina. *USDA Technical Bullentin* 617–633 p.

Isbell, R.J., R. Reeve and J.T. Hutton (1983) Salt and sodicity, pp. 107–117, in Thompson, Moore and Northcote, *Land Use in Soils: An Australian Viewpoint*. Division of Soils, CSIRO, Melbourne. Australian Viewpoint Division of Soils CSIRO, Melbourne.

Lopez Bermudez, F. (1995) *The Field site: Murcia*, pp. 38–60 in Medalus II Mediterranean Desertification and Land Use, Project 1, Phase II 1993–1985 *Basic Field Programme* Final Report Imeson, A. C. EV5V-CT92-0128, 282p.

Jansson, M.B. (1988) A global survey of sediment yield. *G. Annaler*. 70 Series A. 81–98.

Jungerius P. D. and H. van Zon (1982) The formation of the Lias Cuesta (Luxembourg) in the light of present day processes on forest soils. *G. Annaler* 64 A 3–4: 127–140.

Kadomura, H., T. Imagawa and H. Yamamoto (1983) Eruption induced rapid erosion and mass movements on Usu Volcano Hokkaido. *Zeitschrift fur Geomorfologie* N.F. Supp Bd 46: 123–142.

Kasnin Grubin, M. and R. Bryan (2007) Lithological properties and weathering response on badland hillslopes. *Catena*: 68–78.

Katra, I., H. Lavee and P. Sarah (2008) The effect of rock fragment size and position on topsoil moisture on arid and semi-arid hillslopes. *Catena* 72: 49–55.

Kilgore, M. and G.A. Curtis (1987) *Guide to Understorey Burning in a Ponderosa Pine Larch Fir Forests in the Intermountain West* US Dept of Agriculture General Tech Report INT 233, Ogden UT US Department of Agriculture, Forest Service, Intermountain Research Station 39 pp.

Koenigs, F.F.R. (1961) *The mechanical stability of clay soils as influenced by the moisture conditions and some other factors* PUDOC Wageningen. V.L.O. 67: 7.

Kvaaerno, H.S. and L. Li Olygarden (2001) (eds) *Excursion Guide International Sympossium on Snow melt Erosion and Related Problems*. 59 pp.

Leaf, C.F. (1974) *A Model for Predicting Erosion and Sediment Yield from Secondary Forest Road Construction*. USDA Forest Service Research Note RM 274.

Libermann Cruz and Qayum, S. (1994) *La Desertificación en Bolivia*, LIDEMA, La Paz.

Loveday, J. and B.J. Bridge (1983) The Management of salt affected soils, pp. 843–855 in Thompson, Moore and Northcote, *Soils and Land Use in Soils: An Australian Viewpoint*. Division of Soils, CSIRO, Melbourne.

Ludwig, J.A., D.J. Tongway and D. Freudenberger, *et al.* (1977) *Landscape Ecology: Function and Management*. CSIRO, Melbourne, Australia.

Martinez, J.A. (1976) The evaluation of soil properties as it relates to the genesis of volcanic ash soils in Costa Rica. *Soil Sci Soc AmJ* 40: 895–900.

Meade, R.M. (1969) Errors in using modern stream load data to estimate natural rates of denudation *Geol Soc Americ Bull* 80: 1265–1274.

Messerli, B., M. Grosjean, T. Hofer, L. Nunez and C. Pifster (2000) From nature-dominated to human-dominated environmental changes *Quaternary Science Reviews* 19: 459–479. In: Past Global Changes and their Significance for the Future (ed. K.D. Alverson, F. Oldfield and R.S. Bradley). *Quaternary Science Reviews* 19, Pergamon-Elsevier, No. 1–5: 459–479.

Moore, I.D. and G.J. Burch (1986) Physical basis of the length slope factor in the Universal Soil Loss Equation. *Soil Science Soc Am Journal* 50: 1294–1298.

Naveh, Z. (1992) A landscape ecological approach to urban systems as part of the total human ecosystem. *J. Nat Hist Mus Inst Chiba* 2: 47–52.

Norton, L., D. Schroeder and W.C. Moldenhaeuer (1988) Differences in surface crusting and soil loss as affected by tillage methods, pp. 64–71, *International Symposium on the Assessment of Soil Surface Sealing and Assessment.*

Onda, Y., W.E. Dietrich and F. Booker (2008) Evolution of overland flow after a severe forest fire, Point Reyes, California. *Catena* 72: 1.

Olive, L.J. and W.A. Rieger (1988) Problems of assessing the impact of different forestry practices on coastal catchment in New South Wales, Chapter 14, in *Fluvial Geomorphology of Australia*, pp. 283–302, Academic Press of Australia.

Ploey, J. de and D. Gabriels (1980) Measuring soil loss and experimental studies, pp. 63–108, in M.J. Kirkby and R.P.C. Morgam, *Soil Erosion*, John Wiley and Sons, Ltd, Chichester.

Ploey, J. de and H.J. Mucher (1981) A consistency index and rainwash mechanisms on Belgian loamy soils. *Earth Surface Processes and Landforms* 6: 319–330.

Ploey, D. and A. Yair (1985) Promoted erosion and colluviation. A proposal concerning land management and landscape evolution. *Catena* 12: 105–110.

Poesen, J.W.A. and H. Lavee (1991) Effects of size and incorporation of synthetic mulch on runoff and sediment yield from interills in a laboratory study with simulated rainfall. *Soil and Tillage Research* 21: 209–223.

Puigdefabregas, J. and G. Sanchez (1996) Geomorphological implications of vegetation patchiness on semi arid slopes, Chapter 47, pp. 1027–1060, in *Advances in Hillslope Processes*, John Wiley and Sons, Ltd, Chichester.

Rice, R.M., F.B. Tilley and P.A. Datzman (1979) *A watershed's response to logging and roads: South Fork of Casper Creek, California* 1967–1976. Res Paper PSW-146. 12 pp. U.S. Forest Service Department of Agriculture, Berkeley, California.

Riezebos, P.A. and R.T. Slotboom (1974) Palynology in the study of present day hillslope development. *Geologie en Mijnbouw* 53: 436–448.

Riley, S. J. (1980) Implications of current models of runoff production to soil conservation practice. *Geographical Survey* 9: 1.

Riley, S.J. (1984) Effect of clearing and roading operations on the permeability of forest soils, Karuah catchment, New South Wales. *Forest Ecology and Management* 9: 283–293.

Roxo, M.J. (2009) Lucinda *Land Care in Desertification Affected Areas from Science to Application* EU Project (http://geografia.fcsh.unl.pt/lucinda/).

Rubio, J.L., M. Sala, R. Josa and R. Cerni, R. (1991) (eds) *Excursion Guide-book. Conference on Soil Erosion and Degradation as a Consequence of Forest Fire*, 3–7 September 1991, Barcelona-Valencia. ESSC (European Soc. Soil Conservation). Pub. UIMP.

Sang-Arun, J., M. Mihara, Y. Horaguchi and E. Yamaji (2006) Soil erosion and participatory remediation strategy for bench terraces in northern Thailand. *Catena* 65: 258–264.

Schouten, C.J. (1983) Budget if water and its constituents for Lake Taupo New Zealand. Dissolved loads of rivers and surface water quantity quality relationships. *I.A.S.H. Pub.* 141: 277–297.

Swanson N. P. A.R. Dedrick and H.E. Weakly (1965) Soil particles and aggregates transported in runoff from simulated rainfall. *Trans ASEA* 437–440.

Targulian, V.O. and P.V. Krasilinikov (2007) Soil system and pedogenic processes: self-organisation, time scales and environmental significance. *Catena*, 71: 373–381.

Ternan J.L, A.G. Williams, A. Elmes and R. Hartley (1996) Aggregate stability of soils in Central Spin and the role of land management. *Earth Surface Processes and Landforms* 21: 181–193.

Ternan J., L. A.G. Williams, A. Elmes and C. Fitzjohn (1996) The effectiveness of terracing and afforestation for erosion control on Rana Sediments in Central Spain. *Land Degradation and Development* 7: 337–351.

Ternan, J.L., A.G. Williams, A. Elmes and C. Hartley (1996) Aggregate stability of soils in Central Spain and the role of land management. *Earth Surface Processes and Landforms*: 181–193.

Thompson, C.H., A.W. Moore and K.H. Northcote (1983) *Soils and Land Use in Soils: An Australian Viewpoint*. Division of Soils, CSIRO, Melbourne.

Trimble, S.W. (1974) *Man Induced Soil Erosion on the Southern Piedmont. 1700–1970*. Soil Conservation Society of America, Ankeny, Iowa.

Trimble, S.W. and A. C. Mendel (1995) The cow as a geomorphological agent – a critical review *Geomorphology* 13: 233–253.

Wishmeier, W.H. (1976) Use and misuse of the universal soil loss equation. *Journal of Soil and Water Conservation* 31(1): 5–9.

Xu Jiongxin (2006) Sand dust storms ina and around the Ordos Plateau of China as influenced by land use change and desertification. *Catena*, 65: 279–284.

Yair, A. and Klein, M. (1973) The influence of surface properties on flow and erosion processes on debris covered slopes in an arid area. *Catena* 1: 1–18.

Yair, A. and H. Lavee (1974) An investigation of source areas of sediment and sediment transport by overland flow along arid hillslopes. Erosion and Sediment Transport Measurements proceedings of the Florence Symposium *IAHS* 133, pp. 433–446.

Yair, A. and H. Lavee (1985) Runoff generation in arid and semi arid zones 183–220 *In Hydrological Forecasting*, Eds. Burt T and Anderson. Wiley.

Yair, A., D. Sharon and H. Lavee (1980) Trends in runoff and erosion processes over an arid limestone hillside, Northern Negev, Israel. *Hydrological Sciences Bulletin* 25 (3): 243–255.

Zehetner, F. and W.P. Miller (2006) Erodibility and runoff-infiltration characteristics of volcanic ash soils along an altitudinal climosequence in the Ecudorian Andes. *Catena* 65: 201–213.

6

Responses to land degradation from perception to action

6.1 Introduction

One hundred years ago agriculture could be seen to be having a great impact on land degradation and erosion in the United States of America. This impact resulted in the abandonment and afforestation of huge areas in New England and the Appalachians. Tens of thousands of farmers suffered hardship and left the land. Bennett *et al.* (1936) documented the magnitude and impact of erosion and warned about the consequences if no actions were taken. They were able to set up research stations to quantify the soil loss, both in tons of soil and loss of agricultural production. When the extension of rain fed farming extended into the semi-arid areas of the mid-west where rains were unreliable, the loss of the vegetation and top soil enabled wind erosion to remove vast amounts of the exposed subsoil. For weeks, dust darkened the skies in areas as far away as Washington, polluting homes and motivating the setting up and financing of the United States Soil Conservation Service.

Bennett pointed out:

> It seems to take something like a disaster to awaken people who have been accustomed to great national prosperity, such as ours, to the presence of a national menace. Although we were slowly coming to realize that soil erosion was a major national problem, even before that great dust storm, it took that storm to awaken the nation as a whole to some realization.

His response and that of others was to perform the necessary actions that resulted in the implementation of soil conservation and protection legislation and the establishment of the United States Soil Conservation Service. Figure 6.1. showing the dust storm approaching Stratford is an iconic image and haunting reminder of the Great Dust Bowl and Depression. Dust storms are today a major source of atmospheric dust and influence clouds and rainfall.

Professor Pim Jungerius (2006) stated, in connection with The Netherlands:

> Up to the 1960s–70s land use in The Netherlands was largely soil dependent. Now grasslands and maize are grown everywhere independent of soil type. Growing

Desertification, Land Degradation and Sustainability, First Edition. Anton Imeson.
© 2012 John Wiley & Sons, Ltd. Published 2012 by John Wiley & Sons, Ltd.

Figure 6.1 Dust storm approaching Stratford, Texas. Dust bowl surveying in Texas. (Image ID: theb1365, Historic C&GS Collection. Location: Stratford, Texas (Photo Date: April 18, 1935. Credit: NOAA).

maize is considered normal even on low-lying alluvial grounds bordering brooks, or on peat soils. Peat , which contains maybe 90 per cent moisture must be kept wet and prevented from irreversibly drying into light aggregates that are easily blown by the wind.

Setting and oxidation of peat soils can only be limited if water levels in Summer are within 25 cm of the ground surface. But water levels are kept lower for purposes of grass production and carrying capacity. Through oxidation, a considerable percentage of the lowland peat areas is in danger of disappearing within the next decades, including the important geological information they contain about sea level and climatic changes and their ecological functions. Increased CO_2 production, sea level rise and encroachment of settlements are some of the other problems the peatlands are facing. This has already happened in many places, for example in the Fenlands of England.

While at one time cattle from Denmark and the North of Germany were brought here to be fattened up for the markets of Holland and even Antwerp, now economic production is hardly possible in many of the peat areas. Sheep instead of cows now dominate these characteristic Dutch peat-grasslands that are rich in ditches. Even nature organizations have financial problems managing these areas and consider turning them into forest swamps and reed lands. Although this is a more sustainable use from the point of view of peat restoration and preventing oxidation, CO_2 production and loss of geological information, many of these grasslands are Natura 2000 areas for meadow birds such as the black-tailed godwit of which 90 per cent of the west European population breeds in The Netherlands. Furthermore, they are the most traditional and characteristic Dutch landscape, often having kept Early Medieval parcelling.

In China, the principles and methods of sustainable land and water management have been probably known for at least six thousand years. The sustainable management of land and water resources requires that the design and management of things that involve the land should be harmonious with critical natural processes that conform to the principles of physics, chemistry and nature.

Sustainability criteria

For actions and responses to be sustainable they must conform to the holistic scrutiny of the single system perspective:

• The actions should address the causes not the impacts.

• They must be at multiple levels and different scales.

• They must be wanted and understood by society.

• They should be explained in terms of functions, capital or services.

• They must consider change.

• They must preserve soil functions for future generations. (Bruntland)

Table 6.1 taken from Van der Ancker and Jungerius (2006) is useful as it provides an overview of the pressures and causes to which research is responding in policy cycles.

6.1.1 Searching for reality in case studies

Identifying and evaluating Soil Conservation and Protections Strategies for Europe was one of the objectives of SCAPE (see Imeson *et al*. 2007) which had the goal of supporting scientifically the development of European Soil Protection law. It approaches case studies for a range of different purposes. By focusing discussion on concrete real examples, more insight is obtained into the true nature of the issues that are being faced. The real examples being studied can be used to focus the exchange and development of ideas. Most case studies were either used to identify successful actions and strategies or to examine particular topics that the researchers' attention became focused on as the project developed. Case studies were also used from other countries to see how they had dealt with soil protection. They formed a south–north transect from Alicante in the South to Oslo in the North. Case studies revealed many common strategies that have been used with success.

Attention was given to understanding in these case study areas which actions had been successful and which had failed. The aspects discussed ranged from finance, policy and economic instruments to technical and ecological measures of soil conservation. Case studies outside of Europe enabled an evaluation to be made of, for example, the development of soil conservation in Australia, the USA and Israel.

Table 6.1   The developments in soil science in response to threats and forces in society (Adapted from Van der Ancker (2006)).

Date	Problems	Threats	Driving Forces	Soil R
19th century	Nutrient depletion, adverse effects of the introduction of artificial fertilizers	Loss of production	Securing and increasing food production, population pressure	Study of the effects of fertilizers; start of soil science, defining soil as a system
19th century	Land reclamation in colonial areas and agro-economic advice		Economic gain, population pressure	Soil maps and soil suitability maps
1930s	Dust bowls	Loss of agricultural land	Food security, loss of a livelihood for many farmers	Start of soil erosion and soil conservation research
20th century	Gullying of agricultural lands, flooding	Damage to infrastructure, houses, cars and some loss of agricultural production	Prevention of damage and costs	Research on infiltration, overland flow, sealing, soil structure, gullying
Mid 20th century	Development aid	Famine, nutrient depletion of agricultural grounds, loss of lands through soil erosion	Improvement of living conditions in developing countries, population pressure	Soil surveys and soil suitability maps, soil erosion and soil conservation research
Mid 20th century	Land re-allotment, advice on specific soil problems	–	Improvements in cost of production, government guided land use changes	Soil maps and soil suitability maps for land planning, development of ecosystem thinking
Second half 20th century	Toxic chemical pollution	Risk for human health	Diseases and fear of diseases	Soil research on toxic levels, indicators and criteria and cleaning techniques

Second half 20th century	Excessive acids and nutrients N and P, directly but also through atmospheric deposition, salinization as a consequence of irrigation	Pollution of drinking water, health risks, algae bloom, disappearance of flora and fauna from nature areas	Safeguarding high quality and quantity of drinking water, preventing human and animal diseases, safeguarding biodiversity	Research on soil–water interactions, development of computer models, effects of acids, pH, N, P and salt levels on water quality, flora and fauna, criteria, levels and indicators
Start of the 21st century	Health of the soil system	Degraded soil systems, loss of biodiversity	Securing future food production, minimizing adverse effects and reversing deterioration of agricultural and natural soil systems, soil health	Research on soil fauna, humic substances, sealing, soil structure
Start of the 21st century	Mainstreaming into other policies	Loss of flora and fauna caused by changes in the soil system, loss of sites and areas with scientific, educational, historical and aesthetical values, large-scale loss of spatial variation and traditional and characteristic landscapes, water management problems	Minimizing adverse effects by using the qualities of the different soil systems instead of changing the soil qualities to fit our purposes; conserving the history of the land(scape) for scientific and educational purposes and as quality of our daily living environment and for touristic purposes; recovering of lost qualities	Research on ecological soil management and regional soil system development; on soil as part of nature areas and the small-scale relationships between soil qualities, geological and geomorphological processes and flora and fauna; appointing benchmark soils for sustainable agriculture; conservation of natural and cultural heritage soils; research on techniques to integrate geodiversity and geoheritage in spatial planning and land management from governmental up to farm level through concepts such as resilience, sustainable use and panarchy

The case study sites were:

- Alicante (ES) which is representative for the Mediterranean biogeographic region located in the dry Mediterranean zone.

- Cinque Terra (IT), representative for the Mediterranean/continental biogeographic region, located in the humid Mediterranean zone.

- The Montafon region (AT), representative for the Alpine biogeogaphic region.

- Southern Norway, representative for the Boreal biogeographic region.

All of these areas were considered to be environmentally sensitive areas. Climate, slope or rock type as well as socio-economic circumstances meant that there were many threats to the soils present in these areas.

The Alicante and Murcia case study in Spain was interesting because the region is undergoing many rapid changes in land use. A lot of data is available on the different threats facing the soil. The results are available from many past or ongoing EU or national research projects. The region also contains badlands. The region is within the Target Area of the Spanish National Action Plan of the UNCCD. Tourism and irrigated agriculture are the main economic activities. Formerly dry land farming was very important activity. Large areas have been abandoned and are now covered with scrub or forest. Large areas are also frequently subject to wildfires. The field visit was organized jointly with other sister projects concerned specifically with restoration (REACTION) or desertification (MEDRAP)

The SCAPE excursion visited a large restoration project. The climate is semi-arid but there is a large inter-annual variability in precipitation so that there are often periods with droughts or relatively high intensity rainfall.

The Cinque Terra, (Italy) case study enabled a consideration of terraced management to be examined. The three illustrations in Figure 6.2 show a) the situation at one site in 1950, b) in 2000 and c) in 2010. The abandonment of terraced land is very common in many Mediterranean areas and on steep slopes the terraces and the soils they retain can be lost to erosion and landslides. Terraces as a case study were compared from different areas, including Malta, Turkey and North Africa. The Cinque Terra region was made into a National Park and has the status of a UNESCO world heritage. How the park status helped the region to protect its landscape and to prevent the degradation of the terraces is without doubt an important example for other regions. In many parts of the world National Parks with thousands of visitors provide an instrument not just for protecting the soil but also for informing visitors about the issues at hand. The strategies many National and Regional Parks enact in Canada and the USA could serve as a model for Europe. The aim is to help people experience and understand the heritage value of the soil and landscape and this can only be done first hand.

Landslides occurring in Mediterranean areas, often linked with degradation of the vegetation cover and poor maintenance of cultural landscapes due to land abandonment, have raised the attention of decision makers in many countries (Figure 6.2).

The Montafon region (Austria) **case study** studied the specific problems of mountain areas. Mountain soils can be very vulnerable to erosion and compaction and mass

Figure 6.2 Land degradation in the area of the Cinque Terre UNESCO world heritage site due to land abandonment. Left: Terraced landscape in 1950. Centre: Actual (2000) situation with extensive area being abandoned. Right: Simulation of landscape in 2010 after extensive landslides due to the collapse of the terraced land management system (*Source*: Cinque Terre National Park).

movements. Forests with a direct protective function against rockfall, snow avalanches and landslides play a key role in landscape management in the Alpine Region. Such forests are managed in a way that they also protect their own sites against erosion and shallow landslides. In that sense, forest management, which mainly consists of selective 'close to nature' interventions, contributes to soil conservation. Tourism and hydro-electric power generation are major sources of income for the region. In the Stand Montafon, a regional land management and political body which deals with forest, land and water management as well as with tourism, good practice and community action is demonstrated. In both the Montofoon and Cinque Terra, the local people had managed to ensure that capital generated in the region from other sources (tourism and energy) was able to support the conservation and protection of the land.

The Southern Norway case study focused primarily on the boreal zone where transforming marginal grasslands into arable farming land has much increased erosion. The erosion processes lead to the pollution of drinking and fishing water resources (blue algae). Legislation and a set of technical measures was developed to decrease the amount of soil erosion and to improve water quality. Case studies were presented from most Scandinavian countries. In the field, it was clear that land levelling after the Second World War was a major cause of the erosion problems in the region. It was also clear that very steep slopes were being cultivated and that rill erosion was active. It was particularly enlightening for participants from Portugal and Spain to encounter similar problems in Norway or Austria that they were used to at home.

6.1.2 Key findings

Positive experience

Throughout the world, vast numbers of people are performing actions that are successfully contributing towards soil conservation and protection. The picture is far from bleak. If one looks around, or turns on the television, reads a paper or magazine, more often one is confronted with a negative rather than a positive example in the field of soil conservation or the environment as a whole. Yet, in much of the area, things are going reasonably well. The authors concluded that it is a human feature to take the good things that surround us for granted instead of nurturing them and to focus on things that are negative. The problem is that the data and information that could be used to accurately demonstrate what is good or bad is either not present or not in place. Also people do not realize that actions can be changed or stopped immediately in connection with matters such as population growth and pollution.

Unfortunately it is a political fact of life that indicators demonstrating that things are getting worse is often used in order to claim more resources. It is not that the threats to the soil are not real, it is just that they are not always fully understood or explained. There are some places in Europe where soil erosion and contamination are happening at alarming rates and the consequences for the environment are tragic. Most communities in Europe, however, are trying to conserve and protect their environment. To explain things, it is best first to understand change, time and soil functions.

Positive conclusions

Local action groups and NGOs   Thousands of local action groups throughout the world are involved in partnership actions. Some like those dealing with land care are involved explicitly with soil and water but others are concerned with preserving national and cultural heritage. Tens of thousands of world citizens are not only acting but are training and passing on their values to young people. It may be true that the soil is under-represented in words, but how can biodiversity be improved without improving the soil as a habitat? The soil should be included in nature conservation.

Soil threats are local and bounded in place and time   The case studies from Holland and Norway demonstrated that when soil erosion occurred society actually tackled it. This was the policy cycle in action. The direct trigger of much soil erosion in Europe has been land levelling and land consolidation. This has been the cause of much offsite damage. The erosion was the result of a one-off bulldozing of the land. Soil erosion models and concepts need to take advantage of this fact. The soil and farming systems are resilient and people will adapt to control any problem. Our luck is the extreme soil erosion risk is not related to rainfall but to land use policy. The policy of land consolidation in the Netherlands and in Norway was all that were needed. It was not the policy that was wrong, but the way it was allowed.

Best practices   By means of case studies SCAPE is able to promote guidelines and training instruments of best land management practices. Land users can be introduced to management techniques and other options for land use which are less degrading and which stress alternative combinations of functions.

Natural parks   A similarity found throughout all different workshops is the positive value that is brought about by the creation of a natural park. Making an area a UNESCO heritage site is especially important. The implementation of a natural park can be explained as a good practice. Not only does it increase the awareness of our vital resources, such as soil, amongst a bigger public, as people go these parks to enjoy 'a sniff of nature', but it also will significantly contribute to raising educational awareness levels concerning soil protection and conservation. Furthermore, in general terms, it ensures that soil conservation and nature protection measures are implemented within these natural parks and can be assessed in the long or short term on effectiveness, mostly showing, considering the case studies presented, positive outcomes in regeneration of species, biodiversity, increase in soil organic matter content, soil quality, and so on. Concerning the interdisciplinary nature, positive outcomes are also found in economic status; the preciousness of a natural park also increases tourism incomes, for which, for instance, Parco nazionale della Cinque Terra was an outstanding example. In this park, the amount of visitors is kept to a certain figure per day in order not to overpopulate the park which would have negative impacts. Also within the natural park local commodities are made and often derive from an 'ecological' background, and which are bought by people visiting the park, sharing some natural heritage.

Demonstration farms and Networks   Support by extension services is very positive. This can include helping land users set up trials or experiments to perfect their management techniques and solutions.

6.2 Environmentally sensitive areas

6.2.1 Introduction

The policy of environmentally sensitive areas (ESAs) was conceived to protect endangered ecosystems threatened by environmental change. It was typically applied to physically and functionally distinct land units or biotopes, such as riverine meadows, or freshwater coastal lagoons and the main concern was the loss of biodiversity and habitat. It was stressed by Thornes (1996) that particularly in Mediterranean Europe the notion of environmentally sensitive areas was appropriate to desertification. Although desertification is widespread throughout Mediterranean Europe, some areas are clearly more sensitive than others. How could these desertification sensitive areas be defined and compared both today and in the future?

To answer these questions a research programme was set up to investigate ESAs in Target Areas where there was a high degree of data availability and information. Identifying areas sensitive to desertification brings with it the problem that desertification can be an insidiously slow process with effects that are not necessarily obvious and which may be considerably separated in time from the causative factors. The first task of the ESA research was, therefore, to develop the conceptual and practical tools for identifying critical areas, establishing threshold conditions and making comparisons between areas. The different disciplines and experience of the various MEDALUS research groups meant that a variety of concepts and procedures was used to identify ESAs in the target areas (Imeson 1997; Kosmas 1998, Lopez-Bermudez and Basso 1999). A common methodology evolved (Kosmas *et al.* 1999) that as a first step required establishing the spatial patterns of existing land degradation. This pattern was deduced from studies of key indicators of soil, climate and management qualities to which critical values could be given.

The approach had to be both simple and flexible in order to cope with different physical and socio-economic conditions, and different levels of data availability and knowledge of the underlying causes of desertification. The great contrasts between the Target Areas and the complexity of the desertification problem does not allow for the simple transfer of indicators between target areas. Nevertheless the indicators could be used and combined by weightings to classify areas as being critical, potential, or at no risk (Kosmas 1999). Sensitivity is evaluated according to criteria of erosion, resilience and persistence.

Environmental sensitivity at the regional scale   To be relevant for management, the Target Area studies have a focal scale ranging from 1:20,000 and 1 to 200,000. At the coarser regional scale (Kirkby *et al.* 1999), the sensitivity to desertification has been analysed and compared with regional precipitation and vegetation, data obtained from remote sensing and existing land cover information. If the general trends occurring within the Target Areas are considered at the coarse scale of the regional investigations (Kirkby *et al.* 1999), there is useful overlap which allows the Target Area studies to be embedded in the regional ones. Furthermore, the differences occurring within the Target Areas revealed by regional scale indicators enable differences in sensitivity resulting from underlying factors of geology, geomorphology and climate to be used as a basis for stratifying the selection of field sites where studies are being made to underpin indicators. Conducting a regional scale investigation can be considered to be the first preliminary phase of an ESA analysis.

Sensitivity (Brunsden and Thornes 1979) is often used with an abstract or qualitative intention. However, it can also be quantitatively calculated from the relative rates of 'loss', 'recovery' and persistence. For land degradation by soil erosion this requires information about the soil erosion rate (E); the resilience of the soil (R); and the depth or volume of erodible soil (P), all of which can be theoretically measured and quantified at specified temporal and spatial scales. Sensitivity to erosion can be calculated as:

$$S = (E - R)/P$$

where E and R are in rates of erosion (M/year) and P is the soil depth (M). The difficulty of obtaining the data and information needed to calculate sensitivity as described in the equation depends upon the detail and resolution that are needed. At the regional scale, the influence of climate, lithology and land use are so dominant that regional differences in sensitivity can be obtained from maps, remote sensing images, climatological data and readily available information. At the scale relevant for management and mitigation, such approaches give too little resolution and are too simplistic.

Techniques available range from the use of models, field studies of indicators and the response unit approach in combination with remote sensing. The response unit is generally a section of slope with relatively homogeneous soil and vegetation characteristics that reflect the history, processes and characteristics of the site under the influence of climate and land use.

6.3 The European policy, response, and governance

Soil conservation and protection in Europe are not managed at the European level and there is no specific European soil conservation legislation enacted in any country. At the European level there are various 'Directives' and legislation (for example, with respect to water, nitrates, sewage sludge and wildlife habitat) which provide opportunities for soil protection. The lack of European institutions means that each country and region may have its own local policies, priorities, and legislation that define the context within which soil conservation activities take place. The approach of the EU and most countries has been to integrate soil protection and all other environmental issues into other policies. What this means in practice is illustrated for Italy as a case study later.

There is nevertheless, great similarity in the approaches to soil conservation adopted by most countries. They all also use the same soil conservation training books and are strongly influenced by the practices in the USA. There is a continual exchange and diffusion of scientific and practical information. This is facilitated by the European Union framework programmes and COST Actions.

Most of the European Countries are party to the United Nations Convention to Combat Desertification. The affected countries have National Action Plans (NAPS) to Combat Desertification and these have identified priorities such as ecosystem restoration and forestation. These priorities are used to identify the themes treated in the UNCCD CRIC reports (see, for example, Imeson *et al.* 2007). The European Union supports regional collaboration (Regional Action Plans) and is promoting the exploitation of the synergies that are present between the different Rio Conventions. It is also helping develop methods for combating land degradation and for raising awareness.

The European Union and governments such as Spain and Italy have since about 1992, been increasingly concerned about soil erosion and they have initiated a number of research and monitoring activities. An environment has been created in which scientific research is usually focused on critical but relatively narrow objectives. There is seldom any management of the outcomes or funding of follow-up activities. Another focus is on the training of scientists and the development of human capital. There is a good general scientific knowledge about best practices in soil conservation and protection.

A useful overview of soil erosion issues and examples of best practices in Europe can be found in Boardman *et al.* (2005). The first 450 pages of the book review soil erosion in each of the 34 countries and then another 400 pages describe processes. The final conclusions focus on reducing erosion risk. The working and technical group reports produced for the European Soil Strategy on erosion, organic matter, research and monitoring can be downloaded from the JRC soil homepage. These analyse the drivers, pressures, state, impacts and responses to erosion in the European Community (see Reference and further reading at the end of this chapter).

6.3.1 The value of land as real estate

The reality of soil conservation in Europe and in the individual countries can best be described as being agro and real-estate centric.

There is as yet no overarching policy, programme or institutional framework present for preserving or protecting the soil functions and eco-services that protect people from flooding and damage from sedimentation. The public at large is not yet aware of how economic activity, in particular agriculture, is impacting upon ecosystems and their biological and hydrological cycles.

In Europe, soil and land are thought of as real estate and are seen as a resource that farmers or anyone can legitimately exploit for their livelihoods or profit. Ownership does not often bring many obligations of stewardship or governance. As mentioned earlier, the European Union has developed a 'soil strategy' which includes implementing a 'Framework Directive'. Details of this and of its history can be found on the DG-ENV site. A European Soil Forum was established to analyse the threats to European soils and to provide the political and scientific support for a Directive. This process has increased awareness about the threat to the soil. In spite of these efforts by many, there has never been an actual intention to incorporate soil conservation into an integrated strategy of watershed management that would have had a large actual impact.

Soil erosion and the work of soil conservation extension services is seen as something that should help farmers overcome the problems they have with on-site damage in fields. This is why the cost benefit aspects of soil erosion are stressed by DG-ENV that has organized information on 'soil' as being within the domain of 'agriculture' in its organogram (see DG-ENV web page). Reducing the costs to the farmer are supposed to motivate him/her to perform soil conservation activities. Agricultural policy and farmers are not held accountable for the off-site damage they cause. Protection from the off-site damage caused by erosion is sometimes sought in 'soil conservation' but is increasingly less so. River channel engineering is often seen as an alternative. European governments do not usually apply the polluter-pays principle in soil conservation. So erosion is a consequence mainly of the agricultural policy of the organizations that are responsible for establishing soil conservation legislation as well.

In some cases, soil conservation and protection are usually theoretically the responsibility of a Ministry of the Environment and Spatial Planning but their actual interest in the soil is marginal. Responsibilities for land and soil conservation have been mainstreamed into different sectors and there is a lack of money or leadership with respect to cross-cutting problems that affect society mainly in the long term.

Every best practice handbook in soil conservation stresses the need to have an integrated approach that brings together soil, water and land use management in one responsible authority. This is the case in countries like New Zealand and South Africa which have excellent approaches, as well as in China. Yet the approach of most governments in Europe is to leave soil conservation and protection to agriculture. In mountain areas, soils are often protected from erosion because these areas are used for obtaining water. They are kept under forest and laws that protect the water supply in catchment source areas and also achieve soil conservation.

The approach of the EU has been to rely on models rather than to actually measure sediment loads in rivers. This was because of the perceived experience of monitoring, the claims of modellers regarding their ability to represent hydrological processes, and the difficulty of obtaining and combining data.

Erosion is treated mainly as a hydrological process and it is assumed that up-scaling can be done based on soil physics and hydrological events.

The impact of the Universal Soil Loss Equation on both erosion and soil conservation research and how this is translated into management plans has been immense.

The European Environment Agency has produced a report on erosion risk in Europe based on the Pasera model. This expresses a kind of potential erosion pressure that exists in an area. It is essentially a derivative of the USLE concept that considers the relative weight of different factors. In the United States, there is concern that this results in an over estimations in the actual amount of soil loss. Erosion risks result mainly from socio-economic drivers and everywhere or nowhere is at risk according to human actions that can be halted overnight. Forecasts should therefore start with this.

The Italian and Spanish National Action Plans to combat desertification have produced many technical guidelines. The Spanish soil erosion monitoring network has documented methodologies, and research institutes are developing innovative ways of improving water availability in restoration activities. The French Cemagraf organization that has developed methods for reducing erosion and runoff from degrading areas is a source of technical knowledge.

6.3.2 Challenges in European soil policy development

It was found generally that land degradation and erosion (and desertification) are main-streamed into national policies of sustainable development and that these are co-ordinated by the Ministry of the Environment. The main causes of erosion today are unsustainable agricultural practices so that successful policies that address erosion should address this. The reform of the common Agricultural Policy (CAP) and the policy of cross-compliance seems to be successful in some countries where farmers receive money for maintaining healthy soils, increasing organic matter and biodiversity. The success of different policies has been evaluated and the impacts are relatively small because of other pressures.

Nevertheless, in many countries where a serious problem is the flooding caused by erosion, the policies that are being applied are targeted at the downstream river channel rather than at improving or restoring the water regulation capacity of the soil and landscape that is simple to do. The public perception, and that of insurance companies is that climate change is the cause and that it is not the land use that is to blame.

The EU developed a soil strategy to address the threats facing European soils and part of this involved establishing a Soils (Framework) Directive. This was initially supported by many countries. The soil strategy was a useful way of raising awareness but the support for the development of a European Soil Conservation service is not noticeable. Most people do not understand the benefits.

Most countries in Europe have a farmers' advisory service and farmers' unions where support is given. Soil conservation is then specifically within the context of supporting the farmer. The farmers are not usually held responsible for the damage they cause. The extension services are mainly to help the farmers become more profitable. In some countries such as Holland, Hungary and Germany there are guidelines regarding cropping and farming on steep slopes which are complied with, but this is not the case in the UK, for example, where arable crops can be grown on steep slopes. The EU provided funds to develop extension services in some countries but these are not evident on the ground. It would be simple for the EU to dedicate a small amount of always the billions it gives to farmers to research and extension in soil conservation governance.

The mandate of the European Soil Forum was to set up working groups to analyses and report on the threats to European soils. Technical working groups, each with about 40 members, analysed soil erosion and conservation using the DPSIR (drivers, pressures, state, impact and responses). As already mentioned the reports can be downloaded from the JRC web site. Information about best practices can be found in the report on responses. The report on monitoring erosion concluded that it was virtually impossible to measure erosion and that the best approach was to use models.

Figure 6.3   Dick Arnold (U.S. Soil Conservation Service, retired), Luca Montanarella (European Soil Bureau) and Hanoch Lavee, discussing lessons for Europe at the Cinque Terra case study site (Credit: Anton Imeson).

The adoption of best practices and principles is not generally promoted by the governments who influence what farmers and foresters do by means of land use and agricultural policy. For a full discussion see Wilson (2005), who explains why policies to protect the soil and prevent erosion are not implemented. In Europe one can see examples of Best and Poor Practice together.

The policy of the European Community, seems to be to use money that was formerly given to support livestock or crop production in cross-compliance schemes. Farmers provide a service by preventing themselves from causing erosion. This is the opposite situation in much of the world where farmers subsidize governments and cities through cheap food. Both lead to land degradation as farmers occupy sensitive areas as they increase the area cropped.

Table 6.2 gives an overview of the different types of Best Practice and measurement practice at different levels. Figure 6.3, shows a scientific mission at the Cinque Terra site, which is an example of one of the Best Practices described in Table 6.2.

6.3.3 China

In contrast to Europe, in China soil and water conservation receive great attention. The new revision to the Law on Water and Soil Conservation was adopted at the 18th Meeting of the Standing Committee of the Eleventh National People's Congress of the People's Republic of China on 25 December 2010, and will have entered into force as of 1 March 2011. Figure 6.4 shows one of the soil erosion research stations that was visited during a scientific exchange. One aim of the work is to experiment on how to retain more soil and water on slopes and at the same time select new crops for the farmer, such as tea, that combine higher incomes with less erosion. The area in the photo has soils

Table 6.2 Examples of best practice in Europe (Credit: Anton Imeson).

Category	Indicator	Examples of best practices in Europe
Government organization and support of soil conservation and protection activities	Appropriate land and other laws that include soil functions Detailed soil protection laws, institutional arrangements and capacity Public interest and awareness about soil conservation and protection Archiving of material that is freely available Quality and detail of reports submitted to the UNCCD. Organization of meetings by responsible ministries	The Italian and Spanish national action plans to combat desertification which have Soil Conservation Guidelines, scientific and technical support and an integrated approach The Spanish soil erosion monitoring network that has developed measurement methods The French Cemagraf organization that has developed methods for reducing erosion and runoff from degrading areas The EU 5th Framework programme that linked integrated research on erosion and land degradation with stakeholders.
Best practices at Community Level	Demonstration projects Extension services Training and education of existing staff in new approaches to soil conservation Awareness raising through National and regional parks Adaptive management approach to land use planning Protection of public health from agricultural chemicals and the occurrence of cancer. Application of soil conservation laws by authorities	The Cinque Terra Unesco Heritage park in Italy Soil Conservation implementation in The Netherlands and Germany The farmer's union in the United Kingdom Agricultural extension for example in The Netherlands The promotion of geo-diversity and heritage in Europe Biological farming and slow food in Italy (Cinque Terra). Protection of drinking water quality in French rural communities
Best practices at implementation level	Detailed guidelines and regulations. Knowledge and data about the true state of the soil and land Long term perspectives Stakeholder participation and ownership. Local discussion fora.	Use of dynamic GIS to manage local resources (Austria) Soil conservation integrated into policies for water, development and land use etc. Soil conservation practices that retain water on slopes and soil health

(*continued overleaf*)

Table 6.2   (*continued*)

Category	Indicator	Examples of best practices in Europe
	Use of management practices that promoting soil structure, soil vegetation cover and restrict tillage at critical times	Training of land users in the use of simple tools to monitor status of critical soil indicators (e.g. soil stability test, spade test), as for example in Germany
Application of scientific principles and paradigms	Paradigms used to explain erosion and soil conservation The efficiency benefits that paradigm shifts allow. The use and misuse of the Universal soil loss equation The breadth of the consortia engaged in the development of solutions (Witgenstein)	Adaptive management explanations (see South Limburg, The Netherlands example by Dorren and Imeson). Soil conservation monitoring and data collection implementation in Spain

Figure 6.4 Soil Conservation Research Station, Habin Province, China (Credit: Anton Imeson).

that have developed from granite and they are very sandy and erodible. The terraces are constructed as a kind of landscape architecture.

Wu Bangguo, chairman of the Standing Committee of the National People's Congress, said at the end of the meeting that the revised law on water and soil conservation would be of great significance to improve the country's capacity in disaster prevention and improvement of environmental conditions.

Soil erosion is the one of the major environmental problems. Soil and water conservation is now an urgent and strategic task, considering the basic condition in China, said Minister Chen Lei.

The new law has been expected to be a key measure for addressing serious water and soil losses in China, alleviating rural poverty and solving environmental problems.

In the next five years, another 230 000 square kilometres of eroded land and more than 20 000 small watersheds will be brought under control. A total of 368 million ton of annual soil loss will be reduced, according to the Central Government planning authorities.

6.4 Applying the adaptive systems approach explicitly

The soils and recent sediments that we see around us are part of a continuously changing landscape. The changes taking place can be considered over different periods of time, for example, days, years, centuries or millennia, and at different spatial scales. The soil conservation practitioner has to be concerned with and understand all of these scales and at the same time give advice to clients who lack his/her insight. To help them with similar problems, ecologists developed different frameworks for dealing with change and scale. An early framework was known as hierarchy theory (Allen and Star, 1982, O'Neill et al., 1986) and it is very simple to apply (see Chapters 2, 3 and 4). Even earlier in ancient civilizations, philosophers developed concepts that described changes and patterns in nature and applied these to predict soil productivity and plan farming (see Book of Changes, Western Zhou Dynasty p. 24 in Xiao and Jinquan (2008)).

According to the aim of the stakeholder, such as the government department requiring criteria for identifying and protecting areas of outstanding value, a level of interest within the geo-ecosystem or landscape is first defined.

An example could be that you are interested in the valley bottom. The spatial scale of this level of interest is the area that you could see easily from this spot, e.g. 100 by 100 m, and this could be the width of the floodplain or terrace. The theory states that the organization of this level of interest, or actually any level of interest, is explained by at least three levels:

1 The focal level, which is the area mentioned earlier and in which we are directly interested, which is, in other words, directly concerned with the objectives of the user.

2 A coarser, higher level of scale, associated with relatively broader spatial and temporal scales, at which changes occur more slowly. In the example, this means what is happening in the drainage basin as a whole; not just at present but also in the past and in the coming decades, centuries and longer. At the level of interest of the stakeholder these are too slow to affect the dynamics of what is happening. They do constrain the changes that could take place.

3 A lower level, at which changes occur rapidly on fine spatial and temporal scales. This level could refer to the spatial scale of a soil pit or excavation that we might dig

in the ground and the processes that are taking place there, such as the earthworms burrowing in the soil, the growth or decay of plant roots, the deposition of microscopic parts from the atmosphere. It also involves the water cycle and interactions with the river.

In real landscapes, it is also necessary to look at how things are connected with one another, so that measurements that describe or indicate this are studied. This includes the influence of buffering and storage. Therefore, connectivity is an important element of the landscape and structure.

Understanding what is happening at a certain level of interest requires that we should purposefully analyse what is happening at both broader and finer (spatial and temporal) scales. If a certain level of interest is studied within the framework of a hierarchical system, it is often the case that this certain level, which we considered stable and unchanging, is in fact actually changing or even unstable. This is because change or disturbance could take place at another level within the system. This also affects the level we are interested in. Regarding specifically the concept of change, this means that change in landscape systems can only be understood fully if the concept of scale and connectivity is considered as well. An example from fluvial geomorphology (Dorren and Imeson, 2006) illustrates this. When there is a change in base-level, that is if the land rises relative to the sea, the larger rivers in the area react to this. They start to incise into the landscape as the land rises, and the mean gradient of the river, measured between the upper part of the catchment and the sea level, increases. Therefore the running water increasingly has more energy to remove soil material or to incise into bedrock. Small rivers, in tributary catchments, where farmers have their agricultural fields, also react by incising the underlying terrain. If the agricultural fields in the tributary systems are looked at in isolation, these are considered not to change, apart from some slow but constantly ongoing changes, such as biological, physical and chemical changes in the soil itself, slow weathering that produces more soil from the parent material, activities of the farmer that change the soil and some water that erodes particles from the surface of the soil. Why is soil erosion such a local problem in both Spain and Norway, for example? This is because both of these regions have undergone dramatic uplift of several hundreds of metres, in the recent geological past, and the continuing adjustment of fluvial systems makes erosion almost inevitable.

Many processes can be represented by an adaptive cycle, in which four distinct stages have been identified: (i) exploitation or growth; (ii) conservation; (iii) release or collapse; and (iv) reorganization. The adaptive cycle exhibits two major transitions. The first, from exploitation to conservation, is the slow, incremental phase of growth and accumulation. The other, from release to reorganization, is the rapid phase of reorganization leading to renewal. The first is predictable with higher degrees of certainty. The consequences of the second phase are unpredictable and highly uncertain (see Chapters 3 and Chapter 4)

A panarchy, as defined by Holling (2000) and Gunderson and Holling (2002), represents a hierarchical structure in which both human and natural systems are linked together in adaptive cycles. By examining complex natural systems within this structure, it should be possible to identify moments or periods within a single cycle where the system is most receptive to actions that create positive change and enhance sustainability.

6.4.1 A loess area in The Netherlands

The example from South Limburg in The Netherlands illustrates the application of the framework (Dorren and Imeson, 2006).

The landscape of South Limburg is formed by a number of plateaus, which are incised by river valleys. Many of these are dry valleys, which are the remnants of a colder and moister glacial past. For a large part, South Limburg is covered with a layer of loess mostly 2 m but sometimes it is even 20 m thick. The loess overlies coarse-grained Quaternary fluvial sediments, Tertiary sands and Cretaceous limestone. The loess was deposited between 12 000 and 20 000 years ago. During the last 10 000 years (the Holocene), when temperatures increased, the process of soil formation resulted in Luvisols that are characterized by an A, Bt and a C- horizon. The climate of the area is temperate oceanic, with rainfall in all seasons and an annual average precipitation of 750 mm. In the summer, rainfall intensity can be quite high, which sometimes leads to soil erosion. On the steeper slopes, both the A horizon and the Bt horizon have been removed and therefore the C horizon is exposed. In lower areas, considerable amounts of colluvium have been deposited.

The main driving forces that have changed the functioning of the landscape in South-Limburg during the last 15 000 years may be generalized as a) the deposition of loess and b) colonization and use of the landscape by modern man. The impact of this is summarized in the large first part of the adaptive cycle shown in schematic form in Figure 6.5. In this figure, the axis of time follows an imaginary point that moves along the depicted cycle in the graph.

The starting point may be thought of as 12 000 years BP at a moment when loess began to be deposited on the pre-existing postglacial landscape. The history of one place can be schematized along a time-line. The two axes in the figure are described as the potential for erosion and the regulation capacity of the landscape, which is, in other words, to which degree the landscape is able to perform its regulating function by buffering and transmitting ecosystem processes. Examples of these are transportation of material though the landscape by rivers, intermittent streams or wind at different scales, migration of plant and animal populations, etc.

The gradual deposition and accumulation of loess profoundly influenced the hydrology. A loess layer behaves as a giant sponge. A 10 m thick loess layer could retain 4 to 6 m of rain, which was possibly also five to ten times the annual rainfall. Although its water retention makes it ideal for agriculture in a humid region, when it was deposited, it buried and fossilized the drainage system. Groundwater recharge would have dropped, springs would have dried up, dry valleys would have formed and a new land surface would have been created. In terms of the evolution of the landscape and its functioning, South Limburg would gain a highly fertile loess soil but this was at the cost of losing the drainage system. At the same time, pedogenesis resulted in Luvisols due to an increase in temperature, as mentioned before.

Human beings settling in South Limburg enjoyed the benefits of the loess soil. These initially increased the fertility of the Luvisols that would have been particularly resilient to disturbance because of the positive effect of organic matter and the calcium from the calcium carbonate that the original loess contained, on soil structure. Gradually, however, calcium carbonate was leached from surface soils, which would slowly become more erodible.

Agriculture in Neolithic and later Roman periods has been shown by many palaeo-ecological investigations to have had some impact on erosion. In the figure, about 3000 to 1800 years ago, we allow the adaptive cycle to experience a downward collapse as soil resources were redistributed by erosion. Sunken lanes were formed and soil accumulated as colluvium in valley bottoms. It is likely that some actions at that time were deliberately targeted at soil protection, such as the construction of hedgerows to accumulate sediment behind them. This formed terraces known as 'graften'. This may be thought of as a reorganization that led to a restructuring of the landscape. However, it is well known that the introduction of the plough in the early Middle Ages and the Little Ice Age also provided stresses that caused erosion and land degradation. Loss of the productive functions of the soil was then reflected in abandonment and migration, which was a temporal reorganization of the human system.

At the other end of the time-line, the second small cycle in Figure 6.5, which represents the last century, first shows a net accumulation of loess in the terraced landscape. But after that period it shows the impact of land consolidation and reallocation and modern farming, which led to erosion (the downward loop in the small cycle in Figure 6.5). In South Limburg, this meant that small-scale plots, which still existed in the fifties and sixties, were suddenly transformed into large agricultural fields. As a consequence, small hedges, trees and shrubs growing on the edges of the 'graften' disappeared. Land use changed from a diverse mixed agricultural/natural area to mainly maize, wheat and sugar beet. The combination of these agricultural practices and heavy rainfall events resulted in huge erosion problems in the eighties. Tons of fertile soil were removed from the agricultural fields and were deposited in lower parts of the landscape. These so-called off-site effects of soil erosion were even more damaging. Sewage systems in the villages were clogged, which resulted in large mudflows on the streets. These led to considerable damage to infrastructure, as many of the villages in South Limburg were built in the

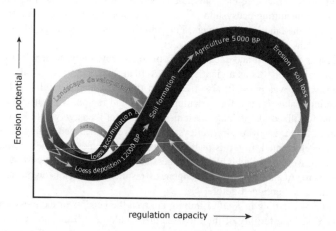

Figure 6.5 Representation of the adaptive cycle of the South Limburg case (see the text for explanation). The x-axis represents the regulation capacity of the landscape, the axis of time follows an imaginary point that moves along the depicted cycle in the graph (Credit: Anton Imeson and Luuk Dorren).

lower parts of the dry-valleys, which is of course exactly were all the water accumulates in case of extreme events.

Conclusion

The adaptive management and panarchy analysis is based on an understanding of processes at different scales. Understanding is much deeper than that we would have had from a statistical methodology in which we tried to interpret change from analysing the influence of different factors at different sites. It includes scale time process and change.

For example, in the case of soil erosion, at the moment most legislation to control soil erosion gives priority to controlling it where it has just taken place – when no soil is left. When a gully is formed, the conditions that were present and which caused it to appear are changed. It makes no sense to invest money strategically and differently in places that are in different stages of the adaptive cycle. Expressed in a different way, it is essential to consider time. Nearly all of the soil conservation work in the world is planned and implemented using two-dimensional concepts of space, so that unfortunately the consequences are not only a waste of effort, but they also destroy aspects of the system that might otherwise not be at risk.

Natural systems have a limited number of states of attraction in which they exist. These are strongly influenced by the geology and the way rocks weather, climate and life (including man). Hierarchy theory and panarchy enable an holistic interpretation of change and risk to be formulated by the consultant for the end user. This can be tailor-made to his/her level of interest. They could provide a framework that enables geologists, biologists and social scientists to participate in a richer dialogue.

6.4.2 Responding to managing fire

Many studies have shown that erosion after forest fires is minimal. This is the case in many areas and the reason is that infiltration rates immediately following fires are high. This was the case in south west Japan where there was a decreasing erodibility in time and an increasing plant cover (Chinen 1987)

Fischer (1984) outlines a procedure for fire management planning for wilderness areas and parks. According to Fischer, the Wilderness Act in the USA sees fire as a natural process that has shaped the character of the American Wilderness. Ecosystems are fire dependent when they require periodic perturbations by fire, as is the case in the eucalyptus forests in Australia, the Mediterranean forests and surrounding areas.

Fire management policies, those of total fire control, contained fires so that they were stopped. In the USA in the past and in Europe today, a Fire Control policy was applied to all lands regardless of classification or primary use. There was an apparent conflict between wilderness management and the Fire Control policy that was evolved to become a policy of fire management. (Moore 1974). There are different definitions according to Fischer, depending on whether it is based on Management Philosophy or Management Action.

As a management philosophy, it means that fire should be considered when developing land and resource management objectives. As a management activity, it is about the inclusion of fire considerations in land management plans to protect forests and rangelands from unwanted fire and the use of fire to accomplish management objectives.

6.4.3 Response to fire

Wilderness fire management is a deliberate planned response that considers the consequences. The responses can be to ignore it, attack it or allow it to burn according to a pre-determined plan. This last option means that it is treated as a prescribed fire. The terms planned ignition and unplanned ignition mean that use can be made of any fire that starts because it is planned in the sense that it is intended, anticipated or expected but is unscheduled.

The different elements involved in planning are described and explained here. Also the links with other plans are mentioned and examples of case studies are illustrated from different parts of the USA.

Prescribed burning an example

Kilgore and Curtis () prepared a guideline for prescribed burning in Ponderosa Pine Larch Fir Forests in the Intermountain West. They interviewed more than 35 experts to develop detailed recommendations which are an excellent source of information for people interested in evaluating this strategy as an option.

This was valid for four different cover types which are described in detail in visual assessment Guides for estimating the amount of woody fuel. They point out that there have been many studies for the burning of Ponderosa Pine in areas from Arizona to Washington. They point out that there is a tendency for managers to think in terms of natural fire cycles, that will say if fire is known to have occurred every 6, 25 or 200 years but in fact it is better to look at the actual fuel. They studied 12 Districts of their Districts on four million acres of Commercial National Forest in Eastern Oregon and Western Montana and 1.3 million acres in the Pacific North West. Their general recommendations were:

- To burn in the Spring with a small crew and use natural or ready-made fire breaks.

- Set a minimum size for the burn, below which it is not economical, say 200 acres and a 4 to 8 hour burning period

- Avoid false starts by careful planning and monitoring burning conditions.

- The resources objectives should be fuel reduction, site preparation for conifers and wildlife habitat improvement.

- Other benefits could be insect and disease abatement, species manipulation, aesthetics.

Adverse impacts include attacks by beetles and, of course, there is always the possibility of soil degradation and runoff.

They found that caution is required because some species are harmed by fire, such as the Grand Fir or White Fir as they can become deceased two years after the fire. Burning under Lodgepole was found to damage white pine, spruce and cedar hemlock because of crown characteristics that lead to excessive scorch or thin bark.

There was often relatively too much litter on the north facing slopes that were damper and this meant that the fire temperatures were higher and could damage the soil. A low intensity burn should therefore be carried out first.

Experienced fire burners were trained using the BEHAVE system. Chance of success is not improved by poor field reconnaissance and inadequate field data. Site specific data is needed.

Before organized fire suppression in the early 1990s Kilgore and Curtis point out that fires occurred naturally at 5 to 25 year intervals. This kept the forest open and was good for browsing wildlife. They proposed different burning strategies for north and south facing slopes: the former could be burnt in the late Summer or early Autumn because they were more moist.

Experienced burners could use the slope to control burning. Less wind is needed on slopes less than 30 per cent. On steep slopes, the funnelling of smoke and heat occurs.

Experts recommended that altitudes below 4500 feet be buried in the Spring and higher areas in the Autumn. There is a relation with soil moisture because the middle third of the slope tends to be dry and there is more risk of high temperatures in the so-called thermal belt. The Guidelines describe all kinds of rules of thumb that they have developed regarding, for example, how to estimate the moisture content of pine leaves. This simply involves bending them and observing how they break. This is important local knowledge.

The final conclusions in training staff for prescribed burning are:

- Teach patience in training your burning staff.

- Use natural and logical boundaries.

- Avoid burning when there are species that can be damaged such as White Pine.

- Have a simple burning plan or format.

- Do not be afraid to burn if conditions are good.

- Know the relationship between fuel burn and fuel moisture.

- Proper preparation of site and plans.

6.5 Responding with laws to protect the land and soil

6.5.1 Introduction

One of the greatest challenges is in translating knowledge and understanding of land degradation and desertification into legislation. An Environmental Law Group, partly working with the IUCN, has written specialized documents that aim to help this process (see the Guidelines of de Boer and Hannan (2004)). The principles that they propose and which have often been used are shown here.

The objective of this chapter is to provide information about the legal principles of applying soil conservation and protection laws in theory and practice. Two countries are given as examples of how the Convention is being implemented. The approach of Romania was very advanced because the government attached a high priority to the soil. Italy has a long tradition of soil protection and there are government research institutes that are providing scientific support.

6.5.2 The implementation of sustainable land use in the context of the UNCCD

The need for more coherent legislative codes, policy instruments and strategic frameworks is one of the main challenges and opportunities of the UNCCD (Hannam and de Boer 2002).

General Principles of legislation being applied in the countries studied and by the Convention

Hannan and de Boer list the following general principles for drafting national soil legislation:

1 General global responsibility to soil.

2 Entitlement to a healthy and ecologically sustainable soil environment.

3 Ecosystem approach must be applied in all aspects of planning and decision making.

4 Sovereignty and responsibility with respect to own policies.

5 International cooperation (global partnership).

6 Monitoring of global soil health and condition.

7 The precautionary principle.

8 Maintenance of biodiversity.

9 Polluter pays.

10 Principle of prevention.

11 Information and participation.

12 Co-operation within states: public authorities, associations and private persons shall co-operate to protect the ecological integrity of the soil environment at all levels of governance.

13 Globalization.

14 Transboundary issues.

15 Obligation to notify other states.

16 Legal action against another state.

17 Protection of soil at time of armed conflict.

18 Role of women in sustainable use of the soil.

19 Role of youth in sustainable use of the soil,

20 Role of indigenous people and local communities in sustainable use of the soil,

21 Protecting cultural aspects of soil.

In the EU, Europe Principle 10, 11 and 12 are being applied. The European Framework Soils Directive includes many other principles. EU Regional development emphasizes the role of youth and women.

6.5.3 National legal and institutional frameworks and regulatory and non-regulatory strategies

States vary in the degree to which they want a regulatory based law. In the long term, a comprehensive policy may be more convenient than strictly legal approaches.

Regulatory and non-regulatory based strategies

These requires statutory soil plans that prescribe legal limits and targets; the issuing of licences or permits to control soil and land use; binding agreements between state and individuals that set limits and standards; use of restraining notices and prosecution for failure to follow standards.

Non-regulatory strategies involve education and awareness-raising, soil research assessment and monitoring, financial support for extension, and extensive use of participatory facilities. There is also a need for development of ecologically sustainable soil use standards, development of soil resource management, protection and incentive based programmes.

It is clear that in Europe nearly all countries follow a non-regulatory path which is consistent with the Convention. The EU Soil Strategy applies the regulatory approach with respect to soil pollution and contamination. Cross-compliance mechanisms require setting standards but at the moment there are no accepted indicator systems in place.

Short- and long-term timeframes in developing legal and institutional frameworks

Short-term approaches are based on a short implementation time-frame and involve minimum changes to an existing legislative regime, fewer related laws and minimal rearrangement of institutional and human resources. Long-term approaches require substantial reforms of existing laws, policies and sectoral changes. This is obviously preferable.

With respect to the cases we are going to deal with, Italy and Romania have a long-term approach.

Hannan and de Boer 2002 describe four different frameworks, two short term and two long term:

Framework 1: This involves making minor amendments to existing laws to define clearly the role of existing institutions to soil management. This could involve introducing a set of sustainable soil objectives into existing laws; procedures that define the roles and responsibility of administrators; or procedures to develop a state soil management strategy.

Framework 2: This involves introducing a substantial amendment into existing land management law to identify the tools of the state and public in soil management. This requires the evaluation and assessment of soil ecosystems, research, planning and management and the development of human resource. It includes enabling public participation and supporting people's rights.

Framework 3: Soil management law based on the concept of ecosystem management. This requires placing the soil in a central position. It requires strong institutions with skills in ecology, soil evaluation, etc. In the EU, this is hardly possible because different legislation has been developed for different areas. Soil is mainstreamed into other issues.

Framework 4: Integrated sustainable soil law. This approach would be an excellent basis for implementing the Convention. Some countries such as China and New Zealand have achieved this.

6.5.4 Methods of developing legal and institutional frameworks

DeBoer and Hannan propose a stepwise approach which can be summarized as:

1 Preliminary phase of identifying key issues in relevant operational environment and law.

2 Analysis of existing law in relation to accepted standards (basic legal and institutional elements to be included in the structure of an individual instrument for its effective implementation). For the relevant legislation, isolate the specific articles, etc., relevant to soil management and categorize them Determine the legal and institutional profile at the national level

3 Determine the specific characteristics of the legal and institutional profiles and their capacity. Document the principles and strengths and weaknesses of laws and instruments, prepare recommendations and soil management guidelines; identify areas for legislative and institutional improvement.

6.5.5 National legislation for implementing the convention: some issues

According to Hannan and de Boer (2002), the purpose and intent of legislation should be clear. By embedding legislation in sustainable development strategies, which is the accepted wisdom, clarity is lost. Desertification is mainstreamed and forgotten.

De Boer and Hannan define what they call *objects and elements of soil legislation*:

The *object* is a group of statements that express a policy, attitudinal or strategic position. Together these statements should establish firm goals, targets and general standards for the administration to achieve sustainable land management. For example, to monitor land use activities to identify different forms of land degradation at the earliest possible stage.

The *element* describes rights and responsibilities such as the duty to protect and conserve the soil for future generations or the right to participate in land use decision making activities, etc.

Next, an *organizational system* needs to be included in whose function it is to carry out the duties prescribed.

We could say that in the case of the countries studies, this is always extremely clear. There is always an authority assigned with well defined responsibilities. The responsibility could be assigned to a particularly ministry but administratively dispersed among a number of government organizations (e.g. forestry, agriculture, water and regional planning).

The different elements that need to be assembled are those of a) a soil authority; b) a co-ordinating function; c) distribution of responsibility; d) levels of responsibility; e) general functions of the soil authority, functional divisions of the authority, head of the soil authority, a soil advisory body, and a soil advisory committee.

These elements were present in both case studies presented here.

6.6 European law and the requirements of the convention

The current implementation of the Convention is taking place within the influence of European programmes and directives and national policies.

The EU Framework Programme has Seven Environmental Thematic Strategies:

• Air Pollution (adopted 21/09/2005)

• Prevention and Recycling of Waste (adopted 21/12/2005)

- Protection and Conservation of the Marine Environment (adopted 24/10/2005)

- Soil (adopted 22/09/2006)

- Sustainable Use of Pesticides (adopted 12/07/2006)

- Sustainable Use of Resources (adopted 21/12/2005)

- Urban Environment (adopted 11/01/2006)

The policy areas are currently grouped in the following environmental themes within which actions that help reduce land degradation can be integrated:

- Air

- Biotechnology

- Chemicals

- Civil Protection and Environmental Accidents

- Climate Change

- Environmental Economics

- Enlargement and Neighboring Countries

- Health

- Industry and Technology

- International Issues

- Land Use

- Nature and Biodiversity

- Noise

- Soil

- Sustainable Development

- Waste

- Water

These environmental themes are mentioned in the CRIC 5 reports of Italy, for example, as being areas of policy where policies aimed at mitigating desertification can be applied.

Integration

The EU member states have adopted the principle of integration. Consequently laws that address desertification become scattered. Although the responsibility for desertification lies with the environment, it is gradually becoming embedded in more areas of policy.

The NAP of Romania is conceptually, very advanced. It actually applies the concepts of **natural social and economic capital** that are promoted in the Millennium report as one of its ways of achieving integration and linking social and physical processes of land degradation. As time has progressed so has the effort to have a comprehensive strategy of sustainable development that is spatially explicit.

6.7 The European soil strategy

In September 2006, the Commission adopted a comprehensive EU strategy specifically dedicated to soil protection. It includes both addressing desertification and SLM (Sustainable Land Management). Figure 6.6, shows scientists, practitioners and environmental law specialists, at Selfoss, Iceland preparing their recommendations for the European Union and also the Selfoss Declaration (Chapter 8).

The Communication (COM(2006) 231) sets the framework. It explains why further action is needed to ensure a high level of soil protection, sets the overall objective of the Strategy and explains what kind of measures must be taken. It establishes a ten-year work program for the European Commission.

Figure 6.6 Conference in Iceland that brought together environmental law experts and European and national experts in soil conservation. Selfoss, Iceland 2005 (Credit: Anton Imeson).

The proposal for a framework Directive (COM(2006) 232) describes out common principles for protecting soils across the EU. Within this common framework, the EU Member States will be in a position to decide how best to protect soil and how use it in a sustainable way on their own territory.

The Impact Assessment (SEC (2006) 1165 and SEC(2006) 620) contains an analysis of the economic, social and environmental impacts of the different options that were considered in the preparatory phase of the strategy and of the measures finally retained by the Commission.

The directive is legitimized by the findings of an Advisory Forum and five Working Groups that were set up, which produced the following reports:

- Volume 1: Introduction and executive summary

- Volume 2: Erosion

- Volume 3: Organic matter

- Volume 4: Contamination and land management

- Volume 5: Monitoring

- Volume 6: Research, sealing & cross-cutting issues

Each of these reports is comprised of many very detailed Task Group reports that provide a valuable source of information. These were prepared by hundreds of unpaid scientists and experts. The reports and other documents can be downloaded at the CIRCA address of DG Environment. The reports on Desertification are included in Volume 2. which can be obtained at http://ec.europa.eu/environment/soil/pdf/vol2.pdf.

6.8 Romania: A model national action plan

Romania signed a law adopting the Convention in 1997 (Law 629/1997). The Former Romanian President took a strong interest in land use, agriculture and soil and took personal interest in the need to improve conditions. For this reason the National Action Plan then received considerable resources so that it not only contains much data, but it is also written at a very high level of scientific appreciation. It applied enlightened and modern concepts that make it even by today's standards far ahead of the simplistic approaches found in action plans that lack motivated interest. This was another monument, just like the palace in Bucherest, that provides a glimpse of former times.

The conceptual basis for the regulations for sustainable land management is in the notion of capital. The report says:

> The sustainability of the natural capital in the area under desertification must start from 'agroforestry' and suppose the balanced relations between agricultural and forestry ecosystems. The political and socio-economical premises concerning natural capital are:

• the environmental protection actions and measures must occupy important place in all national programs of economical development

• to establish the responsibilities of states institutions and of the organizations for a sustainable development

• non-government organizations implication in all decision levels to aware the environment protection.

The effects of droughts, soil degradations and desertification are reflected in natural capital degradations (natural, part-natural, artificial ecosystems). For the attenuation of these effects it must to take into account the politic framework by:

• the soil degradation and over exploitation;

• the replacement of some forests ecosystems with others;

• the degradation and over exploitation of water resources;

• the diminution of food resources from domestic and wild animals by conserving and amelioration of natural ecosystems;

• the promotion of specific agrotechnical measures for extending areas under aridity;

• the overloading of traditional energy resources (wood, coal).

These reflect the notions of controlling land degradation in Romania.

Legislative framework

An integrated approach was used. Legislation was in the areas of:

• Improvement of water use legislation.

• Perfection of legislation on soil protection.

• Improvement of legislation on badlands reclamation and halting of torrential phenomenon.

Promoting of legislation framework to combat drought and desertification
   The National Action Plan refers to the following laws as being important.

L 58/1994 - To ratify the Convention concerning the biological diversity signed at Rio de Janeiro on 5 June 1992 (Of. J. no 199/2 August 1994)

L 137/1995 - Law of Environmental Protection (Of. J. no 304/29 December 1995)

L 7/1996 - Law of Cadastral Survey (Of. J. no 61/13 March 1995)

L 26/1996 - Forestry Code (Of. J. no 93/8 May 1996)

L 51/1996 - To approve GO 25/1995 for implementing and financing research-development activities (Of. J. no 134/27 June 1996)

L 103/1996 – Law of hunting fund and game protection (Of. J. no 235/27 September 1996)

L 107/1996 – Law of water (Of. J. no 244/8 October 1996)

L 137/1996 – To approve GO 33/1995 related to measures for collecting, recycling and re-introducing in the productive circuit all kind of reusable waste (Of. J. no 264/28 October 1996)

OM 125/1996 – To approve the Procedure regulating the economic and social activities having an environmental impact (Of. J. no 73/11 April 1996)

HG (GD) 168/1997 – For service and product regime that could endanger the life, health, work security and environmental protection (Of. J. no 85/8 May 1997)

OM 201/1997 – To approve the procedure authorizing the activity of picking, capturing and acquiring plants and animals which belong to the wild flora and fauna within our country in order to marked them on the domestic and foreign markets (Of. J. no 92/16 May 1997) To improve the legislation regarding the degraded soil improvement and torrential phenomena removal

To review and up-date the methodological norms concerning the forest-pasture development works (simultaneously with the necessary fund raising)

OM 399/1997 – To approve the methodology for implementing, keeping and managing the water cadastral survey of Romania (Of. J. no 111/4 June 1997)

HG (GD) 329/1997 – To adopt some measures for removing the effects of natural calamities which have damaged in November 1995 the national forestry fund and afforested pastures in Covasna, Harghita, Mures and Bistrita Nasaud counties

OM 615/1997 – To approve the Procedure of issuing the agreement of crossing the dam dykes and other water development works protecting against floods, and Technical Guide for designing and developing works for crossing the dykes, dams and other developments made to protect against floods (Of. J. no 241 bis/15 September 1997).

OM 449/1998 – To approve the methodology for certifying physical and legal persons that may perform field studies, draw up technical and economic documentation and develop land reclamation works in the forestry field (Of. J. no 268/17 June 1998)

L 107/1999 – To approve OG (GD) 81/1998 for some measures necessary to improve and afforest the degraded lands (Of. J. no 304/21 June 1999)

L 141/1999 – To approve OG (GD) 96/1998 for regulating the forestry regime and managing the national forestry fund (Of. J. no 355/27 July 1999)

OM 264/1999 – To approve the Forestry Technical Norms for managing the forest vegetation existing beyond the national forestry fund (Of. J. no 233/25 May 1999)

L 1/2000 – To re-constitute the property rights on farming and forestry lands required according to the Low 18/1991 and Low 169/1997 (Of. J. no 8/17 January 2000)

L 73/2000 – Concerning the Environmental Forestry Fund (Of. J. no 207/11 May 2000)

L 159/2000 – For completing the Low of Environmental Protection 137/1995 (Of. J. no 512/22 October 2000).

The National Action Plan (NAP)

The basic strategy was to choose the four themes:

- Agricultural and forestry sustainable development.

- Biodiversity conservation and natural resources.

- The prevention and reduction risks in natural hazards occurrence.

- The improvement of quality of life, especially by rural development in the areas exposed on desertification, lands degradation and drought.

   The general objectives are described as:

- to prevent and combat of desertification, drought and land degradation in those territory exposed on desertification;

- to prevent and combat land degradation in humid areas.

   Priority was given to:

- the development and improvement legislation

- institutional development

- human resource development

- science and technology

- rural development in affected areas.

The organizations involved were:

- Ministry of waters, forests and environment protection (MAPPM)

- Research institutes of MAPPM

- Environment protection agencies

- Forestry inspectorates

- Forestry manager's offices

- Ministry of Agriculture and Food (MAA)

- Academy of Agricultural and Forestry Sciences 'Gh. Ionescu Sisesti' (ASAS)

- National Society of Land Improvement

- National Company Romanian Waters.

A number of actions are described. Those employed in rural areas are used as an illustration.

Rural areas

Water supply for rural development

- Completion of energy resources by alternative methods

- Improving the local climate for prevention of droughts, land degradation and combat desertification

- Improving of soil

- Prevention and combat wind and rain erosion of soil

- Re-use of abandoned crop land

- Improving of degraded pastures

- Diversifying of farming yield

- Maintaining and preserving the biodiversity

- Monitoring trends in drought and desertification trends.

6.9 Italy and the convention

Italy ratified the UNCCD on June 4, 1997 becoming a country Party as both an affected and a donor country. The Focal Point of the UNCCD is headquartered in the Ministry of Foreign Affairs, DG. Cooperation for Development.

Background

For more information, reference is made to the National Action Plan of Italy (1999) itself and to the Progress reports that the National Committee released in 2002 and 2006. Italy also submitted reports describing the support given as a donor country. A comparison of the 2002 and 2006 reports shows how the guidelines for combating desertification being applied in Italy developed in response to new policies and laws addressing sustainable development. In 2006 Italian objectives are coincidental with the environment policy of the EU as reflected in the 6th Framework Programme. Italy has a long history of addressing land degradation and Italian scientists were amongst the first Europeans to quantify these from the 1960s onwards. The National Action Plan shows that from the outset, combating desertification was the responsibility of all Ministers and that money was to be committed for these tasks, Italy also made Institutional arrangements making it possible to work with its partner countries in Annex IV in many areas of common interest. Linking the work to the programmes of regional and water authorities was effective. There are many aspects of the Italian programme that make it a valuable example for the reader. The added value of research and training is apparent.

The National Strategy for Sustainable Development   In the context of the commitment to achieve sustainable development through the integration of its three pillars – environmental, social and economic – the Italian National Environmental Strategy for Sustainable Development (NESSD) was developed by the Ministry of the Environment and Territory, also in accordance with the 6th EU Environmental Action Plan and the guidelines of Barcelona 2002 European Council. The NESSD was approved by CIPE on 2 August 2002 (CIPE deliberation n. 57 of 2 August 2002).

The planning process had been developed starting from a Communication submitted by the Ministry of Environment to the Parliament on October 2001. The drafting of the strategy has been negotiated with all relevant stakeholders including Ministries, environmental NGOs, Trade Unions, Enterprises, local authorities (Regions).

The Italian NESSD contains four broad priority themes, which reflects the ones stated in the EU's 6th Environmental Action Plan:

Climate and atmosphere red on national Green House Gases' emissions in pursuance of Kyoto's Protocol;

forests expansion to increase atmospheric-carbon sinks;

the promotion and support of international co-operation programmes to spread the Best Available Techniques and curb global emissions;

stratospheric ozone depleting gases' emission cut.

6.9.1 Areas of policy

The main areas of policy are **Environment** and **Territorial Planning**.

Desertification was integrated into the National Environmental Strategy for sustainable development which involved several funding Ministries. It makes use of regional development and water management policies, as well as agriculture and forestry and research.

The implementation of the Convention was made part of the Italian National Environmental Strategy for Sustainable Development (NESSD). This was developed by the Ministry of the Environment and Territory. It is based on three pillars: environmental, social and economic sustainability.

It is in compliance with the 6th EU Environmental Action Plan and the guidelines of the Barcelona 2002 European Council.

The NESSD was approved by CIPE on 2 August 2002 (CIPE deliberation n. 57 of 2 August 2002).

The planning process began with a Communication by the Ministry of Environment to the Parliament on October 2001. The drafting of the strategy was negotiated with all relevant stakeholders including Ministries, environmental NGOs, Trade Unions, Enterprises, etc.

Laws

The following laws are listed in the Italian National Reports.

Law n. 36/94, which governs the use of water resources and establishes that water use must be directed towards saving and resource renewal, so as not to harm available water resources, environmental liveability, agriculture, aquatic wildlife and flora, geomorphological processes and hydrogeological balances.

Law n. 183/89, which led to the establishment of the river basin authorities and which calls for the drafting of hydrographic basin plans in order to implement a policy to prevent phenomena of hydrogeological instability, to protect soils, for water purification, and for the organisation, use and management of water resources.

Legislative Decree n. 152/1999, which generally reorganized the topic of protecting water from pollution by subdividing jurisdiction among the State (and within individual ministries), the Regions and the local authorities.

Law 93 of 23 March 2001 acknowledged the need to pursue the work taken up by the National Committee and the action programmes of the regions and basin authorities by allocating funding to pursue the National Committee's activities and for the regions' initial activities.

National Budgetary Law (DPEF) 2007–2008, on the designation of environmental priorities for the National Budget Law, including desertification among the priority areas (under discussion in the Italian Parliament). At national level, it is evident that the main acts pertain to the functioning of the NCCDD and to the implementation of the NAP.

The importance of the regions

The implementation of the Convention in Italy is organized to a large extent at the regional level. This means that Italy can interface combating desertification with the regional development and other policy at an operational level closer to the problems.

The documents that effectuate this are:

The Italian Region Action Programme, IRAP, to Combat Desertification. Some regions established Italian Region Committees, IRCCDD, as requested by the IRAP;

Calabria: the **IRCCDD** was established by the Calabria Regional Act (Del.G.R.) n. 659/2003 and **IRAP** approved by Calabria Region Act (DGR) n. 418/2002;

Basilicata: the **IRCCDD** was established by the Basilicata Regional Act (Del.G.R.) n. 742/2001 and the **IRAP** was approved by River Basin Authority Act 2000;

Sicily: the **IRCCDD** was established by the Sicily Regional Act (D.P.Reg.) n. 171/2000 and the **IRAP** was approved by the Environment and Territory Assessorate Act on 24/07/2003;

Sardinia: the **IRAP** was approved by the Sardinia Regional Act (Del.G.R.) n. 14/2/2000;

Marche: the **IRAP** was approved by the River Basin Authority Act n.3/2000;

Veneto: the **IRAP** was approved by the Veneto Regional Act (Del.G.R.) n. 388/2000.

The National action plan of Italy

Italy approved its National Action Programme on 22 July 1999. It set up a working group within its VI Commission on Sustainable Development consisting of representatives of the National Committee to Combat Drought and Desertification.

The Ministries of the Treasury, Budget and Economic Planning, the Environment, Industry, Transport, Public Works, Scientific Research, Agricultural and Forestry Policies, Foreign Affairs, and Foreign Trade were required within 90 days to send to the Sustainable Development Commission and the National Committee to Combat Desertification, an outline of the resources allocated in the ordinary budgets of each ministry involving:

• soil protection;

• sustainable management of water resources;

• reduction of the impact of productive activities;

- land restoration;

- information, training and research.

These were targeted at programs and measures to combat drought and desertification in vulnerable areas within Italy and in developing countries, according to development co-operation priorities.

Duties

The tasks of the National Committee, with the contribution of technical and scientific institutions and bodies, were described as:

1 To support Italian regions and watershed authorities to identify desertification vulnerable areas (art. 20, paragraphs 2 and 3 of Legislative Decree 152/99).

2 The adoption of standards and methods better suited to understanding, preventing and alleviating desertification phenomena in 'vulnerable areas'.

3 The preparation of the Italian contribution to the Northern Mediterranean Regional Action Programme aimed at ensuring adequate participation in the coordination works with the Annex IV partners.

4 The gathering of uniform soil data for all of Italy based on the activities of the National Soil Monitoring Centre, the regional Soil Services and other offices with similar duties, in close working relationship with the European Soil Office.

6.9.2 Implementation of the NAP in the regions

The regions were required to develop measures and strategies in the form of specific programs to combat drought and desertification in vulnerable area. These had to comply with the special status of individual regions and autonomous provinces (art. 20, par. 2 and 3 of Leg. Dec. 152/99) and in the procedures described in Law 183/99, of the Italian Regions and watershed authorities.

Responsibilities

These programmes must include:

- The preparation of an integrated programme of measures of prevention and mitigation involving both rural and urban areas which integrate the use of traditional knowledge and that of new technologies, based on an inventory of the above and on a land informational outline of the region;

- A framework consistent with the overall objectives of the national economic policy

- Pursue the alleviation of desertification and drought effects that may help consolidate and develop employment in the affected areas;

- The use of local community resources;

- A specific training, education and information activities

- Measures of an agricultural, forestry, civil and social nature that must involve inter-sectoral action and the greatest possible number of public and private participants.

In addition, as prescribed by the UNCCD, the following must be included:

- monitoring and evaluation assessment of social and economic aspects.

The monitoring activities called for in the programmes must be carried out both in the preliminary appraisal, in the form of a preliminary evaluation, during the work, and at its conclusion to evaluate the results achieved. In addition to environmental aspects, social aspects (in terms of new employment, improvement in quality of life, etc.) and economic aspects (cost/benefit analysis, opportunities for economies of scale, etc.) must also be taken into consideration. The results obtained would make it possible to identify the best practices to combat drought and desertification that can be extended to areas affected by analogous desertification phenomena.

The results will be disseminated in public information sessions.

These programmes may be adopted as part of sectoral emergency plans called for under Law 183/89 affecting the priority sectors of:

- national implementation of the Community agricultural policy; 'Agenda 2000';

- Regional Operating Programmes (R.O.P.) for the use of structural funds.

The priority sectors of the regional programmes are:

Soil protection

Sustainable management of water resources

Reduction of environmental impact from productive activities Land restoration.

National actions

The National Committee to Combat Drought and Desertification first set the priorities for the National Action Programme and for the regional programmes and programmes of the Mediterranean Basin authorities.

Guidelines for combating drought and desertification (for approval by the CIPE) were prepared in close collaboration with the National Program for Climate Change Research.

The Guidelines identify the following possible measures for information, training and research:

- Development of public-information programmes by government offices;

- Promotion of information campaigns by public and private enterprises and associations through accords with government offices;

- Survey of research activity in Italy on drought and desertification;

- Analysis and evaluation of strategies to prevent and combat drought and desertification;

- Study of the causes and processes of desertification and the evolution of the phenomenon in Italy;

- Evaluation of the environmental, social and economic implications and consequences of drought and desertification;

- Development of research programmes in association with the international scientific community and international programmes;

- Dissemination of know-how and new acquisitions in scientific research;

- Scientific and technical support for government offices;

- Extension of information to the other countries in the Mediterranean Basin;

- Support for strengthening the clearing-house mechanism;

- An inventory of traditional know-how and technologies aimed at reproducing them with modern techniques.

The current situation can be found in the CRIC 5 report. One very significant action has been the creation of a research fund of 2 million Euros that supports research and extension. There is no room here to list all of the activities so reference is made to this report.

References and further reading

Adeel, Z, and U. Safriel (lead authors), (2005) Dryland systems, in R. Hassan, R. Scholes, and N. Ash, eds, *Millennium Assessment, Ecosystems and Human Well-being. Volume 1: Ecosystems and Human Well-being: Current State and Trends*. Island Press, Washington, USA. pp. 623–664.

Allen, T. F. H., and Starr, T. B., (1982). *Hierarchy: perspectives for ecological complexity*. University of Chicago Press, Chicago, 310 pp.

Ancker J. A. M. van den and P. D. Jungerius (2006) *Geodiversity and Geoheritage within the framework of the EU Soil Strategy* Scape Position paper, 42 p. 3D Environmental Change, Netherlands.

Arnold, D. (2004), Lessons for Europe: the experience of the U.S. Soil Conservation Service. 49–54 in van Asselen, van S, C. Boix-Fayos and A. C. Imeson (2004) *Briefing papers of the second SCAPE workshop in Cinque Terre (IT)* 13-15 April 2004 220 p 3D Environmental Change, Netherlands.

Asselen, van S, C. Boix-Fayos and A. C Imeson (2004) *Briefing papers Of the second SCAPE workshop in Cinque Terre (IT)* 13-15 April 2004 220 p 3D Environmental Change, Netherlands.

Asselen, van S (2004) *Briefing Papers Of the third SCAPE workshop in Schruns* (AU)11-13 October 2004 (128p).

Basso F., Bellotti A., Faretta S., Ferrara A., Mancino G., Pisante M., Quaranta G., and Taberner M., (1999) *Application of the proposed methodology for defining ESAs: The Agri Basin* In *'The Medalus project Mediterranean desertification and land use. Manual on key indicators of desertification and mapping environmentally sensitive areas to desertification*. Edited by: C. Kosmas, M. Kirkby and N. Geeson. European Union 18882. pp: 74–79 ISBN 92-828-6349-2.

Benyamini, Y., 2004, Measuring and monitoring soil erosion for soil conservation and soil protection in Israel. 147–158 Asselen, van S, C. Boix-Fayos and A. C. Imeson (2004) *Briefing papers Of the second SCAPE workshop in Cinque Terre (IT)* 13-15 April 2004 220 p 3D Environmental Change, Netherlands.

Bennett H. H. (1932) *Lectures on Soil Erosion: Its Extent and Meaning and Necessary Measures of Control* (11/04–05/32) Address delivered in connection with the South Carolina Teacher-training program by H.H. Bennett, Chief, In Charge Soil Erosion Investigations, Bureau of Chemistry and Soils, U.S. Department of Agriculture, at Spartanburg and Clemson College, November 4, 1932; Columbia and Rock Hill, November 5, 1932. NRCS, Natural Resource conservation Service, U S Department of Agriculture.

Bennett H. H. (1936) *Soil Conservation and Flood Control* (07/25/36)Address by H.H. Bennett, Chief, Soil Conservation Service, U.S. Department of Agriculture, before the Connecticut Engineering Congress, Bridgeport, Conn., July 25, 1936. NRCS, Natural Resource Conserevation Service, U S Department of Agriculture.

Boatman N, C. Stoate, R. Gooch, C. R. Carvalho, R. Borralho, G. de Snoo and P. Eden (1999) *The Environmental Impact of Arable Crop Production in the European Union, Practical Options for Improvement*.

Boardman, J. and J. Poesen (2006) editors: *Soil erosion in Europe*, Wiley 855p.

Bork, H. (2003) State-of-the-art of erosion research - soil erosion and its consequences since 1800 AD. *Briefing Papers of the first SCAPE Workshop*, C. Boix-Fayos, L. Dorren and A. C. Imeson, 11–14. 3D Environmental Change, Netherlands.

Bonanini, F., 2004, In the Cinque Terre; cultivation is culture. Asselen, van S, C. Boix-Fayos and A. C. Imeson (2004) *Briefing papers Of the second SCAPE workshop in Cinque Terre (IT)* 13-15 April 2004 220 p.

Brunsden, D. and Thornes, J. B., (1979), 'Landscape Sensitivity and Change', *Transactions of the Institute of British Geographers*, 4 (4), pp. 463–84.

Bruntland, G. H. (1987) *Report of the World Commission on Environment and Development: Our Common Future Our Common Future* / Brundtland Report (1987) United Nations World Commission on Environment and Development. United Nations.

Cerda, A., 2004, Lessons and experience of soil conservation in Spain. Asselen, van S, C. Boix-Fayos and A. C. Imeson (2004) *Briefing papers Of the second SCAPE workshop in Cinque Terre (IT)* 13-15 April 2004 220 p 3D Environmental Change, Netherlands.

Chinen, T. (1987) Hillslope erosion after a forest fire in Etajima Island Southwest Japan. *Processus et mesure de lérosion Ed du CNRS* 1990210.

CIRCA (information) Library - CIRCA - Communication & Information Resource Centre. General documents EUROSTAT CIRCA, .circa.europa.eu/Public/irc/dsis/hasaw/library - Cached -

Costanza, R., d'Arge, R., Groot, R. de, *et al.*, (1997). The value of the world's ecosystem services and natural capital. *Nature* 387, 253–260.

COST (Information) COST (European Cooperation in Science and Technology) is one of the longest-running European instruments supporting cooperation among scientists and researchers across Europe.

Demicheli, L., (2004), Monitoring and preventing soil loss: impervious surfaces and human activities. Asselen, van S, C. Boix-Fayos and A. C. Imeson (2004) Briefing papers *Of the second SCAPE workshop in Cinque Terre (IT)* 13-15 April 2004 220 p 3D Environmental Change, Netherlands

Descroix, L. and Gautier, E., (2002). Water erosion in the southern French Alps: climatic and human mechanisms. *Catena* 50 (1), 53–85.

Dorren L. K. A, and A. C. Imeson (2005). Soil erosion and the adaptive cycle metaphor. *Land degradation and development 16*, 509–516.

European Commission (1992) *Council Directive 92/43/EEC of 21 May 1992 on the conservation of natural habitats and of wild fauna and flora*. European Commission Environment, European Commission, Environment.

European Commission (2000) WFD *Directive 2000/60/EC of the European Parliament and of the Council establishing a framework for the Community action in the field of water policy"* European Commission Environment.

European Commission, (2002) Communication from the Commission to the Council, the European Parliament, the Economic and Social Committee and the Committee of the regions. *Towards a Thematic Strategy for Soil Protection*. Brussels, COM (2002) 179 Final. 35 pp.

European Commission (2003) Report from the Commission to the Council and the European Parliament on implementation of Council Directive 91/676/EEC *concerning the protection of waters against pollution caused by nitrates from agricultural sources for the period 2004-2007* [COM(2010)47].

European Commission (2006) *Report on the activities and support provided by the European Community to combat desertification in countries in Asia, Latin America and Caribbean, Central and Eastern Europe in the period January 2001 -2005* submitted to UNCCD CRIC 5 prepared by Imeson, A. C. Koning, P.C. Kisterman H and Wolvekamp P. S. ENV 2006-12800. 74 p. UNCCD.

EU Soil Forum (2003) First meeting of the Advisory Forum on the Soil Thematic Strategy. 23 April 2003 – Brussels. Document N°3 – Version N°2. Specific Mandates. European Commission, Brussels.

Goldstein, R. J. (2004) Environmental Ethics and Positive Law pp 1-37 in *Environmental Ethics and Law* Ashgate 677.

Gunderson, L. H. and Holling, C. S., (2002). *Panarchy: understanding transformations in human and natural systems*. Island Press, Washington, DC, 507 pp.

Gunreben, M., (2004), Soil quality standards in respect of water and wind erosion in Lower Saxony, Germany. 183–194 Asselen, van S, C. Boix-Fayos and A. C. Imeson (2004) *Briefing papers Of the second SCAPE workshop in Cinque Terre (IT)* 13-15 April 2004 220 p 3D Environmental Change, Netherlands.

Hannam, I. D. (2000). Soil conservation policies in Australia: successes, failures and requirements for ecologically sustainable policy. pp. 493–514, *in:* E. L. Napier, S. M. Napier and J. Tvrdon (eds). *Soil and Water Conservation Policies and Programs: Successes and Failures*. Boca Raton, Florida: CRC Press.

Hannam, I. and Boer, B., (2002). *Legal and Institutional Frameworks for Sustainable Soils*. A preliminary report. IUCN Environmental Policy and Law Paper No. 45.

Heidegger M (1954) *The Question concerning Technology and other essays* in, New York Harper and Row

Holling, C. S., (2000). Theories for sustainable futures. *Conservation Ecology 4*(2), 7. [online] URL:

Holling, C. S. and Meffe, G. K. (1996) Command and control and the pathology of natural resource management. *Conservation Biology* 10(2), 328–337.

Imeson, A.C, 2004, The use of indicators in soil erosion and protection. In Sustainable Land Management (SLM). pp 71–82 in Asselen, van S, C. Boix-Fayos and A. C. Imeson (2004) *Briefing papers Of the second SCAPE workshop in Cinque Terre (IT)* 13-15 April 2004 220 p 3D Environmental Change, Netherlands.

Imeson, A.C., O. Arnalds, L. Montanarella, A. Arnouldssen, L. Dorren, M. Curf and D. de la Rosa, (2007) *Soil Conservation and Protection in Europe (SCAPE). The Way Ahead.* European Soil Bureau, Ispra Italy.

Joyce L. A. (1989) An analysis of the range forest situation in the United States 1989-2040. A technical document supporting the 1989 USDA Forest Service RPA Assessment *General Technical Report RM* 180 Rocky Mountains Forest and Range Experimental Station.

Jungerius, P. D. and A. C. Imeson (2005) Globalisation, sustainability and resilience from the soil's point of view. Briefing Paper of the 5th Scape Workshop Iceland. pp 75–87 Arnalds A (2005) *Strategies Science and Law for the Conservation of the World Soil Resources* International Workshop, Selfoss Iceland September 14-18 2005 Rit LBHl nr. 4 Agricultural University of Iceland ISSN 16700-5785 270

Kapur, S., 2004, Natural and Man-Made Agroscapes of Turkey: Sites of Indigenous Sustainable Land Management (SLM). Pp 71–82 in Asselen, van S, C. Boix-Fayos and A. C. Imeson (2004) *Briefing papers Of the second SCAPE workshop in Cinque Terre (IT)* 13-15 April 2004 220 p.

Kilgore, B. M., Curtis, G. A. (1987) *Guide to understory burning in ponderosa pine-larch-fir forests in t h e Intermountain West.* Gen. Tech. Rep. INT-233. Ogden, UT: USDA, For. Serv., Intermtn. Res. Sta. 39 p.

Kirkby, M. J. (1999) *Regional desertification indicators (RDIs).* In: The Medalus Project, Mediterranean desertification and land-use manual on key indicators in Kosmas C, Kirkby, M. J. and Geeson, N. (1999) *The Medalus project. Manual on key indicators of desertification and mapping environmentally sensitive areas to desertification* European Commission Community Research EUR 18882, 94 p.

Kirkby, M. J. (2009) Desertification the broader context. Pp 41–50 in *Advances in studies on Desertification Contributions to the International Conference on Desertification in Memory of Professor John B. Thornes* (edit A. Romero Diaz, F. Belmonte Serrato, F. Alonso Sarria and F. Lopez Bermudez).

Kohl, B. and Markart, G., (2004), The importance of soil protection and conservation in mountainous areas for hydrological purposes. Asselen, van S (2004) pp 27–30 in van Asselen, S. Briefing Papers Of the third SCAPE workshop in Schruns (AU) 11-13 October 2004 (128p) 3D Environmental Change, Netherlands.

Kosmas C, Kirkby, M and Geeson, N. (1999) *The Medalus project. Manual on key indicators of desertification and mapping environmentally sensitive areas to desertification* European Commission Community Research EUR 18882, 94p.

Lang A and Bork, H. R. (2006) Past erosion in Europe pp 465–476 in Boardman, J. and J. Poesen (editors) *Soil erosion in Europe*, Wiley 855 p.

Lavee, H. and Calvo-Cases, A., (2004), Lessons and Experience gained from 20 years of measuring soil erosion and related data in the Mediterranean: Future challenges and the way ahead. van Asselen, van S, C. Boix-Fayos and A. C. Imeson (2004) *Briefing papers of the second SCAPE workshop in Cinque Terre (IT)* 13-15 April 2004 220 p 3D Environmental Change, Netherlands.

Lopez Bermudez F. (1995) *The Field site: Murcia*, pp. 38–60 in Medalus II Mediterranean Desertification and Land Use, Project 1, Phase II 1993-1985 Basic Field Programme Final Report Imeson, A. C. EV5V-CT92-0128, 282p.

Lopez. Bermudez F. A Romero Diaz, J. Martinez-Fernadez and J Martinez Fernandez (1996). *The El Al Field Site: Soil and Vegetation Cover*. Pp 169–188 in Brandt J. and Thornes J. B *Mediterranean Desertification and Land Use* Wiley.

Moore, W. R. (1974) Towards the future, land people and fire. *Forest Management* 3, 3–5.

Moss T and Heidi Fichter (2000) *Regional pathways to sustainability. Experiences of promoting sustainable development in structural funds programmes in 12 pilot areas European Commission* EUR 19401, 174 p.

Nachtergaele, F. (2004) Land Degradation Assessment Indicators and the LADA project. in Asselen, van S, C. Boix-Fayos and A. C. Imeson (2004) *Briefing papers Of the second SCAPE workshop in Cinque Terre (IT)* 13-15 April 2004 220 p. 3D Environmental Change, Netherlands.

O'Neill, R. V., D. DeAngelis, J. Waide and T. F. H. Allen. (1986). *A hierarchical concept of ecosystems.* Princeton University Press.

Role, A. (2004) Experiences in Malta on the management of terraced Mediterranean landscapes. 87–97 in Asselen, van S, C. Boix-Fayos and A. C. Imeson (2004) *Briefing papers Of the second SCAPE workshop in Cinque Terre (IT)* 13-15 April 2004 220 p. 3D Environmental Change, Netherlands.

Rosa, de la, D. (2004) Site-specific soil protection strategies by using a Mediterranean land evaluation decision support system. in Asselen, van S, C. Boix-Fayos and A. C. Imeson (2004) *Briefing papers Of the second SCAPE workshop in Cinque Terre (IT)* 13-15 April 2004 220 p. 3D Environmental Change, Netherlands.

Roxo M. J. (1994) Field site: *Lower Alentejo, Portugal.* In: Medalus II, project 1, 2nd annual report, Brandt J. & Geeson N. (Eds.), London, UK.

Roxo, M. (2004) Long term monitoring of soil erosion by water Vale Formoso Erosion Centre – Portugal. pp 37–38 Asselen, van S, C. Boix-Fayos and A. C. Imeson (2004) *Briefing papers Of the second SCAPE workshop in Cinque Terre (IT)* 13-15 April 2004 220 p 3D Environmental Change, Netherlands.

Scherer, J. (2004) The importance of soil protection in Vorarlberg: the most important soil-related environmental problems and measures. pp 27-30 in van Asselen, S. *Briefing Papers Of the third SCAPE workshop in Schruns (AU)*11-13 October 2004 (128p).

Sprague, L. A., Mueller, D. K., Schwarz, G. E., and Lorenz, D. L. (2009) *Nutrient trends in streams and rivers of the United States, 1993–2003*: U.S. Geological Survey Scientific Investigations Report 2008–5202, 196 p.

Strauss, P. (2004) Effectiveness of soil erosion protection measures in Austrian agriculture in van Asselen, S. *Briefing Papers Of the third SCAPE workshop in Schruns (AU)* 11-13 October 2004 (128p) 3D Environmental Change, Netherlands.

Thornes J. B. (1996) Introduction pp 1–11 in Brandt and Thornes *Mediterranean Desertification and Land Use.* Wiley 554 p.

Thornes J. B. and Burke S. (1996) *Actions taken by national governmental organisations to mitigate desertification in the Mediterranean. Concerted Action on Mediterranean Desertification* Kings College, University of London.

Vente, de, J. (2004) Evaluation of reservoir sedimentation as a methodology for sediment yield assessment in the Mediterranean: challenges and limitations. 139–146 in Asselen, van S, C. Boix-Fayos and A. C. Imeson (2004) *Briefing papers Of the second. SCAPE workshop in Cinque Terre (IT)* 13-15 April 2004 220 p. 3D Environmental Change, Netherlands.

Zdruli, P. (2004) Enhancing networking and exchange of information in the Mediterranean region: The MEDCOASTLAND Thematic Network. Pp 169–182 in Asselen, van S, C. Boix-Fayos and A. C. Imeson (2004) *Briefing papers Of the second SCAPE workshop in Cinque Terre (IT)* 13-15 April 2004 220 p 3D Environmental Change, Netherlands.

United Nations (1992) *Earth Summit Convention on Desertification*, Brazil, 3-14 June 1992. Department of Public Information UN.

UNCCD (1999) *Italy National Action programme to combat drought and desertification*, Rome, 9 p. UNCCD Bonn.

UNCCD (2000) Romania '*National Action Programme Concerning desertification, land degradation and drought prevention and control*, 117 p UNCCD Bonn.

UNCCD (2007) *10-year strategic plan and framework to enhance the implementation of the Convention* 2008-2009, COP 8 Madrid 3-4 September 2007 UNCCD Bonn.

Wilson G. A. and H. Buller (2001). *The use of socioo-economic and environmental indicators in assessing the effectiveness of EU Agri-Environmental Policy*. European Environment 11 297–313.

Wilson, G. A. (2009) Rethinking environmental management - ten years later: a view from the author. *Environments* 36 (3): 3–15.

Wischmeier and Smith Wischmeier, W. H. and D. D. Smith. (1978). "*Predicting Rainfall Erosion Losses*: A Guide to Conservation Planning." Agriculture Handbook No. 537.

Xiao Jietu and Li Jinquan (2008). *An outline history of Chinese Philosophy*, (I) Foreign Language Press Beijing China ISBN 978-7-119-02719-7, 434 p.

Glossary or Footnotes

CEMAGREF: (Explanation) L'institut de recherche en sciences et technologies pour l'environment, Grenoble, France

CAP: (Explanation) European Union Common Agricultural Policy

MEDALUS: (Information) Mediterranean Desertion and Land Use. The acronym of integrated research projects into the complex causes of desertification on Desertification, supported by EU research programmes between about 1990 and 2001

MEDRAP: (information) The name of a Concerted action funded by the European Union to support the northern Mediterranean regional action programme to combat desertification between January 2001 - March 2004

Natura 2000 Natura 2000 is the **centrepiece of EU nature & biodiversity policy**. It is an EUwide network of nature protection areas established under the 1992 Habitats Directive. The aim of the network is to assure the long-term survival of Europe's most valuable and threatened species and habitats. It is comprised of Special Areas of Conservation (SAC) designated by Member States under the Habitats Directive,

PESERA: A European soil erosion risk model Pan-European Soil Erosion Risk Assessment PESERA, Soil Erosion, Soil erosion estimates, PESERA, Pan-European Soil available at eusoils.jrc.ec.europa.eu/esdb_archive/pesera/pesera_download.html -

Part III

Global Desertification Impact and Response

7
Global desertification today

7.1 Desertification today

At the scale of the planet, the extent of desertification and land degradation is easy to observe from a number of sources, including Google Earth that is now replanting virtual trees. Nearly all of the earth is covered by degraded ecosystems. Much less water is being recycled by far less water from far shallower and warmer soils than it did when there was forest. Roots then extended tens of metres into the deeply weathered profiles and the evaporation of the water cooled the area and produced local rainfall. The rainforests also collected water from the atmosphere. All of the local changes in hydrology have an emergent effect at a higher scale whereby the soil and water temperature of rivers increases, there is less infiltration, groundwater levels drop and springs dry. The irrigated agriculture providing most of the food has increased the aridity because of the impact this has on the non-irrigated areas. It is unsustainable to the extent that the water has all been used and large areas contaminated and salinized.

Six hundred years ago the land cover would have looked completely different. Much of the world outside of Europe and Asia would have had a more natural vegetation cover, a high proportion of which would have been forest. Five thousand years ago it would have been more different still, before the spread of agriculture and the domestication of animals and metal working transformed the world.

During millions of years, global and zonal patterns in the vegetation and soil had evolved and the ecosystems that were adapted to and responsible for this are gone. The many illustrations in Europe, South America, Africa and Asia reveal large areas of degraded land with respect to its former state. This means they no longer provide agricultural products or natural resources like they once did. Natural regeneration and restoration is mixed because of human pressures. In places restoration and regeneration actions have been accomplished and many countries have been able to protect significant areas of natural areas that preserve biodiversity and hydrological functions. Restoration may be driven by both business and ethics.

The global or zonal patterns in the land, soils vegetation that existed before this land cover and land use changes have left their imprint and memory in the soils and vegetation that we see today and these still provide many ecosystem goods and services and functions including the seeds for survival. However, much of the life that created this is extinct or unable to live in the new man made environment. Gradually in time and also as the biodiversity decreases, so less organisms and animals remain to maintain in particular hydrological services.

Desertification, Land Degradation and Sustainability, First Edition. Anton Imeson.
© 2012 John Wiley & Sons, Ltd. Published 2012 by John Wiley & Sons, Ltd.

At the global level, responses to land use change are also delayed. These then also include things such as large dams on the coastal areas that then receive too little fresh water. Flooding in Lisbon and Bangladesh have been demonstrated to be delayed responses to erosion that took place much earlier, in the case of Lisbon by perhaps 70 years and in Bangladesh, several thousands of years. Similar delayed responses follow deforestation as they have done in Brazil and the Philippines, Indonesia, Mozambique and Vietnam.

What global land use transformations reveal is that on most of the area receiving 300–2000 mm per year of rainfall per year, where the soils and vegetation was adapted to this, there is now a steppe-like vegetation cover during the growing period and at other times the land is bare of vegetation and fallow. This is desertification at a global scale.

From Oslo in Norway to Faro in Portugal along a transect of land that had Mediterranean forest ecosystems in the South, Temperate deciduous forests in the centre and coniferous taiga type forests in the North, most of the area is now not covered with vegetation at all during much of the year and at others it is covered with grasses or corn and sunflowers. This has changed the heat and water balances at the local level and globally altered the climate and soil.

The hydrological processes and balances have been totally transformed so that the hillslopes and river channels are no longer adjusted to what the land and soil was adjusted to during the preceding ten thousand years or so. An identical or comparable situation exists in the USA, South America, Australia and Africa, so everywhere there are floods, droughts and landslides and billions needs to be spent on flood insurance and protection.

Local becomes global

The recent images shown in Figures 7.1 and 7.2 were selected to illustrate two continental areas, one in Asia and one in America.

Figure 7.1 features the Darya River Floodplain, Kazakhstan, Central Asia. (The work of the NASA or MODIS team who made this possible is greatly appreciated.) It was posted on 1 November 2010.

As regards Figure 7.2, this is part of a water district – the Magic Valley Ground Water – that helps manage water taken from the aquifer. In 2006, another irrigation district on the Snake River Plain, A&B, believed that some of the farms in its district had run short on water, resulting in a poor harvest. Because A&B has senior (older) water rights, Idaho law allowed them to issue a water call, a demand that junior water right holders, including Stevenson, draw less water from the aquifer.

Dean Stevenson has farmed the plains of south-central Idaho most of his forty-seven years. Like all farmers, he worries about things like the price of sugar beets and malt barley or the cost of gasoline, but most of all, he worries about water.

He is right to worry. The 4000 acres he farms with his father and brother receive on average 10 inches (about 25 cm) of rain per year. The water that sustains the sugar beets, barley, wheat, and potatoes is pumped from the Snake River Plain aquifer. Every drop is rationed. (Acknowledgement goes to HolliRiebeekDesign by Robert Simmon, 21 January 2010, for the American material (see Figures 7.2a, b and c).)

Figure 7.1 The river flows for 2200 kilometres from the Tien Shan Mountains west and northwest to the Aral Sea – note the dying waterbody at the low point of the basin. Water has been withdrawn from the river for agriculture for many decades. Although the Syr Darya is the second largest river flowing into the Aral Sea, its discharge is not very large and it is easily depleted. Central Asia's most important cotton-growing region is concentrated in the floodplain of the Syr Darya. Half the river flow is controlled from reservoirs, and half from direct water take-off from canals. In contrast to the intensive agricultural use of water shown here, water control in the mountain valleys upstream is oriented more toward power generation (Credit: NASA Modis team).

Dynamic reality

One issue in many environments is that human settlements and buildings are in fixed locations, and in environments where geomorphological or landscape processes are adjusting and changing the thresholds required for producing flood runoff. This is human-induced erosion in the sense that people choose to live in dynamic coastal zones and floodplains or in areas with high volcanic activity and risk of forest fires.

Areas of loess provide another example of this. When loess was deposited in West Europe, in the Middle East and China, it acted like a large sponge that could store most of the rain that fell on it. There was less groundwater recharge, springs dried up and rivers became dry or disappeared. Under the forest through the activities of the life present in loess, soils form that had excellent water retaining properties and there was no erosion. In South Limburg, the Netherlands, erosion began 2000 years ago when wheat was introduced by the Romans and there was the start of forest clearance. Under wheat and maize, loess develops a very weak structure so that there is crusting and a large increase in runoff. Of course, it is possible, at the next level of the slope, to manage farming and construct terraces, so that the water retention properties of the landscape increases and there is no flooding. When gullies incise into loess they lower irreversibly lower groundwater which leads to see page and slope instability and maybe badland like conditions, that impair that become difficult to farm without causing more erosion.

Similarly, to provide raw materials for industry and food, much of the land is covered with corn or maize. This also releases substances in the soil that lead to a very weak soil structure, so that soils slake and develop surface seals, and therefore produce high

(a)

(b)

Figure 7.2a and b   Agriculture is the largest industry in Idaho, but large areas of the state rely on irrigation to provide water for crops. Irrigated farms in southern Idaho use water from both the Snake River and the Snake River Plain aquifer (Source: Figure 7.2a NASA Modis team and Figure 7.2b. Photograph ©2005 p.m.graham).

amounts of flood runoff. The large amounts of water and fertilizer and herbicides being used have made most groundwater a risk to drink. This has resulted in the large environmental cost of providing bottled water. Rivers and springs have disappeared as water is abstracted for irrigation. Herbicides and insecticides have led to soil degradation, soil compaction and have made soils and crops both toxic and cheap (Cerdà 2009).

Future food crises are being predicted by advertising companies of the multinational companies, which are claiming that world population will increase by 2 billion and will need to be fed. Many claim that there is a global food crisis and that the answer is to further intensify and industrialize agriculture. Most independent scientists believe that traditional organic farming as practiced in India is more productive and that in any case society should confront the issues of population growth, lifestyles marketing and consumerism that affect what people want and expect. Society could plan for 2 billion

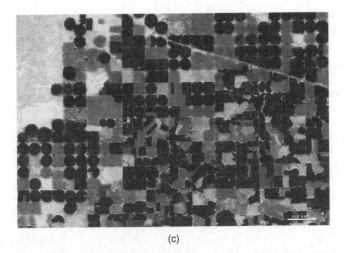

(c)

Figure 7.2c Water Use on Idaho's Snake River Plain. (Posted January 26, 2010.) This image, based on data collected by the Landsat 5 satellite on August 9, 2006, shows evapotranspiration from vegetation on the Snake River Plain in south-central Idaho. Fields of irrigated crops are dark blue squares or circles, showing that the growing plants are taking up and transpiring water. Fallow and recently harvested fields are lighter blue. Surviving on the scant rain that falls on the high desert, the surrounding natural scrubland uses far less water. The scrubland, shown in the upper left corner of the image, is tan and pale blue. The diagonal line across the upper right corner of the image is a road (Credit: NASA Modis team).

people less in 2030 as we all have the freedom of choice. Global desertification occurs because there is no global governance or organization to give leadership and regulate internationally operating companies and nations which are then the only source of environmental knowledge for most people and land users. This lack of knowledge was one of the reasons mentioned by Bennett (1932) for the dustbowl in the USA.

From the adaptive management analysis of the problem it can be deduced that the food and energy crisis land degradation are inevitable if the natural resources and labour being used for the support and benefit of people in poor regions is lost to them. International companies and governments have a very difficult and delicate task in avoiding collateral damage in social, human and natural capital when resources are appropriated and developed in other countries. Taking resources from the system so that the production is transferred away from the small person or group who are self-sufficient and productive but have no power. There is a great capacity to produce food on much less land when people are rewarded more for what they produce.

Plants and ecosystems interact with the soil and rocks to create environments for themselves that help them to modify their own local climate. At the same time, they are having an impact on the regional and global climate by regulating the heat and water balances. Humans and other animals mainly require plants that can photosynthesize sunlight as a source of food or energy. In their interactions with other plants, some have gained a competitive advantage. Falkenmark and Rockstrom (2004) shows how during the last three hundred years the proportion human appropriated water has increased from virtually nothing to 70 per cent. The impact of this on the ecosystems and inhabitants is immense.

Procuring and acquiring services functions being used in other countries

For example, if a golf course is built in Crete in Greece or Faro, Portugal by Dutch or Belgian investors, with the help of investors and pension funds, the services that land once provided are no longer available for the people who once used it. The land that was part for their capital, as it may have given them the benefits of water, food recreational and psychological or spiritual functions, has been lost to them, unless they are stakeholders and willing actors in the process. In Holland and Belgium, Italy, France and Germany, there can be planning process that buffer and protect people from investments because people are more aware of the process. A duty of care and love for the environment has resulted in the development of what can be thought of as ethical capital that is part of the social contract between citizens and the state and which legitimises the power of the state. During the warring states period in China and later it became apparent that the only countries that had a future were those that placed the well-being of the people first. A slave system, in which the rule to rule came from heaven, was replaced by a feudal system as in Europe. The financial benefits of land ownership are often very high because of agricultural policies and limited accountability.

Colonization and the spread of cash crops in America, Asia and Africa has had a similar effect. Although the discovery that palm oil could be used to make soap instead of animal fat lead to the creation of thousands of jobs in the UK and the rise of Unilever, the need for this was a result of marketing and the product could have been made locally. Nobody thought it was moronic or unnecessary to cut down all of the world's rain forests then and today so that all can drink coffee and have soap. People are proud of Unilever and what it achieved for the economic benefit it brought. The challenge is to be able to reverse these processes so that our needs and wants are positive and bring about the restoration of ecosystems. Even if nature remains to many people just an economic resource, restoration could increase the quality of life and provide new resources and benefits for all.

The price of desertification

Just as there is overwhelming evidence that human-induced climate change is threatening the capacity of ecosystems and economies to provide the goods and benefits that society has become accustomed to, there is similar evidence that desertification is having the same impact (Rosenschweig *et al.* (2008); Stern 2005). International Scientific Monitoring Programmes (for example, those co-ordinated by the IGBP 2007, IHDP 2007 and GLP 2007), are measuring and providing explanations for the changes being monitored by the Earth Observation programmes (for example, by NASA 2007 and the ESA (2006). Although desertification is not always treated as a synthesizing concept to explain the observed changes, this is often evidently the case (for example, Lambert 2009). Climate, change-biodiversity and desertification are increasingly being viewed as being simply different indicators of the impact that different human activities and appropriations are having on the Earth's interacting climate and landscape geo-systems systems. What the research and monitoring demonstrate is the unequivocal destruction of terrestrial ecosystems and the impact that this is having not just on the climate but also on flooding and the security of food supplies.

International concern about the impact this is having is raised in *The Millennium Ecosystem Assessment Synthesis Report*, which highlights as one of its four main findings that:

> Humans have changed ecosystems more rapidly and extensively in the last 50 years than in any other period to meet rapidly growing demands for food, fresh water, timber, fibre and fuel. It states that more land was converted to agriculture since 1945 than in the 18th and 19th centuries combined. More than half of all the synthetic nitrogen fertilizers, first made in 1913, ever used on the planet has been used since 1985. That this has resulted in a substantial and largely irreversible loss in diversity of life on Earth is established.

The consequences of this for the goods and benefits that soils and landscapes provided are dramatic and could affect the future ability of the Earth to remain a suitable habitat for man. Each human requires 0.5 kg of oxygen each day that has to be provided by (1.5 kg of plant growth). If only the real-estate value of land, or its short-term economic use are considered and its other functions ignored, the impacts will be felt by society as the disappearance of services and benefits gradually manifest themselves.

The UNCCD: national versus world interests

The UNCCD has great importance as the International Organization responsible for co-ordinating actions necessary to combat desertification. An achievement of the UNCCD has been to require and help countries to develop National Action and Regional Action Plans and to report on the progress that has been made in so-called CRIC reports on the implementation of the Convention. Both the CRIC reports and the National Action Plans provide an immense source of information regarding conditions in the countries and in many cases provide explanations and evidence describing the impact desertification is having on ecosystem goods and benefits. For example, desertification as a result of deforestation and non-sustainable land use costs Bangladesh more than two billion dollars per year. A review of the support given by the EU to countries between 2001 and 2005 (Imeson *et al*. 2005) illustrated that although the consequences of desertification are well understood, most countries lack the means to tackle them, for example in the area of soil protection and land protection.

The advances in the scientific understanding of desertification and the ability to monitor it mean that several of the principles embodied in the Treaty could be advanced. Carbon accounting has raised awareness of the impact that transporting food over long distances has on carbon and other pollution. Research has demonstrated the links that exist between local and global scale processes. Air pollution and dust from industrial or industrialising countries cause changes in patterns of rainfall, making some areas more arid. The distinction between affected and non-affected countries applied by the Convention fails to convey the message that everyone is involved.

Similarly, similar types of landscape and soil have similar desertification problems irrespective of the country or Annex (the regions that the UNCCD uses to group countries that have similar problems, e.g. The Northern Mediterranean Annex); they are in specific types of geo-ecosystem that respond in similar ways to desertification.

Two related questions concern the links that the Convention has emphasized regarding aridity and poverty. Land degradation processes such as erosion occur with most severity in humid areas where the rainfall has more energy. When we look at where land degradation occurs it is not more evident in the dry regions of the world.

The UNCCD faces many challenges at its upcoming Conference of the Parties, if it is to develop strategies and actions that are necessary in response to the new knowledge that has become available regarding the degraded condition of vast areas of the earth's ecosystems. Although the forces that are driving desertification are increasing each year, on the other hand, the scientific understanding needed to address this is at hand. There is increasing realization that soil and land protection, that restore carbon and life to the soil, make sense if the levels of atmospheric carbon are to be reduced and for future oxygen levels to be maintained. Advances in the areas of monitoring and research mean that the COP has if it wants, access to real-time remotely sensed data describing the ecological health of every square metre of earth. New paradigms can help remove the barriers to the implementation of the Convention that have been hitherto present.

The millennium ecosystem assessment synthesis report

The first of the four main findings has been already briefly presented above. The four findings are given below in full for the reader, who is also referred to http://undp.by/en/undp/news/world/04-04-05-04.html:

- Humans have changed ecosystems more rapidly and extensively in the last 50 years than in any other period. This was done largely to meet rapidly growing demands for food, fresh water, timber, fibre and fuel. More land was converted to agriculture since 1945 than in the eighteenth and nineteenth centuries combined. More than half of all the synthetic nitrogen fertilizers, first made in 1913, ever used on the planet has been used since 1985. Experts say that this resulted in a substantial and largely irreversible loss in diversity of life on Earth, with some 10 to 30 per cent of the mammal, bird and amphibian species currently threatened with extinction.

- Ecosystem changes that have contributed substantial net gains in human well-being and economic development have been achieved at growing costs in the form of degradation of other services. Only four ecosystem services have been enhanced in the last 50 years: increases in crop, livestock and aquaculture production, and increased carbon sequestration for global climate regulation. Two services – capture fisheries and fresh water – are now well beyond levels that can sustain current, much less future, demands. Experts say that these problems will substantially diminish the benefits for future generations.

- The degradation of ecosystem services could grow significantly worse during the first half of this century and is a barrier to achieving the UN Millennium Development Goals. In all the four plausible futures explored by the scientists, they project progress in eliminating hunger, but at far slower rates than needed to halve number of people suffering from hunger by 2015. Experts warn that changes in ecosystems such as deforestation influence the abundance of human pathogens such as malaria and cholera, as well as the risk of emergence of new diseases. Malaria, for example, accounts for 11 percent of the disease burden in Africa and had it been eliminated 35 years ago, the continent's gross domestic product would have increased by $100 billion.

- The challenge of reversing the degradation of ecosystems while meeting increasing demands can be met under some scenarios involving significant policy and institutional changes. However, these changes will be large and are not currently under way. The report mentions options that exist to conserve or enhance ecosystem services that reduce negative trade-offs or that will positively impact other services. Protection of natural forests, for example, not only conserves wildlife but also supplies fresh water and reduces carbon emissions.

The MA board of directors who produced another report entitled *Living Beyond Our Means: Natural Assets and Human Well-being* said in a statement:

> The over-riding conclusion of this assessment is that it lies within the power of human societies to ease the strains we are putting on the nature services of the planet, while continuing to use them to bring better living standards to all.

They went on:

> Achieving this, however, will require radical changes in the way nature is treated at every level of decision-making and new ways of cooperation between government, business and civil society. The warning signs are there for all of us to see. The future now lies in our hands.

In May 2002, UN Secretary-General Kofi Annan set out proposed priorities for the WSSD under the innovative 'WEHAB' framework, recognizing biodiversity and sustainable ecosystem management as one of the five priorities: water, energy, health, agriculture and biodiversity.

It would be logical to replace this approach with that of the single system. Without a policy that puts protecting the environment from further degradation and restoring things (as a consequence of human actions) as a main goal, the environment might be sacrificed in the name of human happiness, democracy, energy, food and water.

Crucially, the WEHAB working group paper on biodiversity highlights the need to shift focus from the proximate causes of biodiversity loss to the underlying causes. It focuses on two key Action Areas: integration of biodiversity in country development programmes and economic sectors; and halting the loss of biodiversity and restoring, if possible, biodiversity in degraded areas, as part of reversing loss of environmental resources.

7.2 Global balances and fluxes

Some information about global balances and fluxes is given here.

The IGBP (The International Geosphere Biosphere Programme)

Many studies have been undertaken as part of the IGBP programme that reports on land degradation processes. Newsletters and power point presentations summarize important developments and place them in a policy context. Unfortunately the IGBP does not specifically treat desertification and land degradation as a cross-cutting theme.

The Global land project

This succeeds the International Land Use and Land Cover Project. This supported many investigations into different aspects of desertification and the reports are a good source of further reading. One of its programmes is called *The consequences of land system changes* and this focuses on feedbacks between people and ecosystems, that are critical to Earth System science. Feedbacks are changes in the delivery of a broad range of ecosystem services, such as agricultural productivity, clean air, potable water and many others.

Feedbacks to ecosystems are understood in terms of changes in regimes of decision-making related to land management, and may also include the feedbacks of societal changes to these processes. These changes may be actual or perceived changes, or mediated by broader social, demographic and economic forces.

Consequences of Land System Change   The consequences of land system changes brought about by land use and global environmental changes, including feedbacks between people

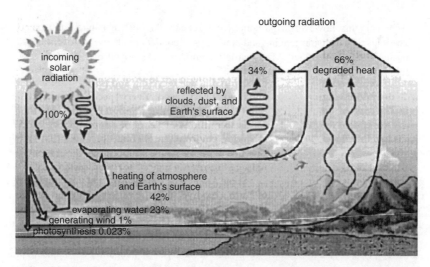

Figure 7.3   Solar energy transformations (Source: NASA Langley Research Center). The figure shows the flow of solar energy in our world. About 33% of the Sun's energy is reflected right back out to space. About 42% goes into heating the atmosphere and the surface of the land and waters. Another 23% goes into the work needed to evaporate water from the oceans and a further 1% goes into driving the atmospheric circulation or winds. Only about 0.02% of the Sun's energy is captured by plants in the process known as photosynthesis. This small amount forms the base of the energy pathways for nearly all life forms.

and ecosystems, are being studied. Feedbacks to people are the ecosystem services, such as agricultural productivity, clean air, and drinking water. Feedbacks to ecosystems are changes in regimes of land management, including feedbacks of societal changes to these processes. These changes may be direct – induced by actual or perceived land system changes – or may operate through broader social, demographic and economic forces in shaping local land use decisions.

Loss of ecological services affects the viability, productivity and stability of the coupled socio-environmental system.

7.2.1 Global fluxes today

Figure 7.3 provides some information about energy and water balances.

Carbon dioxide, water vapour, suspended water droplets and ice crystals in the clouds are more effective absorbers in the infrared part of the electromagnetic spectrum, particularly for wavelengths greater than 8 μm. As the spectrum of longwave terrestrial radiation from the Earth surface extends over wavelengths 3 μm to 30 μm, with a maximum emission at 10 μm, a significant proportion will therefore be absorbed in the atmosphere. About 7 per cent of terrestrial radiation passes directly into space, the remainder being absorbed. Transmission through the atmosphere is in a narrow window. An extremely important window occurs in the absorption spectrum of water vapour between wavelengths 8.5 μm and 11 μm, within which falls the wavebands of maximum emission in the terrestrial radiation spectrum. The atmosphere therefore allows most solar radiation

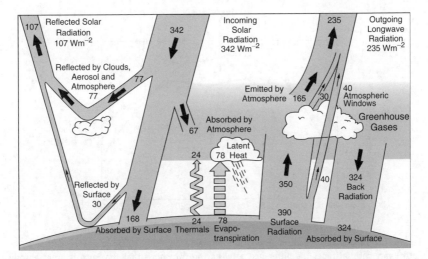

Figure 7.4 The Earth's annual radiation budget. The numbers are all in W/m² (Watts per square meter). Of the incoming radiation, 49% (168 ÷ 342) is absorbed by the Earth's surface. That heat is returned to the atmosphere in a variety of forms (evaporation processes and thermal radiation, for example). Most of this back-scattered heat is absorbed by the atmosphere, which then re-emits it both up and down. Some is lost to space, and some stays in the Earth's climate system. This is what drives the greenhouse effect (Figure adapted from Kiehl and Trenberth, 1997).

to pass through it, but inhibits the passage of terrestrial radiation. This is commonly referred to as the greenhouse effect.

In Figure 7.4, it can be seen that the absorbed radiation is re-emitted, as the atmosphere acts as a radiator. Because of relatively low temperature, generally less than 300 K, atmospheric radiation is longwave and of low intensity. Some of the emissions pass into space, but approximately 60 per cent returns to the Earth's surface systems as counter-radiation. How the energy balance varies with latitude can be seen in Figure 7.5, and it is this together with the rotation of the earth and properties of the ocean that are responsible for the global climate. One place where deserts occur is where the air moving from the equator towards the poles descends.

The sediment transported by runoff transports with the eroded sediment all of the **phosphorus** from the land. The salinity of the oceans is derived from erosion and transport of dissolved salts from the land. The eutrophication of lakes is primarily due to phosphorus that is applied in excess to agricultural fields as fertilizers, and then transported overland and through rivers. Both runoff and groundwater flow play significant roles in transporting **nitrogen** from the land to water bodies. Runoff also plays a part in the **carbon** cycle, again through the transport of eroded rock and soil.

The water cycle is driven by solar energy. Eighty-six per cent of the global evaporation occurs from the oceans, reducing their temperature by evaporative cooling. Without the cooling effect of evaporation, the greenhouse effect would lead to a much higher surface temperature of 67°C, and a warmer planet. The world water cycle is schematically shown in Figure 7.7 with estimates of the amount of water involved. The very small amount of

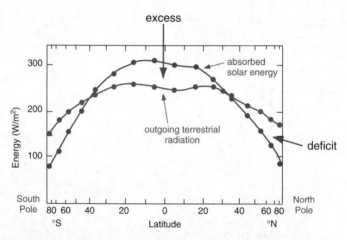

Figure 7.5 Shortwave radiation (from the Sun) and longwave radiation (heat emitted by the Earth) vary with latitude. The difference between the two shows that the Earth is a net absorber of energy (i.e. absorbed energy > outgoing energy) in the tropics, and a net emitter (outgoing energy > absorbed energy) in the polar regions. This is a plot of *zonal mean* radiation; that is, it shows how the radiation varies with *latitude* but not *longitude*. If you imagine a circle around the globe at each latitude, the radiation has been averaged around the circle, because in this case the variation with longitude is less interesting than the variation with latitude (from ClimatePrediction.net, 2008).

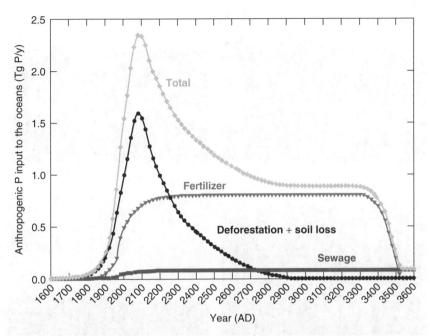

Figure 7.6 Reconstruction and projections of anthropogenic phosphorus delivered to the oceans as a result of several processes, including fertilization, deforestation and soil loss, and sewage. The projection is based on reports of population and arable land published by the World Health Organization and the Intergovernmental Panel on Climate Change. The fertilizer drop off coincides with the depletion of known P reserves. The total integrated anthropogenic input of P (1600–3600 AD) is 1860 Tg (from Filippelli, 2008).

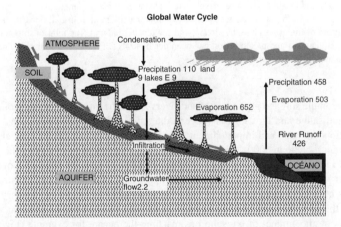

Figure 7.7 The world water cycle is a biogeochemical cycle but also a key component of the cycling of all bio-geochemicals. The values are in 1000 km^3 per year (Credit: Anton Imeson).

(a)   (b)

(c)   (d)

Figure 7.8 Global pressures of fire and tourism
Forest fires and tourism are having global impacts on desertification for many reasons. Figure 7.8a
and b shows the experiments by Prof. Rubio and his team who are investigating the impact of
repeated forest fires on soil and land degradation. The effect is to produce landscapes such as that
at Col de Rates, nearby (Figure 7.8c). Fires occur frequently because of the benefits they provide
economically to the local people. Fires have a large impact on the atmosphere just like the tourists.
The increase in air traffic has been responsible for reducing the rainfall in parts of Murcia because
of the pollution of the atmosphere by aircraft and the global dimming. The relationship between air
traffic, global dimming and precipitation has been demonstrated. Figure 7.8d shows Benidorm from
the sea (Credit: ERMES, P. Rubio and A. Calvo).

fresh water in the soil and groundwater and rivers is significant. Much of the groundwater
is fossil and saline and most of the water in the atmosphere is from the oceans.

Irrigation, drainage and impoundment have had a major impact on the land and water
discharge for more than 5000 years. Controlling water to grow crops has been the primary
motivation for human alteration of freshwater supplies. Today, of course, demands for
freshwater are for irrigation, household and municipal water use, and industrial uses.
There has been a dramatic increase in water appropriation during the last century as well
as during the past 300 years. But it is not just the amount of water that is dramatic, it is also
the impact on the amount of phosphorous reaching the ocean, for example (Figure 7.6).
This figure shows the different sources of phosphate and how they have increased as a
consequence of human actions and how they are projected to be in the future.

Figure 7.9 Challenges faced in procuring and using water resources in an areas of active river channel processes near Tarije Bolivia (Credit: Anton Imeson).

Symptoms of physical water scarcity include severe environmental degradation, such as river desiccation and pollution; declining groundwater tables; water allocation disputes; and failure to meet the needs of some groups. Figure 7.9 from near Tarije Bolivia, illustrates the reality of the global water problem. The steep and active braided river has a high energy and sediment transport that destroys infrastructure. There are very limited groundwater resources, and floods follow droughts. Floodplain sediments have been contaminated by mining and areas suitable for farming are scarce so the river channel is used irrespective of risk. People consume contaminated water and crops.

Because it is difficult to separate evaporation from transpiration, they are combined as evapotranspiration (ET). Evapotranspiration represents the water supply for all non-irrigated vegetation, both natural and crops. Runoff is the source for all human diversions or withdrawals for irrigation, industry, municipal uses, navigation, dilution, hydropower, and maintenance of aquatic life including fisheries (Allan, 2006).

- Withdrawals: agricultural withdrawals $=$ average water application rate $(12\,000\,m^3/ha) \times$ world irrigated area $(240 \times 10^6\,ha$ in $1990) = 2880\,km^3$. Assuming 65% is consumed, $1870\,km^3$.

- Industrial water use is estimated at $975\,km^3$ and roughly 9% $(90\,km^3)$ is consumed. Remainder is discharged back into environment, often polluted.

- Municipal use is estimated at $300\,km^3$ per year, of which $50\,km^3$ (17%) is consumed.

- Evaporation from reservoirs is estimated to average 5% of gross storage capacity of reservoirs $(5500\,km^3)$ or $275\,km^3/yr$.

Table 7.1 ET estimates appropriated for human dominated land uses.

ET Estimates Appropriated for Human Dominated Land Uses

Land Type	NPP co-opted ($\times 10^9$ metric tons)	ET co-opted* (km^3)
Cultivated land	15.0	5,500**
Grazing land	11.6	5,800
Forest land	13.6	6,800
Human occupied areas (lawns, parks, etc.)	0.4	100**
Total appropriated	**40.6**	**18,200**

A total of 26.2% of terrestrial ET is appropriated (18,200 cubic km/69,600 cubic km)
*Assumes 2 g of biomass produced for each litre of water evapo-transpired
**Adjusts for share of ET requirement through irrigation (from Postel *et al.*, 1996)

- In-stream flow needs are estimated from pollution dilution, assuming that this suffices to meet in-stream needs. A common dilution term is 28.3 litres per second per 1000 population. Using the 1990 population yields a dilution requirement of 4700 km^3. If half of water received adequate treatment, the dilution requirement is reduced to 2350 km^3/hr.

- Combining these estimates (see Table 7.1) indicate that humans appropriate 54% of AR. Human use of Evapotranspiration ET (18,200 km^3) plus runoff (6780 km^3) constitutes 30% of total accessible RFWS and 23% of unadjusted RFWS. Figure 7.9 illustrates another global problem, which is that of the contamination of the water and sediments by mining, in many cases hundreds of years ago, but sometimes still today. This river, near Tarije like very many others in Bolivia has alluvial sediments that have been contaminated by mining wastes, which is affecting the health of the people who require the land in the valley bottom for agriculture and water. Another health problem is cancer related to the spread of bracken, which is eaten by cattle and contaminates the milk.

    Water conservation through better planning, management and technologies offers great promise. Figure 7.10 shows per capita water withdrawals in the USA from 1900 to 1995. Per capita water withdrawals began to decline in 1985, despite continued population growth. More efficient agricultural and industrial water use accounts for this trend.

7.3 Case study: desertification and the crash in property prices

During a field visit in October 2009 by a delegation of Chinese soil conservation experts, to Italy and Spain, the European experts, drew attention to the recent increase in erosion

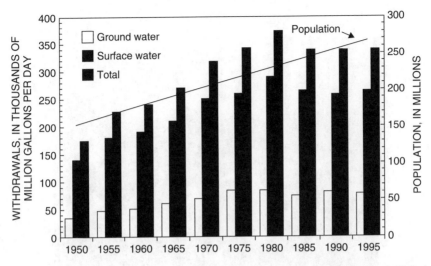

Figure 7.10 Trends in fresh ground- and surface-water withdrawals, and population, for the United States, 1950–1995. Note that per capita water use peaked in 1985, and has since declined (from Allan 2006).

and sedimentation as a consequence of the financial crisis that started in 2008. In many cases, land degradation and desertification are linked to markets that provide money for schemes that affect and fund land use changes or building activity. Erosion and land degradation can cause a loss of investments that triggers a crash in a market because people cannot pay back loans. Similar situations occur all over the world when the financial support for activities is withdrawn and people abandon what they are doing.

In Figure 7.13, this land should never have been classified as suitable for building construction because of its known properties, obvious from the fact that it usually forms badlands. When it is wet, it becomes like porridge. Figure 7.13 shows the erosion that occurred at this location near Mula, Murcia, Spain as a consequence of heavy rainfall in September 2009. The soil surface should always be protected from erosion and dispersive soil material should never be allowed to be on the surface. If left alone, the salt at the surface will be washed out and natural vegetation can grow on the lands and they can also be farmed with good results. But the subsoil with its salt must not be allowed to come onto the surface or gullies will form. Dispersion is one of a number of critical processes because it directly affects both the water and soil conservation regulation processes so that there is both flooding and erosion.

Property development is another problem, because of the intrinsic difference between financial values in the field of investments with real actual values in the economy that has to do with things that actually exist. More than 95 per cent of all money transactions are for financial trading and speculation. In Figure 7.11, the impacts of construction and how these are managed in Florence are being discussed by Dr. Torri and his Chinese experts. Figure 7.12 shows the reservoir near Florence and one of the areas near it that are affected by abandoned construction sites. Getting people to pay interest on money that does not exist for 20 to 40 years can only work if the land has real economic

Figure 7.11   The management of the erosion at a building site in Florence being discussed with Chinese experts (Credit: Anton Imeson).

Figure 7.12   Region near Florence, where property development suddenly ended without considering the consequences for soil erosion and sediment (Credit: Anton Imeson).

Figure 7.13 During the last year because of a building crisis in Europe work has stopped on many building construction sites. In places land was left bare and buildings uncovered on land that is very erodible because of its dispersive properties (Credit: Anton Imeson).

value and is safe. One difficulty is that there is no independent scientific advice that farmers or developers can get because the real business is not helping the landowner but selling loans, insurances and mortgages and statistically it might not matter because most investments are probably sound. As long as land use policy is driven by investments, then investors who are both the property developers and the government are creating a future asset that will bring in revenue to support the local and national political process. The result is that the costs of the land degradation flooding and sedimentation today are in the real economy where money can either be found for managing them or not.

Although the causes and processes of land degradation desertification are nearly always obvious such as here and known for thousands of years, whenever a disaster occurs, the main approach by governments is to make another inventory of the problem and to propose research that describes what is happening again. The general opinion is that development is positive and that people benefit from it but if it gets out of control the consequence are floods, landslides and soil degradation, both of the land and the sea. Criteria are needed to evaluate whether or not things remain within an area of attraction that benefits society and to find where the limits are. As many examples will show, these are understood but irrelevant in terms of how investments and economic development drive change.

7.4 Brazil

Land degradation processes are very intensive in Brazil ever since it was settled by Europeans (Darwin's Beagle Diary). In the North East, about 15 per cent of the land is semi-arid and affected by land degradation processes and recurrent drought. The government launched its National Action Programme to Combat Desertification. The agricultural developments and environmental impacts causing desertification are related to cattle ranching, soy and corn agriculture. The expansion of agriculture for biofuel/ethanol production is considered (sugar cane) to have led to major expansions of industrial agriculture into new areas.

Land degradation takes on many different aspects according to the geographical and historical setting.

In the dry northeastern xeric shrub land and thorn forest, is adapted to arid conditions and there is a short rainy season. As in similar biomes in other parts of the world (the Summer), there is little foliage or undergrowth during the summer and soil temperature are at least 60°C.

More than 40 million people live in the North East of Brazil and there are large numbers of sheep and goats. Cotton was important. Forests were cleared for ceramics and other industries. The Savanna (Cerrado) and the areas adjacent to have different vegetation types and are maintained by fire. The rainfall is high (1000–1500 mm annually), but the rain falls between April and October. These are perfect conditions for soil erosion, as they are in Kenya, for example. The rate of deforestation has been very high and more than 75 per cent of Brazil's original forest cover has already been lost. Cattle ranching and soy plantation agriculture are currently the main causes of deforestation and land degradation. Cashew is a native product of the Cerrado. Wood is used on a large scale to produce charcoal (80%) for industry.

Soil scientists point out that although the soils have some favourable characteristics, these are also negative because they inevitably lead to degradation and erosion (high seasonal rainfall, dry season, depth and texture). The soil tends to be acidic and lacking in nutrients. Agricultural development meant road-building and mechanization, clearing of natural vegetation, reduction of acidity with the use of lime, and the intensive use of fertilizers, herbicides, and pesticides, in other words, all of the things that cause high rates of erosion in Spain (Cerdà 2010). The importance of soy in this area and its profitability has become well known.

The environment was changed to make it suitable for soy and there is evidence that this is not sustainable. In Mato Grosso wind erosion is active.

Land use change in the Amazon is mainly driven by the expansion of cattle ranching, often by people moving from areas where soy has taken over. The expansion of transport infrastructure, opening up the Amazon for small farmers, commercial farmers and cattle ranchers, is facilitated by soy. Once the rainforest canopy is opened, the land dries and, the understorey vegetation becomes prone to fire. Fires meant to clear land burn out of control, making the forest more vulnerable to fires caused by lightning. Fires are now common in the Amazon region.

Although illegal, large amounts of forest destruction and erosion are being caused because the forest is seen as a source of charcoal for the manufacture of pig iron transit to China.

It seems that clearing the forest actually has reduced the amount of evaporation and precipitation. Moisture-laden air masses moves inland from the Atlantic and crosses the Amazon towards the Andes. Land clearance reduces the recycling of rainfall inland. When rain from the Atlantic fell on rainforest, about one quarter was discharged back to the Atlantic Ocean, and three fourths evaporated into the atmosphere, either directly or through transpiration, and was then carried further inland to again come down as rainfall. This explains how rainforests get their name. It also explains why rainfall is heavy throughout the Amazon basin and south of it, in the Cerrado, as well. When rain falls on land that is cleared for grazing or cropping, the runoff/evaporation ratio is reversed as roughly three fourths of it runs off, returning to the sea, leaving only one fourth to evaporate and be carried further inland. Thus the loss of millions hectares of Amazonian forest a year is slowly weakening the water recycling mechanism that brings water to the agricultural regions of the Cerrado.

7.5 Namibia

The DRFN is a Namibian non-governmental sustainability organization aiming to enhance decision-making for sustainable development through research, training and consultancy in the country's land, water and energy sectors.

The DRFN provides objective, relevant and professional services supporting decision-makers of all walks of life – from communities to traditional and local authorities, to the highest decision-making bodies and individuals in government and the private sector – by developing, disseminating and implementing scientific, fact-based and analytical options that form the backbone of policy development, planning and implementation, thereby contributing to Namibia's sustainable development.

In a statement made in Windhoek (Kruger 2006), the director of the DRFN summarized the situation as follows:

> There was a struggle to provide sustainable livelihoods for the rural population and not allow desertification. Everywhere, water is scarce and on the grasslands of the central plateau and limited grasslands to the north, where half the population live, people are confined between the Namib desert, stretching 1400 km along the coast and the Kalahari to the southeast. Namibia has too little arable land to for its 1.8 million people, two million livestock, and current levels of agricultural production. The project manager of the Desert Research Foundation in Namibia, said 'planting trees and other traditional methods of combating land degradation were all good ideas, but in the final analysis, more Namibians needed to look for livelihoods outside agriculture'. Lack of alternative income-generating opportunities is a major obstacle. He explained that Namibia's cattle population is beyond the carrying capacity of the land. 'We are not only concerned about overgrazing, but also about the large numbers of cattle that are destroying the environment', principal technician in the Ministry of Agriculture, Water and Rural Development, Ruben Ngenda, told IRIN.

Since livestock mean status, herds are not reduced. Further, many people still rely on wood as fuel so trees are being cut down.

The policy is to encourage people to take ownership of the resources. Communities have to be in the driver's seat, said Kruger. 'The absence of secure tenure rights on land in the communal areas had contributed to the failure of communities to maintain grazing pastures and invest in resources like irrigation systems.'

Water scarcity is a perennial problem, exacerbated by unstable rainfall patterns. Rationing is commonplace, especially in the summer months, when town councils usually implement restrictions on watering gardens and washing cars with a hose, and urge people to shower or use less water for bathing.

The country depends mostly on its underground aquifers during severe droughts, and the use of reclaimed water. According to a water engineer in Windhoek Municipality, Ammo Peters, Namibia is the only country in Africa, if not the whole world, that purifies water directly from sewerage waste.

In the past few years, Namibia has opened negotiations with its neighbours, Botswana and South Africa, to be allowed to tap water from the Zambezi and Orange rivers, but until an agreement is reached, the country is forced to more effectively exploit what water resources it has.

'Aquifers are a sustainable source of water and we need to recharge them regularly to ensure that the water table does not go down to unacceptable levels,' said Peters. Rainwater accumulated in dams will in future be injected into aquifers, so as to overcome the problem of evaporation, which robs Namibia of almost as much water as it receives each year.

Experts from Egypt, Spain and South Africa are working with the government on a three-year research programme into storing water in aquifers, with the aim of benefiting local communities and improving the country's water management system.

Land use change and desertification in Indiana

This area suffered from severe soil erosion in the 1930s at the time of the dust bowl and many farmers had to leave the region because the productive capacity of their land had been lost and they could not pay back the loans they had taken to buy tractors.

Two hundred years ago, when European settlers first arrived, the upland areas of southern Indiana in the area of the Hoosier National Forest, Crawford and Norman uplands consisted of mainly oak and old growth forest and these were found on mainly glacial sediments and limestones. The land was considered as too densely wooded to be useful.

The forest was cleared as quickly as the settlers could manage but forest was sometimes left on the steeper slopes at first but when the forest service began to buy land in the 1930, very little of this was left. Today's forest was systematically replanted since then (Sieber and Munson 1994). The wild life and biodiversity were prolific and included the Eastern bison and passenger pigeon but many animals were overhunted and disappeared from the region by the late 1880s, including deer and wild turkey. The farmers predominantly grew corn and raised hogs on the steeper areas which were relatively isolated.

The region experienced a gradual economic decline between 1915 and 1950. The farms on the steep slopes with poor soils could not compete with the larger scale farming on flat lands. In the 1920s and 1930s came massive erosion. This occurred with the introduction of mechanised tractors.

A 1935 map of soil erosion made by the U.S. Soil Conservation Service showed that between 75 and 95 per cent of the land was affected by sheet erosion and gullying. The land was described as 'ten year land' as during ten years of tillage by the customary methods, the soil washes away so that further tillage is unprofitable. Farmers could not pay taxes and were forced to abandon their holdings. This environmental devastation was accompanied by the economic problems of The Great Depression.

As a result of this, a national forest was formed in south central Indiana which was officially much later designated as the Hossier National Forest. In 1935 a contemporary newspaper states that the Forest Service had more than 2000 offers of more than 2000000 acres of land – this is equivalent to the areas of hilly land in the area, which had suffered the most erosion.

During the 1930s Indiana acquired other large areas of land. From a policy point of view it was effective in that it acquired vast amounts of poorly maintained farmland and put it under one management scheme. A forester from that period said that at that time erosion had left gullies everywhere and that the only topsoil that was left was in the Ohio River. Only a few pockets of old-growth forest remain. The Federal Government supported the replanting through the Civilian Conservation Corps (CCC) that President Roosevelt initiated during his recovery programme.

Flooding in Indiana

The June flooding in Indiana was caused by heavy rain falling upon saturated soils at a time when streamflows already were much above normal. A wetter than normal Spring preceded the June flood in Indiana. Precipitation totals in central and southern Indiana for the period March–May 2008 ranged from 123 to 180 percent of normal (Indiana State Climate Office, 2008). Rainfall amounts of 1–3 in. on May 30–31 and 1–5 in. on June 3–4 in parts of central and southern Indiana resulted in above-normal streamflows in the days prior to the June flood (National Weather Service, 2008). On the basis of the USGS WaterWatch Recent Streamflow Conditions map for June 5, 2008, daily mean streamflows at many USGS streamgages in central and southern Indiana (with 30 or more years of record) were either much above normal or were record highs for June 5 (U.S. Geological Survey, 2008). On June 6, an abnormally high amount of moisture from the Gulf of Mexico was available for thunderstorms, and a nearly stationary frontal boundary was in place across south central Indiana to enhance thunderstorm development and anchor a common storm path (David Tucek, National Weather Service, written commun., June 2008). A strong inflow of Gulf moisture, lifted by the frontal boundary, resulted in frequent to nearly continuous showers and thunderstorms of moderate to heavy rainfall intensity for 12 to 16 hours on June 6–7 (David Tucek, National Weather Service, written commun., August 2008).

A map of estimated precipitation totals prepared from NWS radar data (Thomas Adams, National Weather Service Ohio River Forecast Center, written commun., 2008) shows rainfall totals ranging from about 2 in. to more than 10 in.

The recurrence interval is the average interval of time within which the given event will be equaled or exceeded once (American Society of Civil Engineers, 1953, p. 1221). For example, the 100-year rainfall is the rainfall that would be exceeded or equaled, on long-term average, once in 100 years. Recurrence interval relates the magnitude of an event to a probability of occurrence and does not imply that the event will happen at regular intervals; for example, two 100-year floods can occur within the same year at the same location. The reciprocal of the recurrence interval is the **annual exceedance probability**, which is the probability that a given event magnitude will be exceeded or equalled in any given year (Hodgkins *et al.* 2007). For example, the annual exceedance

Figure 7.14 Information Provided On November 11 2010, a wall of sand blew across eastern China. The airborne sand entirely hides much of the North China Plain, Shandong Peninsula, and the Bo Hai from view in this true color image, taken mid-morning by the Moderate Resolution Imaging Spectroradiometer (MODIS) on NASA's Terra satellite. Weather stations in several cities on the North China Plain reported blowing sand and poor visibility in the hours it took the storm to pass.

The fast-moving dust was blowing east from the Gobi Desert, where the massive storm originated the day before. After this image was taken, the dust moved towards the Korean Peninsula, where world leaders were gathering for the Group of 20 summit. A weather station in Seoul reported that the dust had reached Korea by 9:00 p.m. on November 11.

Such large dust storms are common in China, but the storms usually happen in the spring, when fronts from Siberia sweep southeast across the Gobi Desert. Late autumn and winter dust storms are rare (Credit: NASA Modis team).

probability of the 100-year peak flood streamflow is 0.01. In other words, there is a 1-percent chance that the 100-year peak flow will be exceeded or equaled in any given year.

7.6 Dust and sandstorms in China

One of the largest environmental problems today are the dust sandstorms that are shown in Figure 7.14 affecting air quality and health. The sandstorm in November 2010 shown in Figure 7.13, illustrates the extent of the problem and the impact this is having today in the region.

In response to the devastating sandstorms that swept across China in 2000, a conference was called by the UN to examine and analyse experience in combating and controlling them. They are seen as both a cause and consequence of desertification. Dust storms and sandstorms are also the major erosion processes in Iceland where vast amounts of soil are lost, leaving bedrock surfaces behind (Arnalds 2010).

The physical processes of sand and dust transport were described by Bagnold. Wind transport occurs as a result of the specific conditions described in Chapter 3, with the roughness of the soil and the soil moisture content being key factors. Drought means that there is less vegetation for animals to eat so that grazing animals create conditions where wind erosion can take place (Youlin *et al.* 2001).

The impacts of dust storms include reductions in livestock forage and fuelwood, reduced water availability, sand encroachment on productive land, increased flooding and reduction of crop yields. These disrupt life and increase poverty, migration and refugees.

A comprehensive review of dust storms is given by Wang Shigong *et al.* (2001).

Dust storms are also a huge mobile source of pollution. On the other hand, they have positive effects. Sahara dust can blow up to 480000 tons of sand and dust to the north east part of the Amazon valley (Wang). The sand is often alkali and it can play a positive role in neutralizing emerging acid rain in Japan (Qua Zhang *et al.* 1994). The presence of dust has an impact on the atmosphere and wind.

References and further reading

Alcamo, J., Döll, P. Henrichs, T., Kaspar, F., Lehner, B., Rösch, T. and Siebert, S. (2003) Development and testing of the WaterGAP 2 global model of water use and availability. *Hydrological Science Journal.*, 48, pp. 317–338.

Allan, D. (2006) *Human Appropriation of the World's Fresh Water Supply*. University of Michigan. Available online from http://www.globalchange.umich.edu/globalchange2/current/lectures/freshwater_supply/freshwater.html (Accessed 03/06/2008).

Allegra, C. (2008) *Final report Water Cycle IUCN*, Gland, Switzerland August 2008 38p.

American Society of Civil Engineers (ACE) (1953), *Report of the subcommittee on the joint division committee on floods:* Am. Soc. Civil Engineers Trans., v. 118, p. 1220–1230. . . .

Arnalds, O. (2010) Dust sources and deposition of Aeolian materials in Iceland, *Iceland Agricultural Science*, 23, 3–21.

Balmford, A., Bruner, A., Cooper, P., *et al.* (2002) Economic reasons for conserving wild nature. *Science* 297, 950–953.

Bennett, H.H. (1932) *Soil Erosion: Its Extent and Meaning and Necessary Measures of Control* Address delivered in connection with the South Carolina Teacher-training program by H.H., Chief, In Charge Soil Erosion Investigations, Bureau of Chemistry and Soils, U.S. Department of Agriculture, at Spartanburg and Clemson College, November 4, 1932; Columbia and Rock Hill, November 5, 1932.

Cerda, A. (2010) Herbicide versus Tillage. Soil and water losses at the El Teularet soil erosion experimental station *Geophysical Research Abstracts*. [np].

Chawla, L. (2002). *Growing up in an urbanising world*. Unesco/Earthscan Publications Ltd., London, UK.

Climate Prediction net (2011) Data source http://climateprediction.net/

Cowie, A., Schneider, B.C. and Montanarella, L.D. (2007) Potential synergies between existing multilateral environmental agreements in the implementation of land use, land-use change and forestry activities *Environmental Science and Policy* 10, 335–352.

Costanza, R., d'Arge, R., Groot, R. de, *et al.*, (1997). The value of the world's ecosystem services and natural capital. *Nature* 387, 253–260.

Crain, W. (2000). The Importance of Nature to Children, in: *Encounter – education for meaning and social justice* 13 (2), 4–12.

Darwin, Charles (1845). *Journal of researches into the natural history and geology of the countries visited during the voyage of H.M.S.* Beagle *round the world*. London: John Murray. 2d ed.

Descroix, L. and Gautier, E. (2002). Water erosion in the southern French Alps: climatic and human mechanisms. *Catena* 50 (1), 53–85.

ESA (2011) http://www.esa.int/esaCP/index.html European Space Agency portal.

Falkenmark, M. and Lundquist, J. (1998) Towards water security: political determination and human adaptation crucial *Natural Resources Forum*, 22, 37–51.

Falkenmark, M. and Rockström, J. (2004). *Balancing Water for Humans and Nature: The New Approach in Ecohydrology*. London: Earthscan.

Filippelli G.M. (2008) The global phosphorus cycle: Past, present, and future *Elements* 4 89–95.

Gleick, P.H. (1996) Water resources. In: *Encyclopedia of Climate and Weather*, ed. by S. H. Schneider, Oxford University Press, New York, vol. 2, pp. 817–823.

Gleick, P.H. (1999) Water Futures: A Review of Global Water Projections. *In*: F. R. Rijsberman, ed., *World Water Scenarios: Analysis*. London: Earthscan.

Gleick, P.H. (2000) *The World's Water 2000–2001. The Biennial Report On Freshwater Resources*. Island Press, Washington D.C., 300 pp.

GLP (2011) www.globallandproject.org/ - Global Land Project Portal.

Gordon, L.J., Steffen, W., Jönsson, B.F., Folke, C., Falkenmark, M. and Johannessen, Å. (2005) Human Modification of Global Water Vapor Flows from the Land Surface. *Proceedings of the National Academy of Sciences of the United States*, 102 (21), pp. 7612–7617. Available online from http://www.pnas.org/content/102/21/7612.full.pdf (Accessed 30/06/2008).

Tresury, H.M., Stern, N. (ed.) *Stern Review: The Economics of Climate Change* H.M, Treasury http://www.hmtreasury.gov.uk/media/6/9/Table_of_Contents.pdf.

Hodgkins, G.A., Stewart, G.J., Cohn, T.A., and Dudley, R.W. (2007) *Estimated magnitudes and recurrence intervals of peak flows on the Mousam and Little Ossipee Rivers for the Flood of April 2007 in southern Maine*: U.S. Geological Survey Open-File Report 2007–1146, 13 p.

IGBP (2011) IGBP Portal *(International Geosphere Biosphere Program)* Access to global data http://www.igbp.net/

IHDP (2011) (IHDP *International Human Dimensions Program on Global Environmental Change*) Portal http://www.ihdp.unu.edu/

Imeson A.C., Koning, P.C. Kisterman H. and Wolvekamp P.S. et al. (2006) *Report on the activities and support provided by the European Community to combat desertification in countries in Asia, Latin America and Caribbean, Central and Eastern Europe in the period January 2001–2005* submitted to UNCCD CRIC 5 prepared by Imeson. ENV 2006-12800. 74 p. UNCCD.

Kahn, P. H. and Kellert, S.R., (2002) *Children and nature: psychological, sociocultural and evolutionary investigations*. MIT Press, Cambridge, U.S.A.

Kahn, P. H., (2001). *The human relationship with nature*. Development and culture. MIT Press, Cambridge, U.S.A.

Kiehl & Trenberth, (1997) Earth's Annual Global Mean Energy Budget. *Bull. Amer. Meteor. Soc.*, 78, 197–208.

Kruger AS. (2006) *Desert Margins Programme (Namibia): Towards participatory rangeland management in the eastern communal areas of Namibia: A case study from Orukune, Okaari and Omazera villages*. Windhoek (Namibia): Desert Research Foundation of Namibia (DRFN).

Kroll T and Kruger A S (1998). Closing the gap: bringing communal farmers and service institutions together for livestock and rangeland development. *J Arid Environ* 1998; 39: 315–23.

Lambert, F., Delmonte, B., Petit, J. R., Bigler, M., Kaufmann, P. R., Hutterli, M. A., Stocker, T. F., Ruth, U., Steffensen, J. P., and Maggi, V (2008).: Dust-climate couplings over the past 800,000 years from the EPICA Dome C ice core, *Nature*, 452, 616–619, 2008.

Leopold, Aldo: (1948) *A Sand County Almanac, and Sketches Here and There*, Oxford University Press, New York, 1987, pg. 81.

Millennium Ecosystem Assessment (2005a). *Ecosystems and Human Well-being: Volume 2 – Scenarios*. Island Press, Washington, DC, 515 pp. Available online from http://www.millenniumassessment.org/en/Scenarios.aspx#download (Accessed 18/06/2008).

Millennium Ecosystem Assessment (2005b). *Ecosystems and Human Well-being: Synthesis*. Island Press, Washington, DC, 155 pp. Available online from http://www.millenniumassessment.org/en/Synthesis.aspx (Accessed 20/06/2008).

Milliman, J. D., Farnsworth, K. L., Jones, P. D., Xu, K. H. and Smith, L. C. (2008). Climatic and anthropogenic factors affecting river discharge to the global ocean, 1951–2000. *Global and Planetary Change*, 62, pp. 187–194.

Morlock, S. E., Menke, C. D., Arvin, D. V., and Kim, M. H., (2008), *Flood of June 7–9, 2008, in central and southern Indiana:* U.S. Geological Survey Open File Report 2008–1322, 15 p., 3 app.

National Weather Service (2011) Source of weather data http://www.weather.gov/

NASA (2011) Source of information and images http://www.nasa.gov/multimedia/imagegallery/

Pagiola, S., Bishop, J. and Landell-Mills, N. (2002). *Selling forest environmental services: market-based mechanisms for conservation and development*. Earthscan Publications Ltd., London, UK, 299 pp.

Pretty J. (2003). Social capital and the collective management of resources. *Science* 302(5652): 1912–1914.

Putnam, R. D. (2000). *Bowling alone: the collapse and revival of American community*. Simon and Schuster, New York, 541 pp.

Rosenzweig, C. D. Karoly, M. Vicarelli[1], P. Neofotis[1], Q. Wu[3], G. Casassa[4], A. Menzel[5], T. Root[6], N. Estrella[7], B. Seguin[7], P. Tryjanowski[8], C. Liu[9], S. Rawlins[10] & A. C. Imeson (2008) Attributing physical and biological impacts to anthropogenic climate change *Nature* 453, 353–357.

Seely, M., P. Klintenberg and A. S. Kruger, (2008). "The unmet challenge of connecting scientific research with community action" in Lee, C. and T. Schaaf (Eds.), *The future of drylands*. UNESCO, Tunis, pp. 687–697.

Qu Zchang, Xu Bao-yu, He Hui xia (1994) Some enlightenment from a sandstorm occurred in northwest China. *Arid land geography* 17, 1, 63–67.

Sieber. E. and Munson C. A. (1994). *Looking at History Indianas Hoosier National Forest Region 1600–1950* Indiana University Press, Bloomington and Indianpolis 131.

Schmitt, A., Dotterweich, M., Schmidtchen, G. and Bork, H.-R., (2003). Vineyards, hopgardens and recent afforestation: effects of late Holocene land use change on soil erosion in northern Bavaria, Germany. *Catena* 51(3-4), 241–254.

Tibbetts, J. (1998). *Open space conservation: investing in your community's economic health*. Lincoln Institute of Land Policy, Cambridge, USA, 24 pp.

Topfer. K. (2000) *The Triple Bottom Line Economic, Social, Natural Capital – United Nations' "Global Compact"*. UN Chronicle Summer 2000.

Turner, W.R., Nakamura, T., Dinetti, M. (2004) Global urbanization and the separation of humans from nature. *BioScience* 54 (6), 585–590.

UNCCD (2007) *10-year strategic plan and framework to enhance the implementation of the Convention* 2008–2009, COP 8 Madrid 3–4 September 2007.

Wagner, G. (2004) The Economics of Tree Hugging: GSAS Student Endorses "Green Accounting". Harvard GSAS Bulletin 33(6), pp. 1 & 3.

Wang Shigong, Dong Guagrong, Shang Kezheng and Chen Huizong (2001). Progress of research on understanding sand and dust storms in the world pp 29–48 in Yang Youlin, Victor Squires and Lu Qi. (editors) 2001 *Global Alarm: Dust and sandstorms from the Worlds drylands*. United Nations Publication No E.02.II. F.50 343 p.

Yang Youlin, Victor Squires and Lu Qi. (editors) (2001) Global Alarm: Dust and sandstorms from the Worlds drylands. United Nations Publication No E.02.II. F.50 343.

Explanations

WEHAB (2002) WEHAB framework (Frameworks for Action). World Summitt on Sustainable development Johannesbourg http://www.un.org/jsummit/html/documents/wehab_papers.html

8
Desertification, ecosystem services and capital

8.1 Introduction

Originally, desertification was used was to describe the development of desert-like conditions in sub-Saharan Africa. Indicators of desertification included the loss of vegetation cover, a reduction in soil depth because of soil erosion, and a reduction in the productive capacity and water-holding properties of the soil (see Chapter 3). These conditions resulted in a higher soil temperatures and albedo which could increase air temperature. There would be less rainfall, rivers would dry up, low crop yields and too little to feed the cattle or pay tax. With the broader view of desertification explained in Chapter 1, then all of the other processes described in Chapters 4 and 5 come into play. The actions described in Chapter 6 then in different ways address land degradation. In this chapter, Chapter 8, the emergent impacts of land degradation are introduced with respect to the notions of ecosystem services and capital.

The impacts of land degradation and desertification are thus experienced as either a) a gradual loss in the capacity of the soils and landscape to provide what it once did in the way of goods and services and as such a loss of capital; or b) their complete and sudden loss. UNESCO and UNEP, from 1960 onwards (Odingo 1980), saw desertification as causing a loss in the capacity of the soil to produce crops, or to support the existing ecosystems. One of the processes is the physical and financial removal (creating debt) from the landscape of systems on the ground of the natural capital that has accumulated there in the form of both goods and money.

The concept of soil functions has been explained in Chapter 1. Soil functions are listed in Figure 8.1.

Soil erosion and degradation resulted in a large loss of organic matter, and this is an important source of carbon. Many people interpret the low carbon content of the soil as making it a potential carbon sink. This would then be one of its services (Figure 8.3).

The Millennium Ecosystem Assessment, in 2005, of the impact of human-induced ecosystem change on ecosystem goods and services warned that ecosystems have been changing more rapidly and extensively in the last 50 years than in any other period. The degradation of ecosystem services could be a barrier to achieving the UN Millennium Development Goals that have been set. Reversing the degradation of ecosystems is a real challenge requiring major policy and institutional changes. It is said that it would

Desertification, Land Degradation and Sustainability, First Edition. Anton Imeson.
© 2012 John Wiley & Sons, Ltd. Published 2012 by John Wiley & Sons, Ltd.

Soil functions

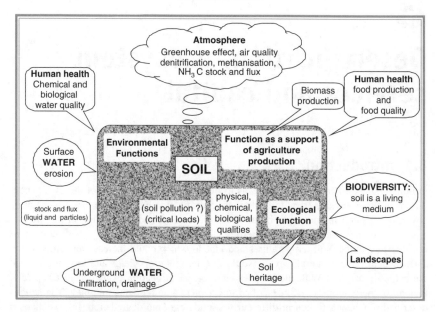

Figure 8.1 Soil functions (*Source*: Robert 2001)

'Private and, as well as public land performs a number of functions that cannot be restricted to the benefit of a single landowner. Land degradation has an immediate effect on the productivity of the land for the owner, but has also, and more importantly, substantial off-site effects with in many cases relevant economic, social and health related implications for the community.'

require changes in the way nature is treated at all level of decision-making and new ways of co-operation between government, business and civil society. The description of degradation used in the Millennium Assessment study incorporates processes of desertification. In a sense, it refers to desertification at the global level, whereas the UNCCD is focused on the impact that desertification has on people living in specific areas.

Ecosystem goods and services include things that the land and soil provide to society: tangible things such as water, food, oxygenated air, protection from floods and landslides but also services that have aesthetic or cultural value. Sometimes the concepts of air, land, management and soil quality are used to describe the different degrees to which ecosystem goods and services are being provided and utilized by communities. Changes in soil quality or health can be used as a tool for investigating the negative impacts of desertification (see Chapter 3).

Environmental economists have estimated the monetary value of all of the world's ecosystem services as being between 16 and 54 trillion dollars (Costanza *et al.* 1997). That humans were consuming a higher proportion of these goods and services than could be sustained in the long term was stressed by Leopold in 1948 but also by Huxley in 1894. Different proportions or types of goods and services are used by people living within and outside of any area. This means that it is involved and complex to establish exactly all of the impacts of desertification on all services provided to people in a global economy. The realization today is that when land is appropriated from nature or there is a change in land use, in most cases, there is too little attention given to the way the provision of goods and services is changed and to the long-term consequences of this for future generations.

8.1.1 Impacts of desertification

Desertification is a complex process of the simultaneous degradation of soil, water resources and vegetation, which can affect natural, semi-natural and agricultural systems, as well as other human activities. Figure 8.2 provides a summary of the ecological processes of desertification, as well as their consequences in terms of damages to the natural and human environment.

The complex of desertification process diminishes the productive capacity of the environmental system (see Figure 8.2). This productive capacity can be described in terms of 'functions of the environment' (De Groot 1992). Functions of an environmental system can be subdivided into four main groups (namely production, regulation, carrier and information functions). Land degradation and desertification could result in a decline of the performance of a particular function. Therefore, an integrated assessment of the impacts of desertification should consider all environmental functions performed, which may include agriculture, forestry but also functions such as sedimentation control and provision of habitat to wildlife. A tentative list of potential impact of desertification is shown in Table 8.1.

The EU task group of the Soil Strategy focused on the impact (Task Group 3 report) on those critical functions which has been singled out as more sensitive to desertification (Imeson 2000). These are explained in detail elsewhere. They are:

1 Water and nutrient regulation function.

2 Soil and water conservation function.

3 Ecosystem restorative function.

The goods and services provided at the 'landscape level' are very often compromised by activities at the 'farm level'. Responsibilities for regulating the hydrological cycle can be defined at the farm level and this is where soil conservation comes in.

The impact of an alternative land use practice on the services provided by unpolluted runoff being enjoyed elsewhere is the responsibility of the land owner when the polluter pays principle is applied.

Globally, land use conversions from forest to agricultural production have over the centuries been removing or reducing the capacity of the soil and land to regulate the hydrological cycle. The long-term consequence of this are soil loss, soil compaction and increased flooding and land sliding at the regional level. The capacity of the main river channels is reduced by landslides and channel erosion so that there are more frequent inundations. Figure 8.4, is specifically intended to show that in areas such as this in

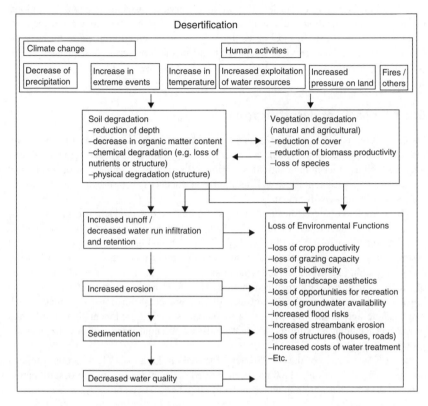

Figure 8.2 Schematic overview of the driving forces and consequences of desertification (From Hein 2002).

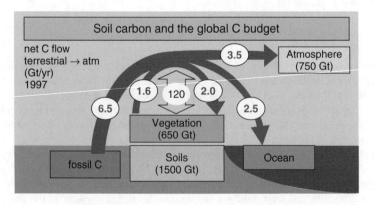

Figure 8.3 Global carbon cycle (*Source*: M. Robert, 2004).

Table 8.1 Checklist of the potential costs of desertification and land degradation (From Hein 2002).

Function	Description	Potential impacts
Regulation functions		
1. Water supply	Better groundwater availability and moisture retention, through good infiltration of rainfall	Loss of ground water resources
2. Water regulation	Lower runoff and flood risks, due to good infiltration of rainfall, or to retention of water in ecosystems.	Loss of surface water resources, and/or increased flood risks
3. Soil retention	Vegetation cover important against erosion	Increased erosion leading to loss of productive capacities of the oil and/or to sedimentation
4. Soil formation and maintenance of fertility	By litter formation and organic matter addition, or by accumulation of sediments.	Loss of resilience of ecosystems because of negative impacts on the soil formation processes
5. Carbon sequestration	Sequestration of carbon in biomass	Loss of the amount of carbon sequestered
Production functions		
6. Food supply	Production of dryland crops.	Loss of productive capacity of the land
7. Grazing	Sheep and goat grazing.	Loss of pasture quality
8. Raw material	Fibre for fabrics	Loss of possibilities to extract raw materials
9. Genetic resources	Old cultivated varieties, or wild plant species diversity.	Loss of genetic diversity
Habitat functions		
10. Refugium	As habitat for natural species	Loss of biodiversity and nature
Information functions		
11. Recreation	Drylands may provide opportunity for tourism and recreation, including outdoor activities	Loss of opportunities for recreation
12. Historic information	Heritage value of traditional agricultural practices	Loss of historic information
13. Aesthetics	Valuable scenery	Loss of scenery
14. Existence/bequest value	Desert landscapes or water resources may have special value in regions of water scarcity.	Impacts on landscapes

Figure 8.4 This part of northern Sardinia enjoys the benefits of a healthy landscape and soils that provides the basis for high social, economic and natural capital. The olive tree is said to be more than 2000 years old (Credit: Anton Imeson).

Sardinia, as well as in much of mainland Europe, natural areas and forests are becoming assets, generating billions of Euros both with respect to the products they generate and tourism. The area produced no runoff during the very intensive thundesrtorms that occurred in August and provides cork and acorns as well as flood production.

Changing cultural habits to stop desertification challenges cultural identity. In Iceland for example, the soil conservation service has in spite of its success not been able to control grazing in the mountains (Figure 8.5). In the Mediterranean and many arid regions water is appropriated from rural areas for parks and gardens. Figure 8.6 shows an area near the Acropolis in Athens where trees improve the microclimate but this requires significanat amounts of irrigation (Figure 8.7). The impact that global warming is having on these ecosystem services and the ensuing costs for society has been recently reviewed by the IPCC Working Group II (2005). At the meeting photographed in Figure 8.8, the discussion was adaptation. Restoring large areas of land using a geoengineering approach would be a positive adaptation. Desertification is both an impact and driver of climate change and at the same time a consequence of biodiversity loss. At the global scale, the vegetation, soil and land cover regulate the world's climate. This regulation is being performed differently by the surfaces and land use with which it is being replaced. Over

Figure 8.5 Sheep being rounded up in Iceland. This is an annual event which is not just about meet but an expression of Icelandic culture (Credit: Anton Imeson).

Figure 8.6 Constructing terraces and growing trees is an excellent strategy in Athens for lowering the summer temperatures. It is several degrees less hot in the shade (Credit: Anton Imeson).

Figure 8.7 is illustrative of the huge amount of water that is used by gardens in, for example, Athens and Madrid. Areas outside of these suffer water shortages (Credit: Anton Imeson).

Figure 8.8 The Working Group II of the IPCC at Mexico, discussing Impact, Adaption and Vulnerability to Climate Change. The degradation of the soil affects the climate, biodiversity and land degradation as different aspects of one system (Credit: Anton Imeson).

vast areas of the planet, the albedo and energy balances have been altered in a direction that is reducing the amount of oxygen being produced by the vegetation, so that CO_2 content is increasing for this reason too.

One of the functions and services that land provides is, as for most people, that of property and real estate. It is viewed as a source of raw materials. The costs of many things today has become relatively cheap. They would not only be expensive, if the costs of environmental degradation were not externalized from the prices, but would also probably be unable to be made. The relative value of goods decided by some countries, which excludes environmental costs, means that an ever increasing proportion of the ecosystem goods and services of the world is ending up in their cities.

The European Union in its CRIC 05 (2007) report to the UNCCD, in which it described the lessons it had learned, said:

> The underlying causes of desertification are related to human activities that often produce and use natural resources in unsustainable ways. Organisation and practice play key roles in influencing the degree of pressure that human activities place on nature. Thus, ecological degradation and impoverishment are the products of social and economic interventions and the institutional context. They stimulate competition among diverse actors at local, national and global levels. This in turn gives rise to overexploitation of resources and exclusion from assets (productive, environmental, or cultural).

8.1.2 The causes

The changing concepts of desertification have been explained in Chapter 1. A thorough analysis of the changing definition of desertification was recently made by the European Union. Problems of desertification were seen as being of special importance to Africa. Today, it is apparent that the land and soil of most of the world's ecosystems require binding international agreements to protect them, not just those in Africa. The view that desertification is increasingly being viewed as occurring almost everywhere and seen as affecting everyone is also held by some governments (Spanish National Action Plan 2007). New paradigms of desertification propose a close relationship between desertification, loss of biodiversity and climate change (Montanarella 2006). It follows, then, that since the economic cost of climate change has been accepted by the general public (Stern 2006), there should be enough public will to include actions needed to combat desertification as one of the policies that address climate change. Today, the concept of the ecological footprint has become common knowledge and concern. The links and relationships between carbon-transport-profit-land degradation poverty and migration are common knowledge (Rubio 2007). The ecological footprint is now used as an indicator of desertification in the Spanish National Action Plan. New paradigms of desertification incorporate the ecological footprint and its link with ecosystem goods and services (Rubio 2007).

A key driver of desertification (but also of climate change, biodiversity, migration and poverty) is the unprecedented appropriation and use of the goods and services provided by ecosystems (as a result of economic development, population growth and increasing consumption). However, it is about how our wants and expectations are created by marketing and the efforts that are being made to create markets and jobs. How the economy is linked to the environment in most econometric models misses the point as it is mainly based on statistics and ignores the reality of the actual processes and causes. Nevertheless, changes could be implemented with much less negative impact if concepts of adaptive management were followed. The Adaptive Management concept links land use change policy to the appropriate spatial and temporal scales and also to ecosystem functions. It also enables feedbacks and scale to be introduced into the discussions.

Applying this theory, say, five thousand or more years ago, Darwin pointed out that there was no feedback preventing humans from multiplying and reproducing and using more and more of nature other than dictated by common sense. Also positively rewarded, were the civilizations, natural and cultural values and behaviour that evolved after the discovery and use of fire, the use of bronze and iron, and the discovery of money. The benefits that these gave when a clan or country possessed metal tools and weapons and higher agricultural productivity, included food surplus for trade or building monuments. In reality, the capital of the natural forests was consumed for many reasons that included the need of weapons for armies, and to produce silver and gold for jewels and coins, In Elizabethan England and in much of the world it was also used to stay warm in winter and cook food. Genetically these things were reinforced because those who had metal and cut down forests fastest eliminated, or enslaved and gained power over, others and their resources. There was a seeming paradox in that to become successful and civilized as a country it was necessary to develop institutions that organized things in an atmosphere of trust which required leaders being benevolent and letting the people live well and happily. At the same time it was this organization and success that enabled them to scale up the rates of natural resource consumption.

The conclusion of this introduction is that in actually making use of the services nature provided, the earth has become less productive because of the transformations brought about.

8.1.3 Different phases of natural resource exploitation

The history and changes in the use of natural resource use and land degradation can be visualized using the concepts of change and dynamic systems described in Chapter 3.

The concepts of adaptive management and panarchy as explained by Gunderson and Holling (2002) is linked to resilience which can also be thought of as indicating how capital accumulates at different levels which change in time. According to the principles of the adaptive cycle, the flow of goods and services is linked to a cycle in which there are stages of accumulation, release, re-organization and exploitation. This cycle applies to both ecosystems and economics considered here as a single system. The concept differentiates between processes (providing services) that operate at different rates (e.g. fine scale, focal scale, and coarse scale). At each level positive feedback creates structures and relationships that constitute capital and a resource. It is a useful framework because it enables governance to be organized at the appropriate scales and to plan and understand change. Examples of its application to improve agricultural goods and services can be found at the resilience alliance.

People behave in ways that are attractive to them and this influences their choices to migrate or act. The attractiveness of different states can be mathematically modelled. Conceptually it is possible to think of two states, one desertified, the other not, which are separated by a threshold. The processes, things are getting better, or things are getting

Figure 8.9 This giants tomb in Sardinia is probably a relic from an agricultural society three to four thousand years ago (Credit: Anton Imeson).

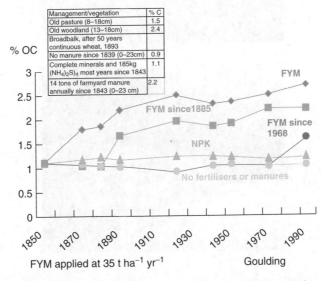

Figure 8.10 Organic carbon in topsoil under different land management practices over a time period of more than 100 years (*Source*: Goulding *et al.* 2003).

worse, mean that there are positive feedbacks which maintain these conditions. At a different scale this applies to land use practices such as the application of farmyard manure over a long period and the benefits this brings. Figure 8.10 shows how long term the effects are of manure applications and the time scale of the changes of the responses in the soil to what people do.

8.1.4 Ecosystem, functions, service and capital

The terms ecosystem functions, service and capital have a long history in ecology, economics and soil science. Functions are seen as being analogous to those of ecosystem goods and services. The applications of soil function were applied in soil science and soil conservation by Rubio (2000). The ancient oak forest in Figure 8.11 was disturbed by the road that impaired and disrupted the services it was providing. As a consequence there

(a)

(b)

Figure 8.11   (a) This oak forest on a very steep slope in Sardinia is providing very many functions that are impaired when a road is constructed. The road caused erosion. (b) shows how to prevent erosion and flooding a gabion was constructed (*Source*: A. C. Imeson 2011, Nuoro, Sardinia).

are high rates of sediment transport and there is a threat to the village. Soil conservation works were constructed to slow down and reduce storm runoff.

Ecosystem services are the processes by which the environment produces resources utilized by humans such as clean air, water, food and materials. The Millennium Ecosystem Assessment classified ecosystem services as follows:

- Supporting services: The services that are necessary for the production of all other ecosystem services including soil formation, photosynthesis, primary production, nutrient cycling and water cycling

- Provisioning services: The products obtained from ecosystems, including food, fibre, fuel, genetic resources, bio-chemicals, natural medicines, pharmaceuticals, ornamental resources and fresh water

- Regulating services: The benefits obtained from the regulation of ecosystem processes, including air quality regulation, climate regulation, water regulation, erosion regulation, water purification, disease regulation, pest regulation, pollination, natural hazard regulation

- Cultural services: The non-material benefits people obtain from ecosystems through spiritual enrichment, cognitive development, reflection, recreation and aesthetic experiences – thereby taking account of landscape values.

As the concept of ecosystem services defined in this way includes almost everything, it is clear that these can only be considered at a general level. An explanation of the significance of the concept of ecosystem services can be found in the work of Costanza and others (Costanza *et al*. 1997). 'Quadruple bottom line' – also known as 'Four Capital Accounting' – into the economic landscape takes into account the impact of social, built, natural and human capital when assessing global markets and challenges like desertification. Studies of ecosystem services have been a step towards determining what might be our natural capital. It was thought that once ecosystem valuation and biodiversity metrics are more widely accepted, there will be less difficulty determining when a baseline value for an ecosystem has been reduced. The problem is that what one perceives depends on who one is and where one lives. It is necessary to consider all of the beneficiaries of services and to negotiate differences.

Pivotal events

Pivotal events occur when there is enough good will to change things and people feel empowered to act. They included the IPPC Third and Fourth Assessment of the Climate Change Convention and the Millennium Assessment of the Convention on Biodiversity. They also include conferences, for example such as that organized in Valencia on soil functions (2000) and the meeting in Iceland on Soils, Society and Global Change (2007). Also there is the European Soil Strategy (2006) that amongst other things set up working groups to report on the threats facing European soils. These included a cross-cutting report on desertification. Its recommendations provide important markers, for example working internationally to produce an ATLAS of Desertification as the EU JRC is doing or major conferences. Research projects have a special task on desertification and can make recommendations that are presented at side events of the UNCCD. Examples of present and recent pivotal research projects in Europe that provide information about desertification include LUCINDA (Roxo 2007) that provided booklets in five languages, and DESIRE that is a major current EU project comparing ways of addressing desertification at hotspots all over the world. DESURVEY, DeSurvey, is another project using mainly remote sensing to assess the vulnerability to desertification and develop early warning metholgies. Other events are the WOCAT programme that is making a catalogue of methods used to combat land degradation and the LADA global land degradation assessment initiative of the FAO. The development of land degradation tools and assessment methodologies have been developed and made available by the NRCS (Natural Resource Conservation Service) in the USA.

Other pivotal evens can be floods, famines and natural disasters.

The Millennium goals of the United Nations (www.undp.org) set out principles and involve intentions to address land degradation.

The Millennium Ecosystem Assessment authors came to the following conclusion: the capacity of ecosystems to provide goods and services is being reduced by desertification and land degradation.

> The changes made to ecosystems contributed to substantial net gains in human well-being and economic development. But these gains have been achieved at growing costs in the form of the degradation of many ecosystem services, increased risk of non-linear changes, and the exacerbation of poverty for some groups of people. These problems, unless addressed, will substantially diminish the benefits that future generations obtain from ecosystems.

The Millennium Ecosystem Assessment authors made it clear that the degradation of ecosystem services could grow significantly worse in the next decades and is a barrier to achieving the Millennium Development Goals.

Evaluations and reviews are regularly made by the EU of all of the projects on land degradation and desertification issues that they support, and to compare these with the National COP and CRIC reports. This gives insight into how far countries thought that land degradation was affecting key goods and services. Such studies specifically review EC policies; EC financial instruments; and EC assisted projects which support the implementation of the UNCCD. It concluded that the EU also sees desertification in the context of economic losses.

The opinion is that land degradation can no longer be perceived as being only an environmental problem: it is also a driver of economic loss and stagnation, poverty, insecurity and migration. In most countries, a high proportion of income, employment and export earnings stem from agricultural production and other land-based activities. Despite growing urbanization, the majority of poor people still live in rural areas. In the absence of significant economic diversification, access to land and the sustainable management of natural resources are preconditions for improving the livelihoods of poorer groups. They are also a precondition for greater social security. Land degradation abatement is of importance to prevent and alleviate poverty, ensure local food security, and for agricultural growth. It is a means to avoid conflicts over scarce resources and to cut migration from rural areas to overcrowded cities. In the face of climate change and climatic variations, investment in land-use-based coping strategies by local populations is a matter of survival.

8.2 Interactions between desertification and ecosystem services

The Ecosystem Assessment Synthesis Report mentioned earlier pointed out that humans have changed ecosystems more rapidly and extensively in the last 50 years than in any other period to meet rapidly growing demands for food, fresh water, timber, fibre and fuel. A world food and energy crisis is claimed by some to exist. That this has resulted in a substantial and largely irreversible loss in diversity of life on Earth is true but there are also large areas such as some areas in Sardinia where there is a very large natural and social capital. The future ability of the Earth to remain a suitable habitat for man should become an issue. Each human or human size animal requires 0.5 kg of oxygen each day that has to be provided by (1.5 kg of plant growth). If only the real-estate value of land, or its short-term economic use are considered and its other functions ignored, the impacts will be felt by society as the disappearance of services and benefits gradually manifest themselves.

None of the Millennium goals that the UN and Europe wish to meet will be possible if the soils and land on which we rely for oxygen, water, food and regulating hydrological and geo-chemical cycles that make the world habitable are in fact depleted of life that sustains natural and social capital.

Because the Earth's carrying capacity is threatened, in order to avoid catastrophic breakdown of ecosystem services, the reader can see that the comprehensive reform in global financial institutions is indeed urgent but because nothing yet has happened it is unlikely to come from the visions of bankers and economists.

A global indicator of the pressures causing desertification and biodiversity loss is the HANPP (Imhoff and Lahouari Bounoua 2006). The HANPP is an indicator that enabled the integrated bio-physical and human drivers to be seen. Primary production indicates how much plant material can be produced and this is obviously highest where there is most energy and water. It is in units that give the proportion of the amount of primary production (gC/Yr) appropriated by humans and it was developed by GSFC of NASA (Nature 2006). Humans annually require 20 per cent of NPP generated on land.

NASA

Although desertification is presented as a typically African problem, in fact, as the areas of India, China and Europe are where human pressure is greatest because of the high population densities and the life-styles of people who place a higher demand on resources. The pressures on ecosystems are least in the dryland regions where people use relatively little of the production produced. The amount of plant-based material used varied greatly compared to how much was locally grown. Humans in sparsely populated areas, like the Amazon, consumed a very small percentage of locally generated NPP. Large urban areas consumed 300 times more than the local area produced. North Americans needed almost 24 per cent of the region's NPP.

Where people consume much more primary production than is produced, the effect of the ecosystem foot print can be deduced. Vast amounts of biomass have to be moved from the areas of low appropriation in Africa and South America. The dependency on imported food in the sink areas parallels the dependency on oil.

Some people suggest that if the producing areas had better legal control over their own land where food or bio-oil production are located, they could have laws that regulated land use and which encouraged soil protection and conservation. On the other hand, when laws exist they are not applied unless this is the wish of the government and public. The example of Brazil exporting iron to China was mentioned in Chapter 6.

The impact of desertification on hydrology can easily be observed and there are hundreds of indicators such as the length of days with no flow in a river. The water balance equation and almost every hydrological parameter can be used as an indicator of desertification.

Runoff and water movement on slopes create patterns which also indicate change and how the water regulation functions are being performed. Soil aggregate stability and permeability are used in the USA (Herrick *et al*. 2004) to assess the health of ecosystems. These enable the impact of, for example, overstocking and soil compaction to be assessed. Ladar measurements enable high resolution images to be constructed of the surface of the vegetation and soil. They have been used to measure plant growth. This method enables the soil fertility changes to be monitored.

Restoring the soil capital

In 1890, Huxley describes how organisms in the soil create capital for themselves in the form of a habitat that they create around them. At that time, successful farmers managed the soil fauna to promote a healthy soil in which micro organisms flourished and created a habitat for themselves that made the soil fertile and productive for humans too. There is a symbiotic relationship between the farmer and the soil by virtue of the other life that was in the environment. The actions of the farmer and the way the soil is managed are part of the capital creation process. With the advent of modern agriculture, only the agricultural production was considered by the encomiasts as being of value, so that the life in the soil and our dependency on it is forgotten. Gradually, in many places, the soil structure declined, soils become compact, they could hold less water and soil degradation occurred. Figure 8.12 from near Yichang in China shows how an area that was degraded and experiencing much erosion can be transformed by changing the land use as part of an integrated soil and water conservation program. The restoration of natural capital after a forest fire occurs naturally as the forest grows and this is illustrated in the erosional response of the forest in Valencia (Figure 8.13).

Basically as Chapter 4 explained, it is very simple to increase this capital by, for example, improving the water retention properties of the soil, the soil water storage capacity. Techniques for doing this were developed by the CSIRO in Australia and they can involve very simple things such as creating more shade, using natural hydrophobic substances and terra cotta. When the water limitations of degraded soils are removed they suddenly become a capital asset that can produce crops or water.

The best indicator of this ecosystem function is the soil structure, bulk density or porosity. The impact of repeated fire on these soil properties has been described by Rubio, for example. Soil aggregates under forest have a very large surface area and can

Figure 8.12 Restoring natural capital in China. These two areas were degraded and to make farming viable assistance was given to help farmers build terraces and select crops such as tea that give high income and better protect the soils (Credit: Anton Imeson 2011).

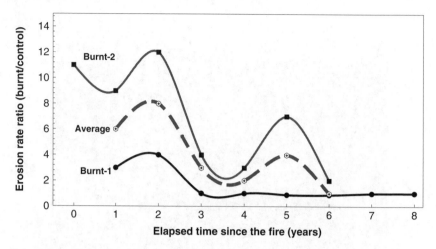

Figure 8.13   Erosion rate ratio (Burnt/Control) at the Aísa valley soil erosion experimental station, Central Spanish Pyrenees. from Cerdà 2006. This figure illustrates the natural recovery of the soil conservation function after fire in Spain.

resist being broken down by rainfall. On modern farmland, this roughness, created by soil micro organisms, is not present. In Spain, under shade the soil can have a good structure but in unshaded areas it is absent and soils do not provide a soil and water nutrient regulating function.

One of the first research projects supported by the EU developed a spatially dynamic systems model of Senegal (1991). The model, advanced for its time, linked the weather and climate with models of agricultural production and land degradation and was run to test the impacts of climate and different policies on both the economy and land degradation. One outcome was that whatever policy was tested in Senegal and other countries, and no matter how good the climate became, poverty always increased. The explanation was simply that to maintain the government and all its organisations too many resources were taken away from the largely rural population for it to make it possible for them to farm sustainability. Relationships between wealth and desertification are very complex and dynamic. The risks are periods of change when people lack the knowledge and experience needed to assess the consequences of the changes caused by new policies (Wilson 2007).

8.3 The impact of desertification on ecosystem services

The implications for desertification sensitive services in the Mediterranean will be illustrated, using the Millennium Assessment classification.

Supporting services

The impact on soil formation is rock specific. Shallow soils caused by erosion could actually increase weathering in places. Soils will be concentrated by wind and water erosion into smaller areas where dust and sand or colluvium accumulates. Warmer soils and less rainfall and lower vegetation cover will mean less photosynthesis and primary production. Changes in soil depth will locally increase or decrease evaporation and change nutrient and water cycling.

Soil degradation and higher temperatures will reduce the soil aggregate stability, lead to crusting. Soil compaction and bulldozing will reduce soil fertility. Frequent fires and erosion will reduce soil resilience and lead to soil degradation. The altered water balance will lead to salinization and sodicity, reducing productivity. The water cycle will be drastically altered so that there is a great decrease in percolation and runoff.

The disruption of the vegetation cover alters the soil surface temperature. Many investigations in Spain have compared soil temperature and moisture profiles under shaded and not shaded areas. Shade is so important that it is manipulated deliberately as a strategy in restoration.

Provisioning services

As a consequence of the above, large areas will lose their ability to provide sufficient water for irrigation, many areas will have thinner soils no longer able to support crops like wheat (as is already happening in Greece). Natural rainwater harvesting both above and below ground could improve the amount of water for irrigation but at the same time promote salinity. Forest fires will be more frequent because of higher wood and soil temperatures reducing timber production. There will maybe 40 to 80 per cent less fresh water. The impacts will be long term.

Regulating services

The benefits obtained from the regulation of ecosystem processes, including air quality regulation, climate regulation, water regulation, erosion regulation, water purification, disease regulation, pest regulation, pollination, natural hazard regulation, will all be impacted on by desertification.

The air, like the soil will be hotter, and more often transport dust. There will be less oxygen being produced as there is less photosynthesis. The regulation of the climate by the soil fauna will be much reduced both in duration and intensity. Water regulation will become less by an order of magnitude so that there is much more frequent flooding. New pests will appear. The erosion and runoff will concentrate hazardous substances and chemicals at hot spots. There will be less water to maintain flows in rivers, which will disappear for longer periods during dry seasons.

Cultural services

These non-material benefits people obtain from ecosystems (e.g. through spiritual enrichment, cognitive development, reflection, recreation and aesthetic experiences – thereby taking account of landscape values) will be profoundly changed. When landscapes are such as those of dahesa no longer provide enough services, they will be abandoned by the people who lived in them. Without the people who created the landscape, it can not be preserved as a functioning system unless it is able to provide other services such as those linked to tourism.

Table 8.2 Positive and negative effects of the capital assets with respect to land degradation in the area of Yéchar (Murcia, Spain) (Authors: Carolina Boix-Fayos, Joris de Vente, Michael Stocking and Juan Albaladejo).

Capital assets	Positive effects	Negative effects
Natural	Fertile land when water is available Favourable lithology and topographical positions for farming, gentle slopes Barley cultivation provides good vegetation cover	Extension of irrigated agriculture led to a decrease of interest in dry land farming Lack of maintenance and vegetation cover, leading to land degradation
Physical	Access to market, roads, industry, improved equipment	Low subsidies in dryland farming and conservation mean less interest for farmers to make use of physical assets for conservation and/or maintenance of production (Opportunity Cost)
Human	Knowledge transfer to maintain terraces from one generation to another.	Human capital limitation because of labour constraint as young people are not interested in dryland farming. The land is left fallow.
Social	The Cooperative is a key to subsidies Farmers help each other in the transfer of knowledge, technology and physical work	Cooperative can marginalize certain farmers
Financial	Good living when farmers have access to pay prices of irrigated land Start-up capital for young farmers	Lack of a suitable subsidy system leads to land degradation Low market price for dryland crops that can prevent land degradation

Some very interesting findings were made in a research project that interviewed farmers regarding how they saw the different types of capital. A summary of the authors' work was presented as a case study in SCAPE (2006) from which Table 8.2 was created.

They compared two contrasting situations in Yéchar and Campos del Río and found that land degradation was affected by many things affecting the resources for farming available to land users. Tables 8.2 and 8.3 summarize the positive and negative effects of changes in capital assets on soil erosion in both municipalities studied.

As mentioned in Chapter 6, the UNCCD NAP (National Action Plan for Romania) illustrates how concepts can be applied in practice. It designed and implemented its Action Plan based on the concepts of natural, economic and social capital. It presents detailed analysis of the soil and land qualities and how the degradation of these reduces the productive capacity of the land and influences aridity.

The strategy of the United Nations Convention to combat desertification that was put in place nearly 30 years ago envisaged the development and application of methodologies

Table 8.3 Positive and negative effects of the capital assets with respect to land degradation in the area of Campos del Río (Murcia, Spain). Land degradation, soil conservation and rural livelihoods: a case study in Spain (Authors: Carolina Boix-Fayos, Joris de Vente, Michael Stocking and Juan Albaladejo).

Capital assets	Positive effects	Negative effects
Natural	Fertile land when water is available Soils relatively easy to work in a wide area, relatively low stoniness compared to surrounding areas Many plots located in favourable topographical positions for farming	Dominance of marly lithology which is easily erodible Many farms located on slopes of more than 7° High evaporative demand
Physical	Access to market, roads, industry, improved equipment Existence of a canning-food factory which guarantee a minimal income Most of the plots have access to water from the water transference schemes	Lack of initiatives with respect to farming, the canning-food factory offers a secure job with a low income
Human	Knowledge transfer for transformation of land from terraces system to land-levelling system Ready availability of cheap labour (immigrants)	Abandonment of traditional terrace systems when the farmers do not have access to financial capital for transformation in irrigated land (drip irrigation and land levelling) Part-time farmers discriminated against in access to subsidies Age factor: old farmers do not have access to loams for transformation of the land and young people are less interested in farming, as a consequence plots are abandoned
Social	Existence of a development agent in the City Council which offers all the facilities to access subsidies and extension courses Farmers help each other in the transference of knowledge, technology and physical work	No agricultural cooperative Negative social pressure on pioneers to start with alternative land management, more sustainable and environmentally friendly, versus the traditional farming Lack of education on sustainable agriculture, no interest when extension services offer innovation and educational courses Agricultural activities are seen as a part-time job, complementary of activities such as work at the canning-food factory and construction works
Financial	Good living when farmers have access to pay prices of irrigated land Secure income from the work at the canning-food factory	Lack of a suitable subsidy system leads to land degradation Low market price for dryland crops that can prevent land degradation No use of the available subsidies

that integrated the physical and socio-economic drivers of desertification and used them as tools to develop for mitigation and the development of indicators (Odingo 1980). The notions of soil or land function, capital and goods and services are very valuable because they enable areas to be compared that are otherwise different.

Long-term monitoring programmes have been established by the scientific community to establish the changes taking place in the earth systems (for example, those co-ordinated by the IGBP 2007 IHDP 2007 and GLP 2007). Research is being co-ordinated to advance understanding of the changes being monitored by the new Earth Observation programmes (for example, by NASA (2007) and the ESA (2006), and the significance of this for governments has recently been described by van de Leeuw 2007).

Attempts of countries to be self sufficient in agricultural products mean that marginal and unsuited areas are brought into production. There is no problem at first but sooner or later land and soil degradation occur. An example of this is illustrated by the wheat campaign in Portugal, which resulted in the conversion of traditional Montado farming systems being converted into wheatfields. In Figure 8.14, wheat production in Portugal is shown and the changing relationship between the area sown and yield illustrates the impact of erosion and soil degradation on this ecosystem service. The high outputs were not sustained and the area under wheat in 1974 is only half that in 1950 (For more information see Roxo).

Global programmes have not often been developed or analysed with land degradation, soil protection or desertification as synthesizing concepts to explain observed changes. Nevertheless the impact of desertification can now clearly be seen, as illustrated by the figures in this book. They can now be observed by the public at large who have access to detailed up-to date images of the earth's land cover (for example, via NASA or Google

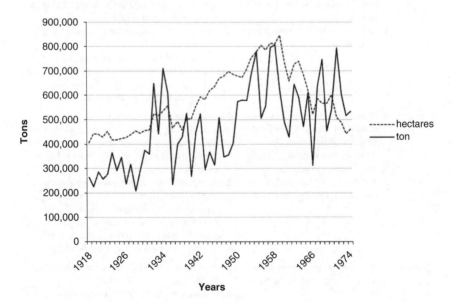

Figure 8.14 Wheat production in Portugal (sown areas and production yield) (From Roxo).

Earth). The massive land degradation taking place in, for example, Brazil, Borneo, The Philippines and Vietnam, for example, or even in the EU can be seen by the public who currently associate the flooding, landslides and natural disasters with climate change and not with the disruption of ecosystems that have lost their water and soil conservation services or functions. The flooding in England almost every year would not have occurred if the soils had not lost their capacity to retain and hold water. The public perception is that climate and not agriculture or land use policy is responsible. Data contradict this. The cost of losing all of these functions for future generations is in the order of many trillions of Euros (Stern 2006).

The destruction of the habitats of organisms on which we depend for the soil and all of its functions is a reason why valued ecosystem services are disappearing. Whether this destruction involves erosion, soil compaction, contamination, salinization or it is done for food or wood production, mineral extraction or tourism, each time the area of the soil and land providing the regulation functions (hydrology, oxygen and nutrients) becomes less and carbon increases. Fortunately, soil and landscape scientists know how these systems can be restored. A programme of soil and land protection that reversed desertification and restored alternative functions and values to the land within two decades is completely feasible.

In its early publications UNESCO and UNEP thought that it would take 30 years at least to restore the functions of degraded ecosystems. The fight against desertification was seen as a long-term affair, Landscapes and soils have to continually have their functions reinvented by succeeding generations.

On the other hand, some processes such as clay illuviation or organic matter accumulation and other functions depend on slow processes in the soil that behave like time-bombs. Suddenly a critical threshold will be reached and a gully may form. In some cases there are cyclic periods of soil formation and erosion that are sometimes independent of man and sometimes not. These have been studied in investigations of colluvial and alluvial sediments where records exist of past conditions.

There are cases when the disruption is a natural consequence of something that triggered it tens or hundreds of years earlier. This is the case in Spain where gully incision is also influenced by uplift. Also in Norway, disruption is driven not by land use change but by an isostatically driven sea level decline.

To breathe or not to breathe

When climate change research began about 15 years ago, the soil and land use change were thought to be the greatest source of carbon. The claim that the increase in atmospheric CO_2 is due to industrialization is only partially true because perhaps more was the result of the agricultural revolution that is still occurring today. The residence time of CO_2 in the atmosphere is 200 years. All of the oxygen in the atmosphere is produced by plants. They take up the CO_2 respired by animals and produce the oxygen that animals breathe. Each human require 0.83 kg of oxygen per day and for this there must be 1.5 kg of living plant (estimated as produced daily about 26 m^2 of crops. Should the world population increases from 6 to 7 billion, we need more not less plants in living soil).

The reduction in atmospheric CO_2 that occurs each year in the Summer of the Northern Hemisphere is attributed to the uptake of carbon during the period of plant growth. Each year there are more people with animals exhuming carbon and a much smaller area of land (covered by cities or crops that are not really active in oxygen production) so that this could easily explain the increase in carbon. However, the critical issue is how much oxygen is being produced and consumed by the weathering of rocks exposed by erosion and by machines and livestock. At the time of the dinosaurs, the oxygen content was higher (perhaps even 34 percent).

For thousands of years people have gradually consumed the natural resources that were present and created an environment in which only a selection of plants and animals adapted to man can live. Chapter 1 explained the causes of this and why and how it happened, Chapter 2 showed how this could be demonstrated with indicators, and Chapters 4, 5 and 6 described the key processes that are influenced by people in ways that can either cause land degradation or reverse it. Individual countries like China, Japan, Iceland and New Zealand have demonstrated the role of a National Soil and Water Conservation service and legislation that can help restore soil functions. Organization is needed to use all of the unemployed natural human capital in a world soil and water conservation effort comparable to that took place in the USA, Iceland and Cape Verde. It could be inspired by efforts now being made in China to create a harmonious environment for society. Historians point out that in the past China was able to achieve prosperity precisely because the country had the technical knowledge and the highly motivated Civil Service required to maintain soil and water conservation. This is maybe comparable with the US Corps of Engineers and the Rijkswaterstaat in The Netherlands.

Responsibility and ownership of global services can include an ethical based compact between governments and the earth's citizens to maintain the ecological integrity so that there is no further degradation of goods and services.

References and further reading

Allan, D. (2006). *Human Appropriation of the World's Fresh Water Supply*. University of Michigan. Available online from http://www.globalchange.umich.edu/globalchange2/current/lectures/fresh water_supply/freshwater.html (Accessed 03/06/2008).

Balmford, A., Bruner, A., Cooper, P., *et al.* (2002). *Economic reasons for conserving wild nature*. Science 297, 950–953.

Briasouli, E. (2008) Land use policy and planning, theorizing, and modeling: Lost in translation, found in complexity?' *Environment and Planning B* Vol. 35: 16–33.

Castillo, V. A. Arnoldussen, S. Bautista, P. Bazzoffi, G. Crescimanno, A. C. Imeson (2004) *Soil erosion Task 6 Desertification*. Reports of the Technical Working Groups, Vol II erosion Editors (L. Van-Camp, B. Bujarrabal A. R. Gentile, R. J A Jones L. Montanarella, C. Olazabal Senthil-K. Selvaradjou R. Jarman, M. Robert and José Luis Rubio) DG Environment, Brussels

Cerda, A. (2010) Herbicide versus Tillage. Soil and water losses at the El Teularet soil erosion experimental station *Geophysical Research Abstracts*. [np].

Cowie A*, Schneider B. C and L. D. Montanarella (2007) Potential synergies between existing multilateral environmental agreements in the implementation of land use, land-use change and forestry activities *Environmental Science and Policy* m 10, 335–352

Costanza, R., d'Arge, R., Groot, R. de, *et al.*, (1997). The value of the world's ecosystem services and natural capital. *Nature* 387, 253–260.

Dorren, L., Berger, F., Imeson, A. C., Maier, B. and Rey, F., (2004). Integrity, stability and management of protection forests in the European Alps. *Forest Ecology and Management* 195(1-2), 165–176.

European Commission (2006) *Report on the activities and support provided by the European Community to combat desertification in countries in Asia, Latin America amd Caribbean, Central and Eastern Europe in the period January 2001–2005* submitted to UNCCD CRIC 5 prepared by Imeson, A. C. Koning, P.C. Kisterman H and Wolvekamp P. S. ENV 2006-12800. 74 p. UNCCD

Falkenmark, M. and Rockström, J. (2004). *Balancing Water for Humans and Nature: The New Approach in Ecohydrology*. London: Earthscan

Gleick, P. H. (1999). *Water Futures: A Review of Global Water Projections*. In: F. R. Rijsberman, ed., World Water Scenarios: Analysis. London: Earthscan.

Gordon, L. J., Steffen, W., Jönsson, B. F., Folke, C., Falkenmark, M. and Johannessen, Å (2005). Human Modification of Global Water Vapor Flows from the Land Surface. *Proceedings of the National Academy of Sciences of the United States*, 102 (21), pp. 7612–7617. Available online from http://www.pnas.org/content/102/21/7612.full.pdf (Accessed 30/06/2008).

Goulding, K. W. T. and Poulton, P. R. (2003). Des experimentations de longue duree sur la recherche en environnement. Un exemple pris en Grande Bretagne. *Etude et Gestion des Sols* 10, 253–261.

Groot, de R. S. (1992) *Functions of nature: evaluation of nature in environmental planning, management and decision making*, Wolters-Noordhoff, Amsterdam: 315 pp.

Heidegger M (1954) *The Question concerning Technology and other essays* in, New York : Harper and Row.

Hein (2002) Checklist of the potential costs of land degradation and the benefits of mitigation measures. Internal Report MEDACTION. Work Package 1.3.(in EU Soil Strategy Task Group Report on desertification)

Huxley T. H. (1893) III Evolution and Ethics and IV Capital the Mother of Labour (1890) *Selected works of Thomas Huxley* Westminster Edition, Appeltons, 334 p.

Imeson, A. C. (2004) Indicator strategies of characterising desertification sensitive areas in regional Action Programmes p 342–357 in *Medrap Concerted Action*, NRD Sassiri. Italy Enne G and D. Peter editors

Imhoff, M. L. L Bounoua, T Ricketts, C Loucks (2004)- Global patterns in human consumption of net primary production Nature, 2004 - nature.com *Nature* 429, 870–873 (24 June 2004)

International Forum (2007) *Soils, Society and Global Change* 31 August – 4 September, Selfoss, Iceland.

IPCC Working Group II (2011) *Working Group II report Impacts, Adaption and Vulnerability AR*4 Fourth Assessment report contribution of Working Group II to the Fourth Assessment Report of the Intergovernmental Panel on Climate Change, 2007 (editors M. L. Parry, O. F. Canziani, J. P. Palutikof, P. J. van der Linden and C. E. Hanson (eds)) Cambridge University Press, Cambridge, United Kingdom and New York, NY, USA.

Leeuw, van der S. (1998). *The Archaeomedes Project - Understanding the natural and anthropogenic causes of land degradation and desertification in the Mediterranean*. Luxemburg: Office for Official Publications of the European Union.

Leopold, Aldo (1948): *A Sand County Almanac, and Sketches Here and There, 1948*, Oxford University Press, New York, 1987, pg. 81.

King County (2011) Public information on Soil Health http://your.kingcounty.gov/solidwaste/natural yardcare/soilbuilding.asp

Malthus (1798) *An essay on the principle of population as it affects the future improvement of society*, J. Johnson London

Millennium Ecosystem Assessment (2005). *Ecosystems and Human Well-being*: Volume 2 – Scenarios. Island Press, Washington, DC, 515 pp. Available online from http://www.millen niumassessment.org/en/Scenarios.aspx#download.

Milliman, J. D., Farnsworth, K. L., Jones, P. D., Xu, K. H. and Smith, L. C. (2008). Climatic and anthropogenic factors affecting river discharge to the global ocean, 1951–2000. *Global and Planetary Change*, 62, pp. 187–194

MODIS (2011) MODIS (The Moderate Resolution Imaging Spectroradiometer) is a key instrument aboard the Terra EOS AM and Aqua EOS PM satellite. It is a source of global data and information on current land degradation and desertification impacts http://modis.gsfc.nasa.gov/

Montanarella. M. A. Cowie, U. Schneider (2007) Potential Synergies Between Existing Multilateral Environmental Agreements in the Implementation of Land Use, Land-Use Change and Forestry Activities – *Environmental Science and Policy*, 10, 335–352.

Odingo, R. S. (1990) The definition of desertification: its programmatic consequences for UNEP and the international community. Desertification Control Bulletin 1990 No. 18 pp. 31–50.

Pagiola, S., Bishop, J. and Landell-Mills, N. (2002). *Selling forest environmental services: market-based mechanisms for conservation and development*. Earthscan Publications Ltd., London, UK, 299 pp.

Pretty J., (2003). Social capital and the collective management of resources. *Science* 302(5652): 1912–1914.

Robert, M (2001) *Soil carbon sequestration for improved land management;* World Soil Resources Report 96 FAO Rome 57 p traductions française et espagnole en 2002.

Rosenzweig C, G Casassa D. Karoly, A. C. Imeson, C. L., A. Menzel S. Rawlins, Terry L. Root, B. Seguin and Tryjanowski (2006) Chapter 1: *Assessment of Observed Changes and Responses in Natural and Managed Systems*, In IPCC WG II Report, IPCC Working Group II (2011) Working Group II report Impacts, Adaption and Vulnerability AR4 Fourth Assessment report Contribution of Working Group II to the Fourth Assessment Report of the Intergovernmental Panel on Climate Change, 2007 (editors M. L. Parry, O. F. Canziani, J. P. Palutikof, P. J. van der Linden and C. E. Hanson (eds)) Cambridge University Press, Cambridge, United Kingdom and New York, NY, USA.

Roxo M. J. (2009) Coordinator of Lucinda Project (*Land Care in Desertification Affected Areas from Science to Application* EU Project (http://geografia.fcsh.unl.pt/lucinda/

Rubio J. L (2009), Desertification and Water Scarcity as a security challenge in the Mediterranean pp 75–92 in Water Scarcity, *Land Degradation and Desertification in the. Mediterranean Region*, NATO Science for Peace and Security Series C: . . . Environmental Security, Springer Science

Stern, (2006P Stern Review: *The Economics of Climate Change* http://www.hmtreasury.gov.uk/media/6/9/Table_of_Contents.pdf

Tibbetts, J., (1998). *Open space conservation: investing in your community's economic health*. Lincoln Institute of Land Policy, Cambridge, USA, 24 pp.

Tongway, D. (1994) *Rangeland Assessment Manual*, Division of Wildlife and Ecology, Canberra (ISBN 0643 555437), 69 p.

Topfer. K., (2000). *The Triple Bottom Line Economic, Social, Natural Capital - United Nations' "Global Compact"*. UN Chronicle Summer 2000.

Turner, W. R., Nakamura, T., Dinetti, M. (2004). Global urbanization and the separation of humans from nature. *BioScience* 54 (6), 585–590.

United Nations (1992) *Earth Summit Convention on Desertification*, Brazil, 3-14 June 1992. Department of Public Information UN. New York.

UNEP (1991). *Status of Desertification and Implementation of the United Nations Plan of Action to Combat desertification*. UNEP, UNEP/GCSS.III/3 15 Oct. Nairobi 8 8 p.

UNCCD (2007) *10-year strategic plan and framework to enhance the implementation of the Convention* 2008-2009, COP 8 Madrid 3-4 September 2007.

Valencia (2000). Third ESSC (European Soil Conservation Society) International Congress *"Man and Soil at the Third. Millennium"*. 28 March-31 April, 2000. Valencia (Spain) Proceedings published 2005.

Wilson, E. O (2005) *The Future of Life*, Time Warner Books London 229 p.

9
The way forward: global soil conservation and protection

9.1 Introduction

Chapter 1 argued that the knowledge, understanding and experience with sustainable land management can be applied to restore many ecosystem functions that have disappeared and prevent land degradation and desertification. In other words, rivers and forests would return and ecosystems would be restored. At the local level in the field, it involves simple actions that gradually restore soil quality and soil functions. These replace those that are degrading them and raise fertility by improving the micro climate and water availability. At a policy level, all land would have the functions of protecting people from natural hazards, soil and water conservation and the restoration of degraded natural areas that would provide clean water to urban areas and for agriculture.

This can happen but it requires public approval and support and actions that we all take in our own way to improve the health and quality of the land so the functions on which we depend can return. The hierarchy in ecosystem processes means that these produce emergent benefits later in time and in a meaningful way contribute to true sustainability in the form of the capital that future generations can use and which is stored in the soil and landscape. The main actors in this are our allies in nature.

The anthropogene

Writing in the current number of the popular *National Geographic Magazine* Neumann and Rotmann (2011) wrote an article called 'Enter the Anthropogene the Age of Man', a term from Paul Crutzen. The dramatic photos raise public awareness and this is an important step in generating support for the actions that countries can take to protect and restore land. All that needs to be done is for a start to be made in putting the environment before energy and in managing and regulating agriculture and industry. Environmental protection and restoration would generate capital and wealth, produce meaningful work and a healthy population.

Some brief conclusions from Chapter 1 are:

Globally, land degradation and desertification is a consequence of our human civilization and the way it has evolved and developed through the exploitation and use of nature.

Desertification, Land Degradation and Sustainability, First Edition. Anton Imeson.
© 2012 John Wiley & Sons, Ltd. Published 2012 by John Wiley & Sons, Ltd.

This included the impacts of agricultural and industrial activities, including mining and metal working, the harnessing of river and groundwater and the appropriation of these from natural areas. The instinct that man has with other animals to breed prolifically so that natural processes are overwhelmed, unless society develops the capacity to organize and protect the environment, is often mentioned

In forestry, agriculture and farming, in most places in the world there are examples of sustainable and non-sustainable production. Scientists have become expert in establishing vegetation under harsh conditions and in restoring landscape functions.

The possibility is that the continued degradation of the natural world might be so advanced that too little water, land and other life is left over to guarantee a sustainable future for our species (Wilson 2005). This is a major cause of aridity and climate change.

9.2 Iceland

When in 2005 in the Selfoss Call for Action in which desertification, soil conservation and environmental law experts met, several actions and recommendation were made that have been applied in this book (use of functions and adaptive management, integration into a single system, cause and effects and processes). What emerged from this were the following recommendations:

- Actions that restore soil quality and health or which stop actions that degrade and pollute the environment could be implemented with immediate effect if there were a plan and leadership.

- Soil fertility can be improved by improving the hydrological properties of the soil and the services these provide. Incomes can be improved at the same as the land degradation is lessened.

- The current way markets operate in finance, agriculture and industry internationally lead to the disappearance of the all kinds of capital at the level of the soil and landscape. Land use changes of this kind invariably cause suffering, poverty, famine and migration to cities. At the same time, there is profligate waste of food as people overeat and supermarkets dispose of unsold products. The wealth of nations disappears into the huge added value of water and very low cost products at excellent margins.

- Governments gain access to the natural resources of other countries that have perceived natural resources by means of companies that act internationally, for example, Brazil, The Ukraine, Guyana, Latvia and Mozambique.

Decisions about development and land use policy are made by regional and national governments. Laws are either not in place or are not being applied. There is no information available to local authorities, who may not even exist and in any case have no influence or sufficient power to restrain people from changing the land use to grow coffee, soya or whatever. Hannan and de Boer (2002) provide valuable guidelines for soil conservation and protection law working with the IUCN. The photograph in Figure 9.1 was taken just

Figure 9.1   Inspiration from the past. The Great Wall of China (Credit: Anton Imeson).

Figure 9.2   The other great walls of China are the millions of terraces that protect the land and which have been part of the cultural landscape for thousands of years (Credit: Anton Imeson).

north of Beijing. If is was possible to stop the Mongols by thinking big we can apply this to desertification. The inspiration in Figure 9.2, might be that however degraded the landscape, for example as in Haiti, it is possible to act and do something. At all levels, the productive functions and services of the soil can be recreated by human labour.

9.3 The call for action

9.3.1 Call for action on the conservation and sustainable use of global soil resources

Statement of the participants from 20 countries at the international workshop, strategies, science and law for the conservation of the world's soil resources, selfoss, iceland, 14–18 september 2005

'Soils are vital for society. Soils are vital to humanity and to natural ecosystems. In many parts of the world, soil degradation, ranging from comprehensive soil nutrient loss, decrease in biological productivity and habitat, decrease in food security, increase in natural disasters and ecosystem degradation, is driven by, among other things the globalization of trade, production incentives, contamination and mismanagement. This results in substantial and increasing detrimental effects on society and on natural ecosystems. Consequently, action is needed to reverse soil degradation and promote their conservation and sustainable use.'

The achievement of conservation and sustainable use of soils

'We consider that, despite highly developed levels of scientific and traditional knowledge about soils, there is inadequate recognition of the fragile state of the world's soils, the fundamental role that soils play, the need to improve their protection for the benefit of society, and the intrinsic value of soils. New policies and incentives, the application of existing knowledge, new and strengthened national legislation and an international instrument are required to reduce soil loss and degradation.'

International action is urgent

'A programme of action is required urgently on an international, regional, national and local level to address the conservation and sustainable use of soils. Such a programme of action will contribute to meeting the global goals on sustainable development agreed in the 1990 Millennium Declaration, the 1992 World Summit on Sustainable Development, as well as in the international Conventions on Biological Diversity and Climate Change and the Convention to Combat Desertification.'

'We recognize the potential synergy between these Conventions, and we call on governments to use all these tools in a concerted and coordinated manner to achieve improved soil conservation.'

'The draft international instrument on the Conservation and Sustainable Use of Soil, agreed in principle at this meeting, sets out the range of measures required. We place particular emphasis on financial incentives, national legal mechanisms and strategies, transboundary cooperation, education and knowledge sharing, capacity building, and engagement of all stakeholders.'

Support required

'To ensure that an international instrument on the Conservation and Sustainable Use of Soil is developed, and national soil institutions and national legislation are strengthened:'

'We request the United Nations Environment Programme, the United Nations Development Programme, the Economic Commission for Europe and the Economic and Social Commission for Asia and the Pacific, the, Food and Agricultural Organization, the World Meteorological Organization, the scientific community including the International Council of Science, the International Social Science Council and the Consultative Group on International Agricultural Research to provide technical and policy assistance.'

'We call on the international donor community, in particular the World Bank, the Global Environment Facility, the European Bank for Reconstruction and Development, the Asian Development Bank, the Islamic Development Bank, as well as the European Community International Fund for Agricultural Development and bilateral donor agencies, to provide the financial means.'

'We request the IUCN and its Members and Commissions to continue to promote and support the development of both an international instrument and the drafting of national soil legislation.'

The following recommendations were made:

Recommendations by the working group on soil conservation and protection in europe

1 A Soil Directive is needed which makes it possible to develop instruments targeted for use at national and regional levels, and to ensure that sustainable use of soil is encompassed in other Directives and national and regional regulations and initiatives.

2 In addressing the maintenance and improvement of soil status the instruments should consider all soil functions and the role of soils for future generations.

3 Systems should be developed where farmers are encouraged to pursue environmentally sound practices which promote the conservation and protection of soils.

4 Instruments need to be developed which operate at different spatial scales.

5 To ensure public and institutional support and understanding for the maintenance and improvement of soil status, a key element is the development and use of education/communication systems at a number of levels and where appropriate targeted at different audiences.

6 When formulating actions previous knowledge and experiences about the behaviour and use of soil and other environmental components should be taken into account.

7 Keys should be developed to enable regional and national soil data to be linked with the European Soil Information System making it possible to use standardized soil information at different levels of application.

8 The development of an adequate soil monitoring system is needed with clear cross linkages with other environmental information.

9.3.2 Recommendations from the working group on desertification – the road forward

Main issues and recommendation from the working group on: desertification; the road forward

1 'Desertification' has a low political priority in Europe. Annex IV of the UNCCD covers only land degradation in Mediterranean countries, thereby excluding areas of northern Europe (including Iceland) that have relevant land degradation problems (and solutions). Desertification should not be considered as a process in isolation, but as an important controlling factor or influence on climate and biodiversity, sustainability, and soil protection (all of which have higher priority in Europe).

2 The scientific underpinning of understanding desertification crosses the interface between physical and social sciences, and the processes for controlling and managing desertification cross the interface between science and policy development and implementation. This creates a complex and large network of actors. However this is an opportunity to treat land degradation holistically, integrating science and institutions, departments and to bring desertification into other agendas (e.g. rural development, agricultural practice). It is also an opportunity to exploit synergies between the Rio Conventions. At the local level it is an opportunity to create networks of successful mitigation schemes.

3 The UNCCD could benefit from increased independent scientific input and scrutiny. There should be an independent panel of science experts providing input to the UNCCD, analogous to the IPCC. At present the Expert Group for the CST does not necessarily fulfil this function.

4 To effectively combat desertification, a change in perception of desertification through education is needed, presenting it as a cross-cutting issue of relevance to a range of agendas important to society such as environment, culture, landscape.

5 There is a need for well-structured information about desertification at a number of levels (students, farmers, policy makers, and scientists) and in relation to other environmental issues (biodiversity, climate change, rural development planning...). Research should focus on the application and implementation of existing tools and knowledge.

9.4 Europe

A european global and european soil conservation and protection service

The SCAPE (Soil conservation and protection strategies for Europe project) identified a gap between how soil protection and conservation should be organized to meet goals of sustainable land use and the current situation in Europe.

These are the arguments that applied to several other countries.

There is a consensus that co-ordination is needed by the agencies responsible for European soil conservation in areas of education and training, monitoring, archiving and research. If a for the EU trivial percentage of the money that is going to be used for soil conservation and protection activities in regional development and agriculture could support a co-ordinating organization, this would be exceedingly efficient. It would greatly increase the effectiveness and prevent inadvertent impacts of policies.

Expert scientific and practical knowledge in support of soil protection needs a long-term mandate. Soil conservation and protection is a long-term commitment, just as afforestation programmes are. They need to be organized over long periods of time.

An organization has a both a memory and a capacity to foresee problems. Complex land use planning decisions should be scientifically sound and anchored in different disciplines (see Briassoulis 2005). Soil Conservation and Protection should be embedded in an overall strategy that includes all 'systems and sectors'. An example of how this could be achieved is provided by New Zealand (Grinlinton 2002 and 2005). With its different Directives and national legal traditions Europe has a special challenge: there has to be a focal point where soil functions are considered.

Co-ordination actions are also needed to explain and communicate soil threats. Without co-ordination people speak different languages and there is wasteful duplication of effort. A soil conservation service would have the task in providing stakeholders with the knowledge and data they need. The USA provides us with a demonstration. The Environmental Protection Agency (EPA) has a scientific strategy with clear action plans. A few years ago principles of watershed ecology and risk management provided a conceptual underpinning. Everyone in the USA could see how all of the different issues and processes are holistically linked. Citizens can better judge the impacts of land use and other policies. The USA makes vast amount of data and information freely available to whoever needs it. The contrast with Europe, that only has effective national monitoring in some countries, is great. Europe is at a huge hidden competitive disadvantage with the USA and other countries because of the lack of coordination in this respect.

Soil conservation service and stewardship

A soil conservation service could give support to national and regional authorities. It is not simple to develop and organize complex integrated programmes of the kind that are needed and co-ordination would reduce costs.

The following essentials were developed by Dick Arnold.

Dick arnold: the seven essentials for a meaningful programme of soil conservation

- **A perception that the problem requires the attention of the European Union to effectively solve problems of functional degradation of soil and land resources**. Use foresight and an inclusive ethic to sensitize yourself and others.

- **An organic act by an appropriate legislative body to create an agency** or organization that will design and implement programs to meet the objectives/mandates intended by that legislative body. There should be guidelines on what is excluded from the intent/mandate of such an agency.

- **Continuing appropriations to conduct the business of the organization** need to be timely and sufficient to establish the structure, technology information, and a discipline-based, holistic delivery system capable of being modified as conditions change. This implies a legislative oversight of the conduct and results of the agency it has created so that additions, deletions, and guidance lead to more effective and efficient delivery and implementation of measures to conserve and protect soil and land related resources.

- **Appropriate information about the resources to be conserved and protected**. Soils have been studied for more than 100 years but the information commonly is fragmented, incomplete, and identified by different systems of classification. Soil mapping is often at different scales and have individual or unique map unit legends, thus it is desirable to have an integrated compilation of maps and databases that are consistent for the purposes intended. Soil correlation, soil map correlations, and database correlations are vital to have effective sources of information in support of any proposed program on soil and water conservation and protection. The US established the National Cooperative Soil Survey in 1899. It has federal leadership but includes state agricultural experiment stations, state conservation agencies, other federal agencies, and recently private soil consultants. This informal organization proposes, tests, and evaluates concepts for soil survey standards and activities in the USA. They maintain their technology information in manuals, handbooks, and now Internet access for identification, classification, mapping, interpreting, and publishing soil information for the USA.

- **Information about technologies designed to conserve and protect resources** specified by the legislation is available and can be adapted, adopted, and made readily available to a delivery system that promotes and assists in implementing resource management systems that result in appropriate conservation and protection. Considerable research data is produced throughout academia, government, and private organizations that can be compiled, evaluated, and formatted in a consistent way for use by specialists and lay people. In the US there has been a long evolution of the Field Office Technical Guide (FOTG) from hard copy handbooks and manuals to the present format for e-government. It is on the Internet. Definitions, standards, and specifications for measures included in resource management systems are given in considerable detail to guide the decisions and implementation of conservation measures.

- **A flexible organizational structure designed to provide the functions and technical services required to carry out the legislated mandates**. As the legislation modifies existing programs and/or adds new areas of emphasis the structure of the organization must be able to adapt to the changing conditions. The problems are complex – pedological, ecological, social, economic, political – and need to be addressed in a holistic manner. Sometimes specialists need to be hired or trained to implement new programs or enhance existing ones. The partnerships with state agencies, private companies, and other federal/national agencies may indicate revisions of cooperative agreements about sharing information and providing effective delivery of appropriate technologies.

- **Monitoring of resource conditions and evaluation of agency accountability**. The intent of creating a conservation agency is to promote the sustainability of environments for the good of people and life in these habitats, now and far into the future. The expenditure of public funds suggests that accountability is relevant to the conduct of business, and the status of the resource conditions are needed to determine the effectiveness of existing efforts and changes of emphasis that may be needed to improve the implementation of appropriate resource management systems.

9.5 Support to the UNCCD

It is now generally appreciated that both the global economy and the global climate are major drivers of environmental change. In a world linked by flows of information, energy and capital, changes somewhere can have an unintended impact almost anywhere. Protecting the functions of the soil in Europe should be part of broader sustainability criteria when land planning decisions are made.

The issue is: how can the global drivers of soil and land degradation be moderated and incorporated into soil conservation strategies?

In particular the impact of world trade agreements, export subsidies, technological innovation and the development of new markets needs to be given attention in order to avert global scale soil and land degradation. This is in fact a major driver of climate change. Examples of catastrophic global scale soil loss and land degradation can be seen in many continents and contexts. These include the current high rates of wind and water erosion and desertification in China, due to a combination of drought and economic development; the catastrophic erosion now taking place in Vietnam as a result of cutting down rain forest to grow coffee; and the erosion in Brazil to produce soya.

Decisions about development and land use policy are made by Regional and National Governments. Laws are either not in place or not being applied. There is no information available to local authorities, who may not even exist and in any case have no influence or sufficient power to restrain people from changing the land use to grow coffee, soya or whatever.

The UNCCD

The UNCCD has not really provided governments with the tools that are needed to regulate land use. It was not given the resources, mandate and authority to deal with the impact that our Civilization has had and is having on natural resources. Although many organizations are very serious about stopping desertification, organized society as a whole is not yet engaged. And yet without stopping desertification, we can never tackle climate change or safeguard biodiversity.

9.6 The importance of international co-operation

Internationally co-ordinated collaboration can be very effective in protecting the environment. Encouraging, strengthening and improving the science behind the programmes of International Organizations that are directly dealing with the issues (for example, FAO, GEF and, of course, the UNCCD) would be highly beneficial. Effective organizations need commitment, capacity and knowledge. There are obviously huge differences in the resources and capacity of different countries, so that the collaboration of nations in regional or even better global action plans is helpful. International and bilateral support is useful (e.g. from UNEP, FAO or INCO) and can be vital in providing resources necessary for nations and organizations to co-ordinate their activities.

International Conventions are important because they provide legally binding agreements, in which governments and international organizations commit themselves to implement action plans to tackle shared problems.

Addressing the Global Dimension of Land degeneration:

✓ Strengthen the scientific instruments of the UNCCD so that land degradation is detected early (e.g. with remote sensing).
✓ Land degradation Impact assessments should be on the shelf.
✓ Soil Conservation Services are needed for training, monitoring and data archiving. These should have a supra national regional mandate.
✓ A GMES or GEO system to provide information on actual conditions
✓ Raise awareness
✓ Develop land ethics and legislation.
✓ Use synergy between different conventions.
✓ An IPCC for soil conservation is needed (IPSC).
✓ Make inventory of Natural Resources.

Earth observation and soil protection

Until now, one of the main difficulties faced by the UNCCD is that there is no real accurate way of measuring or checking the claims made about the implementation of the convention. New advances in remote sensing now mean that it is possible to track and monitor desertification everywhere. Organizations can now be provided with up to date information of problems so that they can be immediately tackled. One of the tasks of an International Panel on Soil and Land Conservation would be to monitor and provide information. Archiving and organising information could be linked to a programme such as GEO. Recent advances in protecting forests in Northern Brazil have been achieved because there is a more or less real-time monitoring at the scale of individual trees.

References and further reading

Arnold, D., (2004), Lessons for Europe: the experience of the U.S. Soil Conservation Service. 49–54 in van Asselen, van S, C. Boix-Fayos A. C. Imeson (2004) *Briefing papers of the second SCAPE workshop in Cinque Terre (IT)* 13-15 April 2004 220 p 3D Environmental Change, Netherlands.

Adeel, Z, and U. Safriel (lead authors), (2005). Dryland systems, in R. Hassan, R. Scholes, and N. Ash, eds, *Millennium Assessment, Ecosystems and Human Well-being. Volume 1: Ecosystems and Human Well-being: Current State and Trends*. Island Press, Washington, USA. pp. 623–664.

Balabanis, P., D. Peter, A. Ghazi and M. Tsogas (1999) *Mediterranean desertification: Research results and policy implications*. EUR 19303. European Commission, DG-Research.

Bosselman K and D.; Grinlington (2002) *Environmental Law for a sustainable society*. New Zealand Centre for Environmental Law Monograph Series Vol 1.

Briasouli (2010) (LEDDRA Project: Land and Ecosystem Degradation and Desertification. *Assessing the fit of responses to land and ecosystem degradation and desertification*, EU 7th Framework Programme, http//Leddra.aegean.gr

Bigas, H. Gudmundur I. G., L Montanarella and A. Arnalds (2009) *Soils, Society and Global Change Proceedings of the International Forum 31-August-04 September. Selfoss Iceland*. European Commission 2009. JRC EUR 23784 EN.

Conacher A, M. Tonts and J. Conacher (2004) Education and land-use planning for sustainable agricultural development in Western Australia *Land Degradation and Development* 15 299–310

Crete (1996) *International Conference on Mediterranean Desertification*, 1996 October 29- 1 November Proceedings Vol 2 Research Results and policy implications Vol 2 EUR 19303.

GEO (2011) Portal for global observations http://www.earthobservations.org/

Greiber T. (1973) *Payments for ecosystem services, Legal and Institutional Frameworks* Environmental Policy and Law Paper No 78 IUCN 314 p.

Gunderson, L. H., Holling, C. S., (2002). *Panarchy: understanding transformations in human and natural systems*. Island Press, Washington, DC, 507 pp.

Hannam, I. and Boer, B., (2002). *Legal and Institutional Frameworks for Sustainable Soils*. A preliminary report. IUCN Environmental Policy and Law Paper No. 45.

International Forum (2007) *Soils, Society and Global Change* 31 August – 4 September, Selfoss, Iceland.

Holling, C. S., Meffe, G. K. 1996. Command and control and the pathology of natural resource management. *Conservation Biology 10(2), 328–337*.

Holling, C. S., 2000. Theories for sustainable futures. *Conservation Ecology 4(2), 7*. [online] URL: http://www.consecol.org/vol4/iss2/art7

Peter, D, 2000 *Mediterranean Desertification. Research results and policy implications*. Proceedings of the International Conference 29 October to 1 November 1996 Crete, Greece EUR 19303, 616 p.

Makhanya E. M. (2004) Demographic dynamics and land degradation at Ratau Lesotho, in the context of rural sustainability *Land Degradation and Development* 15, 257–269.

Meadows, M. E. (2004) Land degradation and development: geographical perspectives Guest Editor's Foreward p.201 Land Degradation and Development Meadows, ME (ed.), 2004. *Land Degradation and Development: Geographical Perspectives*. Special Issue of *Land Degradation and Development* 15 (3): 201–349.

Millennium Declaration (1990) *The United Nations and the International/Millennium Declaration Development Goals* (MDGs) http://www.un.org/millenniumgoals/

World Summit on Sustainable development (1992) http://www.un.org/events/ Johannesburg 2002.

Neumann j and E. Rodtmann (2011) Enter the anthropocene Age of Man *National Geographic Magazine*, March 2011 p 60–84 (includes contributions from other authors).

Rubio, J. L. and V Andreu (eds) (2009 *Human and Socio-economic consequences of*) Campus de Excelencia Universidad las Palmas 272 p.

Thornes J. B and Burke (1996) *Actions taken by national governmental organisations to mitigate desertification in the Mediterranean 1996*. Concerted Action on Mediterranean Desertification.

Wilson, G. A. (2009) Rethinking environmental management - ten years later: a view from the author. *Environments* 36 (3): 3–15.

Appendix A
Soil basics

Soils form by interaction of the earth's crust with atmospheric and biological influences. Bedrock is the ultimate source of the inorganic component in soils. When rock is exposed at the surface of the earth's crust, it is broken down into smaller and smaller fragments by physical forces. The fragments may be altered or decomposed by chemical reaction of mineral matter with water and air. Hundreds, thousands, or even millions of years may be required for the **weathering** or physical and chemical alteration of rock to produce the ultimate end products in soils. Once particles reach a sufficiently small size they can be moved by wind, water or ice when exposed at the surface. It is common, therefore, for small particles to be moved from one location to another. A single particle might occur in several different soils over a period of 100 000 years. Eventually, these particles or their decomposition products reach the ocean where they are re-deposited as marine sediments.

Soils are dynamic bodies having properties that reflect the integrated effects of **climate** (atmosphere) and **biotic activity** (micro organisms, insects, worms, burrowing animals, plants, etc.) on the unconsolidated remnants of rock at the earth's surface (**parent material**). These effects are modified by the **topography** of the landscape and of course continue to take place with the passage of **time**. Soils formed in parent materials over decades, centuries, or millennia may be lost due to accelerated erosion over a period of years or a few decades. There are five key factors in soil formation:

1 type of parent material

2 climate

3 overlying vegetation

4 topography or slope

5 time

Desertification, Land Degradation and Sustainability, First Edition. Anton Imeson.
© 2012 John Wiley & Sons, Ltd. Published 2012 by John Wiley & Sons, Ltd.

The type of parent material influences the soil pH, structure, colour, etc., in a profound way.

High-rainfall climates tend to have less-fertile soils, due to rainwater's effect in leaching nutrients down to lower levels of the soil profile, and have more acidic soils. Low-rainfall climates tend to accumulate salts near the surface and have generally higher soil pH (basic).

Soils that form under coniferous forests tend to be more acidic than those under deciduous forests, and root action is also critical in soil formation.

Soils generally have a harder time forming on steep slopes, due to runoff of soil particles during rain events.

The more time a soil has to form, the deeper its profile will be.

The American soil scientist Jenny (1941) developed a system for explaining soils as a function of parent material, time, drainage, slope, organisms, vegetation, erosion and management. Patterns of soils occurred in the fields that reflected the interplay of these factors. Similar soils occur again and again under similar geo-ecological conditions. It is a paradox that although each soil is different in terms of its exact appearance and properties, soils tend to evolve into a relative limited number of types. A catena is a sequence of soils that occurs on a slope as the soil forming factors vary in a consistent way (Figure A.1).

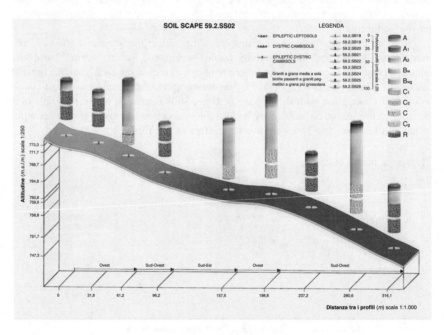

Figure A.1 A soil catena along a slope (*Source:* Madrau *et al.* 2003).

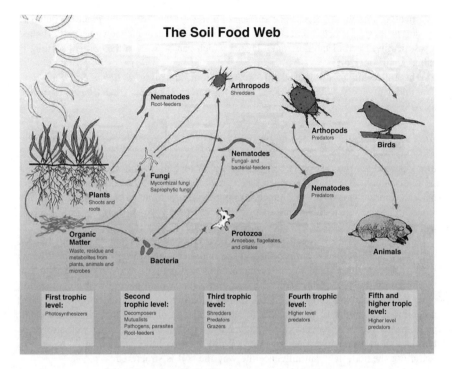

Figure A.2 The Soil Food Web (*Source:* USDA NRCS).

Former soil scientists generally mapped the boundaries between different soil types on the basis of parent material and slope, producing maps that expressed a deep understanding of the processes responsible for soil formation.

Mineral matter, organic matter, soil water and **soil air** are the four major components of a soil. The proportions of these components may vary between horizons in a soil or between similar horizons in different soils. The ratio of soil water to soil air depends on whether the soil is wet or dry. The mineral matter, composed of particles ranging in size from the sub-microscopic to gravel or even rocks in some cases, accounts for the bulk of the dry weight of the soil and occupies some 40 to 60 per cent of the soil volume. Organic matter, derived from the waste products and remains of plants and animals, occurs in largest amounts in the surface soil, but even here seldom accounts for more than 10 per cent of the dry weight of the soil.

Soils are classified based on their **parent material, texture, structure**, and **profile**. Parent material is what the soil was made from, usually mostly inorganic rocks. A soil that has <20% organic matter (O.M.) is a **mineral soil** while one with >20% O.M. is an **organic soil** (i.e. peat). Texture refers to the proportion of sand, silt, and clay in the soil; sandy soils are called light or coarse-textured, whereas clay soils are called heavy or fine-textured. Clay tends to increase the water-holding capacity of the soil. Loamy soils have a balanced sand, silt, and clay composition and are thus good for plant growth. Structure refers to the aggregation of soil particles into platy, prismatic, blocky, spherical, or crumb-like clods. The surface of a soil reveals very little about the depth of the soil or its subsurface characteristics. A vertical cross-sectional view of a soil is called a **soil profile**. Each of the horizontal layers, which can be seen in the vertical section, is called a **soil horizon**.

The following part is based on excerpts from: *A Guide to Better Soil Structure*, Cranfeld University, Silsoe, National Soil Resources Institute, 2002 (Presented at the SCAPE workshop in Cinque Terra).

What is soil structure?

Many people tend to confuse a soil structure with texture. A soil's texture is the bricks (a mix of sand, silt and clay), which when stuck together with organic matter and other natural "mortar" make up the larger all-important structural blocks (aggregates). The structure of the soil is the arrangement of blocks around which the roots grow and air and water move.

Just like our houses, a soil is made up of a number of different 'building' blocks, which are described according to their shape and size using fairly easily defined terms such as blocky or granular, fine or medium. Soils that naturally have a good structure in the long term have a 'stable' soil structure, those that would naturally lose aggregation have an unstable structure. In general, a well-structured topsoil (first 30 cm) will have a continuous network of pore spaces to allow drainage of water, free movement of air and unrestricted development of roots. A subsoil (below 30 cm) can be well structured but also allow water to permeate slowly. While there is little people can do to modify texture of the soil, they can influence the way the soil is structured.

Soil structure is important because:

- It is the plumbing system for the soil which controls water flow and air flow

- It provides space and a protected home for roots, germinating seeds and soil fauna

- It affects farming operations, for instance the easiness of cultivation

- It affects the impact of landuse on the environment; the amount of run-off and erosion, the amount of nutrients and/or pollutants lost in drainage, runoff and erosion.

Soil structure holds a vital, but often overlooked role in the sustainable food production and the well-being of society (Bronick and Lal 2005).

Soil chemistry

Soluble salts generally disassociate in water into two component ions, one that is positively charged (***cation***) and one that is negatively charged (***anion***). The ability of the salt to dissolve is directly related to the solution's pH, or relative concentrations of hydrogen (H+) and hydroxide (OH−) ions. Higher pH indicates the soil has more OH− than H+, and is thus ***basic*** or ***alkaline***. Lower pH indicates the soil has more H+ than OH−, and is thus ***acidic***. Neutral pH, where a solution has equal concentrations of

H+ and OH−, is 7.0. Important soil cations include aluminum (Al^{3+}), ammonium (NH^{4+}) calcium (Ca^{2+}), magnesium (Mg^{2+}), potassium (K^+), and sodium (Na^+). Important soil anions include bicarbonate (HCO_3^-), chloride (Cl^-), carbonate (CO_3^{2-}), nitrate (NO_3^-), orthophosphate ($H_2PO_4^-$), and sulfate (SO_4^{2-}).

The soil community

Soil organisms are integral to soil processes, including nutrient cycling, energy cycling, water cycling, processing of potential pollutants, and plant pest dynamics. These processes are essential to agriculture and forestry, and for protecting the quality of water, air, and habitat (NRCS 2004). One teaspoon of good grassland soil may contain 5 billion bacteria, 20 million fungi and 1 million protoctists. Expand the census to a square meter and you will find, besides the creatures already mentioned, perhaps 1000 each of ants, spiders, woodlice, beetles and their larvae; 2000 each of earthworms and millipedes and centipedes; 8000 slugs and snails; 20 000 pot worms, 40 000 springtails, 120 000 mites and 12 million nematodes. If you would envision the soil as a city, it is to put it mildly, densely settled (Wallace 1999).

Soil organisms can be described by their functions in a soil (Coleman and Crossley 1996; Wardle 2002). There are:

- *Decomposers:* Bacteria, actinomycetes (filamentous bacteria), and saprophytic fungi degrade plant and animal residue, organic compounds, and some pesticides.

- *Grazers and predators:* Protozoa, mites, nematodes, and other organisms "graze" on bacteria or fungi; prey on other species of protozoa and nematodes; or both graze and prey. Grazers and predators release plant-available nutrients as they consume microbes.

- *Litter transformers:* Arthropods are invertebrates with jointed legs, including insects, spiders, mites, springtails, centipedes, and millipedes. Some litter transformers, especially ants, termites, scarab beetles, and earthworms, are 'ecosystem engineers' that physically change the soil habitat for other organisms by chewing and burrowing through the soil.

- *Mutualists:* Mycorrhizal fungi, nitrogen-fixing bacteria, and some free-living microbes have co-evolved together with plants to form mutually beneficial associations with plants.

- *Pathogens, parasites and root feeders:* Organisms that cause disease make up a tiny fraction of the organisms in the soil. Disease-causing organisms include certain species of bacteria, fungi, protozoa, nematodes, insects, and mites.

References and further reading

C.J. Bronick and R. Lal (2005) Soil structure and management: a review. *Geoderma* 124: 3–22.
Coleman, D.C. and D.A. Crossley (1996) *Fundamentals of Soil Ecology*. Academic Press, San Diego.

Jenny, Hans (1941) *Factors of Soil Formation. A System of Quantitative Pedology*. McGraw-Hill.
NRCS Soil Quality–Soil Biology (2004) Technical Note No. 4. Soil Biology and Land Management.
SOIL BIOLOGY CLASSROOM ACTIVITIES, The Soil Biology Web Page (from the NRCS Soil
    Quality Institute) at http://soils.usda.gov/sqi; URL: http://organiclifestyles.tamu.edu/soilbasics/
    soilformation.html; URL: http://pas.byu.edu/AgHrt100/classif.htm.
Wallace, P. (1999) The soil bank. In: Whole Earth 96, Celebrating soil – Mother of all things.
Wardle, D.A. (2002) *Communities and Ecosystems: Linking the Aboveground and Belowground
    Components*. Princeton University Press. Princeton, New Jersey.

Index

accelerated erosion 16, 25
actions and causes 7–8, 67, 133
actual desertification 9, 13, 239
actual geomorphological processes 16
adaptation of culture 8, 25, 32, 142–3,
    273
adaptive cycle 32–3, *33*, 64, 185, 204,
    206, 276
  case 204–5
adaptive management 204
adaptive management as response 185
adaptive systems application, The
    Netherlands 207
  Case 209, *210*
Aesthetic value and function 5, 46
afforestation Spain Case 171
Allegra 2008 102
aggregation indices 70, *see* soil
agricultural efficiency 10
agricultural revolution 11
agriculture appropriation of water 7, 103
agrocentric response to sustainability 49
Allen et al 1984 122
Amazon Forest 6
Ambers et al 167, 168
Andean forest 174
Andersen et al 47
Annex 4 UNCCD (Northern
    Mediterranean) 61
answers to land degradation 201
Anthropogene 293
Antrim, Northern Ireland 88, *89*
appropriation of resources 243
aquifer, management 179
aquifers safe yield 179
Aral Sea 238, *241*

Argentina 32
aridity 8, 17
Arizona 149
armouring 160
Arnalds 7, 46
Arnold Dick USGS 300
Arroyo development 134
Athens water use impact 273–4, *273,*
    274
Atlantic rain forest, Brazil 30, 155
Atlantic States, human
    impact Case 169
Atlantic States, Pennsylvanian
    Rivers 169
Atlas of soil biodiversity 279
attractiveness and desertification 62, 127,
    275
Australia 24
  Cairns *79*
  logging impact, Karuah Forest, NSW
    170
  wheat, Towoomba, Queensland 160
Austria, protection forests 84
awareness of desertification 6

Badlands 12, 18
  Canada 136
  Spain, badlands Bolivia *147*
Bangladesh desertification cost 245
Barbados 5
Belgian Ardennes 18
benevolent actions 62
best practices 198, 203, 205, **206**
Biodiversity as indicator 67
Blue Ridge Foothills Virginia 168
Boix-Fayos and others 162, **286, 287**

Desertification, Land Degradation and Sustainability, First Edition. Anton Imeson.
© 2012 John Wiley & Sons, Ltd. Published 2012 by John Wiley & Sons, Ltd.